REVOLUTIONARY HUMANISM AND HISTORICISM IN MODERN ITALY

REVOLUTIONARY HUMANISM AND HISTORICISM IN MODERN ITALY

EDMUND E. JACOBITTI

NEW HAVEN AND LONDON
YALE UNIVERSITY PRESS

Published with assistance from the
Kingsley Trust Association Publication Fund
established by the Scroll and Key Society of Yale College

Designed by Sally Harris
and set in IBM Press Roman type.
Printed in the United States of America by
Edwards Brothers Inc., Ann Arbor, Mich.

Library of Congress Cataloging in Publication Data
Jacobitti, Edmund E   1938–
    Revolutionary humanism and historicism
in modern Italy.
    Bibliography: p.
    Includes index.
    1. Italy–Intellectual life. 2. Humanism–
History. 3. Croce, Benedetto, 1866–1951. 4. Histori-
cism. I. Title.
DG450.J3   945.09   80–23619
ISBN 0–300–02479–7

10   9   8   7   6   5   4   3   2   1

To the memory of my mother,
Marguerite Lucille Jacobitti

Religious people live on a shadow.
We live on the shadow of a shadow.
On what will those who live after us live?

Renan

CONTENTS

Acknowledgments   xi

Introduction   1

1   Revolutionary Italian Humanism before the Twentieth Century   11
2   Benedetto Croce: The Search for a Faith   57
3   Aesthetics and the New Culture   75
4   Aesthetics and the Struggle against Positivism   87
5   The New Culture versus Reformist Socialism   101
6   Sorel and Croce: Myth and Faith   125
7   Benedetto Croce: The Otherworldliness of Absolute Historicism   137
8   The Prophet Who Failed   154

Endnotes   165

Bibliography   219

Index   235

ACKNOWLEDGMENTS

I owe a great deal to a group of uncommonly helpful people for this book, and any attempt to present each with the thanks he or she deserves would not be possible here. To Professors George Mosse and Hanna Pitkin, who fifteen years ago helped me into the arena of intellectual history that I now so much enjoy, I owe an unrepayable debt. To Professors Tom Thorson, Stanley Payne, and Sterling Fishman, who provided many a pleasant oasis in those years, I also owe a great deal. With respect to the present manuscript, I would like to extend my appreciation to Professors Renzo De Felice, Max Fisch, Massimo Fittipaldi, Giuseppe Galasso, and especially to Max Salvadori. All have provided me, in one way or another, with valuable assistance, kind suggestions, and helpful advice. Although it would be impossible to mention each by name, I would also like to thank the many kind persons who aided me in the research for this book and who serve in the following libraries and institutions: the Biblioteca universitaria Alessandrina at the University of Rome; the Biblioteca dell'Istituto Gramsci; the Biblioteca dell'Istituto italiano per gli studi storici; the Biblioteca nazionale "Vittorio Emmanuele III" at Naples; and the Biblioteca universitaria at the University of Naples. I especially wish to thank the Graduate School at Southern Illinois University at Edwardsville for its financial assistance.

To Jane Weingartner, who typed for me under the most pressing conditions and who gave unstintingly of her time, I wish to express my sincere thanks. I also wish to thank my family and friends in Naples—in particular, Gianmarco and Sandra Iacobitti and Vittorio and Maria Teresa Iacobitti—who provided me, on various occasions, with months of unsurpassed hospitality as well as invaluable assistance in obtaining research material.

To my wife Suzanne, who by now, I fear, can recite this work from memory, I owe the greatest debt of all. As a professional scholar she took hours of her own time to read this manuscript, and as a wife she took additional hours to encourage me. Without her the book would not have been written at all.

For any errors that may exist here I accept full responsibility; this applies as well to the translations, which are, unless otherwise noted, my own.

INTRODUCTION

Those acquainted with the thought of Antonio Gramsci will doubtless recall his memorable definition of "culture" set out in *Letteratura e vita nazionale.* "Culture," he noted, means "a coherent, unitary, nationally diffused 'conception of life and man,' a 'lay religion,' a philosophy that has become precisely a 'culture,' that is, it has generated an ethic, a way of life, a civil and individual conduct." A "culture," in other words, provides the limits within which human theory and practice must operate if they are to be regarded as normal, as appropriate. Culture is thus similar to what Vico in his *New Science* called "common sense." "Common sense is judgment without reflection, shared by an entire class, an entire people, or the entire human race."

Without a "culture," a "common sense" or "lay religion," life would be wild, unpredictable, quite unimaginable, for any and all conduct would then be appropriate. "Whirl is king, having deposed Zeus," says Aristophanes. The world of culture is, in other words, so bound to the world of practice that even a Marxist like Gramsci noted the superiority of culture over the "merely economic and political."

> The most important element to be discussed . . . is this: whether [Marxism] excludes . . . the importance of cultural and moral forces, really judges as "appearance" the facts of the superstructure. It can be said that not only does [Marxism] not exclude [culture] but the most recent phase of [its] development consists precisely in vindicating . . . and in increasing . . . cultural activity, in [establishing] a cultural front . . . alongside of the merely economic and political fronts.

All bibliographical and biographical references to persons and events are included in the relevant chapters, and none will appear in the Introduction.

This superiority of the cultural front Gramsci called "hegemony," and it was his intention to replace the current national hegemony with a new, "nationally diffused conception of life and man": Marxism. It was a revolutionary idea, for to carry out a revolution is precisely to shatter one common sense and replace it with another. Such revolutions can take place gradually and easily or, more often, suddenly and traumatically with Leninist steel. Moreover, no matter how it takes place, no revolution may call itself successful until it has, by one means or another, replaced an earlier culture and armed its subjects with the new common sense. To generate a new culture, a new "faith," as it were, is then to carry out a revolution, to launch a people into a new era.

No theme is of greater concern to twentieth-century Italian intellectuals than this creation of a new culture. Whether one reads Gramsci or his apparent mentor, the young Benedetto Croce, whether one reads figures as diverse as Giovanni Gentile, Guido De Ruggiero, Gaetano Salvemini, or lesser lights such as Giovanni Papini and Giuseppe Prezzolini, the central concern is everywhere and always the same, the need to make a new Italy, to carry out a revolution in culture that will be the basis and substance of a revolution in every aspect of Italian life. This revolutionary theme in modern Italian intellectual history is still largely unexplored today, and where explored, it frequently remains widely misunderstood. This misunderstanding, moreover, stems only partly from a lack of familiarity with the actual writings of men like Gramsci, Croce, Gentile, and others. A greater handicap is our unfamiliarity with the historical tradition from which these intellectuals sprang and the historical-intellectual context in which they operated. Lacking this knowledge, a student reads a work by Croce or Gramsci and places him either in some abstract context ("liberalism," "Marxism") or in some context familiar to the student but alien to the author (English or French liberalism, German Marxism). Then, having things nicely ticketed and docketed, the student proceeds to see what his author has to say about his "ticket."

To truly understand modern Italian thought requires, instead, an understanding of the context in which it arose and the questions its representatives sought to answer. Our present understanding of this context is quite narrow, the commonest assumption being that after Machiavelli, or at any rate after Vico, Italian thought went into hibernation, an empty parenthesis that endured down to the turn of the present century, when it was closed by the sudden emergence of Croce or perhaps Gramsci. However, by regarding these men simply as refreshing meteors hurled into the twentieth century from the void of post-Renaissance Italian darkness, we quite miss their message.

There are, of course, messages worth missing, but the message of the twentieth-century Italians is not one of them. On the contrary, it seems now suddenly to have become more relevant than ever, for they, more than any other thinkers, have seen, perhaps foreseen, what the Mexican intellectual Carlos Fuentes in February of 1979 described as "the reappearance of cultural factors as a determining force in national and world affairs."

From Algeria to Tanzania to China to Canada, the national aspiration, the need to embody culture in a national state and a national society, is still the strongest moving force as the world plunges towards the twenty-first century. Culture has triumphed over economic determinism.

As pioneers of this discovery of "culture," Italian thinkers deserve our attention, and this is particularly true of Benedetto Croce, the thinker who more than any other has shaped the mind of the modern Italian intellectual—even the mind of Gramsci. So successfully had Croce given his culture to Italy that Gramsci, maturing in that Crocean "hegemony," cast his "rebirth" of Marxism in Crocean terms. "This is the only historical possibility which will permit an adequate rebirth of Marxism. . . . For we Italians, to be the heirs of classical German philosophy means to be the heirs of Crocean philosophy, which is the contemporary world moment of classical German philosophy."

Whether this constituted, as Gramsci hoped, a Marxist conquest of Croce or a Crocean conquest of Gramsci is a matter we shall take up in another volume. Here it is sufficient to note the importance of Croce to Gramsci and to Italian culture in general. By the first decade of the present century Croce reigned over Italian culture like "a lay Pope," as Gramsci once put it. "Not since Goethe," wrote H. Stuart Hughes, "had any single individual dominated so completely the culture of a major European country." Without Croce, without the culture from which he sprang and which he represented, there would have been no Gramsci as we know him; and no understanding of Gramsci is possible without an understanding of the Crocean culture in which he matured. That culture had its roots in the city of Naples, in the traditions of Naples.

As a city, Naples has contributed more than any other, save perhaps Vatican City, to the creation of the Italian mind. Indeed, from Naples has come the only coherent opposition and alternative to Roman Catholic culture. No European state save Italy has had to deal at quite such close quarters with the spiritual and physical presence of the Roman Church. A universal church, a universal faith, with concerns always beyond the particular geographical boundaries of

Italy, the Church nevertheless constituted in the past and to a large extent constitutes today one of the most resilient and powerful forces in Italian life. The very proximity of the Church, however, produced an anticlericalism that has been almost as vital a part of Italian intellectual life as the Church itself, producing in Italy a kind of national schizophrenia which colored and colors still today its intellectual development. Anticlericalist thought in Italy developed, in short, as an alternative culture. This alternative culture, persisting for at least some two and a half centuries, has played a constant philosophical theme in Italy, a theme with variations certainly, but nonetheless a theme whose fundamental message has always been distinctively "realist," distinctively Neapolitan. In place of the Roman religion, with its concern with the afterlife and the Holy Spirit, Neapolitan thinkers have counterposed a lay religion concerned with the human spirit in this life, an ethic and culture celebrating man the creator and product of human history.

Long before Italy became a nation in 1860—indeed long before nearly anyone even thought in terms of an Italian nation—Naples, capital of the Bourbon Kingdom of the Two Sicilies, had begun with Vico this long hymn to man and his worldly power and wisdom. By widening out the path made by Vico, other Neapolitans, like Vicenzo Cuoco and, in the Risorgimento, Silvio and Bertrando Spaventa and Francesco De Sanctis, were, in fact, to prepare a philosophical perspective remarkably akin to that other springboard for modern philosophy, the thought of the left Hegelians in Germany. This modern Neapolitan philosophy had its full flowering in the nineteenth and early twentieth centuries when, in the works of men like Antonio Labriola and Benedetto Croce, it became the culture of modern Italy, the basis for a cultural revolution in nearly all aspects of Italian intellectual life.

Like the thought of Marx—and yet with implications frequently opposed to Marx—the intellectual culture of Naples was humanist and historicist, two terms that since the time of Vico have shaped Neapolitan and later Italian perceptions of man and his place in the world. The foundation of humanist historicism is the belief that a true understanding of man can come only from an objective assessment of man as he is, not as he ought to be, man as he is revealed in the historical record rather than man as revealed in the visions of theologians and philosophers. This study of man as he actually developed in history involved a revolutionary change of perspective, for it constituted a rejection of the well-established belief that only that which is constant can be an object of knowledge. The Neapolitans since Vico have, as a matter of "common sense," rejected Parmenides and the abstract universals of Aristotle, to concentrate instead on

4

the Heraclitean becoming. Unlike those schools of thought that sought the meaning of the flux outside the flux—in the eternal laws first of God, then of nature, and now in the laws of the scientific sociologist—Neapolitan thinkers have looked squarely at man in history, trying to see there some root meaning to the human drama.

Despite this fascination with the concrete, neither Vico nor his later Neapolitan or Italian descendants had any interest in materialism or naturalism. The Neapolitan school saw in materialism not the dialectical materialism of Marx, but the static and eternal materialism of the French philosophes. Even when Marxian materialism was more thoroughly understood, twentieth-century followers of Vico, such as the Spaventas and De Sanctis, remained uninterested in materialism or nature, seeing there, if no longer the remnants of the eighteenth century, only the Kantian "thing-in-itself," an unknowable entity masked forever from human understanding. There was, the Italian humanists held, no point in searching for man outside man, no point in trying to understand man by appealing to something eternal and constant outside of man and history, for nothing stood outside history.

It was this willingness, even this eagerness, to accept man as he was that set Neapolitan humanism apart from the naive "humanitarianism" of both religious and Enlightenment thought. These two movements, however much opposed to each other in practice, shared, as Professor Carl L. Becker pointed out, a heavenly perspective. Neither was willing to accept man as he was, for both believed he could be, or at any rate had been, more. They therefore studied man from the perspective of the ideal rather than the real, and in both cases man came up short. Religious thinkers condemned man for his lost innocence, his inability to live according to divine law, while the philosophe condemned man for his inability to live according to the natural law. It occurred to neither school that both divine and natural law were man's creations, testaments to his glory, standing not as signposts outside of history, but as human footprints along the historical path already taken. Unlike the theologian and the philosophe who saw majesty in God and nature and madness in man, the humanist historicist, precisely because he believed nothing stood outside of history, valued man's history all the more. The humanist, in short, studied history because it was the only thing he could not "doubt." *Ero ergo sum.* To understand what he had become, the humanist turned to see what he had been, from where he had come; he turned to the past.

As he contemplated his history, two paths opened before him—or after him. To some, like Vico, history appeared an endless cycle, an inescapable *corsi e ricorsi* from which man, despite all his efforts—indeed, because of all his efforts—could not escape. On all sides man found himself forced to act in a world created earlier and by others, created not in six days, but continuously. This world was omnipresent and inescapable, forcing man to solve problems seen differently by all, the collective and formless wobble of their contradictory solutions producing that perfect arc of the inescapable *corso.*

To others, however, the *corsi* were escapable precisely because they were man-made and because history was controlled by man alone. The spiral of the *corsi e ricorsi* imprisoned man only because man had not realized the full extent of his power, had not realized that if behind history stood nothing but the human spirit, then man was truly godly, able to chart any course he chose. In the past man had never contemplated himself alone on Nietzsche's limitless sea, seeing around him instead barriers divine and natural that testified to his own impotence. Yet those barriers had been erected, albeit unconsciously, by man himself, and it was precisely those barriers which shielded man from a full consciousness of his absolute freedom. It was those barriers which prevented man from taking or even contemplating those actions necessary for his escape from the *corsi,* his escape from unconsciousness to consciousness. It now remained, therefore, to merely seize conscious control of what man had all along unconsciously "controlled," leaping into a world beyond the *corsi* into that boundless genesis in which man was the creator. This concrete humanism, this hostility to abstract Enlightenment natural laws as well as to the transcendent Christian religion, marks the uniqueness and the prescience of modern Italian thought, the first formulation of that modern equation of humanism and historicism which stated that man and man alone had created this world and therefore man alone had the capacity and duty to remake the world.

This promise, this vision of a human world emancipated from any philosophy that sought to make of man an instrument, prepared the way for Hegel's entrance into Naples—and prepared as well the way for a unique revision of Hegelian thought. At first Hegel had seemed a new Vico exalting historical becoming over the constant "is." Moreover, Hegel seemed not only to satisfy philosophical needs but political needs as well, for with his exaltation of the nation-state Hegel appeared to Neapolitan patriots of the 1840s and 1850s as "the philosopher of the Risorgimento," the prophet of a nation-state foreordained by a world spirit whose will was superior to the private and selfish wills of those hostile to the creation of an Italian nation.

A closer look at Hegel's philosophy, however, revealed a Trojan horse. To Neapolitan thinkers who, like the Spaventas and De Sanctis, had rejected the otherwordly providence of Christianity and the Enlightenment, and even the this-worldly providence of Vico's *corsi,* the Hegelian *Weltgeist,* controlling from above the actions of man below—even if they did produce the nation state—appeared to let in by the back door what Neapolitan thought had already ejected from the front—a superhuman transcendence. Like their left Hegelian counterparts, they therefore chose to relocate the historical *Weltgeist* in the world of men rather than in heaven.

This inversion of the Hegelian dialectic, coming as it did in reaction to all transcendence, however, produced not only a hostility to Hegel's world spirit, but also—quite unlike the Young Hegelians—an absolute refusal to accept any notion of history that prescribed a foreordained course for the historical process. Indeed, Neapolitan and later Italian idealist thought, especially in Croce, refused to accept even the concept of a "philosophy of history," if by that was meant anything more than mere "change." It was testimony to their consistency: a "philosophy of history" ran counter to the whole notion of an immanent and worldly historicism, for it seemed to place the logos outside man, seemed to be a return to rationalism and religion, to *filosofia teologizzante.* Thus, Italian idealism rejected the subtle transcendence of the left Hegelians with the same disdain with which they had earlier rejected the more obvious transcendence of the right Hegelians.

Moreover, this inversion of the Hegelian dialectic, because it came in the midst of the Risorgimento struggle to create an Italian nation, carried with it no revolutionary message to overthrow the state. Indeed, its message was quite the opposite, for it called upon men to set aside every concern save that of building the nation. The fervent nationalism of the Italian Hegelians, combined with their strong belief in man's absolute power to control his own history, was therefore strikingly contrasted with the ideas of the revolutionaries in the left Hegelian movement. This was all the more apparent in the Italian rejection of materialism, for in materialism they saw not only the static mechanics of the eighteenth century but also the root cause of Italy's frustrated destiny. Each person and each class, Italian humanists argued, pursued their own material interests, and in their selfish pursuit, far from advancing the course of history, they prevented it. History was produced by the abandonment of material interests so as to pursue higher ideal interests, interests embodied in the idea of a "culture," of a "common sense" that inspired men to a new "way of life, a civil and individual conduct."

Until men subordinated their private interests to those of the whole, until man chose to act as one, rather than each contradicting the will of the other, Italy would never overcome her backwardness. This was no different after Italy was born than during the long period of her gestation, for even after being born, Italy's proper place in the European hierarchy was on every occasion frustrated by her inability to speak with one voice, by her obvious lack of a "common sense" or "culture."

Neapolitan thinkers were more familiar than most with the problem of trying to impose a single unifying culture upon a land as diverse as southern Italy. Convinced by their philosophy that man alone was responsible for his history, Neapolitan intellectuals had for years tried to shape the course of the South. From the time of the Bourbon Kingdom of the Two Sicilies to the time of the modern Italian monarchy and the present Italian republic, however, these intellectuals had collided with a population whose ideas were always contrary to their own, a population that, though both amiable and delightful, constituted the apotheosis of all that humanist-historicist philosophy abhorred.

To anyone familiar with the unending tumult and hullabaloo that has almost always marked the city of Naples, it is obvious that there, perhaps there as nowhere else, the philosopher will encounter a world unlike anything he has ever encountered before, and the Neapolitan intellectuals who grew to maturity in that city were inevitably to carry with them a notion of a "real world" that fairly demanded the intervention of men who could take charge of history and chart a new course. Alongside "philosophical Naples," in short, there lay another Naples, another world, the teeming, volatile world of the urban and rural masses, the *cafoni,* infamous from the time of Hannibal and Scipio the African down to the present. Steeped in suspicion, superstition, and, most of all, "religion," exhibiting a resistance to change that rivaled that of the monuments at Stonehenge, the humble and explosive southern masses have stupefied twenty centuries of intellectuals and have left their mark upon all modern Neapolitan—and therefore nearly all modern Italian—thought. "Naples is the calamity of the South," exclaimed Gaetano Salvemini.

> It is a vast center of waste and unproductive activity in which half the population makes its way by pickpocketing and swindling the other half. . . .
> The University of Naples, every year, unlooses about six hundred doctors and lawyers and about sixty professors of letters and science, the greater part of all of these being intellectually besotted, morally corrupt, and absolutely incapable of writing ten lines without ten grammatical errors.

It was the same more than a century before, in the Age of Reason. Hearing that he was about to be sent from Paris to Naples, the scholarly Abbé Galiani exclaimed, "Save death, nothing worse could have happened to me." Throwing up his hands at ever luring the Neapolitan into the world of books, he groaned, "Half of humanity has a far greater need of a good husband than a good book, and if that be true of Paris, how true it must be of Naples, where there are only twelve people who can read." Five hundred years ago, in the midst of the Renaissance, the same depressing picture appears in the words of a stunned Viennese who arrived at the city in 1421. "The things I see here," he wrote, "make one glad not to have been born a Neapolitan."

From the point of view of the Neapolitan intellectual, then, two peoples dwelled in Naples, two peoples separated, as Vincenzo Cuoco once put it, by two hundred years and two languages—and yet they were two peoples whose physical proximity made true separation all but impossible. The existence of a cultured elite and a humble mass is, of course, not uncommon, and as the writings of figures as diverse as Mill, Tocqueville, Kierkegaard, Nietzsche, and Ortega y Gasset make plain, it need not lead one to any necessary or inevitable political or social conclusions. What separated the Neapolitan intellectual from his other continental counterparts was his constant confrontation with and frustration by the masses. This confrontation accounts, at least in part, for the Neapolitan humanist's constant preoccupation with such themes as education, religion, and psychology. Most especially it accounts for his obsession with the theme of revolution among a population hostile to revolution, a population led, until very recently, by its feudal priests and barons and always alien to the world inhabited by the humanist historicist.

In one revolution after another the Neapolitan intellectuals sought to bring about a change in the political and social structure of the state, only to have their hopes frustrated by a reactionary populace. The result was that each mushrooming of incipient republicanism turned in the end to elitism, and a history of the political activity of these intellectuals thus takes on the character of a series of parabolic curves—republican and revolutionary ascent, confrontation with the masses, precipitous descent. Each revolutionary takeoff, in short, found itself anchored to the inert mass beneath it, its flight cut short by the unbreakable weight of the hostile populace.

With each attempted revolution the gulf separating elite and mass grew wider and yet unavoidable. From the continued confrontation there developed an elaborate theory of "the two peoples," a doctrine that transformed the task of the humanist into that of freeing men from themselves, making them see that all that reverence they felt for existing authority and for the Almighty was misplaced and ought instead to be directed toward themselves. To discover the human origin of the political, let alone the divine, to discover and uncover the conventionality of all that makes this world orderly and familiar, was, however, more than "one people" could easily give, or force upon, "the other people." The result is an oscillation in Italian thought between attempts to impose a new "culture" from above, through revolution, and attempts to build, through education, a culture below that would eventually turn the pleb into citizen. At either extreme, however, the premise was always the same: only through changing the existing culture could the political and economic order be changed. This lesson, learned first in Vico, has endured down to the present.

It was Benedetto Croce who, in the atmosphere of the Italian and European fin de siècle, most changed the existing Italian culture, and it was he who brought the immanentist rebellion to its zenith. It was he, too, who presided over the decline of immanentism just prior to the Great War. That decline came, paradoxically, because the revolt had been all too successful, because the absolute annihilation of transcendence deprived all thought and action of any meaning. It was not only that the icons of social stability were here overturned, nor even that in the revolt against abstract and mechanical reason, there were occasional enthusiastic endorsements of blind voluntarism and mysticism; rather, it was in not seeing, not seeing "clearly and distinctly," that a victory that had as its *reward* a Kafkaesque void was unacceptable and would lead to the opposite, and not only the opposite, but the opposite extreme. A glimpse of the victory made the warriors shudder, for they appeared to have escaped the "prison" of their transcendent faiths only to have entered a room without walls. As doubt is of the few rather than the many, it could not be made an object of public consumption, for the more it was understood, the more was it rejected. Even for the bulk of intellectuals who had employed immanentism, it appeared to have promised more than it could deliver, hence their near universal feeling of betrayal. In many ways, then, the birth of those extreme movements that characterize this century, and even the reenforcement of the traditional transcendent faiths, lay paradoxically in the iconoclasm of the intellectuals, a Neronian iconoclasm that gave birth to madnesses its authors would later disown or, at best, claim only as illegitimate.

1 REVOLUTIONARY ITALIAN HUMANISM BEFORE THE TWENTIETH CENTURY

The seventeenth and early eighteenth centuries were preoccupied with the problem of skepticism. Natural law theorists of every hue and shade offered different arrangements by which the worldly cacophony might be made a harmonious symphony. Hobbes, Pascal, Descartes, and Vico all tried to connect the Heraclitean world of historical practice with the rational, constant world of theory. Hobbes tried to force the world of practice to conform to that of theory, while Pascal, wringing his hands at the world of history, offered his followers the world of faith. Descartes, meanwhile, peered straight through the world of history only to spy beneath it a world of reason which he never seemed quite able to attach to the world of appearance. Vico's answer was unique, for at least in its mature form, it did not see another more certain world, nor did it glide into Pascalian resignation or Hobbesian defiance of history.[1]

Vico sought wisdom which was, to use the Hegelian formula, both rational and real, a rational and universal explanation of developing history. He was the first in the modern world to see that society did not spring full blown from the sea like Botticelli's Venus nor could it be studied as if it were a modern sociologist's mechanism subject to unalterable and imaginary principles. No Newton could unravel the mystery that was human society unless he saw that the laws that governed society did not regulate its structure but the course of its development—and decline. Society developed; it developed from the primitive to the refined and, then, falling into skepticism, disintegrated, returning man to barbarism only to repeat again this "course the nations run." This *corso e ricorso,* Vico believed, followed a rational and universal law. The theory led Vico to adopt a then revolutionary perspective, the modern view that the

11

flow of history itself ought to be the object of our scrutiny. Vico's recognition of the importance of history was unique in a century that was, on the whole, hostile to history, a century before Darwin, Hegel, and peculiar men like St. Simon and Fourier made the notion of a theory of historical development commonsensical. The Cartesian orthodoxy of the seventeenth century held that the study of history, of the bewildering customs and traditions of men, was quite inferior to the study of the rational and coherent world of theory.[2] Poised on the edge of the "scientific revolution," Cartesian scholars could find no value in anything as obviously silly as the activity of their curious predecessors. The world, Descartes advised unanswerably, would have been better off had its institutions been "devised by some prudent legislator" rather than by the ad hoc responses of one and many through the course of time. The line from Descartes to 1789 is a little smudged but still evident. History, the record of man's responses to local and transient issues, revealed little in the opinion of Descartes and should be forgotten, perhaps abolished, as the Jacobins tried to do later.

Born into seventeenth-century Naples, Vico, in fact, had before him a living example of the traditional separation of theory and practice, the ideal and the historically real. In the latter part of the century that ill-starred city belonged to the realm of the Spanish sovereign Charles II, whose viceroys, garrisons, and infamously corrupt civil servants misruled and plundered the nearly ungovernable populace with the same determination as the armies of bandits who freely roamed the countryside and the countless thieves who marauded the city.[3] Centered in the midst of this tumult, however, lay another world, the nearly five-hundred-year-old University of Naples. There, despite (or perhaps to spite) the bewildering chaos of life, the faculty scholasticized upon the heavenly city of Cartesian philosophy. Were it not that Cartesianism was in vogue even in tranquil areas, one might be tempted to dismiss the prominence of Neapolitan Cartesianism as a reaction to life in Naples, the scholar's equivalent of voluntary exile or emigration; whatever the cause, a greater separation of scholars from the world of history can scarcely be imagined. The philosophic flight from reality was mirrored, as well, in the university curriculum: "Cartesianism had decidedly gained the ascendance. Consequently, the study of languages and of history, literary elaboration, and learned research were despised; mathematics and physics were the only popular sciences; instruction in Euclid had been substituted for the teaching of logic; and short routes to knowledge, easy methods, manuals, and abridgements were in excessive request."[4] Frederick II, "Stupor Mundi," who had founded the university in 1224 to provide realistic administrators for his realm, would have smiled ironically at the present state of his creation.

Like most of his contemporaries, Vico's early philosophical orientation had been Cartesian;[5] the fads of the mushrooming scientific culture—mathematics, geometry, scientific methodology—constituted for him, as for others, the common sense of the new era. At first, in fact, Vico seems to have shared the usual contempt for history, or philology as it was commonly called. Thus, in an early lecture he exclaimed, "You, philologist, boast of knowing everything about the furniture and clothing of the Romans and of being more intimate with the quarters, tribes, and streets of Rome than those of your own city. Why this pride? You know no more than did the potter, the cook, the cobbler, the summoner, the auctioneer of Rome."[6] Unlike his contemporary philosophes at Naples, however, Vico was never content to remain cloistered in the heavenly world of abstract truth, cut off from unmanageable history.[7] True knowledge, Vico believed, had to be of the social world of man, written in the social language of man; it could not be knowledge of an abstract world of mathematics written in the ahistorical foreign language of scientific precision.

Caught up in this search for knowledge of society, Vico remained unmoved by, and suspicious of, the greatest scientific discovery of his age, the discovery that man and nature spoke, or at any rate appeared to speak, the same language: mathematics. Long before Kant, Vico pondered that extraordinary coincidence of languages and began to wonder, as indeed Hobbes[8] and Plato had wondered, from whence came the language of mathematics and geometry, and why were they so reliable. Perusing the pages of Euclid's *Elements,* Vico, like Hobbes in 1628, was amazed—but, he wondered, did nature in fact speak "mathematics" or was she merely "spoken to."

Pondering that irresolvable case of tail chasing, it occurred to Vico that the world of geometry and mathematics was unique, for its precision came not from the material observed but from the observer of the material. We are certain of geometry, he concluded, because we are the author of the geometric proposition. In a 1708 address (*prolusione*) delivered to the University of Naples, entitled "On the Study Methods of Our Times," Vico noted: "We are able to demonstrate geometrical propositions because we create them; were it possible for us to supply demonstrations of physics, we would be capable of creating them [ex nihilo] as well [*geometrica demonstramus, quia facimus; si physica demonstrare possemus, faceremus*] ."[9]

The idea of the conventionality of geometry was, in germ form, the foundation for the later Vichian epistemology, which was to go beyond the abstract conventionality of geometry to include as well knowledge of reality. In the study of Francis Bacon he began in 1707,[10] Vico first saw the possibility of infusing conventional geometric propositions with concrete reality. Bacon had wished to restore (*instaur*, as he called it) science to a useful and practical role in life after the depredations of the schoolmen. He deplored the promiscuous empiricist who produced "tenets of a more deformed and monstrous nature than the sophistic or rationalist school; not being founded in the light of common notions ... but in the confined obscurity of a few experiments." [11] Likewise he rejected the a priori metaphysicians [12] who "have withdrawn themselves too much from the contemplation of nature, and the observations of experience, and have tumbled up and down in their own thoughts and fictions." [13] Instead, Bacon looked for that time when "thought and action may be more nearly and tightly joined and united than they have been." [14] Vico was "drawn to Francis Bacon, Lord Verulam, man of incomparable wisdom both common and esoteric, at one and the same time a universal man in theory and in practice, a rare philosopher and a great English minister of state." [15]

By 1710 Vico had combined Bacon's desire for a conjunction of thought and action with the earlier idea of the conventionality of geometry. It led him to equate knowing with doing, thought with action, and to assert that only those things that man has made can he know. Of those things that God has made, Vico noted, man can have only consciousness.

This new theory of knowledge was set out in the "De antiquissima Italorum sapientia." To know, announced Vico, is to know the cause or origin of a thing, to know how it came into being, and such knowledge is available only to the maker. "To know means in fact to possess the manner or form in which a thing comes to be; while one has [mere] consciousness of those things of which he cannot demonstrate the manner or form in which they came to be [_Scire enim est tenere genus seu formam, quo res fiat: conscientia autem est eorum, quorum genus seu formam demonstrare non possumus_]." [16] The conclusion of the "De antiquissima," therefore, was that true knowledge (_scientia, sapienza_) is acquired only when man is the author of the thing known.

This discovery rested upon a distinction between certainty (_certum_) and truth (_verum_) ("In good Latin," Vico reminded his readers later in the _New Science_, "_certum_ means particularized or, as the schools say, individuated"), [17] between the _product_ of certainty which is mere subjective consciousness (_conscientia_) and the product of truth which is knowledge (_scientia_). While this insight did not at first seem to advance Vico's acquisition of knowledge of history and society, it did allow him to see more clearly the failure of the _cogito ergo sum_. The _cogito_, Vico said, yielded not objective truth, but subjective certainty, _certum_. This was no barrier to skepticism. "The skeptic," Vico explained, "does not doubt that he thinks: he is certain of this fact [_Quin profitetur ita certum esse_] .... He does not doubt that he exists [_nec dubitat se esse_], but he holds nevertheless that his certainty of thought is consciousness, not knowledge [*sed certitudinem, quod cogitet, conscientiam contendit esse, non scientiam*] ; it is a vulgar notion [*cognitionem*] present in any ignorant person. . . . The skeptic denies that by means of the *consciousness* of thought one acquires knowledge of the *being* of a thing." [18]

So far Vico's discovery that knowledge is available only to the creator of the thing known had been confined to the world of mathematics and geometry. It took him another thirty years before he saw the possibility of carrying out Bacon's dream of making knowledge of concrete historical reality as reliable as the knowledge of abstract geometrical propositions. It was in the *New Science*[19] that Vico used these ideas to dramatically extend the world of human creation and hence of human knowledge to the world of history, the factual world of civil society. It was Vico's contention, in fact, that our knowledge of the world of men, society, and history was more real than our knowledge of geometry—and no less accurate either.

"This science," Vico proclaimed, "proceeds exactly like geometry . . . but with a reality greater by just so much as the institutions having to do with human affairs be more real than points, lines, surfaces, and figures."[20]

What had made this sudden broadening of human knowledge possible was Vico's discovery that the world of civil institutions had been made by man. Since the advent of modern science man had slighted the study of the fluid world of history and of history's meaning while concentrating upon the fixed physical world. This was all wrong, Vico said. The moderns, the Cartesians, and those ensnared by the scientific revolution were on a false scent, seeking the impossible, the knowledge of nature[21] or, as a later thinker put it, *das Ding an sich.* Instead, man ought to have turned to those things that he alone had made and that he alone, therefore, could know.

Society is that which is done or made by man and is therefore his *factum*[22] and therefore no longer alien as *certum,* or a mere subjective fact in the mind. In Vico's famous words,

> But in the night of thick darkness enveloping the earliest antiquity, so remote from ourselves, there shines the eternal and never failing light of a truth beyond all question: that the world of civil society has certainly been made by men, and that its principles are therefore to be found within the modifications of our own mind. Whoever reflects on this cannot but marvel that the philosophers should have bent all their energies to the study of nature, which since God made it, He alone knows; and that they should have neglected the study of the world of nations or civil world, which since man made it, men could come to know it.[23]

15

The notion was—is—revolutionary. All that was not of nature was not only knowable to man, but made (*factum*) by man, and for Vico *everything* that "is," save God and nature, was *made* by man. Since man had made it, he alone could have true knowledge of it, just as he had knowledge of geometry and mathematics. Thus, man made the true, *verum,* or as Vico put it, in the language of the schoolmen, *verum factum convertuntur.* But it is not only *verum* that man made and therefore knew, but also *bonum, pulchrum,* and the whole of civil society, its laws and customs, its institutions and values. The idea was unprecedented (or at any rate it was so prudently camouflaged in the true wisdom of *The Peloponnesian War* not to have been noticed in the modern world), but as Max Fisch put it, there were "hints" from which Vico might have derived the idea. Indeed, the "hint" Fisch suggests could not have been more appropriate—or more startling: "In the Vulgate," Fisch notes, "God says, 'Let x be made [*fiat*],' and x is made so [*factum est ita*], and God sees that x is good [*bonum*]. The maker intends; He makes true; and He inspects and passes what He had made."[24]

Until the *New Science,* however, the maker had been God. Now man became the maker and creator of the good, the true, and the beautiful. Thus, man becomes godlike, for the transcendentals became the *factum* of man. Vico "proposes that we cultivate the force of our divine mind in all its faculties . . . [and] proves that the human mind is by analogy the god of man, just as God is the mind of the whole of things." This idea, says Goretti, "especially epitomizes the Renaissance conception of man as mortal god."[25]

In fact, the transcendentals were no longer transcendentals at all but immanent in man. That which because of its abstractness had been altogether unknowable save to the mystic now became knowable to man. The world of abstraction—but also the world of verification—tumbled into the world of human *factum.* Thus, we may say that Vico, instead of adding another transcendental (that of the done or made, *factum*) to the recognized ontological transcendentals, changed the focus from the transcendental to the concrete, to immanentism, or to a new humanism. "Vico's epistemology," noted Edie, "thus establishes a notion of 'human truth.'"[26]

The key that made this immanentism possible, that unlocked the secret of man's godlike power to create, was Vico's discovery that the first men were primitives, that the founders of human society were not sages like Moses, Solon, and Homer, but man-beasts who created by trial and error the civil society that surrounded them. "This discovery," Vico wrote, "which is the master key of this Science, has cost us the persistent research of almost all our literary life."[27]

These early man-beasts, these primitives, responding to particular needs and instincts, were geniuses at invention, Vico said, for they created solutions to problems without models but with imagination. Moreover, these instinctual and imaginative solutions came in response to particular problems, for early man did not think in terms of universal solutions or possess abstract thought of any kind. Thus, in law; "the most ancient laws, we observe, were each concerned to command or forbid in but a single case; only later were they given general application (so incapable of universals were the first people!); and furthermore they were not concerned at all before the acts occurred that made them necessary."[28] This discovery of the ad hoc nature of our primitive forebears' responses to problems shattered all previous assumptions about the origin of society, about its founders or founder. It also called into question all notions of an eternal law of any kind: contract theory, natural law, the eternal law of God. This acknowledgment of the feral origins of humanity, whatever Vico intended, flew in the face of the entire Christian tradition and caused, as well, a lively controversy in Italy between the *ferini* (those who accepted Vico) and the *antiferini.* "To admit the feral state as the starting point for the rise of humanity, and to make the development of society a matter of internal dialectic, was to put the entire structure of Catholic thought in jeopardy."[29] "It is certain," noted Croce, "from an objective point of view that Vico's doctrines implicitly contained criticism of Christian transcendence and theology as well as the history of Christianity."[30] Man was the sole founder of his civil institutions and had founded them without any guidance, without any model. Man therefore ruled over history as God ruled over nature, two divine providences rather than one.

Because the ancients were those who created out of a void the civilizations of the world (the Gentile world, Vico said, for the Hebrews had special guidance),[31] they were called "poets, which is Greek for creators."[32] It is to these poets that we owe civilization—its values, language, and institutions. Baiting the Cartesians, Vico said:

> We shall show clearly and distinctly how the founders of Gentile humanity by means of their natural theology (or metaphysics) imagined the gods; how by means of their logic they invented language; by morals, created heroes; by economics, founded families, and by politics, cities; by their physics, established the beginnings of things as all divine; by the particular physics of man, in a certain sense created themselves.[33]

This extraordinary evaluation of the primitives and their ex nihilo creations allowed Vico to see what his contemporary philosophes had missed. They insisted upon measuring early man by the standard of the immutable natural law, seeing as a result only how far man had fallen short of the ideal. Vico instead saw early man building his society from the terrifying void of chaos, and as a result he saw how far man had come. This radical departure from orthodox Cartesianism is stated by Fisch and Bergin:

> Certainly to posit as the founders of civilization not sages but brutes; to posit as the primitive and therefore basic forms of apprehension not reason but instinct, feeling, intuition, manipulatory inventiveness (that is, the apprehension not of the universal but of the particular); and to posit as the primitive and basic modes of generalization not the universals of science and philosophy but those of poetry . . . was to emancipate oneself at last from Descartes and give a new dignity to these philological and historical disciplines which he had despised as resting on inferior cognitive faculties. [34]

This reversal of perspective provided Vico with the basis for a startling new version of natural law. Far from transcending history, the natural law Vico envisioned was synonymous with it. The natural law described the development of man and man's creations, man's *factum*. It described, in short, everything human—law, truth, and our concepts of beauty, good, and the purpose of society.

To study the course of this natural law, Vico suggested a program as original and revealing as the law itself. Scholars should study not the words of the great philosophers and sages of the past, nor even the deeds of the ancient heroes, but rather the customs and traditions of the mass of men as they traveled through time. The natural law, in short, was "coeval with the customs of the nations" or, to put the matter differently, the natural law was manifest in what Vico called "common sense," [35] *sensis communis*. Common sense was found not in philosophy but in the words of ordinary language that effortlessly slip off the tongue, for when using them, there is no fear of misunderstanding. [36] Common sense had its origin in classical rhetoric. Classical rhetoric persuades by acting on "our instincts, on our passions, which generally become aroused by images . . . and does not seek to justify itself rationally." [37] This is not to say, however, that it is irrational but simply that it does not meet the standards of technical logic. The *ratio geometrica,* with its "quest for certitude [*certum*] which can be translated into a mathematical truth [*verum*]," implies that all knowledge that does not fit into this neat formula is simply not knowledge at all, that it is "the crazy maid of the house," to use Goretti's words. [38] "It is an error," Vico said, "to apply to the prudent conduct of life the abstract criterion of reasoning that obtains in the domain of science. . . . The doctrinaires judge human actions as they ought to be, not as they actually are." [39]

Vico may have found the type of reasoning he valued in the *Topics* of Aristotle. For the dialectic discussed in the *Topics* was the most basic form of

reasoning, allowing men to "reason from opinions that are generally accepted about every problem propounded to us."[40] It was reason, but reason which rested upon opinion and was therefore historical and probable. The Cartesians, however, rejected all that was probable and uncertain, and opinions, the stuff of custom and tradition, were uncertain. Opinions could not be certain, of course, and to expect them to be certain and to disregard all those that were not was the mark of a foolish man, said Aristotle. "It is the mark of an educated man to look for precision in each class of things just so far as the nature of the subject admits; it is evidently equally foolish to accept probable reasoning from a mathematician as to demand from a theoretician scientific proofs."[41] *Topics,* reasoning through opinion, was, in short, Vico's common sense.[42]

"Common sense is judgment without reflection, shared by an entire class, an entire people, or the entire human race."[43] Common sense, in short, is the world's history spoken, albeit unconsciously, by history's actors as they coped with life's needs, making choices dictated by that common sense that, while holding them prisoner, yet allowed them, so to speak, to act freely. "Human choice," wrote Vico, "by its nature uncertain, is made certain and determined by the common sense of men with respect to human needs or utilities."[44]

Vico found common sense manifested in all aspects of life: poetry, religion, myth, as well as deeds and social and civil institutions. All these aspects of ancient life exist today as words, and these words are the record of the human spirit, its footprints; and in the study of these words, in their etymology and in the order of their appearance, there is, therefore, the study of the unfolding of the human mind in history.[45] Words are the external manifestations of the ideas of man, and by learning how ancient man used words to explain life to himself, the historian learned about the development of man. Thus, by looking within "the modifications of the human mind" man discovered the nature of the ancients; by studying what their myths, poems, and legends meant to them rather than to the later historian, man learned the nature of the first men and hence of himself, for to know the origins of a thing is to know a thing.

This appreciation of man's common sense isolated Vico, of course, from the ideas of the humble masses, who would have been horrified at his blasphemous humanization of eternal truth. It also further separated Vico from the Enlightenment tradition. The typical Enlightenment approach was to avoid any examination of the bewildering and contradictory customs, traditions, and common sense of the mass of men, the vulgar wisdom of the herd, and to concentrate instead upon the sublime natural law. "So long as I gave thought only to the manners and customs of men," groaned Descartes, "I met with nothing to reassure me, finding almost as much diversity in them as I had previously found in the opinions of philosophers."[46] Even Rousseau valued the mind of his sovereign horde only before it was contaminated by customs, traditions, and civilized common sense. The eighteenth-century philosophe saw truth as lying somewhere—anywhere—except in common sense; indeed, to him common sense was the barrier that masked the real world of his natural law. If common sense—"prejudice" said the philosophe—could be broken down, then the natural law and natural harmony of nature would begin.

Having concluded that man is the author of his customs and his common sense, indeed his values, and, as a later generation would conclude, even his God, Vico stood before a thoroughly modern abyss. He did not notice. Anticipating that "invisible hand" of Adam Smith, Vico ordered and arranged the potential chaos of his discovery into what he assumed would provide again a rationality for the real.

In examining the customs and common sense of one nation and another, Vico noted an extraordinary thing. A pattern emerged, an ideal and eternal pattern, through which each nation had passed. This pattern, these *corsi e ricorsi,* which were everywhere and always the same, described the rise and fall of the nations, the "course the nations run." It was this pattern that revealed meaning in the *factum* of men. Unlike the natural law of the philosophes, Vico's *corsi* were not abstractions imposed upon unwilling human history but a description of history, of the real, a theory of practice as a later generation would learn to call it. Moreover, precisely because this law was synonymous with history and made by man, it was natural rather than conventional, or merely conventional.

According to Vico's law, man rose from the barbarian era to an age of gods where "men believed themselves and all their institutions to depend on the gods, since they thought everything was a god or was made or done by a god."[47] From the age of gods man passed to the age of heroes, where the founders of society believed themselves to be descendants of the gods and their exploits were therefore immortalized by the early bards and poets. Finally came the age of man, wherein man separated himself from the gods entirely and saw, or thought he saw, immanent within his own nature the power to order his own destiny. Following this last state came the age of skepticism and man then passed back into barbarism, the *corso* thus completed, the *ricorso* about to begin. This cycle of history with its attendant forms of government, its languages, laws, reason, customs is the subject of the fourth book of the *New Science.*

This "ideal eternal law," this "course the nations run," however, does admit of exceptions. Vico did not mean that every civilization must or even would follow the ideal universal pattern described in the *New Science.* There could and would be exceptions caused by extraordinary events, though the ideal pattern remained valid. That a youngster should die accidentally, or for that matter that the majority of youngsters might die accidentally, would not invalidate the universal law that a youth is meant to mature and to die in old age.[48]

The near inevitability of this course the nations run (*corso e ricorso*) Vico attributed to providence. It was providence that accounted for the fact that the ideal eternal law was everywhere and always the same. It was providence that accounted for the disparity between the ends envisioned by individual human actors in history and the ends that their combined efforts produced, for man's private ends were thwarted by a providence that acted in the interest of wider ends.[49]

For Vico this did not obviate man's free will, nor did it mean that the world was not the product of mind.

> It is true that men have themselves made this world of nations (and we took this as the first incontestable principle of our Science, since we despaired of finding it from the philosophers and philologists), but this world without doubt has issued from a mind often diverse, at times quite contrary, and always superior to the particular ends that men had proposed to themselves; which narrow ends, made means to serve wider ends, it has always employed to preserve the human race upon this earth. . . . That which did all this was mind, for men did it with intelligence; it was not fate, for they did it by choice, for the results of their always so acting are perpetually the same.[50]

Not chance, then, but providence working through man has made the world as it is. It is the locus of this providence, however, that arrests the reader. It is, in the *New Science,* nearly everywhere preceded by the word "divine"; yet nowhere does either "divine" or "providence" begin with a capital letter, though God and Science always do. Providence is, moreover, not infrequently compared with the "true God" who guides the Hebrews and "the ordinary help from providence" offered to the Gentiles,[51] leading one to the supposition that providence was to Vico nothing more—and nothing less either—than the collective will of man. This collective will, made manifest in the history of common sense, therefore lay immanent in man as opposed to the transcendent providence of the "true God" who guided the Israelites.

In placing the logos of history squarely within man, or rather in suggesting that Vico lodged it there, one risks imposing the common sense of the present upon a writer who wrote two centuries earlier in a time that only gradually came to accept the notion of Adam Smith's "invisible hand" and, much later, Hegel's "cunning of reason."[52] Nevertheless, the belief in Vico's theory of immanence seems justified, for it is the only theory that remains consistent with Vico's human theory of knowledge, the *verum ipsum factum*, and the human origins of history asserted in the *New Science*. To suppose any continuing role for the transcendent God of history in even the most innocuous fashion seems to fly in the face of Vico's intentions. To preserve God in any fashion, in fact, would, in A. William Salomone's words,

> deprive the world of human history of the very autonomy, "integrity," and responsibility which the *Scienza nuova,* had so arduously discovered in that world. . . . To have reintroduced . . . [at] the very end of the *Scienza nuova,* the purely Christian idea of providence as the ultimate arbiter of the antinomy of history would only have signified that Vico, having let Cartesian reason out the front door of his philosophical structure, was now, practically in the last moment, willing to re-admit theological providentialism through the back door.[53]

After Vico's death in 1744 this earthly providence was to become his most famous and enduring legacy. In fact, down to the present day Vico's work has usually been seen as fruitful only insofar as it confirmed the idea of a human history controlled by man alone and therefore possessing "autonomy, 'integrity,' and responsibility." The other half of Vico's message—the Science of the *New Science*—was ignored by Vico's followers, who did not want to accept the dismal prospect of the inexorable *corsi e ricorsi.* This bowdlerization of Vico began immediately upon his death, for in the dominant Enlightenment culture of Naples, with its belief in progress, liberty, and republicanism, the second message was incomprehensible, for it seemed to deny the very autonomy the first message had promised. In fact, Vico's most ardent—self-proclaimed—followers were themselves caught up in and absorbed by the ideas of the Enlightenment—a silent and unnoticed testimony to the inescapable *corsi* of culture. These "Vichians" soon transformed Vico into a spokesman for precisely those ideas he had so long and vigorously opposed. The *corsi,* they announced, were not the natural law that described the course the nations run, but a record of unnatural and quite avoidable human errors. Now that man recognized himself as author and master of history, the *corsi* could be forgotten and the declines consciously avoided. In short, the more the heirs of Vico examined earlier history and saw its shortcomings, the more they were convinced that the natural law did not provide for failure but for progress; for the law was not in history but outside it, an eternal "clear and distinct" truth which, if followed, would allow man to escape the past. The result of this transfiguration of Vico was the politicization of the *New Science*. Because of their commitment to a "better history" for mankind, the "new Vichians" threw in their lot with the republican and democratic zealots of the Neapolitan Enlightenment.[54] Caught up in the fashionable doctrine of natural law, natural rights, and the natural "equality" of men, they could not imagine that Vico, too, had not been an early, albeit unconscious, Jacobin. Therefore:

> The thinkers of the [Neapolitan] Enlightenment subjected the *Scienza nuova* to a process of dismemberment, disengaging and developing those parts of the work which best fitted their aims and disregarding the others. They were helped in doing this (we should add) by the insufficient organicity of Vico's work. The boldest ones went to the length of seeking in his work some support for the principle of the natural equality of all men (a principle dear to the new believers) and found it in the "poetical characters," who had redimensioned and leveled in a popular way the great figures of secular history.[55]

Those "poetical characters" (Moses, Solon, Homer), who were "leveled" by Vico's *New Science* and whose "leveling" proved so popular to the democratic and egalitarian ideas of the philosophes of Naples, were not, of course, intended by Vico to demonstrate egalitarianism. On the contrary, the bulk of the *New Science* had been devoted to disproving the existence of the historical Homer only in order to prove the absence of any primal law or primal lawgiver. Yet by asserting that history moved forward on account of the common sense of humanity, the work of the many rather than the few or the one, the *New Science* seemed to the late-eighteenth-century Vichians to add historical justification to the revolutionary message they wished to promulgate. It was but a short step from Vico's leveling of Homer and the other ancient "great ones" to a leveling of the contemporary great ones who sat on and around the Bourbon throne of Naples.

As the French Revolution approached, the Neapolitan Vichians became ever more hostile to the Bourbon regime, and with the outbreak of the Revolution in 1789, they were utterly transformed from idle thinkers into superheated Jacobins.[56] To them the revolution proved that man indeed was the author of his institutions. Excitement mounted as the French took Rome in February of 1798, sending into exile the half-paralyzed, eighty-year-old Pope Pius VI. Exiling the pope, however, had unexpected consequences. While it demonstrated the revolutionary power of man to make and unmake his institutions, thereby cheering the Neapolitan republicans, it alienated for a century and more the already suspicious common people of the South, who, steeped in the tradition of religious and secular hierarchy, were dismayed and disoriented by this purely human interference in the given order.

Within a year the French were at Naples, and when King Ferdinand fled to Sicily, the republicans were installed in power by the occupying forces. Transported from the salons to the palace, they did not notice, or affected not to notice, the sullen and bitter stares of the common people, nor did they seem to note the fierce antagonism and bitter resistance the French met everywhere in the kingdom. The natural law, they believed, even though promulgated from above by an elite of seers, would soon win the necessary wide support and a new common sense would result. The republicans believed, in short, that they could dictate common sense, altering the *corsi e ricorsi* by legislative fiat. The republic was named, fittingly enough, after Parthenope, one of those sirens of yore whose seductive melodies had lured ancient mariners to their destruction.

Propped up by French arms, the Parthenopean radicals constituted themselves as a legislative council and grandly swept away the vestiges of feudalism, primogeniture, and religious domination. Their evenings were spent in discussion of civic virtue and attending performances—at the Patriotic Theatre—of Alfieri's *Timoleone*. Alfieri's tragedy was performed

> with the following puff, a perfect sample of the brave new style: "A great mirror of exemplariness, of moral and Republican virtues, was this historic upholder of the rights of man! His modesty, truly worthy of a philanthropic heart, even amid the lustre of his actions and of the acclamations of an entire people familiar with his sublime democratic sentiments, which led him (an object of envy!) to stifle the tenderest voices of nature through heroism, deserves to be admired, to be followed, and to serve as a lesson to the whole regenerated World.
>
> "Patriots of Naples, run hither in crowds to steel your hearts and revive your energies! In order to make the way easy for you the manager offers free entrance to all this evening (May 24), and those who wish to pay at the door will benefit their indigent brothers, among whom this sum will be distributed. Citizens zealous for your country, bring artists, relations and friends! The action is worthy of you."[57]

Out of the initial chaos of the revolution there emerged among the new political leadership Vichian intellectuals like Mario Pagano and Vincenzo Cuoco. Pagano was, without doubt, the most well known.[58] It was he who introduced the bill in the legislative assembly to confiscate the land and property of those who had fled to Sicily with the king, and it was he who elaborated a constitution for the new government. It was "of the Roman type," as Luigi Salvatorelli put it, complete with "archons, censors, and ephors. The population, only recently quieted from shouts of 'Long live the Holy Faith, Long live San Gennaro, Death to the Jacobins,' gave but grudging approval."[59]

Cuoco, the other great Vichian, noting the sullen attitude of the Neapolitans, was more cautious about what the revolution could achieve, though he did not shrink from participation. In a letter to Vincenzo Russo, another conspirator considerably more unrealistic than Pagano,[60] Cuoco expressed concern.

> The project given us by Pagano is not the best. It is better certainly than the Ligurian, Roman, and Cisalpine [constitutions], but it seems to me that it is too French and too little Neapolitan. Pagano's edifice is constructed of material which the French constitution provided him; the architect is grand, but the material of its construction is only clay.[61]

Cuoco went on to point out that every people cherishes in its common sense the memory of its ancient customs. The more enslaved it becomes, the more dear the customs of the past.

> This residue of customs and government of other times, which is found in every nation, is precious to a wise legislator and ought to form the base of his new order.[62] The people always preserve respect for what came to them from their ancestors. . . . Those that wish to destroy it, do they not see that they destroy in this way every foundation of justice and every principle of social order?[63]

Russo was unimpressed, as was Pagano, but meanwhile, outside the Legislative Assembly and the Patriotic Theatre, in the streets of Naples and in the countryside of the Regno di Napoli, the forces who revered those ancient customs—their ancient common sense—began to gather strength.

On February 7, 1799, a scarlet-clad cardinal atop a snow-white horse landed, with eight companions, on the shores of Reggio Calabria. Fabrizio Ruffo, sent by Ferdinand I from his exile in Palermo, began the organization of a ragtag army of peasants, ruffians, brigands, and religious zealots who were called the sanfedisti, those of the Holy Faith. With the formation of the Second Coalition and the consequent withdrawal of the French, the sanfedisti began a bloody, chaotic assault northwards. Ruffo's forces moved inexorably toward Naples, butchering any pro-French citizens who happened to fall into their hands. Meanwhile, at Naples, the legislative council continued its abolition of fiefdom and its emancipation of the very peasants who now surrounded the city. The enraged mob fell upon Naples in a grisly melee that no one dared to halt. With the arrival of the king, a series of "trials" were held, as a result of which Pagano, Russo, and hundreds of others were, if lucky, beheaded.[64] Cuoco escaped this fate, and in 1800 began to set out an account of what had happened.[65]

The *Saggio storico sulla rivoluzione napoletana del 1799* made two points.

In the first place it was a reassertion of Vico's hostility to abstract speculation and in the second it was a fundamental revision of nearly every aspect of Vico's work. In reasserting Vico, Cuoco noted that the Parthenopean Republic had been a failure because of an overestimation of the power of philosophy.[66]

> Imagining a republican constitution is not the same as founding a republic. ... Liberty is not established save through forming free men. Before erecting the edifice of liberty on Neapolitan soil, there were, in the ancient constitution, in the ancient customs and prejudices, in the present interests of the inhabitants, a thousand obstacles.[67]

After Cuoco Neapolitan thinkers were, with only infrequent exceptions, to remain hostile to the whole abstract Enlightenment tradition, preserving forever the memory of 1799 as a kind of insulation against French materialism, rationalism, and optimism. Thus, in the nineteenth and twentieth centuries, Naples was to welcome not positivism and scientific methodology—to which it has always remained hostile—but Hegel and classical German philosophy. It was thus from Naples that Benedetto Croce at the beginning of the twentieth century, while warning against "positivism" and the evil effects of "Encyclopedism" and "Jacobinism," recalled the "sad experience" Italy had suffered because of these ideologies "at the time of the French invasions." He went on to note, "The entire Italian Risorgimento developed as a reaction against that French, Jacobin, Masonic direction." It therefore seemed "impossible" to him that any Italian should take positivism seriously, "impossible" that, "simply to imitate the French, we again import that calamity from which we suffered more than a century ago."[68]

It was not this orthodox Vichian position, however, that was to assure Cuoco a position in history. It was, rather, in his revision of Vico that he was to influence the course of Neapolitan humanism and, after 1860 when that humanism became more widely known and influential, the course of Italian thought as well. To Cuoco after 1799, Vico's science seemed a prison. Man was free to create his own civil history, and yet this history was controlled, despite everything, by the inexorable *corsi e ricorsi.* Evangelizing the message that man was author of his civil institutions had led to the stoning of the evangels, a stoning at the hands of the very persons the message was supposed to emancipate. Yet to accept the futility of human efforts to alter the *corsi* meant withdrawal to an otherworldly stoicism. Cuoco did not intend to surrender to the *corsi.*

The problem was, he decided, that Neapolitan culture was divided into two peoples. The revolution had not been made by the people but against them. It was not an active revolution but a passive one, for its success depended upon winning public opinion *after* the revolution rather than before.

Our revolution was a passive one, the only means of bringing it to a successful conclusion being to win over public opinion. But the views of the patriots[69] and those of the population were not the same; they had different
ideas, different customs, and even different languages. . . . The Neapolitan
nation is to be considered as divided into two peoples separated by two
centuries. . . . Since the cultured group was educated according to foreign
models, its culture was of the few and of no use to the nation, and the
nation nearly despised a culture that was useless and that they did not understand.[70]

The southern peasant, rooted in feudalism and religion, at home in what
appeared to him a natural hierarchy of men and things, possessed a common
sense akin to that of the medieval peasant or, at best, the peasant of the Vendée
in 1793-94. On the other hand, the Neapolitan philosophe, at home in the
salon and living vicariously, if not in fact, at Paris, was content only when contemplating the natural law and, ironically, the equality of man. These two cul-
tures, which until 1799 had lived together in amiable indifference and mutual
incomprehension, became for Cuoco the foundation of his revolutionary revision of Vico. Rereading the *New Science* after 1799, Cuoco noted there Vico's
remarks on the rational *popolo raziocinante* and the irrational *popolo sensiente,*
on the historic role of the *famuli* (serfs) and heroes, and he saw there, or thought
he saw there, proof that Vico, too, had recognized the existence of the two
peoples.[71] It followed, as a matter of common sense, that Vico had meant the
rational to rule over the irrational. Thus was Vico's long campaign against the
"company of philosophes" turned into a campaign in their favor.

To place the doctrine of the two peoples—the one conscious, the other not—
in the *New Science* was, however, to overturn not only Vico's idea that history
was the history of common sense rather than the vision of the rationalist elite,
but to overturn and call into question as well the whole theory of the *corsi e ricorsi,* the whole idea that history—however literally one takes the *corsi*—had a
life of its own. It was precisely this, in fact, that Cuoco meant to challenge. In
Vico the voice of providence had been the collective voice of the nation, the
unconscious and the conscious, the noble and the elite, who, shouting at each
other in worldly disharmony, produced—everywhere and always—precisely the
harmonious *corsi e ricorsi* they all sought differently to avoid. For Vico the
idea that the nation might speak with one voice, asserting one truth, was absurd
and would have nullified the whole idea of a providence that, as he put it, was
"at times quite contrary, and always superior to the particular ends that men had
proposed themselves." In the doctrine of the two peoples Cuoco now sought his
way out of the inexorable Vichian *corsi.* For Cuoco providence became the voice

of the elect, their "particular ends" being frustrated by the unconscious pleb who, because of his abiding ignorance of philosophy, made the *corsi* inevitable.

The gulf between the sanfedisti and the philosophers, however, could not be breached, for the philosopher could not be made to understand the pleb, and, as 1799 indicated, raising the pleb to philosophy was both "dangerous and impossible." The only answer was to put leadership in the hands of an elite who would speak with one voice while educating the masses to toil docilely—and silently—in socially useful capacities. The dictatorship of Joachim Murat was the perfect vehicle for such an endeavor.

In 1806 Napoleon's forces again seized Naples and, in 1808, installed Murat upon the vacant Bourbon throne. Unlike the revolutionaries of 1799, Murat was welcomed by both the upper and lower strata of society,[72] and it was to Murat's Naples that Cuoco returned. Murat's dictatorship was no mere abstraction like the Parthenopean Republic, no mere "representative system" reflecting the cacophony of two different voices. It was a "concrete and living unity" which "possessed at once the life and activity of the particulars, and the weight and energy of their synthesis."[73] It was then merely a question of "educating" the peasant into playing his proper silent role. Cuoco therefore submitted to Murat a lengthy report on "education," noting that "the political problem is a problem of education."[74]

This report, however, was not simply a report on educating the masses to socially useful lives, but a program that was to insure, as the earlier Platonic Republic had insured, that philosophers did not corrupt the men of lead with notions of abstract philosophy, utopian dreams, and poetry. Insulating the masses from metaphysics, Cuoco felt, ought not to be difficult, for the people had an almost natural and Vichian hostility to the abstract and useless. Prior to 1799, Cuoco noted—doubtless recalling Vico's "De nostri temporis studiorum ratione"—education had been "useless," encouraging idle speculation and political adventurism among the few and invincible boredom among the many.

The "rapporto" therefore advised Murat that philosophy and science be concerned not with abstract speculation but with the concrete *art* of life. For Cuoco, "art" meant skill, craft, or usage (*techne,* for the Greeks), and his primary concern was to make philosophy and science into art in that sense of the word. For

> the end of knowing is action. If the sciences are of no use in the smallest concerns of life, if they are not strictly united to the arts, they become gloriously useless or remain imperfect. We will say more: the sciences will remain imperfect, for their foundation is experience and [experience] is the fruit of the skills and practice of life [*figlia delle arti e dell' uso della vita*].[75]

Thus, knowledge, in order to be truly knowledge, must find its confirmation in the practice of life. This is the key to the "Rapporto." Whatever subject fell beneath the scrutiny of Cuoco, be it the cost of education or the subject to be taught, all was evaluated according to the test of its utility for the citizen and the state.

Even at the university level, Cuoco, like Vico, discouraged abstract thought; the Department of Philosophy and Belles Lettres, for example, should concentrate upon the useful and the instrumental. "The philosophy of which we speak is not to be taken in all the broad extension of meaning which such a term might have. In such a case it would mean all that is humanly knowable. . . . But here we intend to speak only on the part of philosophy which used to be called 'instrumental' and which is concerned with the operations of our spirit and its regulation." [76] In the realm of logic, similarly, he explained that men learn either by reason, as in geometry, or by experience. The first is easy: "Two geometric propositions which the professor will analyze for his students will teach them as much as necessary." [77] On the other hand, "the most difficult thing is to teach the students the method of experience." This, he said, echoing and citing Vico's hymn to rhetoric, to common sense, ought to be based upon probability. "The most necessary and most ignored element in logic is the theory of probability. How few times can we hope to reach the truth and how often, on the other hand, are we forced to proceed with nothing more than probability." (Not the probability taught by mathematicians, he added, for that was an abstraction that did not apply to life, an abstraction in which "the regularity of the formula had conquered the reality of the thing.") [78]

The advancement of the masses to useful social life within parameters set out by the state was epitomized in Cuoco's concept of "uniform" education. Education had to be uniform and directed from Naples, Cuoco believed, else upon its arrival in the provinces it be distorted to conform to local tastes and abstract discussions. Texts, methods of instruction, even scientific theories ought to be uniform throughout the state and scrutinized by the state. It was a disagreeable idea even to Cuoco and one not without disadvantages for the progress of science. "This uniformity can produce serious evils for the sciences themselves and can retard the progress of them more than disputes. The Jesuits are an example." [79] How can one obtain, he asked, "that uniformity which facilitates universal instruction without destroying the strength of the individual?" [80] Cuoco's answer was that the central control of education be lodged in a commission whose members would be encouraged to dissent among themselves while enforcing below the will of the commission. "Confidence from below, authority from above," as his French contemporary put it. [81]

29

Cuoco proposed three levels of education: primary, secondary, and university. All citizens would attend the first level, the purpose of which was, significantly, not simply to teach the basic skills of reading, writing, and arithmetic but to provide the population from on high with a common morality or, as Vico would have said, a common sense.[82] "Morality is the primary need of a society, and a common morality is as necessary as morality itself. Whatever be the system one wishes to follow, it must be confessed that morality is an intrinsic property of our mind."[83] Since the need for a morality is a part of human nature, if morality is not provided through education, men will provide it for themselves, and there will then be, Cuoco feared, as many moralities as there are subjects in the kingdom—or worse yet, a morality at the bottom which is hostile to the morality above.

Cuoco's foray into the "political" uses of education was to provide an essential ingredient in Neapolitan humanism, one it was never to lose. Politics and education forever afterwards were, for the humanist, entwined. Consciously or not, perhaps they always had been. What was novel in Cuoco, however—at least since the time of the Greeks—was that education here was catapulted onto a stratospheric level involving cosmic questions about the duty of "the conscious" men to the "unconscious." Because the former believed there were no limits on man's power in the world and the latter believed in a world controlled by divine, natural, and purely impish forces quite beyond our control, the "conscious" men saw their duty in both overinflated and awesome terms. Any doctrine of limited government, of the individual's right to pursue his own self-interest, became treachery against all humanity. As Lenin indicated, such a notion is pregnant with an ascending scale of possibilities, possibilities that can be controlled only by a frank acknowledgment of man's limited power to shape events. Such an acknowledgment came hard after reading Vico and leaving out the *corsi.*

With the defeat of Napoleon, however, any real experimentation with Cuoco's doctrine of education came to an end; the revolutionary Vichians disappeared as rapidly as the French armies. Their legacy, however, was to remain. Abstracted from the mass, the revolutionary humanists of Italy were to revolt again and again after 1799, each time colliding with the "other people," enacting a history of their own *corsi e ricorsi* as they sought to free the pleb from the spiritual and temporal forces that held him prisoner, sought, in fact, to free the pleb from himself.

It was, however, another generation before this humanist culture of Naples would again rise to challenge the official teachings of the Bourbon state and its Catholic ally. Despite periodic outbursts of violence and near incomprehensible revolutionary combinations such as that which produced the Carbonari revolt of 1820, the humanist culture of Naples remained after 1815 and up until about the 1840s an easily controlled and fairly innocuous movement.

Then, in the late 1830s and especially in the 1840s, the revolutionary fever again began to rise. The issues themselves were no longer simply those of 1789, for a new ideology now stirred Italian intellectuals: nationalism. In midcentury, nationalism and humanism coalesced in Italy to provide one of the primary foundations for the Risorgimento. As with the revolutionary spirit of the previous century, this nationalism was anything but a popular movement, especially in the South. Conquered, looted, and plundered for centuries, Italians—especially southern Italians—had long ago given up any notion of a common nation-state. Only a small elite in the South understood the vision of an Italian nation and were willing and anxious to merge the South into the wider context of Italian and European life. This elite, exiled time and again for their revolutionary activities, had become, like those Neapolitan Enlightenment philosophes educated at Paris in the last century, more at home abroad than at Naples, more familiar with European culture than their own native culture. The southern population as a whole, meanwhile, remained rooted in its religious traditions, and when the papacy explicitly opposed Italian unification, the people became dutifully indifferent, if not absolutely hostile, to the Risorgimento. There thus opened again in the Risorgimento itself the chasm between the two peoples of the South, between those who saw the vision of a united Italy and those who followed the antinationalist teachings of the Church.

While the masses remained with the Church, the elite turned elsewhere for support in their quest for a unified state. They found their prophet in Georg Wilhelm Friedrich Hegel. Hegel, of course, is not a name that springs readily to mind as one contemplates the Risorgimento.[84] Yet among patriots, especially at Naples, Hegel awakened a wide and sympathetic following. In the early 1840's, in fact, Hegel was strewn all over the underground nationalist culture of Naples, in literary, political, and philosophical journals, in academies, debating societies, and radical groups of various and not infrequently contradictory purposes. The movement was anything but coherent, save in its hostility to the Bourbon regime. Conflicts between left Hegelians and right Hegelians, nationalist-republican, nationalist-monarchist, and even Mazzinian Hegelians abounded. Hegel, with his glorification of mind, his concept of historical inevitability, and especially his exaltation of the nation-state, found, in stateless Italy, an almost natural following, particularly among southern intellectuals raised in the Vichian milieu.

Writing to Engels at the end of the nineteenth century, Antonio Labriola, another Neapolitan and one of the most brilliant of the founders of Italian Marxism, noted two phases in Neapolitan Hegelianism, the one "private," the other "public." Hegelianism developed "at Naples, privately from 1840 to 1860, and then publicly at the University [of Naples] from 1860 to 1875."[85] The dates were significant: Hegelianism developed "privately" from 1840 to 1860 because it was regarded, quite rightly, by both opponents and proponents, as radical nationalism. Then, in 1860, Italian unification took place, and Hegelianism became "public" because it had remained the ideology of the successful southern patriots who now came to serve the new regime they had helped to build. In serving the new state they continued to propagate the Hegelian nationalist "religion" in order to undo the counterrevolution of the Catholic and Bourbon antinationalists.

Though extremely diverse, the early "private" phase of Neapolitan Hegelianism (1840–60) was dominated by republican and democratic Hegelians, men who believed, as the revolutionaries of 1799, that success was merely a matter of "imagining a republican constitution." Revolutions similar to the one they were promoting at Naples would, they believed, lead inevitably to one large, unified Italian republic. For these patriots, 1848 was what 1799 had been for Cuoco and his followers, the end of their innocent republicanism. The revolution was an utter failure nearly everywhere, but especially at Naples, and the sobered participants, isolated from the mass they sought to free, were clearly bewildered. Three years later Napoleon III's coup d'etat at Paris delivered a knockout blow to republicanism nearly everywhere. The Hegelian patriots, after 1851, turned their attention to the aggressive state of Piedmont, hoping to find there a power that would do from the top what the Italian masses would not do from below. If Italians would not coalesce to produce the state, then the state would, as one non-Hegelian put it, expand to "make the Italians."[86]

Hegelianism had arrived in Italy not from Germany, but from France, in the person of Victor Cousin and through the translations (from German into French) of Augusto Vera. Given the problems of the translations[87] as well as the in-house disputes of the Neapolitan Hegelians, it is not surprising that Hegelianism was almost immediately transformed to meet local as well as personal tastes. That the Bourbon police regarded the Hegelians as subversives only added to the confusion, for the response of the Hegelians was to further obscure the thought of the master with indirect references, inscrutable metaphors, and guarded phrases, producing a liturgy all but indecipherable today. On the other hand, it is said, it "enriched" the writings of the period on such "safe" subjects as literature and history, to which the Hegelians were forced to turn.[88]

One of the leading Hegelian philosophers of the South, and later of the new Italian state, was Bertrando Spaventa, by most accounts, favorable or not, the leading intellectual of the era. As with Vico before him, however, his intellectual ability isolated him from his fellows, and despite his great mind and his contributions to the new Italian state, he was, in the Italy of his day, regarded with suspicion. His lectures at the University of Naples were hooted, his writings frequently rejected by the publishers.[89]

As the philosopher of a state that was as foreign to most Italians—especially southern Italians—as ever the Bourbons had been, Spaventa's real influence did not begin until some twenty years after his death. At the dawn of the present century he was discovered by his most celebrated student and biographer, Giovanni Gentile. From the time of that discovery to the end of World War II, Spaventa remained where Gentile, the "philosopher of fascism," placed him, as the "precursor" of modern thought, the architect of the twentieth-century ethical state. For Gentile, Spaventa was

> the most accomplished representative of our spiritual heritage, who was inspired to study foreign philosophy only to acquire a profound consciousness of the highest speculative needs of modern times, and therefore deepen all the seeds of life that were in our great tradition, from the great thinkers of the Renaissance, heralds and martyrs of the new European thought, to the most noted philosophers who emerged in the nineteenth century from the national Catholic orientation. In him all forces met and were united; with him the old Italy passed and the new began.[90]

Given the fate of Gentile and the ethical state under Mussolini, it is not surprising that few have found it worthwhile uncovering Gentile's Spaventa. Recently, however, new scholars, almost all Marxist, have resurrected Spaventa, and so, like Lazarus, he enjoys a new existence. If Gentile had aimed at establishing a tradition that ran Hegel-Spaventa-Gentile, the new Marxists have their own tradition in mind: Hegel-Spaventa-Labriola-Gramsci.[91] For Giuseppe Berti, Spaventa was the Italian Feuerbach:

> The philosophy of Spaventa, like the philosophy of Feuerbach, is dominated by an anthropological principle. Its object is no longer—as in Hegel—the absolute spirit, but *man* . . . man who at a certain moment separated himself from nature and has created the world. Spaventa, in other words, shared one of the fundamental affirmations of the German left Hegelians, of the philosophy of Feuerbach, that is, that "philosophy must have as its cognitive principle, as its object, not the ego [*l'io*], nor the absolute spirit or the abstract, or even reason *in the abstract,* but the real and total being of man."[92]

Between the thought of Hegel and Spaventa,

there is, therefore, not only a break, there is an abyss. Spaventa affirmed in depth *implicitly* what Feuerbach affirmed explicitly, that is, "whoever does not renounce Hegelian philosophy, does not renounce theology either; because the Hegelian doctrine . . . is nothing more than the exposition, in rational terms, of theological doctrine." . . . If one wishes to say that Hegel was continued by Spaventa it is analogous . . . to our saying that Hegel is overcome and continued by the left Hegelians.[93]

There is more to Berti's claim that Spaventa is no longer concerned with the absolute spirit, but with man—and less. While Spaventa's concern is no longer the *Weltgeist*, neither is it man; it is the state.

This new literature has, on the whole, not much changed the picture of Spaventa given us by Gentile, though articles—unknown to Gentile—attesting to the genuine social revolutionary position of Spaventa in the early 1850s have recently been discovered.[94] The Marxist literature, in fact, tends to confirm the view that Spaventa was the author of the idea of a radical, nearly omnipresent pedagogical state whose purpose was to raise the pleb to citizen, to create the cultural hegemony later called for by both Gramsci and Gentile—however else they may have differed. The Marxist scholars are by no means, however, a unanimous school, but our purpose here is not to explore the in-house polemics of that group, but rather to put Spaventa back into the context of the nineteenth century so as to understand not only the force he represented but also those he opposed.

Like Cuoco, Spaventa represented one of the principal evangelists of a new doctrine being elaborated against sanfedisti feudalism and Catholicism, a kind of lay humanism or religion that celebrated man as creator of his own destiny. Not much is known of Spaventa's early life, and the most reliable knowledge of his political and intellectual activity comes only after 1848.[95]

A caustic Abruzzese, born—fittingly enough—in the town of Bomba in 1817, Spaventa, at his parents' wishes, entered the priesthood[96] and was educated at the seminary in Chieti. Later he became a teacher at Monte Cassino and, in 1840, came, with his equally famous brother, Silvio, to Naples, where he was associated with the nationalist revolutionaries of 1848. With the exception of a single writing on mathematics of 1840 there is little evidence of Spaventa's thought for the next ten years when, exiled in Turin for participation in the abortive '48, he renounced the priesthood, became a Freemason, and began to write in the radical journal *Il progresso*.

If nothing very specific can be said about this lost decade in Spaventa's biography, something can be said about the circles in which he probably traveled,[97] namely among the "Hegelians" of Naples.[98] "The Italian philosophy of the Risorgimento," wrote Bertrando years later, "was German philosophy. Hegel and the other earlier German philosophers were known in Naples before 1848."[99] In the journal *Nazionale* there is a clear expression of this pre-1848 Hegelianism. There one finds as well articles by Silvio Spaventa and—it is tempting to believe, but evidently impossible to prove—also by Bertrando, though the latter, as a cleric, was in no position to air his grudges against the regime publicly. *Nazionale* presented Hegel as the prophet of liberty, a philosopher who saw history as the "story of liberty." Announced *Nazionale:* "Reason alone governs the world, and [reason] has an infinite right to existence. Reason is its own end and this end is liberty. [Thus] the idea of every revolution is necessarily the idea of liberty." The words are Silvio's, but Bertrando would in no way have disagreed.[100] "Reason alone governs the world." They are words to ponder. For Hegel they had implied the instability of a world based on a developing reason, the present always on the verge of the future, the "is" in constant conflict with the "ought," and, depending on whether one emphasized the "is" or the "ought," the "necessity" or the "possibility," a conservative or revolutionary position. In *Nazionale,* it scarcely need be noted, the ambiguous Hegelian position became exclusively revolutionary.

This emphasis upon "liberty" and "reason" led the writers in *Nazionale* to embrace republicanism, Silvio reporting later to Croce that had the king fled during the 1848 revolution, they would not have hesitated a moment in proclaiming a republic. Proclaiming a republic, however, as Cuoco had noted earlier, "is not the same as founding a republic. . . . Liberty is not established save through forming free men." The Hegelians, however, because they believed reason to be in charge of history and also that "reason is its own end and this end is liberty," felt little concern with Cuoco's anxieties. Their purpose was simply to provoke the revolution that would usher in the new era. Eighteen forty-eight was the test not only of the mettle of the revolutionaries but of the mind of history.

In that test, however, it was found that the mind of history lay still with the mass rather than with the elite and that the mass, far from desiring "reason" and "liberty," were content to rest with "authority." The revolution at Naples broke out in February and was followed—in some cases preceded—by violent outbursts all over Italy, indeed, all over Europe. At no other time during the Risorgimento, save in 1859, was all Italy so aflame and all authority so threatened. And yet by August it had all failed. In fact, as far as Naples was concerned, the revolutionary flame lasted only until May 15, when the king's forces attacked the revolutionaries, and the crowds, viewing the whole matter with the apolitical passion of a soccer match, ceased cheering the rebels and began to cheer the Swiss Guards.[101] The revolution had been a short-lived coup d'etat followed inevitably by the repression, imprisonment, execution, and exile of the revolutionaries.

On October 26, 1849, Bertrando went into exile at Florence, his brother having been arrested and imprisoned. After ten months Bertrando moved to Turin, where he received a position as professor of the history of philosophy at the University of Turin and in November and December of 1850 published the first articles that can definitely be attributed to him after 1840.[102] Disoriented, but not yet convinced that republicanism was a total failure, Spaventa in 1850 had had his faith in the people shaken, but not broken—yet.

The journal in which these articles appeared, *Il progresso* (November 1850 to December 1851), was, however, more ambiguous in its republicanism than had been *Nazionale,* ambiguous not only because it was within the confines of the Piedmontese monarchy, the only apparent hope against Austrian oppression, but ambiguous as well on account of its awkward attempt at reconciling the Hegelian "eternal design of reason," as Spaventa called it, with an unreliable popular will. This problem of reconciling popular liberty with an absolute reason became, in *Il progresso,* a nearly omnipresent theme, the writers occasionally wondering aloud whether or not they might have to go further than a republic, might not have to liberate the illiterate masses of *cafoni* not only from their oppressors but from themselves as well. Until the population could be infused with the "eternal design of reason," the state remained a mere abstraction. At this point Spaventa saw his role as that of an evangelist. Little, however, is more infuriating to the evangelist than that vacant shrug of the shoulders that Spaventa received as he urged Italians to abandon their religion and their anarchic individualism and create the Italian state. "The *last* century," he announced to an indifferent audience, "aimed at the absolute liberty of the individual; ours intends the absolute liberty of nations."

Over the next few months and years Spaventa's political temperature began to rise, and gradually there appeared an increasing hostility to Italian individualism and self-interest. Reason was one, was universal, the motor force of history; self-interest and particularism were the enemies of reason. The masses *would* rally, Italy *would* be created—but only when men put aside their prejudices, religious emotions, and individual whims, when men made their individual wills conform to "reason."[103] "Thought is the soul of the universe, the most intimate part of the life of nations. When it descends to the level of the material, the history of a people no longer has a true value, and the events that compose it are not the execution of the eternal design of reason, but simply accidents without purpose or result." Hegel, Spaventa pointed out, had resolved the dilemma left by Kant's positing of an empty formal liberty, a liberty without essence or content; for Hegelian doctrine set out both the form and the content of liberty. The form was the particular subject in action; the content was reason as manifested in the law of the state. Only when the individual conformed to this reason and the citizen submitted his particular will to that reason did true liberty prevail. "The highest duty of individuals is to submit their particular wills to [reason]."[104]

A year later, in early 1851, in a polemic with the Church over the issue of freedom in the schools (*libertà d'insegnamento,* or academic freedom as we would say), Spaventa moved closer to his mature doctrine of the "ethical state," as he called it. The issue revolved around the degree to which the state of Piedmont, with its barely two-year-old constitutional government, could tolerate the teachings of the Church in the schools. Complete freedom to teach meant indoctrination by the Jesuits against the constitution—the death knell to democratic republicanism. The alternative was to have the state present an "official teaching." One can sense the agony of the man as he was tossed to and fro, seeing the danger in both positions.

> Speaking in absolute terms, all those who love liberty and want a full and complete measure of it can only say that teachings must be free. But if the question is turned into the field of reality and practice, if one thinks of the particular social and political conditions of the state, opinions begin to divide, accord changes to discord. . . . We have no need of declaring our wishes. We wish absolute liberty in all the spheres of individual development. . . . But we want liberty to be the true queen and not the victim that the priests of antiquity invoked in order to bury it upon the altar of a sanguinary God.[105]

As the polemic continued, he was forced "to distinguish between the theoretical solution and the practical solution to freedom in the schools."[106]

In September of 1851 came his answer:

> Until the system of governmental authority is on its feet, *able to make the force of its arms felt from the center to all points of the circumference;* until there is a religion of the state, rich, privileged, unassailable; until the supporters themselves of the new liberty are disposed to grant to the government the right of *inspection,* precursor of the right of repression, you will have to put up with the fact that we, not finding the conditions for true and direct liberty, will make use of the privilege we enjoy and will address ourselves *to the responsibility of the government and to the authority of Parliament* to obtain those reforms which are in agreement with the times and required by the new social conditions.[107]

Italian unification was still nearly a decade away, and Spaventa had already concluded that if Piedmont, let alone Italy, were to survive, the state would have to replace the Church as the source of moral and ethical guidance. Even Napoleon III, whose coup d'etat was only four months away, would not aim so directly at such a powerful force. In Italy anticlericalism was a prerequisite for the very birth of the state. Though Spaventa had moved further and further away from his early republicanism, moved closer in fact to authoritarianism, he still believed that if only the church's influence could be curbed, the revolution to create Italy would come from below. With their minds purged of individual interests, religious dogma, and religious hostility to the state, Italians' natural desire for liberty would bring them to see the "reason," the "necessity" of the nation-state.

It began to occur to Spaventa at this point that the "two peoples" of Italy might be made to think more easily as one if the class differences that separated rich and poor were broken down. The elite were bent on satisfaction of their own private interests, interests that the more successfully they were pursued, the more they inevitably divided the nation, leaving the masses in the hands of the Church and the elite in greedy pursuit of money and material wealth. Along with a state-controlled anticlericalism, social equality was also a prerequisite for national unity. Throughout 1851, up to that fateful December at least, the doctrine of equality began to loom larger and larger in Spaventa's mind.

In his research on the doctrine of equality Spaventa examined the 1789 revolution, and, like Marx, he concluded that it had merely replaced a titled aristocracy with a monied aristocracy and that therefore the political revolution needed to be followed by a social revolution if real equality were to be reached.[108] This social revolution was, it needs to be noted, not a revolution for "socialism," which Spaventa rejected,[109] but for nationalism. This nationalism condemned bourgeois self-interest—just as twentieth-century nationalists like Corradini, Papini, and Prezzolini condemned bourgeois self-interest—not for its exploitation of the masses, but for its crass individualism, its anarchic hedonism, which sacrificed the nation to the man rather than the man to the nation. No notion, certainly, of the withering away of the state occurred to Spaventa or to any other Italian patriot of the 1850s. The social revolution was to be within the confines of—indeed, it was designed to produce—the state. It was a mechanism for unification.[110]

Spaventa's dream of a popular uprising to produce a republic of equal citizens was, however, soon shattered by the news from France, that bellwether of nineteenth-century radicalism whose beacon more than any other attracted the attention of Italian radicals. France was already, in early 1851, a political republic when Napoleon III and his henchmen, to the general delight of nearly everyone, overthrew the state. The 18th Brumaire, moreover, was no unpopular coup d'etat but, like Murat's 1808 monarchy, the very expression of the popular will. Elite and mass had revolted, revolted for Napoleon, against not only equality, but against liberty and republicanism. Spaventa was overwhelmed. He wrote to his friend De Meis who was at Paris:

> I do not need to tell you how great was my astonishment at what has happened. Now that everything is dominated by chance and luck, there is nothing to do but watch and observe. There are times when it seems that the necessary and rational laws that govern the life of a people are suspended and the Idea, the Spirit, or whatever the hell it is, is hidden and retires into darkness. ... The true mistress of this world seems to be force and the will of men; life has no value. [111]

Republicanism now seemed an anachronism, and to await a popular movement for anything but authority seemed absurd. The lesson was not lost on Spaventa. If Italy was going to be created it would be from above, not below. Giving up his republicanism, Spaventa threw in his lot with the Piedmontese monarchy—and was roundly criticized for his "treachery." "You were once on the extreme left," read the December 13 issue of *Patria* aimed at Bertrando (and Silvio, who, released from the Bourbon prison at Naples, had also come to Turin), "now you play the moderate without conscience." [112] To De Meis, Spaventa wrote of his admiration for the Turin monarchy and the *Torinesi.* Their Spartan discipline and rustic militarism, so great a contrast with the southerners, led him to see in the *Torinesi* the regeneration of Italy. "Say what you like about these *bulls,*" he wrote, "they are destined by God to be the first start of the Italian regeneration." [113]

It is important to note here that this change from republican nationalism to monarchist nationalism did not change the revolutionary nature of Spaventa's intentions toward the southern peoples nor toward the Church and its influence over those peoples. What changed was the vehicle of revolution. Journalists, philosophers, students, and thinkers did not and could not make a revolution, for this Hegelian no longer believed that history was moved forward by philosophy or "reason" alone. The divine providence of Hegel needed a more earthly, human, and anthropological abode; and it was natural enough that for the Hegelian Spaventa and for many other patriots, the new locus of that providence should be found not in abstract "reason" but in the concrete state of Piedmont, a state staffed and directed by an elite. Here then lies the origin of the so-called ethical state. Even after 1860, when the South was united with the North in the new kingdom of Italy, the mission for many Hegelians remained the same. The nation existed, but many of its inhabitants, sullen and hostile, required conversion.[114]

This post-1848 phase of Hegelianism must be compared, despite certain differences, with the left Hegelian movement in Germany, where a simultaneous effort to invert Hegel and stand him "right side up" also existed. That the Italian patriots, for nationalist reasons, grounded and humanized the Hegelian dialectic in the state rather than in society, that they remained idealists hostile to materialism, while Marx and the left Hegelians became materialists, in no way alters the similar purpose of this inversion of the dialectic. Both were revolutionary. Hegelian providence was in both cases made human, "Vichianized," and men, at least an elite of men, now set themselves the task of controlling history. The dilemma of the Hegelians at Naples was, moreover, just like that of the left Hegelians in the North: how to convince the participants in the historical drama of the course charted by "reason."

In a polemic against Rousseau, Spaventa in 1855 set out in nearly its mature form his doctrine of the ethical state, a state that would provide the parameters of conduct required by and for the Italian regeneration. Rousseau's liberty, noted Spaventa, was formal and without content; it rested upon the artificial convention of the social contract. Moreover, in his reading of Hegel, Spaventa said, he also had noted two difficulties with Rousseau's notion of sovereignty. First, it rested upon the concept of majority rule rather than the rule of reason, the only true sovereign and author of the only true liberty. Second, since Rousseau's sovereignty did not rest upon reason but only human will, every citizen would make of it what he chose, and the doctrine would produce not unity but anarchy and social dissolution.[115] "The will of the majority cannot have the force of law except insofar as it conforms to reason and truth. Reason, therefore, and not the general will, is the supreme law."[116] Whether or not Spaventa saw the danger in what Professor Jacob L. Talmon has recently called the sovereign horde, he certainly saw that in his own nation's case, the general will, the common sense of the masses, was quite out of step with his own view of reason.

Spaventa's support of the monarchist state was soon rewarded as the wily Cavour enlisted the not unambiguous support of Napoleon III in the unification of Italy. And not only did northern Italy fall to the Piedmontese, but, exceeding Cavour's wildest dreams, so too did the South, handed over to the Piedmontese by the enigmatic Garibaldi. Contrary to what the young Spaventa at Naples had thought, the unification had come first at the top and had now to be extended downward, downward upon a people who regarded the Piedmontese as foreigners, more remote than ever the Bourbons had been. *"Restano a fare gl'italiani"* might just as easily have been said by Spaventa.

That task of "making Italians" fell, as far as education was concerned, upon the shoulders of Francesco De Sanctis, Italy's first minister of public instruction. A former revolutionary from the South, a veteran of the Neapolitan '48, De Sanctis meant to accompany the other efforts of the new government to form a national culture with a complete revolution in education, a revolution that would bring an end to the old Neapolitan culture. "The reform of De Sanctis . . . would not have been on its own revolutionary, despite its rapid victory . . . if it had not signaled the twilight of the old Neapolitan culture and the beginning of its transformation into the national culture." [117]

De Sanctis called upon Spaventa to ask him if he would take the Chair of Philosophy at the University of Naples, if he would return to the city they both had tried to free through revolution and try again through instruction. Spaventa accepted, knowing that he would be treated as a representative of the government—that is, as a foreigner, an enemy.

> The men that De Sanctis called to the most important teaching positions had, in the harsh days of their exile, comes to feel themselves citizens of a wider world, and they aimed at the reattachment of the southern culture to the general Italian culture and also to the European culture. Their designation to the Neapolitan University positions signaled, therefore, the end of a regime—and not only in the political camp. They were not men of a party . . . but men of a new faith. [118]

Armed with the new faith, Spaventa set off for Naples, there to propound the new doctrine integrating North and South into a single culture. It was going to be, Spaventa realized, a long journey. He felt, as he arrived in Naples early in 1862, that he had landed in another world.

"How they have been cretinized in these twelve years," he wrote to his brother, Silvio. "It is a horrible thing to think of how many prejudices the average Neapolitan carries with him." [119] On the other hand, he recalled shortly thereafter, things remained pretty much the same at Naples. Infested with bandits, Camorristi, followers of the Bourbons, and followers of Mazzini's Action party, all willing to sell their loyalty for a sinecure with the state, Naples represented that "other Italy" which the new state had somehow to endure or to cure. "The bad thing is," he told Silvio, "that things are still—and will be for some time—in the hands of the rabble; I mean those that have no faith in anything; they are not Bourbons really, nor Italians, but rogues, intriguers, thieves, charlatans, liars, adulators." [120]

Arriving at the University of Naples, Spaventa encountered, as he had expected, a stubborn and hostile audience. Amid hoots and jeers, riot and tumult,
he announced his conviction that the apogee of modern philosophy had been
reached in Hegelian thought, a worldly Hegelianism that replaced God with the
state. This philosophy needed now to be brought to Italy. This would not be
difficult, he felt, for if only Italians would return to the thought of their own
Renaissance, to the thought of Bruno, Campanella, and Vico, they would see
that the path to modern thought led straight from the early Italians to Hegel.
"The true disciples of Bruno, Vanini, Campanella, Vico, and other famous Italians," Spaventa had noted back in 1850, "are not the Italian philosophers of the
last two hundred years, but Spinoza, Kant, Fichte, Schelling, and Hegel." [121]
The Italians, in other words, had been the original source of modern thought
and had merely now to return to their own traditions. All was not lost, Spaventa believed; it was, in fact, just about to begin. "We arrived late after having
been first, that's all." [122] It was not, however, a message to assuage the passions
of either those hostile to Piedmont or those who followed the popular, former
Mazzinian Vincenzo Gioberti. The abbé Gioberti believed—as the title of his
extraordinary book, *On the Moral and Civil Superiority of the Italians,* indicated
—in the primacy of Italy among the European nations. Unlike Spaventa, however, Gioberti believed that Italian primacy rested on the fact that Italy, as the
seat of the papacy, had once been the center of civilization. It would be so
again when a reformed papacy took up the cause of Italian unification. To Spaventa, obviously, papal leadership of the Risorgimento was inconceivable. Moreover, Gioberti's followers soon narrowed the abbé's ideas into a chauvinistic
hostility to all non-Italian thought—particularly Hegelianism. From the day he
arrived, Spaventa wrote to his brother, "certain rumors began against us: blas-
phemers, heresy, foreigners, etc. . . . They say . . . that I am a Hegelian, that is,
a partisan of the devil, that I want to pervert the youth, that I don't know
Italian philosophy." [123] Day after day tumult and chaos followed in Spaventa's
wake. When near insurrection broke out at the university, the rioters, the rec-
tor told Spaventa, had shouted, "Down with German philosophy, long live Gioberti, death to Hegel!" When the demonstrators arrived at the library, Spaventa
reported to Silvio, "a priest—who was there as an assistant librarian—not only
did not object, but said, 'Hold fast, boys, and shout down these pantheists and
atheists that have been placed in the university.' The fact is notorious and the
good priest is still here." [124]

Spaventa's "inverted Hegelianism" involved him in a polemic not only with
anti-Hegelians like the followers of Gioberti, but with many Hegelians as well.
Spaventa's revision of the dialectic had cut him off from the "orthodox Hegel-

ianism" of the South. The leader of these "orthodox Hegelians" was Augusto Vera, whose following in southern Italy (and indeed in the whole world) represented a threat to Spaventa's active nationalism. [125] For Vera, thought, or the idea, still represented the abstract *Weltgeist* of Hegel, a truth torn off from concrete reality, a truth that instead of being historicized into the ethic of the nation, belonged equally and impartially to all nations. According to Spaventa, this left man as alienated from himself as he had ever been under the Christian God. Orthodox Hegelianism, transcending the realities of national boundaries and historical reality, made of truth another abstraction to be worshiped rather than a worldly and national ethic to be lived.

> I know very well what is said by [Vera] . "What does it matter to us if philosophy is Italian or not? We want truth and truth has nothing to do with nationality." Certainly truth transcends nationality; but without nationality it is an abstraction. You can transplant truth as much as you like; if it has not real correspondence with our national genius, it will be truth in itself, but not for us; for it will be something dead. [126]

To counter the Hegel proposed by Vera, Spaventa propounded his earlier inversion of the dialectic by recalling for Vera and his followers the immanentism of Vico. Philosophy did not develop in the abstract minds of philosophers, but in the concrete historical and—for Spaventa—essentially political world. The truth of modern philosophy was that which had been noted by Vico: spirit is immanent and autogenetic. "Development is autogenesis." [127] For Spaventa "only this spirit can conceive of its true self: It is not being or one [*ente*], but ... the Creator." [128] The orthodox Hegel of Vera, from Spaventa's point of view, was merely religion all over again, religion historicized, but religion all the same and therefore not immanence but transcendence. [129]

As a foil to the orthodox Vera, Spaventa constituted, in one sense, essentially the same thing that Feuerbach in Germany represented with his 1841 *Das Wesen des Christentums,* and in fact not a few persons have seen Spaventa as the Italian Feuerbach. [130] Yet—always within the confines of his nationalism— Spaventa went further than Feuerbach, approaching Marx's own aim of changing the world rather than merely contemplating it. He never became a "materialist," for the whole idea of materialism is repugnant to the southern Italian tradition, being tied, probably irretrievably, to the mechanics of the eighteenth century. Still, Spaventa was no less concerned than Marx with the need to focus attention on the concrete social conditions that affect human behavior, the need to ground the Hegelian spirit in civil and human institutions. As in Vico and Marx, the central purpose of Spaventa's mature thought was an immanent, anthropological, and worldly dialectic;[131] and like Marx in particular, Spaventa was concerned that the orthodox Hegelians might make in Italy a theoretical revolution instead of a practical one. It is for this reason that Spaventa relied so heavily upon the role of the state.

The state for Spaventa was an active and positive historical force, a moral and ethical entity. It was, Spaventa maintained, no "mere *ens rationis,* or fiction, a convention of individuals gathered for the satisfaction of their interests,"[132] not simply a "universal abstract" playing a negative role in the conflict of particular citizens.

> The end of the state is the *common security;* this common security is not possible if the state is only a *universal* abstract; negative without interest . . . its own life . . . remain[ing] *outside* the life of the particularity. . . . In that manner the common security is never attained; for [that] activity of the state is purely *mechanical*—simply *material* power and force; and from this force is always subtracted the will and particularity of the individual.

To achieve the common security, the state must be "an essentially *ethical* force, that is, have its own positive, substantial life."[133]

Against the classical liberal conception of the state, therefore, Spaventa maintained that the state was a "great family," an "absolute universality." As common sense and common morality had been the foundations of the states described by Vico and Cuoco, so too with Spaventa was a common and vigorous morality the basis for a healthy state. There was, however, in Spaventa's notion of morality a kind of protestantism that refused to accept mere justification by good works and sought as well justification by faith. The duty of the "ethical spirit" in this "great family" was not that he simply "do the good" but that he have "the *subjective* intention, certainty, and conviction of the good," for no mere "accidental" congruence of will and good would suffice. If all the citizens so comported themselves, then—and only then—would a state exist, for the collective will is the "*substantial, necessary,* common and universal" foundation of the state.[134]

This all-encompassing state extended its grasp, of necessity, to every sphere of thought and action, and Spaventa was particularly concerned that science be included in the culture set out by the ethical state. Spaventa's idealism led him to see spirit as a historically developing anthropological mind, albeit a mind only the elite understood. As with Vico before him, Spaventa was therefore immune to nineteenth-century scientific thought, which equated reason not with historical development but with nature, with physics. To Spaventa, as to Vico, New-tonian physics, whether social or natural, was an abstraction, a form of eternal

truth standing outside of history and long since overcome—intentionally or not—
by Vico and Hegel. No eternal scientific metaphysic was possible, because concrete historical man continually revised or, better, utilized and appropriated the
physical world for his own concrete and necessarily transient purposes. An
"eternal nature" with an "eternal design" would be, in such a view, meaningless.
Neither nature nor God stood outside man's control nor existed independently
of him.

> The main thrust of [Spaventa's] mature work (the entire lengthy polemic
> against naturalism and positivistic mechanism) could be perceived precisely
> in the affirmation that "man is the principle of another world [as opposed
> to the world of nature] and . . . this world is not a simple continuation of
> the natural world but [stands] *above* and *opposed* to it." It was the great
> Vichian discovery which Spaventa celebrated in the lesson dedicated to him
> in the 1861 lectures: the revolutionary conception of man as "historical
> man," which Hegel had consigned to the *Preface* of the *Phenomenology*.[135]

In fact Spaventa went even further than Vico in his idealism, criticizing the
Vichian "dualism" that had originated in the bifurcation of the world into that
natural sphere made by God, which He alone could know, and the historical
sphere, which, being made by man, could by man alone be known.[136] This idealism, this enlargement of the Cartesian *cogito* into a Kantian synthetic a priori,
was the basis for Spaventa's assault on positivism and the scientific perspective.
Science, according to Spaventa, was not an independent metaphysic to be used
as a model for inquiry in any and all areas. Its uses were limited and precise and
needed always to be contained by the philosophy set out by the ethical state.
Science, in short, needed to be "put in its place," as Croce would say later on.
  "It is not that philosophy must become positive, experimental, scientific . . .
it is that the data, the experience, the science must become philosophy. To do
so does not mean that they must cease to be what they are, must deny themselves; but [that] they be understood in the absolute unity which is unity of
knowing."[137] That is, science must not try to replace the "culture" set out by
the elite, but put itself to work within its parameters. The culture would provide the limits within which science would be done. Only in this way, by enlist-
ing every discipline and every intellect in the construction of the new culture,
could an Italian regeneration take place. It was in this overwhelming state that
the "liberalism" of Spaventa perished. Thus, Luigi Russo, commenting upon
the "error of Bertrando Spaventa," noted, "Here was the danger in the ethical
state as it was theorized by our Hegelians: not only art, science, and philosophy were servants of the state, but so was all human activity—religion, morality,

justice. . . . The doctrine of the ethical state, understood as most persons understood it, as a state that directs, teaches, sets moral standards, directs worship, would [be] a theological state, a Calvinist state." [138]

The idea of a national regeneration of culture was, of course, a notion subject to many interpretations, and few Risorgimento thinkers went to the extremes advocated by Spaventa. For many intellectuals of the Risorgimento the ideas of Spaventa were, in fact, usually overshadowed by those of Francesco De Sanctis, the author of the cultural revolution in the South. [139] With Spaventa, De Sanctis shared a desire for a national resurgence that would unify Italy and then launch the new nation into the community of modern European states. Like Spaventa, De Sanctis had been a "Hegelian" revolutionary, an active participant in the Neapolitan '48, a convert to Piedmontese monarchism, and a defector from orthodox Hegelianism. Yet from the outset there were obvious differences between the two men, not the least of which was De Sanctis's inability, despite his fervent patriotism, to share Spaventa's religious enthusiasm for the nation as the sole fount of spiritual sustenance.

The differences between Spaventa and Francesco De Sanctis lie partly in the way in which they encountered, interpreted, and revised Hegel, and partly in the personalities of the two men. Unlike Spaventa, a political philosopher who tried to politicize everything, De Sanctis was both a political actor and a philosopher, a philosopher of aesthetics and literary criticism. "My life," he wrote, in 1869, "has two pages, one literary, the other political, and I cannot excise either one or the other; they are the two obligations of my life which I shall continue to the end." [140]

The greatest interpreter and self-professed disciple of De Sanctis was doubtless Benedetto Croce. [141] The burden of Croce's judgment was to make of De Sanctis a precursor of the Crocean aesthetic theory of the twentieth century and to slight the *etico-politico* De Sanctis. With the rise of fascism, however, and the consequent, though momentary, prominence of Gentile, Croce was forced to acknowledge a liberal political De Sanctis to prevent the threat of a fascist (Gentilean) capture of the famous art critic as a precursor of fascism. [142] However, no sooner had Croce rescued "his" De Sanctis from the right than, from the left, there approached an equally potent movement, also in search of "precursors." Luigi Russo, from the Crocean school itself, began to see in the new ethico-political De Sanctis a form of militantism that others, Croce in particular, had missed. "Until now," wrote Russo, "a recognition of De Sanctis as a *politico-militante* has been missing. It has been missing [even] on the part of his friends." [143] Russo's work—written, it must be remembered, in the worst years of fascism and at the same time as Croce's own paregyric to Giolittian Italy [144]—was also an attempt to rescue the heritage of De Sanctis from the fascists. As Russo's opposition to fascism grew, however, so too did his attraction to the Marxist movement in Italy. A conflict with Croce was inevitable. Having "rescued" De Sanctis from the Gentileans, Croce was not about to see *his* precursor carried off by the left as a precursor of Gramsci.[145]

Shortly before his death, Croce addressed the whole issue of De Sanctis-Croce or De Sanctis-Gramsci. Where had the initial *diade* come from?

> It is very simple. Many years ago in the *Liceo* . . . I avidly read the *Nuovi saggi critici* of Francesco De Sanctis. Everything became clear to me. . . . His concept of poetry as pure form I preserved for a long time. Only after many years . . . did I turn to modify and remodify it . . . arriving thus at [a] form of intuition clearly distinct from affirmations of a realistic character. At that time a very rich aesthetic was born, the corollaries of which even today I have not yet exhausted. But another aspect of the books of De Sanctis disturbed me and left me a bit cold; not being persuaded that, despite the liberty recognized by [De Sanctis] in poetry, literary history could accompany and follow political and moral history, I disregarded the thesis. . . . [Also] I published in 1896 [De Sanctis's] volume of lessons on the liberal and democratic schools. . . . [I also defended] his thought [against attacks by even] Carducci. . . . These facts . . . can explain . . . the formula "De Sanctis-Croce" which grew up spontaneously among readers. As to that other, "De Sanctis-Gramsci," . . . I would be saddened if Italy would alienate De Sanctis from me.[146]

Our concern here will be limited to the development of De Sanctis's political philosophy, first with his attempt to generate a culture that would lead to the formation of Italy and second with his post-Risorgimento efforts to create a new culture for the young nation he had helped to found. The dividing line between these two phases of De Sanctis's career is 1870, the year in which Italian forces seized Rome from the papacy and brought to a close the long struggle for unification. However, because the Risorgimento was not only an event but also a culture, an ethic of theory and practice which had shaped both lives and minds for a generation or more, its conclusion was not only a moment of triumph, but also of emptiness and concern. On the eve of victory a disorienting cultural vacuum loomed. De Sanctis, seeing it, hoped to fill the void with a new culture, a new mission which would link again the realms of thought and action and set Italy on a new course. It was no easy task moving from the "age of poetry," as Croce would call it later, to the "age of prose." Moreover, compared to the years of the Risorgimento, it was bound to seem pedestrian. It was made no easier by the grim social, political, and economic problems facing the young nation.

The "age of poetry" seemed easier by far than the "age of prose," for the enemies of preunification Italy had made the earlier course to nationhood obvious.
After 1870 no obstacles were so clear. De Sanctis hoped, after 1870, to be the
author of a new course for his country.

De Sanctis (1817–83) was born near Naples in the village of Morra Irpina
(now Morra De Sanctis), the second son of a cultured and politically liberal
lawyer.[147] At the age of nine he was sent to Naples to attend the private school
directed by his paternal uncle, and there, in Naples, he was exposed to the creative and revolutionary idealism that, by the 1840s, permeated the city. In 1841,
two years after opening his own elementary school, he received an appointment
as a professor at the Royal Military College and there he remained until 1848.
It was while at the Military College that De Sanctis's early interest in idealist philosophy and aesthetics began to develop, and it is not surprising that, despite
his paymaster, he drifted almost naturally into the revolutionary Hegelian milieu.
Like other Hegelians, he found himself, somewhat vaguely it appears,[148] in opposition to the regime. Whatever form of "Hegelian" he was at that time, years
later he remembered himself as a constitutional monarchist. His hero, he recalled,
was Adolphe Thiers. "In 1830 he was what we were in 1848 . . . parliamentary
government was his ideal. He wanted there to be '*le gouvernment du pays par le
pays.*' His formula was this: '*Le roi regne, mais ne gouverne pas.*' His thought
was of that monarchy '*entourée d'institutions republicaines.*'"[149] In addition to
Thiers's politics, De Sanctis recalled his admiration for the Frenchman's "campaign against the Jesuits and the convents."[150] Political liberalism accompanied
by an almost obligatory anti-clericalism seemed therefore the inclination of
De Sanctis. As 1848 drew closer, De Sanctis may have gravitated—it is not clear
how wholeheartedly—to the Mazzinians,[151] but in February of 1848 when
Ferdinand II (Bomba) was forced to grant a constitution to the kingdom, it was
with great moderation—and near virginal innocence—that De Sanctis stood to
address his students: "A few days ago we were saying times as content as these
will never return! And here we have times even more wonderful and, after those
of Naples, will come those of Italy. . . . But the noble testimony of our joy in
our new rights will be to show ourselves worthy of our new duties. It is a serious
thing, my beloved students, it is liberty and it requires great obligations of us."
In the enthusiasm of the moment—and here he was by no means alone—De Sanctis put his faith even in Pius IX. "You ought to thank God you have been born
under Pius IX. Pius IX does not seem old and severe to me; his heart is young and
he is the idol of the young. You have been born to be his disciples. . . . Now
your task, young men, is to understand Pius IX, he who has so wonderfully understood us. . . . Remember," he concluded, "one does not govern oneself with

poetry, but with history. One does not govern oneself with books, but with the world." [152]

A few months later the optimism faded. In May, during the reaction, De Sanctis mounted the barricades and nearly lost his life. Indeed, one of his best students, Luigi La Vista, was killed at his side in the battle. [153] Shortly afterward De Sanctis left Naples for Calabria. There, hidden by friends, he remained until December of 1850, when he was arrested by the Bourbon police and imprisoned for thirty-two months in the Castel dell'Ova.

In his prison writings [154] one notes the influence of a rebellious Hegel as well as an embittered reaction to Catholicism and a resilient faith in man. The hymn he sang was no longer to Pius IX but to

> Adam . . . the first sinner and rebel. . . . And to Buddha, Prometheus, Socrates, and [the man] Christ, [all] authors of civilization and perpetuators of [Adam's sin], for they were, no less than he, rebels and sinners. I abandon the religious tradition to those for whom sluggishness is the greatest of goods and work a punishment. For me, Adam, in whom was first revealed the spirit in the fullness of its power, is the founder of human dignity; and in him the world, far from declining, began to progress. Man is a force composed of opposites, of evil and good, grief and joy, hate and love, and this is the fulcrum that exalts thought higher and higher in its perpetual struggle with nature towards its inevitable target. When God says to man: the sweat will pour from your brow, he poses in that way the foundation of human greatness; that which He ceases to give us, we acquire the force to take. . . . Let us exalt man as he is, and he is great. [155]

It was while in prison that De Sanctis read Hegel's *Logic* and Rosenkranz's *History of Literature* and translated both into Italian. [156] It was Hegel, especially Hegel's aesthetics, however, that really interested De Sanctis. It is said that having read the first two volumes, he had guessed the contents of the rest and expounded them later in the classroom before Benard had finished his translation of them. [157]

Released from prison in August of 1853, De Sanctis came to Turin, where he encountered Spaventa and the other exiles and became both a Freemason and a supporter of the Savoyards. [158] It was also in this period of exile that De Sanctis's ideas matured and that he began a revision of the Hegelian dialectic. Like Spaventa, he had been sobered by the experience of 1848 and the new "18th Brumaire." Like Spaventa, too, he came to believe that orthodox Hegelianism was another abstraction, like Catholicism, alien to man and hostile to humanist thought. "There are in Hegel," De Sanctis wrote much later in 1879, "two principles that stand at the base of the whole modern movement: the principle of becoming, the basis of evolution, and the principle of existence, the basis of realism. His system has fallen to pieces, but these two principles make Hegel the basis for future thought." [159] Nonetheless, De Sanctis believed that Hegelianism as set out by the orthodox school had become an a priori metaphysic. Writing to argue with the right Hegelian De Meis, De Sanctis exclaimed, "I have never been a Hegelian *à tout prix.* One must be a servant of the truth. . . . But what do you want? I am fed up with the absolute, the ontology, and the a priori. Hegel has done me a great deal of good; but also a great deal of harm. It has been years since I read him." [160]

Like Spaventa, but with quite different results, De Sanctis soon began to enlarge the distance between himself and the orthodox Hegelians. Instead of merely standing the Hegelian system "right side up," however, he began to disassemble it, foreshadowing in the process the later "revisions" of Hegel made by Benedetto Croce. In Hegel the course of history had been seen as the development of thought from inferior forms of "reflection," such as art and religion, to the highest form, philosophy. The modern era, therefore, was characterized by the disappearance, the absorption, of these inferior modes into mature *Philosophie.* De Sanctis revised, not to say reversed, this whole process, running the film, so to speak, backwards in his mind so that philosophy now began in the abstract and descended to the concrete, releasing there the "inferior" forms of thought and action so that they might pursue their own lives independent, or nearly independent, of philosophy. As with Spaventa, however, this was not a materialization of the Hegelian idea, but a grounding of the idea—or ideas— in concrete historical reality. Like the forces of Newtonian gravity, those of Neapolitan "gravity" tended to make it impossible to escape the worldly, and De Sanctis, like Spaventa and Vico before him, rejected any attempt to escape the earth to philosophy as not only futile but self-deceiving. For De Sanctis only religion, or to be precise, only Catholicism, remained, and had to remain, imprisoned by philosophy, for Catholicism was, like orthodox Hegelianism, the enemy of the concrete.

This de-Hegelianization of Hegel produced something else as well, something that distinguished De Sanctis's desire for a national regeneration from Spaventa's. Because De Sanctis had dismantled the Hegelian dialectic before he inverted it—or at least, while he inverted it—the inversion did not produce, as it did in Spaventa and Marx, an all-encompassing metaphilosophy containing at the worldly level all the categories the old Hegelian *Weltgeist* had contained in the abstract. Art, politics, literary criticism, all now grounded in the concrete enjoyed in De Sanctis existences independent of philosophy, albeit shadowy existences, their "distinct" forms being given to them later by Croce. [161] The aim of this separation of art from philosophy was to enhance the appreciation of art in and of itself. "Among the vulgar there remains the opinion that the excellence of the *Divine Comedy* lies in the depth of its philosophy and theology. This idea makes the book quite unpopular, since the vulgar are rather like women who willingly talk of educated men but are bored in their presence. The vulgar admire learned books but they do not read them." [162] De Sanctis began to feel that the Hegelian school of criticism, by its determination to resolve art into philosophy, had destroyed the individuality, the concreteness, the beauty of the work of art. Hegelianism regarded the literary product as a model, an idea, a representative of some higher, quasi-platonic idea.

Modern philosophy [Hegelianism], having arisen on account of an exaggerated reaction against [eighteenth-century] materialism—which now raises its head with vindictive spirit—has contributed a great deal to putting criticism and poetry in a false light. The concept, the ideal, the intelligible, the divine, the eternal, the idea, the type and the archetype, etc.: these are the words of the new poetic, which vulgarizes genius itself into a purely intellectual work. [163]

In place of the form as mere symbol of the idea, De Sanctis posited the form as sufficient unto itself, an organic unity of particular and universal in which "the idea stands incorporated and yet forgotten [*involuta e come smemorata*] ." [164] Philosophy for De Sanctis was therefore separate from aesthetics.

It is outside aesthetics because in aesthetics the idea has already surpassed itself [*ha già oltrepassata se stessa*] ; it no longer exists; what exists is the form. The poet in the heat of inspiration sees images, phenomena, forms, and sees them not as the veil or manifestation of ideas but as forms, that is as beautiful or ugly. He sees the world already formed and in action and does not know on account of what general laws or which metaphysic it has taken that form and operates in that way. Ask Homer and Virgil, Shakespeare and Aristotle what is the idea of their world. They do not know. . . . For me the essence of art is form. Not form in disguise, in a veil, mirror, or whatever the manifestation of a generality distinct from it while somehow united to it; but rather form into which the idea has already passed, and in which the individual has already been realized. This is the proper organic unity of art. Now form is not an idea, and therefore the poet intuits things not ideas. The immortal element in poetry is form, whatever idea may grow out of it. [165]

This discovery of the independent nature, the autonomy, of art opened a whole new vista for De Sanctis. The way of the future, he now believed, lay in

distinction, in distinguishing art, politics, economics—all of what Croce would
later call the "worldly sciences—from theology and philosophy. Hegel therefore
represented, with his all-encompassing theology, his *Weltgeist,* a step backward
from the lay world. Man in his long quest for a monism from which all else
could be derived was on a false scent, snared by the illusion of the one, the medieval, the Orient. The future lay not in recapturing the illusion, but in escaping
it.

Having separated art from philosophy, De Sanctis then turned to politics. As
may be expected, his aim was to emancipate politics from "theology," the otherworldly prison that prevented man from seeing himself as well as from building
his nation here on earth. It was time, he wrote in *L'italia* in 1865, to recall the
heritage of Dante. "When we say thought of Dante we mean especially this: liberation of the laity through abolition of the temporal power [of the papacy]."[166]
De Sanctis's most radical writings were against the Church, and if in the old
Ghibelline ideas of Dante he found a kindred spirit, it was in Machiavelli that he
found his proper forebear. With all his hostility to the Christian order, Machiavelli seemed to De Sanctis to point the way to the future: he was the first prophet
of a lay religion, a humanism that allowed man to work out, on his own, apart
from religion, natural law, or any extraterrestrial limit whatsoever, the nature and
parameters of the human order. Machiavelli foresaw the lay state purged of its
medieval concentration on the afterlife, grounded in civic patriotism and human
institutions. While others, like Savonarola and the Church as a whole at the Council
of Trent,[167] sought to restore the primitive piety and universality of the *Respub-
lica christiana,* Machiavelli saw things "from a different, more elevated, point of
view." The entire medieval era was "in putrefaction, dead already in spirit [*coscienza*], still alive in forms and institutions." There was no point therefore in
leading Italy "backwards and restoring the medieval era," and so Machiavelli "con-
curred in its demolition."[168]

The medieval era had both a theological and a political foundation, and
Machiavelli was the first to propose the modern alternatives to those cornerstones
of medieval life. The political foundation of the Middle Ages had been the papacy and the empire, and it was Machiavelli, said De Sanctis, who had urged man
to replace those "universals" with particular nation-states. According to Machiavelli, said De Sanctis, "the mission of man on this earth, his first duty, is patriotism, the glory, greatness, the liberty of the *patria.*"[169]

In theology and philosophy Machiavelli also pointed the way to the modern
humanist alternative to the Middle Ages: the reversal of the Christian ideals of
"sin" and "virtue." The medieval era, said De Sanctis, had as its theological basis
the notion that "sin lay in attaching oneself to this life" and "virtue lay in the

negation of the worldly life." "Reality" for the Christian "is not what is, but what ought to be and therefore its true content is the afterlife [*l'altro mondo*]. Hell, purgatory, paradise, the world that conforms to truth and justice," [170] these are the realities of Christian thought. Machiavelli, instead, posited the modern age, the modern man, actively creating his own world here on earth. "To rehabilitate worldly life, to give it purpose, to restore knowledge, to re-create the inner forces, to restore man in his seriousness and his activity, this is the spirit that flows through all the works of Machiavelli." [171] In him De Sanctis saw the root form of modern thought—Descartes's *cogito*—and in the *cogito* the beginning of the Kantian revolution, man's active and independent spirit creating and appropriating the world around him.

> Casting out of his world any supernatural and accidental cause, Machiavelli laid the foundation for the immutability and immortality of human thought and spirit, creator of history. This was a complete revolution. It is the famous *cogito* with which modern [philosophy] began. It is man emancipated from the supernatural and the superhuman who, like the state, proclaims his autonomy and his independence and takes possession of the world. [172]

Like Spaventa, De Sanctis had slipped almost naturally into the idea of the *cogito* as pure modern idealism, a creative Kantian synthetic a priori which made of man an earthly god. It is a heady idea, and De Sanctis had good reason to be exhilarated. It was the autumn of 1870 and the French, defeated at Sedan, had withdrawn their forces from Rome, leaving the city open to the Italian armies. "We are therefore proud of our Machiavelli. Praise be to him when any part of the old structure collapses. And praise be to him when any of the new is built. While I am now writing, the bells sound continuously, announcing the entrance of the Italians into Rome." [173]

For the young De Sanctis the physical conquest of Rome and the elimination of the temporal power of the papacy were, of course, only symbols of a much more dramatic philosophical conquest made earlier. The long struggle of man to emancipate himself from the "supernatural and the superhuman" and take "possession of the world" here came to a triumphant conclusion. "The purification and the sanctification of man no longer has its purpose in another life but in this terrestrial life. Man becomes pure and holy, that is to say virtuous, when he applies himself to perfecting what is human in himself and considers himself not as alone and separate, but as a member of a whole that is humanity." [174]

To less philosophical patriots the conquest of Rome was no less dramatic. It seemed to be the logical culmination of the unification process. No city other than Rome, however more suitable, could have served as the nation's capital. Rome, in short, was obvious.

Afterward nothing was to be so obvious. When the city fell an era ended not only for De Sanctis but for the nation that, in microcosm, his spirit portrayed. A political-philosophical conflict, a way of life begun back at the time of Machiavelli, here came to a close. The effect was disorienting. The conclusion of the culture of the Risorgimento required that a new culture be discovered, created, that new limits be found—and attacked. Limits, De Sanctis saw, provided not only the boundaries within which human thought and action were confined, but also the obstacles against which man could struggle, obstacles that gave direction to his action and charted the distance he had traveled. Without limits, without culture or common sense, theory and practice came unhinged—the intellectuals retreating to the world of abstract philosophy, the masses left to toil without meaning or direction. The thesis, in short, was disoriented without its antithesis.

Speaking at Naples in 1872, De Sanctis noted that what makes a people great is "having all its moral forces intact. [But] these forces do not produce unless they are confronted with outside limits. . . . These limits create . . . the goal, which removes vagueness from freedom . . . [and] gives it direction. [Moral] forces are productive . . . only insofar as their liberty is limited. [Moral] forces require a goal just as means require an end." [175] Glancing uneasily about him, De Sanctis found no new linking of thought and action, no new culture being formed to challenge new heights. "In Italy all those limits which used to arouse so much force of life . . . have been weakened, character exhausted, moral forces dispirited, the Church [merely a] vacuous formality; family, *patria*, class, state, every social organism, all public life, empty formality." [176]

Elaborating upon that empty formality, De Sanctis concluded that it was faith which constituted culture, faith which inspired the linking of theory and practice. "At any cost," he wrote, "it is necessary to have a faith, to struggle, poetize, live and die for it." [177] Without that faith, man turned to contemplation: "Lacking faith, philosophy is born. Art descends and criticism arises. History ends and historians appear." [178]

It was to this need of a faith, a common sense or culture, that De Sanctis was to devote the rest of his life. In 1877, in an article entitled significantly "La cultura politica," De Sanctis analyzed the dilemma of modern Italy.

> We have now reached the following state: we no longer know what is right and what is left, what we want or where we are going. . . . Many attribute this to a defect of strength. . . . But [a] defect of strength itself requires explanation. Are we a degenerate and fallen people? I don't think so. . . . Strength is lacking because faith is lacking. And faith is lacking because

culture is lacking. It is useless to deceive ourselves. Strength and faith are
two things that one cannot have at will. When they are not there, they are
not there. We can say to no one: Believe or else.[179]

The constitution of this "culture"—a word De Sanctis began to use more
frequently in place of the ambiguous "faith"—was the most urgent requirement
of post-Christian man. Culture, or lay religion as Gramsci and Croce called it,
was what gave meaning not only to ordinary life but also to politics. "Without
this base politics is done in the void, remains without echo, and is immediately
corrupted." Thus it was for De Sanctis that neither thought (science) nor action
(politics) could transpire without the significance given them by religion, whether
lay or ecclesiastical. The responsibility for the creation of this "culture" lay,
according to De Sanctis, with the intellectuals:

> There is no minister of public instruction who can, by official means, pro-
> mote this culture. . . . We need a center of Italian culture and a valiant nucle-
> us of citizens that express the unity of this culture. . . . This is the greatest
> service that one can render the country. By not engaging in [pure] politics,
> one does the truly political.[180]

This need to create a "center of Italian culture," a "valiant nucleus of citizens," was the heritage De Sanctis was to bequeath to the next generation of
intellectuals and the heritage he received from his Vichian forebears.[181] De Sanctis's idea that effective political action required a surrounding culture derived
from Vico's theory of common sense and would become one of the cornerstones
of Crocean idealism in the next century. For De Sanctis the purpose of culture
was political, because it provided the context in which political action took place.
Without such a context the world of theory and practice would be totally open-
ended, and political activity—and every other activity, for that matter—would be
impossible. Culture, in short, circumscribed and made manageable an otherwise
incomprehensible world. Culture provided the ends, while the narrower and sub-
ordinate realm of the political provided only the means. Hence, "by not engaging in [pure] politics, one does the truly political." This idea of the political
nature of culture would later bear fruit not only in Croce's program of cultural
renewal, but in Gramsci's idea of hegemony. In praising De Sanctis, Gramsci
said that De Sanctis had taught the necessity of having a "conception of life and
of man, a lay religion, a philosophy that had become a 'culture,' that is to say,
generated an ethic, a way of life, a civic and individual behavior."[182]

In many respects De Sanctis's humanism was a continuation of forces already
set in motion within the tradition. By his inversion of the Hegelian dialectic
he had continued the Vichian tradition of hostility to abstract law and theology—

to any "philosophy of history," Croce would say later. Similarly, with his charge to the intellectuals to take on the responsibilities of leadership he confirmed in a moderate manner the doctrine of the two peoples.

Yet there was much in De Sanctis that was new and contributed lasting elements to the doctrine of humanism. Two of these elements especially stand out. First, his particularization of spirit into independent categories, or rather "distinct categories," was to have a major impact on Croce and through Croce on a whole generation of idealists. Second, and perhaps most important, De Sanctis changed the foundations of humanism, broadening it to include not only those patriotic and defensive intellectuals who, like Spaventa, supported the establishment of and preservation of the state, but intellectuals in general. All of them had a responsibility for the nation and for the goals and culture it would create for itself. This was to have, in the next generation, rather remarkable repercussions, for the concern of those later intellectuals was no longer with the creation of a fledgling state against Catholicism but with regenerating a state they believed to have fallen into the torpor of old age. They and they alone had the potion to counteract senility. They looked back to the generation of the Risorgimento as one of youth and vigor, and they meant to recapture its ardor. The next generation of intellectuals, in short, were revolutionaries who aimed not at the creation or even the preservation of the established state, but at unseating it or at least renewing it.

It should not be too surprising that many of these intellectuals should turn to Marxism as a method for this renewal. Marxism gained great popularity in Italy after 1890, and for those who came out of the humanist tradition the similarities between their heritage and Marx were too obvious to ignore. On the other hand, the humanist intellectuals who were attracted to Marx found there the problem of a prescribed course for history. In other words, they found in Marx, or thought they found in him, the problem Cuoco and Spaventa had found in Vico: history had a mind of its own. For revolutionaries determined to make history submit to their own will, this "philosophy of history"—so antithetical to any full-fledged immanentism—had to be overcome. This made Italian Marxists who came from the humanist tradition impervious to materialism in its modern sense and highly susceptible to Marxian revisionism in the fashion of Sorel.

It was Benedetto Croce who, while searching for a new culture to replace the stagnant bourgeois culture he found around him, was to lead Italy into another culture.

2

BENEDETTO CROCE: THE SEARCH FOR A FAITH

An Abruzzese born of well-to-do parents, Benedetto Croce (1866–1952) spent his early years at the family palazzo in Naples. His mother was educated, devout, and interested in art and historical monuments; "I owe to her," he wrote, "the first awakening of my interest in the past."[1] His father devoted himself to managing the family property. The elder Croce's cousins were Bertrando and Silvio Spaventa, and Croce's parents, he said, remembered with horror that Bertrando, before his apostasy, had "celebrated mass in our chapel. . . . Some years later when I was about to set off for the university, my mother called me aside and warned me against attending any of Spaventa's lectures lest the principles of religion be snatched from my breast."[2] Forewarned and forearmed, Croce, it is comforting to note, did precisely what any other mortal would have done—without telling either his parents or Spaventa that he was in the audience. The promise of titillation, however, was not fulfilled. He found the lectures "innocuous," and in any case, Spaventa died shortly thereafter. Croce, however, like most men of his generation, was not to come of age with his religious faith intact. After several years of "great sadness and lively anxiety" over his "vacillations in faith . . . I became distracted by life and I no longer asked myself whether I believed or not . . . and one day it occurred to me, and I said to myself, that I was completely outside religious beliefs."[3] "Distracted by life" is the key phrase. Religion no longer mattered, no longer seemed a part of life. The question now was to find what could replace it.

Shortly after his apostasy Croce returned to Naples. In 1883, while on a family outing to Ischia, Croce, his mother, father, and sister were buried in rubble when an earthquake struck the island. By an odd inversion of accepted religious "signs," the only survivor was the apostate youth, now transformed into a wealthy orphan. The next few years of Croce's life, though personally anguished, left an indelible impression upon him. His guardian turned out to be none other than Silvio Spaventa. Barely eighteen when he came to Rome, Croce was miserable. "Those years were my most grievous and gloomy; . . . laying my head on my pillow at night I strongly desired to not awaken in the morning, and I even had thoughts of suicide. I had no friends nor anything with which to divert myself; I never once saw Rome at night." [4] Yet, as Croce later acknowledged, the years were of tremendous intellectual value. The Spaventa household, next door to the Palazzo Montecitorio, was frequented by deputies, professors, and journalists, with discussions of "politics, law, science and the upcoming parliamentary debates and repercussions." [5] These were the years of Prime Minister Depretis, whose government in 1876 had replaced the party of the Historic Right (*Destra storica*), the party that had created a unified Italy. Although the *Destra* had built the nation, it seemed afterwards to lose its sense of direction. Its opposition to the extension of democracy, its supposedly inglorious seizure of Rome after the French forces protecting the pope had been withdrawn, made easy political targets. The new government of Depretis (the Left, or *Sinistra*), however, was weak and ineffective and, battered by the inevitable and often unrealistic comparisons with the earlier glories of the Risorgimento, it did little to assuage the national hunger for leadership. At Spaventa's home Croce therefore listened to the "sarcasm and vituperation aimed by Spaventa, his friends and visitors" at the new government.

In 1885, Croce attended the University of Rome and there heard the lectures of the great intellectual Antonio Labriola, also a frequent visitor at the Spaventa household and "one whom I greatly admired [for his] evening conversations, crackling with spirit, caustic remarks, overflowing with a new doctrine."

Subject to the same malaise as many others in those years, Croce explained that Labriola's lectures filled "my anguished need to rebuild in a rational form a faith in life and in its purposes and duties, since I had lost the guide of my religion." Labriola was not yet a Marxist but was a follower of the Kantian psychologist J. F. Herbart. In Herbart values remained absolute and secure. Herbart was thus, for Croce—who "had lost the guide of [his] religion"—precisely what was needed. "In 1885 Labriola induced [Croce] to study the Herbartians . . . Zimmermann, M. Drobisch, Strümpell, W. F. Volkmann," [6] Croce, momentarily, found them satisfying. "The Herbartian ethic of Labriola served to restore in my soul the majesty of the ideal, of the ought as opposed to the is." [7] Despite the heritage of Spaventa and the culture of the South, Croce found himself comfortable with a kind of dualism, a belief in the world as it appears and, replacing his religion, a belief in the world as it ought to be. For Croce, this belief in transcendent values remained for years an unquestioned assumption through which and against which historical reality was to be examined. Thus, in 1896 he explained, "Every historical fact can be examined according to a double measure or a double criterion: the obvious moral criterion and the properly historical one. The first is founded on the elementary principles of ethical judgment, the second on the individual persuasions and convictions about the ends of history and the course of progress."[8] While others were, in the absence of religion, seduced by naturalism, positivism, and other ideologies, Croce remained immune. "That platonic-scholastic-Herbartian conception protected me from the naturalism and materialism dominant at the time of my youth."[9]

In 1886 Croce returned to the family home at Naples. He was twenty years old and independently wealthy. For the next few years he buried himself in libraries and began publishing his first works. These works of "pure erudition"[10] avoided problems of a speculative nature, problems about the nature of history, and problems related to values.[11] Croce was, of course, well aware that abstract values, secure for him in their Herbartian armor, were under attack elsewhere. At Labriola's suggestion[12] he had taken up, after the study of the Herbartians, the writings of the contemporary German social scientists, Dilthey and the Southwest German school of Simmel, Rickert, and Windelband. He was sympathetic with their reaction against any attempt to reduce history to a natural science. Dilthey wanted to develop a science of history, but one independent of natural science. The Southwest German school, on the other hand, argued that science was not suitable for the study of history because science's task was to subsume particular facts under general laws. History, they argued, was the study of the particular fact not the general law. Coming from a background of Kantian studies, they asked, what were the conditions under which valid knowledge independent of science could be gained in history?[13] Within a few months these writers were to make a large impact on Croce.

By the spring of 1892 Croce had become dissatisfied with his own writings. Steeped in Kantian notions of absolute values, Croce was also now drawn to Vico, drawn, that is, from the absolute to a concern with the concrete.[14] Croce wondered where and in what way the two came together. He decided to write a different kind of history, one that would bridge this gap. It was to be a work on the spiritual life of Italy from the Renaissance to the present. It was not to be a "political history, but a moral history," not a "chronicle of events" but a "history of feelings."[15] The final work concerned the early part of Italian spiritual life, life under the Spanish domination, *La Spagna nella vita italiana durante la Rinascenza.* The book, however, took some time to finish, for Croce soon found himself worrying "about the method to be followed in the chosen work and in the study of history in general"; and so "I found myself little by little led to the problem of the nature of history and of science; I therefore read many Italian and German books on philosophy and the methodology of history, and also for the first time the *Scienza nuova* [of Vico]."[16]

In May he wrote a series of letters to Donato Jaja, the titular head of the Italian orthodox Hegelian school, announcing his dissatisfaction with his present works:

> I'm twenty-five years old now and it's time to narrow my studies to one of perhaps two fields. . . . I have decided to take up two kinds of studies. . . ; historical studies dealing with the *internal* history of Italy in the last three or four centuries, and philosophical studies dealing principally with the philosophy of history and the philosophy of art. That is my program, at least for the present.[17]

Croce's program of studies was coupled with an attack upon certain tendencies in modern historiography and social science which he found disturbing: the easy dismissal of values by positivists and Hegelian historicists, and the tendency of both these groups to study abstractions rather than the facts of history. He turned first to the Hegelians. He had not yet read Hegel: "I did not think at that time of looking for Hegel in Hegel, partly because my sparse philosophical preparation did not allow it and partly because of a terror created for me by the pages of Spaventa; . . . If the expositor and interpretor was so obscure, what would the original text be?"[18] Nevertheless, he deplored the Hegelians' historization of truth. "Certainly," he wrote in response to them, "geometry was born under given conditions which it is important to determine; but this does not mean that the truths of geometry are something purely historical or relative."[19] Equally disturbing, Croce found in Hegelian historians, especially after reading Vico, a certain "theological" tendency, a desire to study the idea rather than the facts. In April 1892 he attacked Hegelian philosophy in a scholarly paper read to the Neapolitan Academia Pontaniana. "I believe that the fundamental principles and especially the method of that system are entirely erroneous; the dangerous consequences of this error will become clear in particular disciplines."[20] Croce sent off a copy of his paper to Donato Jaja, who was amazed: "Dear Benedetto . . . you are the nephew of Bertrando and Silvio Spaventa, you are a compatriot of Camillo De Meis." And Jaja went on to explain that knowledge of events, "knowledge [gained] with natural and historical methods of research is not enough." Events must be understood. Hegel "does not abandon experience, . . . but wants to understand it and, through understanding it, create a world that is the very world" given in experience, a world of thought which corresponds to the world of action.[21] To Croce this was theology, history based on the presupposition of an idea that directed events. For Croce, Herbartian truths had no control over history; they were touchstones against which history could be evaluated. Was Croce not in the tradition of Vico in his attempt to push through the orthodox Hegelian philosophy to the concrete facts of history? Croce had taken, albeit unconsciously, a few steps down the path opened by Feuerbach.

Having separated himself from the Hegelians, the right Hegelians at any rate, Croce now turned his attention to the positivists. Here he drew upon his reading of the German social scientists, noting that the positivists do not examine history but abstract laws, which they regard as more important than the facts. In a paper of 1893, far more important than the earlier one, Croce set out the essentials of what would, with significant alterations, become his own Philosophy of Spirit. The paper was written in response to Pasquale Villari, professor at the University of Florence, student of De Sanctis, and mentor of Gaetano Salvemini. In 1891, Villari had written a series of articles in *La nuova antologia* asking "Is History Science?"[22] Croce responded in an article entitled "History Brought under the General Concept of Art,"[23] which he read to the Neapolitan Academia Pontaniana on March 5, 1893. The main idea of the article was to draw a distinction between science on the one hand and art and history on the other. It was, in fact, a hasty distinction and one that would trouble the author for almost the next fifteen years. In the category of science, Croce included philosophy, as had Hegel and Schelling. Science and philosophy are distinguished from art and history in that the former subsume particulars under general concepts, while the latter examine particular facts in their concreteness.[24] Croce thus divided intellectual activity into two categories, one containing art and history, and the other containing science and philosophy. "Therefore," said Croce, "either one does art, or one does science."[25] This response, so similar in some ways to the idea of the Southwest German school, separated Croce from the positivists and Hegelians, of course, because however much the two schools differed, neither concentrated on the real events of history. The positivists concentrated on general laws and were therefore "scientists," while the Hegelians concentrated on the idea and were therefore philosophers or, as Croce called them, "theologians."

More important than his separation from the Hegelians and positivists, however, was the long-run effect of his assertion that history, the study of the real, was art. This cut Croce and his school off from the German school, which had sought to find a different, but still scientific, basis for history. Croce sought the basis of history in the antithesis of science—art.

61

By art, of course, Croce did not mean an abandonment of the real. He used the term as Vico used it, that is, to imply the first form of knowledge, that closest to reality. "Art," meant here, as Nicola Petruzzellis pointed out,[26] "representation of reality, knowledge of the individual" fact.

In some respects, then, Croce fit into the humanist pattern discussed earlier. If he had been put off from reading Hegel, had not quite understood Spaventa, he seemed to have absorbed enough of the tradition to feel that positivism as an outgrowth of the Enlightenment had many of the limitations Vico had discerned in Descartes. He also opposed Hegel, but the very opposition indicated an almost left Hegelian preoccupation with concrete human history. Concreteness, the hallmark of the southern intellectual tradition, was what Croce sought and the lack of which he condemned in others. In art, he thought he had found it.

Alongside this assumption that concreteness is the business of historians there was, however, an assumption that seemed to cast Croce quite outside the southern tradition: his continuing great concern with the transcendent truths preserved by Herbart. Croce wished, in other words, to hold stable the Heraclitean rush of events by maintaining above it the ontological *verum, bonum, pulchrum.* Thus, Croce explained in the 1893 essay, "an invincible instinct of our soul forces us to seek the relations which must exist between the supreme ideality of the human spirit, between the true, the good, and the beautiful."[27]

In 1895 Labriola, well aware of Croce's hostility toward positivism and orthodox Hegelianism, sent to Croce his recently completed essay, "In Memory of the Communist Manifesto." Labriola had abandoned his Herbartianism and turned to Marxism after Croce had left Rome in 1886. Croce was anxious to see what had so moved his mentor. The impact on Croce of an ideology rigidly opposed to Hegel's "theological tendencies" as well as to mechanistic positivism, yet vitally concerned with the concrete, may well be imagined. When Croce received the manuscript in the mail he was

> inflamed by the reading of the pages of Labriola. I was taken by the feeling of a revelation that was opening my anxious spirit; I wasted no time and threw myself into the study of Marx and of the economists and of the modern and ancient communists, a study that I had to follow intensely for the next two years.[28]

It was no wonder that Croce was "inflamed." From a theoretical standpoint the ideas of Antonio Labriola, "the great theorist of Italian Marxism and among the greatest teachers of European Marxism,"[29] were clearly the most significant

and original expressed at this time in Italy. His entire conception of historical
materialism aimed at the destruction of all faiths and all cosmic beliefs. Even
though Labriola was a theorist, a *professorissimo,* as the exiled Russian revolutionary thinker Anna Kulischioff once described him,[30] his philosophy was
an attempt to annihilate all speculative faiths so as to stress the practical over
the theoretical. The only thing that mattered was that the socialist "ask himself at every moment: What is the proper thing to say, to do, under the present
circumstances, for the best interests of the proletariat?"[31] To Labriola, Marxism was a *practical* philosophy, *una filosofia della practica.*

> The *philosophy of practice* ... is the pith of historical materialism. ... The
> realistic process leads first from life to thought, not from thought to life.
> It leads from wants and therefore from various feelings of well-being or ill-
> ness resulting from the satisfaction or neglect of these wants to the creation
> of the poetical myth of supernatural forces, not vice versa. ... Historical
> materialism, then, or the *philosophy of practice,* takes account of man as a
> social and historical being. It gives the last blow to all forms of idealism
> which regard actually existing things as mere reflexes, reproductions, imita-
> tions, results, of so-called a priori thought, thought before the fact. It marks
> also the end of naturalistic materialism. [32]

To Labriola, then, the supernatural was mere poetic myth and the positivist
Marxists were the modern equivalents of older theological thinkers long since
overcome by Marx. Labriola's lesson was to forget the supernatural and to work
on practical matters, for man cannot think about the abstract, for "we cannot
think anything except things we ourselves experience."[33] It must be stated "over
and over again [that] it is not given to us to know the thing in itself, the inmost
nature of things, the final cause and fundamental reason of phenomena."[34] Historical materialism is instead, he said, a method, a critical method for understanding history and for proceeding in the present epoch.

> Our doctrine does not pretend to be the intellectual vision of a great plan
> or a design, but it is merely a method of research and of conception. It is
> not by accident that Marx spoke of his discovery as a guiding thread, and it
> is precisely for this reason that it is analogous to Darwinism, which also is
> a method, and is not and cannot be a modern repetition of the constructed
> or constructive natural philosophy. [35]

It is important to note here that Labriola saw Darwinism as a method, not
as a deterministic, semireligious vision leading to the triumph of man. Historical
materialism and Darwinism were critical, analytic, and in a fundamental sense

historical. Historical materialism explained the struggle of humanity to satisfy the necessary prerequisites of life through interaction with one's fellows. History, therefore, was *only*

> the history of society—that is to say, the history of the variations of human cooperation, from the primitive horde down to the modern state, from the immediate struggle against nature, by means of a few simple tools, to the present economic structure, which reduces itself to these two poles: accumulated labor (capital) and living labor (proletarians).[36]

Finally, historical materialism was also the doctrine of the proletariat (the "orientation" of historical materialism "has been determined by the visual angle of the proletariat"),[37] because it taught that the most *effective* way to satisfy our needs was in a classless society.[38]

Historical and cosmic justification are, it is obvious, irrelevant to this conception of socialism, for thought never departed in Labriola from the everyday world of food, shelter, and clothing. Thought to Labriola was practical; it was simple "natural reflection . . . which takes place in us while we follow the satisfaction of our needs."[39] Thought of this type (and there was no other type) was limited, practical, and goal oriented. It was akin to science, which to Labriola was also a practical and natural method of thought aimed merely at satisfying our material wants. (Labriola, for obvious reasons, did not consider the need to "know" as a basis of science.) "In other words, science depends upon our needs."[40] It was for this reason that historical materialism was "scientific" too.[41] In the long run he hoped that a "science in its perfect state will have absorbed [abstract] philosophy."[42]

Thus, acceptance of the philosophy of historical materialism led one to confront the daily and the prosaic, to abandon metaphysical speculation in order better to work the soil in Voltaire's garden. The process was historical and unending, for no eternal truth existed, because no eternal problem existed. "Historical materialism demands of those who wish to profess it, consciously and frankly, a certain queer humility."[43] Labriola if nothing else was humbling.

This "terrestrialization" of philosophy seemed to Labriola to have banished forever the simplistic notion of determinism raised by abstract positivists and to have launched Marxism into the arena of liberty. Marxist philosophy, according to Labriola, obviated the hiatus between theory and practice. Precisely because it was "practical," wrote Labriola, "it implies the elimination of the vulgar distinction between theory and practice."[44]

To all of this Labriola exposed the young Croce. Their common antipathy toward positivism seemed to Labriola a sufficient basis for collaboration. Labriola persuaded Croce to attack Marx's son-in-law Paul Lafargue in order to discredit his rigid materialism. Croce complied in a blistering essay ("Lafargue applies with the greatest facility . . . the new materialist conception of history, which he has reduced to a simple formula that requires only to be pronounced in order to explain everything").[45] During the summer of 1895, Croce and Labriola met frequently ("We saw each other almost every day and took long walks, during which he exposed to me his thoughts, doubts, interpretations, and re-elaborations of the doctrine of historical materialism"), and Labriola began to urge Croce to write something on Marxism for Sorel's journal at Paris, *Le Devenir social.* Sorel had begun publishing Labriola's work in French, and since then the two men had become fast friends. Now Croce was asked to join the group. From that point on the three men labored together to work out a theory of socialism. "We three," as Labriola referred to the group, were to work out a concrete revolutionary strategy for socialism. The triumvirate, however, was doomed from the outset.

Labriola was grounded in the historical concrete and, rara avis, he was quite content to remain there. But what made him think others would? Labriola had created a kind of elitist philosophy for those who could afford the luxury of doubt, but it could never appeal to more than a few.

Croce's reaction was not what Labriola had expected. Croce had been look- ing for a philosophy that took account of and explained the facts, a philosophy, however, that had some standard outside the dialectical warp of history against which history could be measured. From mere facts this could not be attained, and from Labriola Croce had gotten, he felt, mere facts, economic facts at that.[46]

In the spring of 1896, Croce set down his thoughts on these matters in an essay, "On the Materialist Conception of History," which concerned itself with Labriola's recently published *Del materialismo storico.* To Croce it was the "most ample and profound treatment of" Marxism that existed.[47] But what did Croce find in the book? He found that according to Labriola, "so-called histor- ical materialism" was not a philosophy of history.[48] "Labriola does not say this explicitly, rather, in a word he says exactly the opposite. Yet the denial, unless I deceive myself, is implicit."[49]

And perhaps it was. There can be little question that Labriola attacked philos- ophy of history in a Hegelian (metaphysical) sense. Following the lead of the German social scientists who claimed that history was concrete facts, and build- ing upon his own earlier assertion that history was art, not philosophy, Croce explained that "the possibility of a philosophy of history presupposes the pos- sibility of a conceptual reduction of the course of history."[50] The concept of history, however, tells us nothing about the course of history. History was simply isolated facts.[51] One did not have a concept of facts but simply the facts themselves.

A concept of "history" would mean simply "change" or "development" and, as such, means little or nothing. Labriola's constant attempt to destroy theological conceptions of history thus indicated to Croce that Labriola was confused. On the one hand, he rejected anything other than history; on the other, he proclaimed a "philosophy of history." But since "historical movement cannot be reduced except to a single concept, that of development, rendered empty of all that is properly contained in history," [52] Labriola had "abandoned any pretense of establishing the law of history, or of finding the concept to which the complex of historical facts may be reduced." [53]

Labriola had not, of course, reduced history to the simple concept of "development." Historical materialism meant the end of transcendent beliefs or principles in history, but it also meant that the satisfaction of material needs had been isolated as the concrete motor force of the historical process. But Croce, as we have seen, had begun with the bias that this was not all there was to history. Since historical materialism provided nothing else, it therefore became simply an instrument to further the attack on the theological and deterministic philosophies of history. "Historical materialism, is not, and cannot be, a new philosophy of history, nor a new method," he concluded. What was it then, besides an attack upon determinism? Here Croce drew upon Labriola's insistence that historical materialism had to do with the history of social cooperation. Thus, Croce concluded, historical materialism was "simply this: a sum of new data, of new expressions, which enter into the mind of the historian." [54] That is, it deals with economic data that historians hitherto had been wont to ignore. Now they would no longer ignore it.

Historical materialism, moreover, as Croce defined it, had nothing to do with a practical movement like socialism. To be of use in a practical movement it would have to do just what Labriola refused to allow historical materialism to do: provide a faith. Thus, Croce observed: "Deprived of any superfluous notions of finality and providential designs, historical materialism cannot give any succor to socialism nor to any other practical endeavor." [55] Croce had concluded—though he would not make much of it for two years—just what Sorel would conclude in 1907: men participating in great struggles need to know that their cause is just and that it will triumph. Croce needed to know it too.

Like Croce, Sorel had begun to ask himself whether something more than this Labriolan concreteness was not required. [56] "One thing has always been present in my mind," wrote Sorel, "that men who are participating in a great social movement always picture their coming action as a battle in which their cause is certain to triumph. These constructions, knowledge of which is so important for historians, I propose to call myths." [57] But "certainty" was just

what Labriola had removed. He felt no need to supply socialism with any Bergsonian *élan vital,* as did Sorel, nor any neo-Kantian impetus for action, as did
the German Revisionist Eduard Bernstein.[58] He cared, he said, not a whit for
the desire of the simple to make socialism "moral."[59]

It was this unwillingness to provide a constant moral basis for action outside
the dialectic which caused Sorel and Croce to wonder if Labriola's philosophy
could have any practical merit. Before men would act they needed to justify
their action. To "justify" meant to Croce precisely what Labriola wished to
avoid: a reliance on metaphysics. In short, Croce was not a pure materialist, for
he still believed in constant values. "Signor Croce," wrote an exasperated Georgi
Plekhanov, "is jumbled by the common prejudices of the philistine against materialism."[60] And, Plekhanov continued a year later,

> Croce says of himself that in ethical questions he has not succeeded in freeing
> himself from the prison of the Kantian criticism. . . . We would add that the
> "Kantian criticism" has left a profound, indelible imprint on his *entire* con-
> ception of the world. It is precisely in this that the secret of his *critical* exer-
> cises exists. He understands that *Kantianism* is not compatible with the
> historical and sociopolitical conceptions of Marx, which are entirely pene-
> trated by the spirit of *materialism.* Yet instead of completely renouncing
> Kantianism, or turning his back on Marxism, he attempts to ride both horses
> at once, trying to modify Marxism in such a way that it will end by no
> longer being in contradiction with these views with which *it cannot but be
> in contradiction.*[61]

For Croce, in other words, morality and ethical values were too important
to leave to historical materialism, which historicized them and made them concrete. Concreteness was one thing, but to extend it to the world of values was
going too far. "Really," Croce wrote to Gentile, "the difference between me and
Labriola is great with respect to the *scientific form,* and therefore the *historical
weight* of the doctrine. Labriola, whom I hold in very great esteem . . . has carried to excess his horror of *scholasticism* and *abstractionism.*"[62]

This belief in values, this naïveté, as Labriola saw it, led Labriola to suspect
that Croce could never understand a *practical* philosophy because he theorized
too much, pushed words to their logical conclusion, and then discarded a philosophy because it did not explain everything. Labriola wrote to Croce complain-
ing of a *"formal* presupposition or prejudice, that one can know more in fact
than he can know."[63] Croce was too academic, an "intellectual epicurean," one
who theorized and assumed that with thought man could arrive at the truth.
"I want to take this opportunity to tell you . . . [that] this is the road to Pla-
tonism and scholasticism."[64]

But Croce was not to be deterred. Having glimpsed the "truth" of historical materialism ("Marx and Labriola could not but have thought what seemed to me to be true"),[65] Croce began slowly to reject it. "You argue instead of expounding," Labriola wrote somewhat later, "and you argue only with yourself. ... In other words, you argue with yourself in order to find out what use you can make of Marxism but not to find out what it is."[66]

Despite all this, however, a somewhat tenuous collaboration between Croce and Labriola continued. In November 1896 Croce, at Labriola's insistence, wrote for Sorel's *Le Devenir social* a scathing attack upon the Marxist positivist Achille Loria: "Labriola proposed to me that I do to Professor Loria what I had done to Lafargue."[67] Even though Croce could still summon his strengths to attack positivism, however, this did not mean he had acquiesced in Labriola's theories. By the summer of 1897 it was clear that Croce was searching for something more satisfying than historical materialism à la Labriola. By November of that year Croce had on paper some of his most devastating remarks on historical materialism. No longer believing that he was following in the footsteps of Labriola, he read his new essay, "On the Interpretation and Criticism of Some Concepts of Marxism,"[68] to the Academia Pontaniana.

Beginning with a long analysis of Marx's economic theory, Croce again stressed that economics was only one aspect of human nature. Croce therefore reduced the labor theory of value to only "one factor among other factors, or a factor that appears to us empirically as contrasted, diminished, and revised by other factors." It is hardly a "dominant absolute factor." Marxist economics, therefore, is not even a general economic science but instead a study of one isolated economic factor. The value of Marxian economics lies not in its mistaken and abstract theory but in its empirical investigations. It is, in the final analysis, a comparative sociology of working conditions.[69] Marx had exaggerated abstract and arbitrary notions such as surplus value, the labor theory of value, the law of falling profits, and then imposed them upon a concrete world where they did not fit. It was this reduction of Marxism to mere economics, to a single aspect of life, which made it inadequate as a total *Weltanschauung;* a philosophy that dealt with man in such a one-sided and limited way could not be a new faith.[70]

Having dealt with Marx's economics, Croce then went on to see what use historical materialism really had. Continuing from what he had said in his earlier essay, Croce now concluded that the sole use of historical materialism was to provide new data for historians. Historical materialism was a "simple canon of historical interpretation."[71]

"This canon counsels paying attention to the so-called economic substructure of society." It "implies no anticipation of results" and is "useful in many cases, useless in others, and its correct and profitable use depends always on . . . prudence." [72] As such, historical materialism is politically useless and has nothing to do with socialism, which is not an "amoral science" but rather a proletarian ethic aimed at the conquest of power. This last conclusion, the separation of historical materialism from socialism, struck Sorel and was to become the basis for their future relationship. For socialism, according to Croce, had no theoretical justification. Marx was not a theorist, but an agitator, the "Machiavelli of the proletariat" in Croce's inimitable words. [73] (Croce, of course, here saw Machiavelli as an Italian nationalist, not as a political scientist.)

These ideas, so remote from what Labriola had believed to be the essence of Marxism, mark a significant watershed in Italian Marxism. They mark, in fact, the end of Italian Marxism à la Labriola for more than half a century. [74]

So closely were Labriola and Croce and, for that matter, Sorel associated with socialism in the public mind [75] that Croce's views were soon confused with Labriola's. In October of 1898, Bernstein, who had also read Croce's essay, wrote to Labriola to see if in fact the essay represented Labriola's viewpoint as well. Sorel at the same time wrote to Labriola suggesting that Croce's essay be used as the preface to the French publication of Labriola's letters. Labriola himself began to doubt not only Croce and Sorel but his own role in this "crisis of Marxism." Perhaps Croce and Sorel were right. Perhaps Labriola's concreteness, his refusal to give socialism any base other than the materialistic, had contributed to the crisis. "I do not know if this crisis exists," wrote Labriola, "or whether I am its representative or author." [76]

The crisis existed, however, and Labriola soon turned upon Croce and Sorel for their apostasy. To Labriola "we three" became "you two." "You two have written what you have written and this most holy trinity has gone up in smoke." [77] Soon Labriola could see the doctrine he had discovered being torn apart not only in Italy but in Germany and France as well. Something "very serious," something *"real,"* had happened in Germany, he wrote to Croce, something, he still hoped vainly, that Croce would be concerned about.

> Bernstein has been disavowed at the Stuttgart Congress. Bernstein is preparing a book on what is now *valid* in Marxism. He has told me his idea and at the same time has recounted some of his petty gossip: for example, Kautsky refuses to publish articles for him because he is not ready yet to refute them. Kautsky, on his own, writes me of the grave danger of a break with Bernstein. It appears, among other things, that Kautsky has refused to publish some articles in which *Bernstein refers to your writings and mine.* [78]

Croce, however, refused to help and smugly concluded: "Labriola had deluded himself into thinking he had found in me a collaborator." [79] Forced now to make some public declaration as to where he stood with respect to Croce's ideas on Marxism, Labriola appended a postscript to the French edition of his own letters to Sorel, then about to be printed at Paris. After some sarcasm directed at Sorel, Labriola then turned to the major issue: disavowing Croce's last essay.

> Although this work [of Croce's] is supposed to be a free review of my *Socialism and Philosophy* . . . the fact is that aside from some useful observations on historical methods and a few sagacious remarks on political tactics, it contains theoretical enunciations, which have nothing to do with my publications and opinions, *but are rather diametrically opposed to them.* Should I now engage officially in an explicit polemic against the whole dissertation. . . ? Why should I? What good would it do? [80]

This decision not to enter into a polemic left the field to Croce, who now assumed the role of "interpreter" of Marxism in Italy. As Giuseppe Petronio noted, at the end of the nineteenth century "there were two theoretical Marxists: Labriola, already near the end of his life, and Croce." [81] Confused, bitter, and only five years from death, Labriola had become not the founder of Italian revolutionary socialism, but merely the equal, at best, of Croce, who had forever inserted himself into the Italian debate over Marxism.

Croce's experience with historical materialism is also important from a personal point of view, for it constituted a distinct disappointment. He had hoped to find a faith that preserved values intact; instead, he found one that concerned itself only with economics. This did not, however, mean that having seen the weakness or unilateralness of historical materialism, Croce lost interest in the search for a more meaningful philosophy. Croce did not abandon his search for a revolutionary and catalytic faith, in fact, until more than a decade later. What he abandoned in 1897 was only Labriola; his search for a faith that dealt with man as a whole continued. In this pursuit Croce had another encounter which was to affect his life as much as, perhaps more than, his encounter with Labriola. Reading through Croce's rather boldly self-confident manuscripts on Marxism, one finds a rather curious reference. Three times Croce urges his readers to consult another analysis of Marxism, that "of the expert [*talente*] Professor Giovanni Gentile." [82] Nothing too curious perhaps, except that Gentile's analysis of Marxism was diametrically opposed to Croce's.

Born in Castelvetrano, Sicily in 1875, Gentile came under the influence of Jaja when, in 1893, he won a scholarship to the University of Pisa. It was Jaja

who introduced Gentile to Spaventa and the southern humanist tradition as well
as to the German idealists. Much more than Croce, Gentile possessed an extraordinary philosophical instinct and ability, and where Croce, nine years Gentile's
senior, was put off by reading the idealists, Gentile managed them with ease.[83]
This also accounts for the different approaches the two men took toward Labriola and Marx. Where Croce was concerned with practice, with the practical
effects of Marxism, and was disappointed because, as he put it, Marxism could
not "give any succor to socialism nor to any other practical endeavor,"[84] Gentile was concerned with theory and the logical coherence of Marxism, or at
any rate what he conceived Marxism to be. Labriola's remark to Croce that "you
only use" Marxism was no less true of Gentile.

Gentile was, from the time of his first encounter with Spaventa under Jaja,
a zealous convert to idealism. His aim was to end the hiatus between being and
becoming, between the world of Parmenides and the world of Heraclitus, an
accomplishment that he felt had been hinted at in the conjunction of the "being
of God" and the "becoming of God" in the works of, first, Giordano Bruno,
then Spinoza.[85] With these concerns and with the unshakable conviction that
only through idealism could the worlds of theory and practice be bridged, Gentile read Marx as Hegel would have read, say, Engels. It was not until 1897 that
Gentile began to write his own essays on Marx. In the meantime, while still a
student at Pisa, he wrote commentaries on Croce's interpretation of Marx. Indeed, it was through their common, though contradictory, interest in Marx
that Croce and Gentile first met.[86] By 1897 Gentile had drawn his own conclusions about Marxism and set them down in the journal *Studi storici (del crive-
lucci).*[87]

The only thing new in Marx, said Gentile, was the "philosophy of *prassi*,"
and that was new only because Marx had substituted "matter" for "thought."
The concept of the "philosophy of practice" was well known to idealists and
was a legitimate philosophy of history. This is what Croce had missed in his reading of Marx and this was why Croce had seen the theory of Labriola as a mere
canon of historical interpretation.[88]

Gentile went on to explain. If, as the philosophy of Kant maintains, spirit is
not a mere observer, passive before the object given it, then spirit must be the
creator of the object. This "Hegelianization" of Marx, as Aldo Lo Schiavo put
it,[89] led Gentile to conclude that since spirit now became the creator, the dualism of Kant, the thing-in-itself, had at last been overcome, absorbed in the spirit
as a whole. Combining this Berkelian-Fichtian observation with Vico's *verum-
factum-convertuntur* (to be, is to be done, made, created), Gentile went on,
"Thought is real in so far as it poses the object. Either thought is and thinks; or

71

it does not think and is not thought. If it thinks, it creates [*fa,* or makes, as Vico would have put it] . Therefore reality, the objectivity of thought, is a result of its own nature. This is one of the primary results of Marxist realism." The world, the "material of historical materialism, far from being external and opposed to the idea of Hegel, is included in it, in fact is the very same thing—a result Hegelian philosophy gained from the Kantian synthetic a priori."[90]

Gentile's essay of 1897 remained largely unknown for many years, not so much because it presented Marx in a distorted fashion, but because Gentile himself remained largely in the shadow created by Croce. The essay, remarkable for its coherence, possibly contained in germ form what would in 1916 be set out as the mature thought of Gentile.[91]

Despite their differences over what Marxism might mean, by 1898 both Gentile and Croce could agree that if Marxism meant anything at all, it was of little significance. For Croce Marxism was not enough to inspire the pleb, and in any case Italy was too backward to be inspired. On November 23 he wrote to Gentile,

> I'll tell you, as to historical materialism, I no longer wish to concern myself. . . . I got from Marxism what I needed and if I were inclined to political life I would work for the proletarian movement. But even this would be, perhaps, premature in Italy; . . . we cannot allow ourselves the luxury of raising questions that suppose an advanced state of civilization.[92]

The next day Gentile answered:

> To tell you the truth, your sudden decision to concern yourself no longer with Marxism surprised me; but I don't know how I can disapprove since it was always apparent to me that one could get very little that was constructive out of it. Anyhow, Labriola's exaggerations and pretenses are now undone.[93]

The confident, almost superior tone of Gentile's letter to Croce will doubtless arrest readers accustomed to believing that Croce was always the dominant figure in their relationship. At this juncture quite the opposite was true. Gentile's "use" of Marxism had reassured and deepened his earlier conviction that a revival of idealism was essential. Unlike Croce, Gentile knew where he wanted to go. Although Croce, as we shall see, had gained a great deal from his Marxian studies, he remained in 1898 in essentially the same stage of intellectual development as he had been in 1895, when he had first received the letter from Labriola. He wanted to return to his interrupted study of the philosophy of art and history. He therefore remained open to the influence of the younger but more confident Gentile, and it was through Gentile that Croce was educated—better, reeducated—in the writings of De Sanctis, Spaventa, and the Italian Hegelian movement.[94] It would be several years, however, before this influence would bear fruit.

In the meantime Croce returned to his search, in art and history, for some bridge between the world of history and the world of stable Herbartian values. Disillusioned with Labriola and Marx because they paid attention only to *prassi,* disillusioned with the orthodox Hegelians and positivists because they ignored practical life, Croce turned in 1898 to a figure from the past who seemed able to combine ideal values with political action. Francesco De Sanctis had fallen out of fashion during the period of positivist hegemony because, it was charged, his efforts at history were unaccompanied by factual research and documentation.[95] On April 3, 1898, Croce read a lengthy manuscript in defense of the Risorgimento author, "Francesco De Sanctis and His Recent Critics," to the Academia Pontaniana.[96] The paper is revealing, especially about the inner turmoil of its author, caught as he was between the desire to remain concrete and the awareness that total immersion in the concrete would mean abandonment of the ahistorical Herbartian sanctuary. In 1898 Croce tried to preserve both.

He scorned the positivist critics of De Sanctis, explaining that far from ignoring factual life, De Sanctis aimed at integrating literature with concrete history, with life itself, that his purpose was to show the concrete spiritual origins of literature. If De Sanctis was no mere "compiler" of facts, this was because he dealt with "the problems of the soul and of human society."[97] Croce went on—reopening that Marxist parenthesis which he thought he had closed (and not for the last time either)—to explain that "literature has its foundation in the needs of life; these needs give it its seriousness. If the needs were to change, the literature would have to change [*mutando questi bisogni, debba mutare la letteratura*], and if it did not change, it would become rhetorical and academic."[98]

Ideas arose then under determinate conditions, but this did not seem to mean for Croce that these ideas were secondary, superstructural. On the contrary, they had to be held with tenacity, for only in this way could the world of flux, the world of politics, be controlled. "One must recognize the firmness of [De Sanctis's] ethical concepts, upon which alone one can build a healthy political program."[99] It was because De Sanctis had a firm conception of life that he was able to affect the course of political events. This conception of life, this faith, was precisely what was absent from Italy as the century drew to a close. Thus, Croce urged his audience in capital letters to reexamine "Francesco De Sanctis, who had what is usually lacking: A CONCEPTION OF LIFE AND A FAITH."

This "conception of life" allowed the intellectuals to work in the practical world to effect change. After rereading Vico and Cuoco, Croce concluded that even though they had scorned abstract political ideas, it was still through ideas that they were able to affect politics. Thus Vico, while unnoticed as a political figure, had still great effect in the political world "because his concepts, by modifying the intellectual environment, had brought about [*condizzionarono*] new political directions. Precisely this [the modifying of the intellectual environment] was the task of the philosopher and not of the politician, who, instead, directly modifies practical life." [100]

Croce's study of De Sanctis, replacing Marx, signaled a return to the study of the philosophy of art and the philosophy of history interrupted in 1895. [101] Almost immediately Croce encountered difficulties inherent in the position he had taken in the 1893 essay, which brought history under the concept of art. From 1898 to 1902 Croce labored to eliminate the difficulties and to set out a theory of art. The results were momentous.

3 AESTHETICS AND THE NEW CULTURE

Never having accepted Labriola's mundane materialism, Croce departed at the turn of the century from any doctrine that implied that man could find contentment in the satisfaction of material wants. Instead, De Sanctis's pronouncement that man must have a conception of life, a faith, became, for Croce, the basis for an attempted regeneration of the Italian culture now shaking itself loose from the burden of positivism. A new culture that could act as a lay religion guiding man's actions could bring about the same sense of purpose in Italy that had existed during the Risorgimento.

Man, Croce said, could not live without this "sense of religion." Positivism, because it had denied this need, was passing out of fashion, and men would now seek comfort again in a faith so as to make sense of their world. Croce prayed that this would not lead again to the transcendent religion of the Church but rather to a religion based on truth, on man, on the "negation of every form of transcendence."

> Without religion, or rather without this orientation, one does not live, or one lives with a soul divided and perplexed, unhappily. . . . Positivism made the singular effort to leave unsolved the religious needs of men. . . . [But] after the many decades of positivist dominion the religious need has again awakened, all the more demanding for its long denial. . . . Two paths open before us; the first leads back to the old faith, to the church and synagogue. . . . But on this path lies mental suicide. [The other path] promises man the truth, the full truth to be conquered by the force of thought, with the will of the true, with the speculative method proper to philosophy. . . . *The negation of positivism and with it the negation of every form of*

transcendence and belief is what is now called the "rebirth of idealism."...
In its rebirth, philosophical idealism must recognize and take up again its
historical tradition . . . interrupted for some decades by the positivist inter-
regnum. Those four thinkers who form the philosophical quadrilateral of
Germany—Kant, Fichte, Schelling, and Hegel, of which only Kant has continued to be an object of study, though divorced from his nearest disciples
and followers, and badly misunderstood . . . must be recalled to life. . . .
[Let it not be forgotten] that Italy will not be great spiritually except by
the acquisition of its own *religious consciousness*, which is also *philosophical
consciousness*. [1]

Like Vico, De Sanctis, Spaventa, and others within the Italian tradition of
humanism, Croce could not accept materialism, for it provided no faith in man
but, rather, made of man an instrument. Instead of turning to history, however,
as the matrix that resolved the opposites of materialism and idealism, Croce
turned to an idealism that had more in common with Kant than Vico, which
celebrated man's creative *mind* rather than his creative activity in history. It
would be several crucial years before he would see what De Sanctis, after Vico,
had called the "middle way," between the a priori of the idealists and the a
posteriori of the materialists, the way of making all reality and all thought historical.

It is, of course, a fine line, the distinction between materialism and idealism,
a line grown increasingly murky with continued puzzlement over Descartes's
cogito, not to mention the synthetic a priori of Kant. How different were the
conceptions of Vico's *verum-ipsum-factum* and the *cogito,* and yet if one were
to leave out the fact that in Vico it was through doing, through *praxis,* that
knowing was possible, then how similar the notions of Descartes and Vico became. The one had said that to know, or to think, is to be; the other, that to
know is to be done. And where for an idealist can a thing be done but in the
mind? How easily Vico's idea—that in practice, in history, knowledge is made
possible—might be lost and how easily might he be transformed into the anti-
historical Descartes. After the Kantian synthetic a priori, with its implications of
an autonomous—no, omnipotent—mind, the temptation to leave out practice,
to see Vico as a refiner of Descartes and as a precursor of Kant, became, in Risorgimento Naples at any rate, a fairly respectable notion. It was Vico idealized, so
that *factum* became, with *verum,* a mere cognitive activity. Thus, Francesco Fiorentino in the 1860s found it easy to fit Vico into a universal history, a history
that had Vico's historicism culminate in the ahistoricity of Kant. "Thus, Vico
is considered by Fiorentino as the natural successor of the Cartesian *cogito* as

well as the precursor of the Kantian synthetic a priori, indeed of the whole of the *Critique of Pure Reason.*" [2]

Leaving the historical and practical aspect of *factum* out of Vico was not so extraordinary for one who had, as Croce, utterly abandoned Labriola's odd contentment with mere *praxis.* In Croce the difference between Vico and Descartes appeared not as the difference between the *verum-factum* and rationalism, but as the difference between a Cartesian rationalism and Vichian imaginative poetry liberated from rigid logic and a mathematical *raison.* In Croce's *Estetica* of 1902 history, *praxis*, took a back seat to man's creative mind, and faith in man as creator, poet, and artist assumed the primary focus. This extraordinary book of a mere 150 pages (the rest of the text being a history of the criticism of art) was, however, both a theory of aesthetics and a theory of the human spirit in toto. It became for many intellectuals—but never for the masses—the lay culture of De Sanctis, the foundation for a lay religion, which was to replace abstract Catholicism, positivism, and orthodox as well as unorthodox Hegelianism, was to celebrate instead the religion of humanity.

The *Estetica* marked a watershed in Croce's development; the book coincided with his abandonment of transcendence and the philosophy of Herbart as well as the beginning of a long struggle with Hegel. Croce had become an idealist, but for him the ideas resided, at least until the discovery of the "middle way," in the minds of men and nowhere else. There was no *Weltgeist* in Croce's early idealism, for

> I . . . had acquired a sort of unconscious immanentism, not being interested in a world other than the one in which I was actually living and not feeling directly or even at all the problem of transcendence, and therefore not encountering any difficulty in conceiving of the relation between thought and action. [3]

A philosophy of immanentism then, which did not conceive of the relationship between theory and practice, which did not quite digest the dialectic of *factum-verum* but instead saw art as a kind of direct translation of the vision into objectivity, that was the basis for the *Estetica* of 1902.

Few works published in Italy until well into the Fascist period produced an effect quite like Croce's *Estetica.* [4] Part philosophy, part polemic against positivism, it injected itself into that *"crisi del positivismo"* at such a propitious time and with such a devastating effect that later writings of Croce or even Gentile could never quite equal—and in Croce's case, never quite reverse—the course it seemed to set for the anguished, searching, and bored intelligentsia who peered over the top of the nineteenth century and into the twentieth. Hear, for example, the words of the scholar Mario Vinciguerra, later editor of *La nuova Europa,* as he recalled, some fifty-five years later, that unforgettable day when at the age of fifteen he bought his own copy of the *Estetica,* which had so moved his friends: "That day on which I acquired the book in a little shop, I clutched it to my chest and raced home, and unmindful of anything else, I dove within it." And Vinciguerra continued, "I do not evoke this faraway memory for autobiographical vanity, but because my house in those days was not exceptional or isolated. It was not the case of a boy of acute sensitivity; it was rather the spiritual disposition of a great part of our generation . . . who received at the outset, in its original form, the unique [*innovatrice*] word launched by that book."[5]

Eugenio Garin, the great contemporary historian of Italian culture, similarly noted the extraordinary impact of Croce's book. "It must never be forgotten," he wrote, that "the essential impact of Croce upon the Italian culture was largely that of the *Estetica* of 1902. . . . For nearly two decades . . . philosophical Italy, friend or adversary [of Croce], remained tied to a book which today is easily ignored, but at that time penetrated every field of knowledge with a voice that rendered an entire generation Crocean."[6] Even Croce was stunned by the prestige that now surrounded him. It is amazing, he wrote to his friend Karl Vossler, "even I have become a follower of myself."[7]

The impact of the *Estetica* derived from its two great accomplishments. First, it established the independence of art as a human or spiritual activity and did so at a time when art was regarded by positivists, psychologists, and others as either inexplicable or aberrant. Second, it made artistic "knowledge" the basis for philosophical, moral, and practical knowledge at a time when skepticism had called all three into question.

In staking out an independent basis for art, Croce sharpened De Sanctis's earlier separation of art from the other categories of spiritual life. Like De Sanctis, Croce rejected the panlogism of Hegelian thought, which had aimed at resolving or "dissolving" art into philosophy. Instead, Croce vindicated artistic expression as an activity beyond the purview of logic, science, morality, or practical life. Insofar as art was merely an expression of philosophy or morality, so far was it not art. Thus, Spenser's *Faerie Queene* became, on account of its religious content, not art but the "expression of certain aspects of the protestant spirit in England."[8] So pure of the practical was art, Croce said, that the technique itself with which the artist conveys his vision to the canvas or the sculptor forms the bronze has nothing to do with art.[9] When the vision was molded in the artist's mind, the artistic process ceased; when the artist took up his brush or the sculptor his chisel, then practical activity ensued.[10] As Croce had indicated, he saw, on account of his unconscious immanentism, "no difficulty conceiving of the relation between thought and action."

In the realm of aesthetic criticism, Croce's *Estetica* led, in his own work and in that of his followers, to an examination of single examples of art, a book or a painting, for example, as the expression of an artist's momentary vision of a particular subject. The vision was that of the artist. It could be challenged only on the grounds that it was an incomplete vision, a distorted one, unclear in the artist's own mind before he set it down and hence unclear when manifested to others. It could not be judged as "immoral" or "illogical" or even as "impractical." It stood on its own as an aesthetic statement in no need of any other support and in defiance of any nonaesthetic criticism. In short, the choice of content of an artistic expression was not to be criticized. The purity of the vision could be.

> The theme or content cannot, therefore, be practically or morally charged with epithets of praise or blame. . . . Some critics object to the theme or contents of works which they accept as being artistically perfect but unworthy of art; but there is nothing to be done if these expressions are really perfect, save to advise the critics to leave the artists in peace, for they can only derive inspiration from what has moved their soul. . . . The impossibility of choice of content completes the theorem of the *independence of art* and is also the only legitimate meaning of the expression "Art for art's sake." [11]

Similarly, since each artistic expression was a complete statement in and of itself, no attempt should or could be made to compare works of art of different artists. Still less was it possible to categorize a work of art as tragedy, novel, or epic; each was a thing in itself and a statement of itself. The categorization of art into generic types was merely a practical activity and aesthetically meaningless. What did it matter whether or not an artist's tragedy lived up to some abstract form of tragedy? "All the books dealing with classifications and systems of the arts could be burned without any loss whatever. We say this with the utmost respect," he quipped, "to the writers who have expended their labors upon them." [12] And adhering to the time-honored Italian expression *traduttore traditore*, Croce chastized translations as the artistic vision of the translator rather than that of the author. [13] As a logical conclusion to this, Croce also denied the validity of a history of art unless it were a series of monographs written on artists or particular pieces of art. It is in this way that the adherence to concreteness, to particular works of art, was to be maintained. Like the historical concrete, the aesthetic particular was a thing in itself not to be engulfed by any philosophy. This vindication of art was the first achievement of the *Estetica*.

The second, as noted above, was to make art the basis for the rest of spirit's activity. Art not only rested in an impregnable castle secure against the forays of moralists and philosophers, it dominated the horizon. Here Croce took up the basic idea set out in his 1893 essay against Pasquale Villari, where he had explained that history and art were both activities that treated of particular or individual subjects. At the opening of the *Estetica,* Croce set out a full diagram of the spirit, explaining this earlier idea and elaborating it further. Intellectual activity was divided into two spheres, one containing art and history and dealing with particulars, the other containing science and philosophy and dealing with universals, or "concepts" as Croce called them. Similarly, Croce now divided practical activity into two spheres: that which was craft, amoral, occasionally "Machiavellian," and aimed at a particular end, and that which was lofty, ethical, and aimed at the universal good. [14] Although the *Estetica* was primarily about man's aesthetic ability, it was also a complete statement about the human spirit, for it dealt, explicitly and implicitly, with all four of the categories. At the time when it was written, Croce had no intention of adding further volumes to his so-called philosophy of spirit. "When I wrote the first volume I had no idea of giving it . . . two [new] companions; and I therefore designed it to be, as I say, complete in itself." [15] To understand its impact, it is necessary to remember that this was no obscure work on aesthetics but a work that raised aesthetics to dimensions that reached every other aspect of life.

The category that contained art and history, Croce said, rested upon "intuition." Intuition is a slippery word. For Croce it meant the immediate image of a particular thing, and Croce went on to say, in probably the most famous lines in the entire book, that intuitions were expressions. "Intuitive activity possesses intuitions to the extent that it expresses them." [16] This most controversial equation of intuition with expression was the foundation for the *Estetica.* It rested upon the rather solid idea that if an artist, or for that matter anyone else, could not express the intuition, he did not have it. If it was on the tip of the tongue, so to speak, but never objectified into some kind of expression, then it was not a clear intuition.

> Whatever is not objectified in an expression is not intuition or representation, but sensation or nature [*naturalità*] . The spirit does not intuit except by doing, forming, expressing. Whoever separates intuition from expression will never again succeed in rejoining them. Intuitive activity intuits in so far as it expresses. [17]

For Croce the world of nature remained intact, a datum upon which the human spirit worked. The artist objectified the sensations received from nature into artistic expressions, and this objectification, this expression, represented the free, creative activity of the spirit. Unless the sensation was expressed, it remained mere nature. This conception of art linked artistic creativity not to any transcendent *pulchrum* but rather to the human activity of expression. Thus, Croce concluded that it was the form of art which distinguished it from other activities of the spirit. Art was expression. Content was irrelevant, and "we know nothing of its nature." [18]

This equation of intuition and expression with art had the effect of getting around the knotty issue of what constituted beauty by saying it is an "activity" not an object. "The beautiful is not a physical fact: It does not belong to things but to the activity of man, to spiritual energy." [19] Moreover, the equation of intuition with expression rescued art from the positivists [20] and psychologists who had reduced it to irrational instincts, unsatisfied sexual urges, and other catchalls by making it a form of theoretical knowledge. It furthermore raised art from an inferior spiritual form, as it had been in Hegel, to the very first form of knowledge, the way in which all men, artists or not, conceived and transformed the world of nature. The entire perspective of positivism, which viewed man as part of nature, was reversed so that nature appeared inert without man. All knowledge, even science and philosophy, therefore depended upon the artistic intuition: "Every scientific work is also a work of art." [21] Art thus seemed to readers of the *Estetica* to be both emancipated and emancipator. "I loved it," wrote Giuseppe Antonio Borgese (1882-1952) in 1903: "I enthusiastically applauded [*mi piacque entusiasicamente*] the air of vigorous liberty that it introduced into the staid [*chiuse*] schools."[22]

The *Estetica* in one sense marked Croce's adherence to the tradition of lay humanism which flowed out of the nineteenth century. No longer did the individual fulfill himself by pursuing a Herbartian end that lay outside life itself; rather, artistic perfection lay in human activity and was immeasurable by any outside standard. Croce celebrated an almost deified human spirit. "The divine for Croce is not reality separated from man, but that aspect of man or of history which is manifested as development in ordinary life." [23]

Man himself, as artist, appeared divine, for what he did not objectify in expression remained dead nature. The artist therefore gave life to what would otherwise have remained dumb. It was this creative aspect of expression which impressed Croce. The artist created as surely as the Almighty. But Croce did not stop there. It was not only the artist who was creator. All men were creators, for art was not simply the gift of genius bestowed on the few; it was an essential characteristic of every man. Thus, not only objets d'art, but also the particulars of everyday life, were created by the intuition-expressions of the ordinary man.

"It cannot be asserted that the intuition which is generally called artistic differs from ordinary intuition. . . . The limits of the intuition-expressions that are called art as opposed to those that are called non-art, are empirical and impossible to define." [24] Even a child created when through that infantile haze he formed the first objects of his environment and the words created to describe them. Man was not passive nor a receiver, but, as with Kant, active and a creator. Croce devoted an entire chapter to the idea that artistic intuition, that which is created by the artist, is no different in form than the simpler creations of other men: intuition is intuition. In this view intuition became the basis for all man's creations; all were art.

> If an epigram be art, why not a simple word? If a story, why not the news jottings of the journalist? If a landscape, why not a map? The teacher of philosophy in Moliere's comedy was right: "Whenever we speak we create prose." But there will always be scholars like Monsieur Jourdain, astonished at having spoken prose for forty years without knowing it, who will have difficulty in persuading themselves that when they call their servant John to bring their slippers, they have spoken nothing but—prose. . . . The principal reason which has prevented aesthetic, the science of art, from revealing the true nature of art, its real roots in human nature, has been its separation from the general spiritual life, the having made of it a sort of special function or aristocratic club. [25]

This equation of intuition with expression led Croce then to an important point, perhaps the major point: all language was expression and creation. Indeed, the full title of *Estetica* is the *Aesthetic as Science of Expression and General Linguistics.* "Language is perpetual creation. What has been linguistically expressed cannot be repeated. . . . The ever-new impressions give rise to continuous changes of sounds and meanings, that is, to ever new expressions. . . . Everyone speaks, and should speak, according to the echoes that things arouse in his soul." [26] Each man had, as it were, his own dictionary, a dictionary in a perpetual state of revision. Croce went on to affirm, therefore, that his aesthetic theory led to the following: "Thus were synonyms and homonyms destroyed, and thus was shown the impossibility of really translating one word into another." [27]

Croce had just come from a reading of Vico. What he got from it is fairly clear. For Vico the first men were, as we have seen, poets; that is, they were creators. "The first men . . . created things according to their own ideas. . . . By imagining, [they] did the creating, for which [reason] they were called 'poets,' which is Greek for 'creators.'" [28]

For Croce the importance of the *New Science* lay not in its science, in its concept of a universal history, which Croce could not accept from Vico any more than he could from Labriola, but in Vico's discovery of poetic wisdom, the wisdom of the ancients which allowed them to work out, case by case, what proved to be the institutions of society. But what a difference between the fantasies of artists and the fantasies of Vico's man-beasts, the one tested on canvas, the other in the world. Croce's rejection of Vico's cyclical notion of history was inevitable, given his desire to democratize art to the level of every man in the present. For Vico this "poetic" creativity had been confined to the primitive stage of society; for Croce it was a permanent and essential characteristic of the human spirit.[29] Here Croce followed the lead of De Sanctis, who had rejected Hegel's resolution of art into philosophy. Thus Croce: "The aesthetic of Hegel is thus a funeral oration: he passes in review the successive forms of art, shows the progressive steps of internal consumption, and lays the whole in the grave, leaving philosophy to write its epitaph."[30]

Thus, for Croce art was both independent of any other spiritual activity and at the same time an eternal characteristic of human nature. Not only was it eternal, it was the very first form of knowledge, prior to any other and therefore sire of every other form of spiritual activity. Upon intuition rested philosophic, moral, and practical activity. Yet Croce's vindication of art nowhere made plain that these extraordinary powers of creativity were not nearly as potent in real life as they appeared to be in art. It was one thing to express or create an epigram, quite another to create an intuition of the historical situation that surrounded one. Yet Croce cast them into the same realm. The reluctance to accept the idea of a philosophy of history and the consequent acceptance of the idea that history dealt with particulars and individual facts caused Croce to associate history with artistic intuition rather than philosophy; he therefore put art and history into the same category. "Intuition," however, as a category containing both art and history, had certain liabilities. Intuition was not, Croce counseled, to be confused with "perception," for perception implied the reality of the thing perceived. Intuition, since it was both artistic and historical, could imply no such bias. Intuition could be of the real or of the "possible." The former was historical; the latter, artistic. But how was one to know which was before one? Croce did not know.[31]

At the beginning of the work Croce remarked that he had intuition of himself and of the pen with which he was writing, but that he also had an intuition of himself in another town doing something else. Which was real? He did not know. Since 1893, when he had first linked art and history, he had seen the problem. Who could tell whether the expression conveyed was of the real or fantastic? The distinction must be irrelevant. "The distinction between reality and nonreality is extraneous, secondary, to the true nature of intuition."[32] That seeming a bit abrupt, Croce returned several chapters later to the same question, explaining, "History is distinguished in the concrete from pure imagination only as one intuition is distinguished from another: in the memory." [33]

Yet since the memory can do no more than recall the original intuition, the distinction between the real and the imaginary does not seem to have been advanced very far. [34]

The only way to have removed the dilemma would have been to remove history from the aesthetic category, which would have meant, given Croce's system, putting it into the philosophical category. This Croce refused to do, because it would have meant that history would have to deal then with universals, which were not concrete but abstract. Thus, the concept of the universal may be "rich with information, very rich if you like, but however rich it may be, [it is] incapable of obtaining that individuality of historical knowledge to which only aesthetic knowledge attains." [35]

At this early stage Croce was forced to choose between history as abstract philosophy and history as particular—but a particular whose reality could not be verified. He chose, consistently enough, the latter.

There was in Croce, then, a departure from the more concrete traditions of earlier Italian humanism. Where they had aimed at cutting through the imaginary to reach the purely human, Croce had restored the authority of the imaginary alongside of and within the historical real. There is no reason, however, to suppose that Croce really meant to counsel a slipping into the world of make-believe. It is undoubtedly ironic that in order to emphasize that each work of art was an individual concrete entity, each historical fact a particular fact that no abstract philosophy of history could ever grasp, Croce felt compelled to leave the imaginary fact of art and the real fact of history in the same category. [36] As it had been for his predecessors, the concern of Croce was to avoid the universal and abstract so as to concentrate on the particular. The confusion of art and history was an accidental by-product of Croce's real purpose: isolation and study of the individual and an exaltation of human creativity. One has the feeling that at this stage in his thought Croce was aware of the difficulty in distinguishing fact and fancy but believed that in practice they would not be confused, that common sense would keep them apart. Despite this obstacle and despite Croce's departure from the more clearly social concerns of Spaventa and De Sanctis, Croce's early ideas constituted a fulfillment, or at least a continuation, of the forces set in motion by De Sanctis and Spaventa. For Croce, as for his two predecessors, the goal was the rejuvenation of Italian society through the spreading of a lay culture that would worship human institutions, human society, and the human creativity that had produced them. That goal was a priori and unquestioned. Spaventa, De Sanctis, and Croce are all comforted by and rejoice in their faith in man. They fought Hegel and "philosophy of history" because it seemed to them to steal man's freedom, his ability to posit his own end. Hence Croce's rejection of Labriola; hence De Sanctis's and Spaventa's "overcoming" of Hegel. They meant to celebrate man rather than a universal history, and Croce's *Estetica* constituted a major step in the separation of man, the human spirit, from the universal philosophy of history. The isolation of that spirit aimed at giving it new dignity, a dignity beyond the merely economic. It celebrated man as artist and philosopher, as well as practical and moral, and its message was that, like artistic expression, these achievements of man were from within. The struggle in the future lay in the further emancipation of man from philosophy of history and the further glorification of man's creative power. Croce stated the task while commenting upon another advocate of the philosophy of history, Vico. Vico's "error" was, for Croce, precisely his confusion of the "rigid distinction between concrete history and the philosophy of spirit." [37] The real importance of Vico's *New Science,* Croce said,

> has never been fully appreciated, [for] he is still regarded as the inventor of the philosophy of history. . . . The fact is that his philosophy of history, his ideal history, his *Scienza nuova d'intorno alla comune natura delle nazioni,* does not concern the concrete empirical history which unfolds itself in time: it is not history; it is a science of the ideal, a philosophy of spirit. [38]

This "philosophy of spirit" that Croce found in Vico was, of course, the philosophy of the first men, the poet creators who had begun civilization but whose elements still lived in all men today. The struggle in the future, Croce said, must be to overcome Vico and all philosophy of history, "to sever the philosophy of the spirit from history, the modifications of the human mind from the historic vicissitudes of peoples." [39]

Freed from history, man at last would be free to posit his own goals, his own ends, and transcendence of every sort would disappear. The end of man would be man himself. Croce did not note, however, any more than Spaventa and De Sanctis had noted, that by making man an end in himself, he had literally posed a case of raising oneself by one's own bootstraps. The end was so much a part of Croce and so little questioned by him, that he did not see that man was not the answer but the question.

Despite the weaknesses of the *Estetica*—perhaps because of them—the book was received with enthusiasm. Those ideas, coming as they did, in the midst of the crisis of positivism, seemed to offer a total primacy to man's creative power. *"Enfin Croce vint,"* wrote Boileau di Malherbe. "Croce had come and profoundly transformed and ordered our vision of the world." [40] Whereas in the positivism of Roberto Ardigò man had seemed to be no more than a reflex action of nature, now he seemed godlike, a creator. "It seemed to me," wrote Luciano Aneceschi after reading the work, "that I had come into the possession of a golden key." [41] The *Estetica* seemed to reendow man with all the capacities that naturalist determinism had taken from him *and* at the same time to explain the world about man. "The *Estetica* presented itself to us," wrote Vinciguerra, "as the 'open sesame' not only of the world of art, but of the world as art." [42]

The *Estetica,* in short, fell, as Scirocco put it, "like a bomb" upon the positivists and other naturalists. [43] And it was only the first, for with the astonishing success of the *Estetica,* Croce suddenly found himself in a position of authority, a position from which he could advance the state of Italian culture and bring about the spiritual renewal of his country. [44]

4 AESTHETICS AND THE STRUGGLE AGAINST POSITIVISM

The promise of *Estetica* was of a new era, an era beyond mere analysis, beyond the limits set by a constraining positivism and—more significant, at least in retrospect—an era separated from the limits imposed by the confines of history and the past. It is an odd aspect of human nature, one noted earlier by De Sanctis, that while man always has attempted to pass beyond the limits that circumscribe his thought and action, it is only within those limits that his thought and action have significance. In that age of innocence that preceded the present doubt, men believed those limits had come from God or perhaps nature, but by the turn of the present century it was the common assumption of most intellectuals that those limits and forces had been imposed by man himself, for who else save man was the author of history? History for the humanist was the drama of man's testing of the solidity of those limits, a drama that reached its denouement in the present, when man, recognizing the conventionality of the limits, soared into the beyond. But then—and here was the irony—the protagonist discovered the void and tried, as he still is trying, to orient himself. Where to turn but to history, the one constant left, the one thing from which there was no escape? Not knowing where to go, man looked back to see where he had been, turned to see if from the wake he could discover the course. To those who had exchanged the old God for a new "progressive" philosophy of history, the view back revealed a steady course, but Croce was inured against any such faith. He was not discouraged. He saw no advantage in exchanging one God for another when man was sufficient unto himself. It was not a new idea. It was a revolutionary idea.

As Tocqueville has pointed out in his *Ancien régime,* truly revolutionary eras are rare, and even when such eras seem to be at hand, it often transpires that the revolutionary is in reality but the apotheosis of those forces against which he seems in rebellion, caught like ordinary mortals in the forces of history he had hoped to alter. A truly revolutionary cataclysm would escape this unfolding reality and fashion a new one ex nihilo. To many the *Estetica* seemed to endorse such a vision, for to enter its pages was to enter a room with no walls where history was no longer a series of imprisoning forces but a vision indistinguishable from the fantasy created by man in his ordinary aesthetic life. To attack such a conception of man seemed to attack man himself in favor of the confines he had just escaped. Philosophy of history, positivism, naturalism, all were the same, for each removed from man his omnipotence, and it was only because, after the death of Labriola, naturalism and positivism seemed to be the primary opponents of this autonomy, that Croce spoke less of "philosophy of history" and more of "positivism."

> In the last half century the naturalist and mathematical culture has been raised to the level of the supreme cultural ideal; [yet] it is precisely this form which does not represent concreteness of the mind and which explains itself in fashioning empty schemes or manipulating data of experience. . . . As a consequence it has happened that the heroes of the mental world no longer appear, as they once did, as poets, philosophers, historians; but rather, at the exclusion of these, as physiologists, physicists, zoologists. . . . Those new directors of social life are entirely insensitive to art; they ignore history; they sneer like drunken bumpkins at philosophy; and they satisfy their religious needs, if at all, in those sacred . . . masonic lodges and electoral committees. *The philosophical reawakening will have to put the naturalists, doctors, physiologists, and psychiatrists in their place and destroy their arrogance.* [1]

One cannot help but recall here Spaventa's attempt to undo three centuries of Italian culture in order to return to the pure gold of the tradition of Vico. Croce's desire to erase a mere half-century appears more modest, but because of his brilliance, and because, unlike Spaventa, he seemed to say what others then felt but could not articulate, Croce left a far greater mark on Italian culture than Spaventa. Whatever might be said of Croce today, when he mushroomed into prominence in Italy at the turn of the century, he was seen as the leading spokesman of a cultural rebirth whose purpose was to renew and reinvigorate a society most intellectuals found bankrupt. [2] To reorient society required a complete change in perspective.

To put the old culture in its place and establish this new perspective, Croce founded *La critica,* his own journal. With him was the young Giovanni Gentile.

The seriousness of their endeavor was highlighted by Croce himself. "In my work in *La critica* my conscience became tranquil and I felt I had found my place, that [I was giving] the best of myself and carrying out a political task, political in the widest sense."[3]

Croce's use of the word "political" here was the same as De Sanctis's earlier idea that "by not engaging in the political, one does the truly political."[4] Pure politics for Croce, as for De Sanctis and Machiavelli, was a means-end endeavor, and any such activity had to be set in the wider context of an ethic that justified it and made it "common sense." It was to the construction of the common sense rather than the pursuit of the end that the intellectual was to dedicate himself. Such an ethic could not be tolerant, not only because common sense, by definition, does not tolerate every point of view, but because in a real sense the enemy of Croce (as for Nietzsche) was tolerance. This was no lighthearted hymn to intolerance and chauvinism. Croce was not opposed to the tolerance that a self-confident man allows an adversary. What he opposed was empty tolerance, the fruit of cultural dismay and disorientation, that grasping for straws and fads as the sinking man grasps whatever is afloat in order to save himself. "My little magazine," he wrote to Giuseppe Lombardo-Radice, "will be *exclusive, partisan.* . . . We have been ruined in Italy by false liberalism. . . . On principle we will limit ourselves to a few collaborators."[5]

The first issue of the journal boldly announced that *La critica* was not just one more self-indulgent lament. It offered an alternative. The enemies were "the naturalists, the Enlightenment, and the Jesuits."

> We purpose to sustain a *determinate point of view.* Nothing is, in fact, more dangerous to the healthy development of scholarship than the misunderstood sentiment of tolerance, which is, in fact, indifference and skepticism.[6]

The journal was an immediate success. The author of the *Estetica,* the critic of Marxism, a scholar rather than a mere rebel—but no less rebellious for that—Croce spoke with more authority than other critics. Mario Vinciguerra remembered the day *La critica* first came out and when he first saw it in the window of a Neapolitan bookstore:

> That day, before that window, I discovered *La critica,* but I had no need of discovering Croce; on the contrary, I stood ecstatic for a few moments before the issue, for I now had the indubitable proof that the star to which we adolescents were already looking as a guide was approaching its zenith.[7]

And Attilio Momigliano rightly observed that *La critica*

will remain in the history of culture as an example, perhaps unique, of the formative and reformative power of a magazine. He who examines their development during these forty years will see that philosophy and particularly aesthetics, literary criticism, history and historical criticism, the criticism of art, linguistics, law, have all felt the influence of the thought that every two months was spread by that magazine.[8]

Luigi Russo put it even more emphatically as he recalled his first reading of *La critica.* "It was a fascinating and disturbing reading for me. . . . When I read Croce I felt like a loaded powder magazine."[9]

This tremendous success was produced, at least in part, by that "determinate point of view," by that restricted collaboration, in short, by the appearance of a confident sense of direction. The magazine always reflected the guiding hand of its editor, and *this* was the source of its strength. The other contemporary journals, *La nuova antologia, La rassegna contemporaneo, La rivista d'Italia,* seemed, as Renato Serra once put it, to have "been written by a committee." If you want to begin a magazine, "think of *La critica,*" he wrote to Luigi Ambrosini, Carducci scholar and editor of *La stampa.*

> A single issue can appear a little pedantic, arid, curt. But take a whole year: Croce and Gentile, Gentile and Croce. That is their power. It is *they.* They have become familiar, friends to their readers. Every month you await their feelings on books and events.[10]

Among the young, perhaps what was also most important was the constant polemic, the argumentative vituperation poured upon the eminent figures, upon scientists, and upon university professors ("*i signori professori* who for years and years have furnished [us] with books devoid of any thought and passion").[11] Nor, for that matter, was the professors' fear of ridicule to be discounted. Giuseppe Prezzolini, editor of *Leonardo* and future editor of *La voce,* tells us of the disorientation in the universities, where the students read *La critica* for ammunition.

> At least now, before publishing, on the basis of the documents in their butcher shops, a rehash of ten German authors or an approval of some author, the philosophy professor or the student of letters will think more than twice as he sees rise before him the vengeful vision of a review signed, "B. C." or "G. G."[12]

In the early *La critica* particularly it was not uncommon to find entire issues written by Gentile and Croce alone. Gradually others were permitted to write in the magazine as long as they remained faithful to that determinate point of view.[13] One then began to see in *La critica* some of the more famous names in Italy: Adolfo Omodeo and Guido De Ruggiero, for example, both then Gentileans, as well as some of the more obscure but *fedelissimi* Croceans.[14] The common theme of the editors as well as of lesser writers was their antipathy to positivism.[15]

Positivism was a step backward to the eighteenth century. If it were accepted by modern Italians, Italy would be thrown back a hundred years or more and her spiritual regeneration stymied. The link between positivism and the Enlightenment appeared to Croce to open corridors of doors: the eighteenth century had culminated in French imperialism; French imperialism had interrupted the growth of Italian nationalism by fostering the universalism of *liberté, égalité, fraternité,* the battle cry of Jacobins and encyclopedists then, but now, at the turn of the nineteenth century, the rallying cry of the Freemasons. Thus did Croce see in the present impotence of Italy the hand of France under the sway of the old Freemason Clemenceau. What France had once accomplished under the Jacobins—the turning of Italy's nationalism into universalism—she was now attempting with positivism, materialism, and Freemasonry.

> The Masonic mentality used to be called Encyclopedism and Jacobinism in the eighteenth century, and Italy suffered a sad experience at its hands at the time of the French invasions. . . . It can be said that the entire Italian Risorgimento developed as a reaction against that French, Jacobin, Masonic direction. . . . [And] it now seems impossible that at the beginning of the twentieth century, simply to imitate the French, we again import among ourselves that calamity from which we have [already] suffered more than a century ago.[16]

The Masonic-positivistic approach to historical reality, according to Croce, was abstract and naïve. Instead of delving deeply into the problems of the spirit and of philosophy, it sought explanations in moralistic clichés, abstract schemes, and natural law.

> The Masonic mentality simplifies everything: history, which is complicated; philosophy, which is difficult; science, which does not lend itself to firm conclusions; morality, which is rich with contrasts and anxieties. It passes triumphantly upon all these things in the name of reason, liberty, humanity, brotherhood, and tolerance. And with these abstractions it claims to distinguish, in the blink of an eye, good from evil, and classify facts and men according to exterior signs and formulae. A perfect culture for tradesmen,

petty professionals, elementary school teachers, lawyers, and quacks, because it is cheap culture; but therefore the very worst for him who must delve into the problems of the spirit, of society, and reality.[17]

To halt the aping of the French and the idolatry of science, Croce turned his attention to literature, raising from the past and the near past figures who seemed to symbolize Italian greatness and who could become the catalysts for a new resurgence. Such a figure was Giosuè Carducci[18] (1835-1907), whose life needs now to be briefly recounted, for Croce found in him a model of pagan humanism which he invoked for his countrymen in the opening pages of *La critica.*

Born the son of a republican doctor in absolutist Tuscany, Carducci was educated at the university of Pisa, and in 1860, this twenty-five-year-old author of a single volume of poetry was appointed by the new government as professor of Italian literature at the University of Bologna. There, for the next twenty-four years, the poet and, later, senator excoriated Catholicism, Christianity, and, until charmed by the Savoyard Queen Margherita, monarchy. ("I looked at the queen . . . blond and bedecked with jewels, glistening in white. A fantasy came over me.")[19]

A "republican" by birth as well as by instinct, Carducci spent his early life with his father (and his pet wolf),[20] scurrying furtively about the peninsula, his home life a series of parentheses separated by sudden hasty departures just ahead of the police.[21] He seemed never to have gotten over the experience. At the age of forty-eight he wrote, "Every morning I awaken with a furious desire to fight; my first greeting to the sun is a gape like that of Gonnella when he turned into a wolf, *quaerens quem devoret*: the first feeling that healthy life announces to me is the need to fight for existence."[22] Carducci had lived through the greatness of the Risorgimento only to come to feel—as Croce at this point had come to feel—that the greatness had ebbed in the post-Risorgimento years. Carducci stood as a symbol of protest against the present course of history,[23] awaiting the final "republic" synthesis of man and state into an organic unity that erased the individual as it exalted the state, merged the "two peoples" of Italy into a single sovereign Italian whole. The mediocrity of the present Italian leaders, Carducci felt, prevented any such resolution.

In 1882, using the occasion of Garibaldi's death, Carducci compared the greatness of the old warrior with the mediocrity of the present. In that hymn to Garibaldi, that contempt for the present culture, in that longing for a new Risorgimento moved by a new faith, Carducci sounded the dominant motif for the end of the nineteenth century and the beginning of the twentieth in Italy.

Over the tomb of the great Italian waves the flag of the Thousand. But what flag will Italy wave today over the body and urn of its heroes? . . . We are not the descendants of Camillo and Caesar or the nephews of Machiavelli; we are the friends and *concierges* of Bismarck. . . . All this you say . . . will pass . . . and the memory of Giuseppe Garibaldi, leader in the supreme test, will always be with us . . . ? Oh, [but] I tell you in truth that he is quite dead, and the dead, I believe, are too content, having passed once through the portal of the great *perhaps,* to return here again. It is the people who in their memory embalm the great deceased and with restless and longing imagination raise them from the tombs and regarb them in their affection; and to [those] glorious ghosts they implore, beg, and command, *"Avanti! Avanti!* O fathers to [our] rescue." . . . Thus do the Slavs believe that one day Craglievich Marco will arise from his grave and mount a great spotted horse to hunt and battle Turks and Germans. And the German poets sing of Barbarossa asleep in his underground castle until the ravens awake him and the sword, tumbling down and crashing upon the floor, warns him that it is the hour to recreate the Holy Empire. . . . But for such long suffering and pleasant expectations in the midst of anguish, a people must have a great foundation of idealism [*idealità*]. Does Italy have it? I hope so![24]

In Francesco Crispi, the bombastic, ambitious, and ruinous prime minister of the 1890s, Carducci found his Barbarossa[25] and when Crispi blundered into Abyssinia, Carducci hailed the new Garibaldi and set out to inflame the hesitant:

To what point still to push or where to lay down the flag is not to be discussed when one must do battle. It is only important that the flag of the fatherland ought not to fail or retire after ten years of effort; in this we are agreed. Is that not so, Italians? *Sì! Sì!* . . . This army in Africa has shown and shows, before and now, that it is the healthiest, best educated, and most resilient element in the nation, and in it and all that it has promised, the fatherland can surely entrust itself.[26]

Carducci's poetry celebrated a kind of pagan humanism that predated the Christianity he detested. In the *Odi barbari* he praised the ancient Romans whose worldly patriotism had built the empire. Like De Sanctis and Spaventa before him, Carducci sought the liberation of man from centuries of Christian asceticism, and as usual he went one step farther than his predecessors as well as his contemporaries. That one step gained for him the rapt attention of the discontented.

Carducci's liberator was not Machiavelli nor, as with De Sanctis, Adam. Instead he invoked Satan.

Salute, O Satan,
O rebellion,
O vindicating force
of reason!

The sacred send forth to you
incense and prayers!
You have conquered the Jehovah
of the priests.[27]

The *Inno a satana* was written on a single September eve[28] "under the impulse of the fumes of Bacchus," as Basilone put it.[29] It was not published until two years later, and then only under the pseudonym Enotrio Romano, because Carducci "feared that his verses might seem more anti-Christian than antimystical, antiascetic, antimedieval."[30] And if that seems like Lenin "fearing" that he might seem a Bolshevik,[31] it is nonetheless true that in his own immoderate way, Carducci had picked up again the theme of Machiavelli and De Sanctis: man must first rid himself of diversionary philosophy and Christian morality if he was to become truly human, ready to appropriate the world. It was that immoderation, however, that extra step that Carducci took and others did not, that separated Carducci in the minds of Italians from moderates like De Sanctis. Carducci's Satan may have been "reason and nature, the body and the mind, all that revolts against the asceticism, sacerdotalism and obscurantism, which have so often claimed to represent the Christian religion,"[32] but Carducci was a good deal more than a voice against asceticism and sacerdotalism. Carducci came a generation later than, and lacked the philosophical depth of, De Sanctis and the brothers Spaventa. He represented, in fact, the extremist ethic of Mazzini, that antiliberal republicanism that was to plague Italian republicans with an ambivalence and hostility toward the individual and an exaggerated reverence for a state in the hands of "the people." Carducci in fact represented the extreme opposite of De Sanctis and the Vichian historicist culture of Naples, which he ever and wholeheartedly abhorred. Very carefully and aptly choosing his words, Luigi Russo explained the dialectic of late-nineteenth-century Italy:

> The collision . . . between two faiths born simultaneously with the modern world, between the liberal faith and the democratic faith . . . between the coherently liberal Vichians of Naples (we will leave apart the term Hegelian, which was a purely polemical term adopted by men of the time [!]) with their very acute sense of state sovereignty and Giosuè Carducci, the most representative and bold champion of the Mazzinian culture which, agitating for the myth of an extemporaneous popular sovereignty, ended

by supporting a tyranny of the piazza, repudiating the existing state, and the deepest requirement of liberalism itself. [33]

Where De Sanctis was troubled by the worldly task of building a poor and barely united country, Carducci and many of his followers were troubled by the difficulties of attempting the impossible. His inspiration was, therefore, more unrealistic and hence more despairing. To set men free from God and raise Italy to the stature of a great power were Carducci's constant ambitions. In Carducci, "two great rebellions: the patriotic rebellion, the self-assertion of Italy against her foreign oppressors and, deeper and greater, the self-assertion of the pagan humanism of the Renaissance against Catholic tradition and asceticism. . . . [In Carducci] paganism and patriotism go hand in hand." [34]

Carducci never saw this rebellion, this quest, resolved. He left its pursuit to the next generation. They must recapture the spirit of the Risorgimento and its poets, Alfieri, Foscolo, Leopardi, Manzoni.

> The Risorgimento had had the religion of man only with Alfieri, the religion of poetic man with Foscolo, the religion of suffering man with Leopardi, the religion of the working man with Manzoni. The Risorgimento was now exhausted. Carducci taught the absolute necessity of finding again the way of a faith; and he left this, his inner tragedy, as a heritage to the new generation with the obligation that it be fulfilled, that it be transcended and expiated. . . . The legacy of Carducci was thus a giant question mark that required an answer. [35]

Benedetto Croce had not seen Carducci in ten years when, in 1902, he dedicated to the great poet his just completed *Estetica*. [36] The dedication to Carducci was symbolic. Like Carducci calling for the return of Garibaldi in 1882, Croce now seemed to call for the return of Carducci from retirement. Croce and Carducci had met in the early 1880s and by 1888 corresponded regularly, exchanging, after that, copies of each other's works until Carducci died in 1907, one year after he had received the Nobel Prize for literature.

In Carducci Croce found a poet who praised modern man liberated from religion and metaphysics, the inspiration for the transformation of Italian society. Croce's rejection of Marxism and his condemnation of the Enlightenment and the Jacobins ought not to mislead one into thinking Croce was a reactionary or even a conservative at the turn of the century. [37] He condemned eighteenth-century thought because it was too abstract to inspire moral regeneration in any but an elite few; as for Marxism, as set out by Labriola, he believed it too narrow to provide any inspiration at all. What was required was a philosophy with a faith in man, not a merely economic man or a philosophical man, but man in all his aspects. It had to be a philosophy with Italian roots and Italian patriarchs like Carducci and Machiavelli, not a culture imported from France. Such a philosophy had been set out in the *Estetica,* and Croce now turned his critical eye toward finding those who fit into the scheme set out in that book.

The first issue of *La critica,* January 20, 1903, began Croce's analysis of literature, and he began it with a long essay on Carducci. He noted the decline of Italian literature after Leopardi, Manzoni, and Giovanni Berchet and observed, following De Sanctis, "Precisely when Italy was created, the political-intellectual world from which it was born was undone." [38] This "absence of seriousness" in Italian literature Croce attributed to the fact that once Italy had been formed, the nationalist literary culture calling for that formation became abstract and pointless. No new culture, no new purpose had replaced the ideals called for before 1860. The successors to Manzoni, Berchet, and Leopardi merely moralized about the abstract notions of brotherhood popular in the French Revolution or repeated what those three authors had already said, and said better.

To be great, literature must, Croce said, citing the closing remarks of De Sanctis's *Storia della letteratura italiana,* take its content from contemporary life and problems. "What ought modern literature to be?" he asked. De Sanctis, observing the success of the Risorgimento, had long ago pointed the way. "Knowledge having been restored, a life emancipated from the trappings of the classics and romantics having been acquired, new literature will be the echo of contemporary universal and national life." [39] The visions of the poet, whether real or imagined, had to deal with contemporary life and its problems, and in Carducci, Croce felt, this concreteness and pertinence had been crystallized. That De Sanctis and Carducci had stood at opposite ends of the liberal-democratic spectrum did not deter Croce from finding in Carducci the kind of dealing with contemporary life and problems for which De Sanctis had called.

Croce acknowledged that Carducci was a rebel and a pagan, taking pains to remove any pejorative implications from those words, especially the latter,[40] but went on to say that this was only the most obvious aspect of Carducci's work. What caused Carducci to stand above others and what merited his exaltation in modern times was his concreteness, his "relevance." Carducci represented a protest against the abstract, against the "alienation" of man, and a living example of devotion to *human* history. Thus, Croce turned to the "Hymn to Satan."

> The *Inno a satana* is the celebration of human history, of the force of reason and a healthy sense of life: Satan, symbol of nature in antiquity, reappears

as the sorceress, wizard, the alchemist of the Middle Ages, in so far as they planted the seeds of truth and life for the future [*in quante gettavano germi di verità e di vita pel futuro*], as the fragmentary survival of the classical tradition in the poets, as the historians of ancient Rome: until they were affirmed in the Renaissance and the modern world.[41]

It was the Carduccian "concreteness" that caused Croce to link the Tuscan rebel to the left Hegelians and to Vico! Carducci's breathtaking metaphors and fabulous revolts, so unpopular as to require anonymous publications, could be forgotten. What counted was his devotion to man and his hostility to any kind of abstraction. Thus, Carducci appeared to Croce as "that conciliation of matter and spirit, the liberation from the beyond and the unreal, that rediscovery of the meaning of being in being itself, which at the beginning of the nineteenth century had been reached in the idealism of Hegel and, in a more or less imperfect form, was renewed in the neo-materialism . . . [of] the extreme left Hegelians."[42] Croce then went on to link Carducci—Carducci with his hymns to Satan, the barbarians, sorceresses and wizards—to Vico's "philologist"; indeed, Carducci was "truly the poet of history, of the history of civilization and culture: a poet of *Philology*, in the sense of Vico."[43]

It was Carducci's exaltation of man, his emphasis upon human action, which led Croce to an exaltation of Carducci as poet and therefore creator. "If he had been the teacher of the new generation, it must not be forgotten that he had been such because [he was a] poet: he did not give empty forms . . . he gave a really new poetry."[44] In Carducci, Croce found the spirit of the revolt of idealist man against external limits.

"*Decapitaro, Emmanuel Kant, Iddio, Massimiliano Robespierre, il re,*" rang the lines of Carducci's 1871 "Versaglia."[45] Those famous words linking the Kantian revolution in thought, the Kantian decapitation of God, with Robespierre's decapitation of the king, did they not indicate again to Croce the liberating power of Kant's synthetic a priori, the omnipotence of creative man who, as he deified himself, smashed the barriers of religion and monarchy?[46] It was the message of the *Estetica* in verse, and Croce, fresh from a reading of Marx, may have recalled, as Gramsci would later recall when he read Carducci, that passage in Marx's *Holy Family* where the "philosophical language" of the Germans was compared to the "political language" of the French rebels of 1789.[47] Carducci seemed to be, therefore, precisely the figure to lead the new humanism, its "elder statesman" and prophet.

His enthusiasm for Carducci endured, in fact, throughout Croce's life. In the 1928 *Storia d'Italia*, Croce, a much different Croce to be sure, stated the impact of Carducci on Croce's generation in much the same terms he had used in 1903. [48]

Earlier in that *Storia* of 1928 Croce praised Carducci while comparing him to another literary figure, Gabriele D'Annunzio, that "sensualistic, beastly decadent," [49] who to Croce seemed so far removed from Carducci. "My generation," said Croce in his autobiography, "was the generation of Carducci, not of D'Annunzio." [50]

And yet if one glances back to *La critica, La critica* of 1904, D'Annunzio appeared to Croce quite a different, quite a promising figure: "Let us pay homage to Gabriele D'Annunzio, to the marvelous creator [*all'artifice mirabile*], the tireless worker, this tempestuous productive force which is at its maximum strength and which, just now, has given us *Francesca* and *Laudi* and, even as we write, announces the completion *nescio quid maius* of *Figlia di Joria.*" [51]

To many—not least himself—Gabriele D'Annunzio was the successor to Carducci, [52] the logical fruition of those forces Carducci had raised and the hero foretold in the Carduccian inheritance. [53]

Born at Pescara on the Adriatic, Gabriele D'Annunzio (1863–1938) arrived, at the age of eighteen, in Rome and there began a literary career that rocketed him into first national and then international prominence with a velocity so stunning and so swift that within a decade he had nearly eclipsed Carducci. [54] If in the fin de siècle fascination with decadence Carducci seemed to ebb, it was not because of any dissatisfaction with the old Tuscan's eccentricity, but because D'Annunzio seemed even more Carduccian than Carducci.

Like Carducci, D'Annunzio felt himself surrounded by a political and cultural wasteland, and he dedicated his life to giving to his countrymen, by way of remedying the situation, a series of what an earlier age had called "policy examples." These examples came not only in the life he led but in the literature he wrote, literature that was primarily about the life he led or, to put the best face on it, about the life he only wished he led.

Even with the best of efforts, reading D'Annunzio is an unforgettable experience, nearly overwhelming. In an age as jaded as our own there is still something mind-jarring in reading those paeans to narcissism and debauch as well as recalling that those lives strewn in the erratic wakes left by D'Annunzio's satyr-like heroes were, in the public scandal that was his private life, real people, often famous (for example, Eleanora Duse) but just as often innocent unknowns upon whom he trod with gay and self-conscious abandon. [55] Whatever form of apostolic succession one chooses to employ, D'Annunzio will remain one of the most extraordinary apostles of decadence ever to have instructed humanity in the art of self-indulgence. D'Annunzio's heroes make Iago look virtuous—or at least comprehensible. Painted in lurid, voluptuous sensualism, the D'Annunzian hero was a figure steeped in hedonism, devoid of morality, innocent of deep reflection, and intoxicated, as D'Annunzio was intoxicated, only with himself. Such a figure was that modern *condottiero* Andrea Sperelli, the leading character in D'Annunzio's *Piacere* (*Child of Pleasure*), and Sperelli, as Gerhard Masur put it, was an "autoanalysis, if not an autobiography." [56]

Croce read D'Annunzio, of course, before the artist's parabola had reached its peak, but as the tone of his two long articles of 1904 makes clear, he read him with awe. It is no wonder. D'Annunzio seemed to be the living apotheosis of Croce's early *Estetica*. His art was pure image, pure intuition, entirely removed from—not to say antithetical to—the other forms of spiritual life, ethics, philosophy, and practicality. Hence "it is sufficient to keep one's eyes open, to have ears to hear, in order to realize that he has before him an artist, and a great one." [57] Croce went on to take exception to those who called D'Annunzio morally evil, superficial, a mere dilettante. [58] If he was to be called a dilettante, it was necessary to remove "every injurious coloring from the word" and to make it interchangeable with "aestheticism, or the formula 'art for art's sake.'" [59]

There was, according to Croce, no philosophical or moral content at all in D'Annunzio, simply a beautiful expression of the artist's vision. Therefore D'Annunzio was different from Carducci with his classical idealism, Manzoni with his neo-Catholicism, or Leopardi with his pessimism. [60] D'Annunzio was different, Croce said, in that he was not a spiritual guide, but a man who was true only to himself, a man who was like Nietzsche! "D'Annunzio declared once that he was, without knowing it, Nietzschean before Nietzsche; and this seems to me to be true, for Nietzsche's is, more than a philosophy, a temperament, a sentiment rather than a system." [61] It was that sentiment, Croce said, which had produced characters like Andrea Sperelli in *Il piacere*. And, following D'Annunzio, Croce went on to acknowledge the similarity of Sperelli with, of all people, Zarathustra.

In fact, Croce was misled. So anxious was he to find an example of his *Estetica* that he did not see that D'Annunzianism was not simply a pure image but was, in fact, precisely the "spiritual guide" of a good part of that generation. The idea that D'Annunzio could be contained in the particular realm of art, that he would not assault other realms as he was to assault—with bands of followers —the city of Fiume, was naïve in the extreme. Moreover, having just pointed out that D'Annunzio was an artist and not a "spiritual guide," Croce went on to make him nothing less than a guide, not a decadent, but a Renaissance hero. "We look with amazement on this our contemporary, this Italian of exquisite culture, who is in no way humbled by science and philosophy, which he knows [!], nourishes himself on images, translates all into forms and myths, almost as if it were his vital medium, the only atmosphere in which he can breathe and move."[62]

Croce did not see this rejection of the world of science and philosophy, this retreat into a world of symbols and images, as an indication of decadence, nor did he believe "that the fin de siècle period—a meaningless phrase coined by Parisian *boulevardiers*—was a period of decadence." The decadent was quite the opposite: "the natural sciences, garbed as philosophies," for they had "destroyed the world which religion and idealist philosophy used to represent as *cosmos*," that which we ourselves build, "and in place of *cosmos* the scientists have substituted a series of dead and heavy classificatory schemes." There was decadence, too, said this "critic of Marxism," in the world of practice, where the "industrialized bourgeoisie have destroyed the "ideal brotherhood of people" and replaced it with a "single brotherhood, that of the *trusts.*"[63] In a world where science and trusts had become, at the expense of man, the fundamental elements of society, D'Annunzio, the nonconformist who refused to yield to the passing of the world of man, could not be regarded as decadent in the usual sense of the word. On the contrary, Croce affirmed: "I am ready . . . to accept D'Annunzio as an expression of a renaissance. . . . D'Annunzio is one of the surest signs of the renaissance of Italian art, which he has assimilated and knows how to express in its own original way, the spiritual current of the modern world."[64]

In short, Croce saw in D'Annunzio the prototype of the poet-creator, the figure who, through idealism, could point the way to an overcoming of materialism and science: cultural regeneration through art—but with obvious and inexorable consequences in all the other realms, else it could not have sparked the revival. "He is a poet; and that ought to be enough, since the poetic species by divine law is altogether more rare than that of the sages, reasoners, and good counselors."[65]

As early as 1907 Croce would begin to rue his hymn to D'Annunzio, to see him no longer as the symbol of a renaissance, but as the fop and dandy he really was. But by then others had picked up the theme of revolt through art.

5 THE NEW CULTURE VERSUS REFORMIST SOCIALISM

> O patria mia, vedo le mura e gli archi
> E le colonne e i simularcri e l'erme
> Torri degli avi nostri,
> Ma la gloria non vedo
> Non vedo il lauro e il ferro ond'eran carchi
> I nostri padri antichi.
>
> [O my fatherland, I see the walls and the arches,
> The columns, the images, and the solitary
> Towers of our forefathers,
> But I no longer see the glory;
> I no longer see the laurel and the sword carried
> By our ancient forefathers.]

These are the words of Giacomo Leopardi as he contemplated in 1819 the bleak future that the Vienna settlement had seemingly imposed upon his land. Leopardi was out of fashion after 1900, his dispirited resignation to the realities of restoration Italy being seen as a lack of will, a kind of desperate wringing of the hands. Leopardi was the Italian Hamlet whose native hue of resolution had been "sicklied o'er with the pale cast of thought." His impotence had only been transformed into the gallantry of the Risorgimento by men of daring, men of action—Mazzini, Garibaldi, Manin—and because of them, Italy had arisen to nationhood.

Such at least was the picture generally accepted by those intellectuals born after unification,[1] those who, thirty years after the climactic seizure of Rome, saw the promise of greatness for Italy withering in the post-Risorgimento corruption of *l'età giolittiana*. Like Leopardi, they too no longer saw the glory, the laurel, and the sword borne by their forefathers. But unlike Leopardi, they meant to do something about it.

Croce was not, of course, the only one who felt the need for a second Risorgimento. Had he expressed a purely private emotion rather than that of a generation, he would never have achieved such prominence. He was the most prominent figure in a generation of more violent and less reflective men who came to maturity immediately after the turn of the century, men who saw, or thought they saw, in Croce, in his *Estetica* and in his praise for D'Annunzio, the beginning of a new humanist culture. The figures to whom we now turn were men of passion, unimpressed with anything as–to search exactly for the word– mundane as Labriola, men overwhelmed by the poverty of positivism. For them the key to survival was individual liberation, and their revolt constituted an exaggerated and distorted egoism, the final unrestrained exaltation of man against any sort of exterior limit. Where earlier Italian thinkers like De Sanctis had stressed the limited notion of a dialectical freedom in which man had to contend with other historical forces, these men placed a primacy upon man as an omnipotent force. Their goal was action, and "doubt" was not a word in their vocabulary.

"The reign of Hamlet, Pascal, and Leopardi is over," announced Giuseppe Antonio Borgese. "We know by now that even to die requires the will. . . . We know that no one commits a more powerful and savage act of life than he who commits suicide. Likewise the necessity to live no longer frightens us. We are hardened by the fires of action, we new men, we do not tremble upon the ice [which covers] the river."[2]

Twenty-one years old when he wrote that paean to action (entitled, ominously, "The Ghost Ship"), Borgese had just graduated from the Istituto di studi superiori at Florence. The article appeared in a new journal, *Hermes*, which Borgese himself had just begun and which would, in its short two-year life, launch the careers of not only Borgese but many other prominent Italians.[3] Borgese himself had written several articles in the Florentine journal *Leonardo* and had even been permitted by Croce to write in *La critica*, with its determinate point of view. "It has been rather rare," Croce wrote of Borgese in 1903, "for me to read writings so meditated and penetrating on esthetics as those of Borgese."[4]

Borgese's *Hermes*, begun in 1904, symbolized the D'Annunzian desire to carry into action the word-dreams of the Abruzzian poet. Thus, the opening issue announced: "We love and admire Gabriele D'Annunzio more than any other of our modern poets, dead or alive . . . we are disciples of D'Annunzio, as D'Annunzio was the disciple of Carducci and Carducci of Foscolo and Monti." [5]

Hermes was, on the surface, a magazine of art and literature, but there was more there than art for art's sake; it was art for nationalism's sake. Above all, Borgese wrote, as he explained two years later the purpose of *Hermes,*

> we felt ourselves to be Italians and we had and have an uncrushable faith in a next *risorgimento* of all national activities, the intellectual as well as the fantastic, the political as well as the industrial and economic. Our hatred of any form of baseness, falsity, misery meant an increasing desire to hurry and prepare—in the field of our activity—[that] fortunate and marvelous happening. [6]

Not just literature then, but an intellectual, political, industrial *risorgimento*. Hence Borgese acknowledged not only D'Annunzio as his patron, but also Enrico Corradini. Corradini (1865-1931) was the leading nationalist of the era, one of the founders of the Nationalist party in 1910, and in 1904 editor of the bombastic and xenophobic *Il regno.* "Gabriele D'Annunzio is for us a great teacher, [but] . . . we have turned to Enrico Corradini because he is among the few who had courage and intelligence in [that] slobbering generation that preceded us." Borgese (1881-1952), born twenty years after Corradini, counted himself within the new generation which was to take up the course of Italian history charted in the Risorgimento and abandoned in the post-Risorgimento period.

It was a revolt against torpor, and it found its inspiration in the idea of the poet as seer, the poet as creator and leader. Marcello Taddei (1884-1908) was, perhaps, more lyrical in his D'Annunzian sentiments than some others in *Hermes,* but he exposed the demon that motivated its contributors so openly and candidly that it is impossible not to note him. They were all "pilgrims landed from unknown paths upon a faraway land," he wrote, pilgrims "who did not know how to forget the fatherland." After years of immortal pilgrimage, led by "the poets"—that is, by "the heroes"—they made their "inevitable return" to bring about the national resurgence.

> The poets understand the awakening of the *patria* just as they understand the awakening of their souls. Recently in Italy we have witnessed the miracle of a poet that returned to the *patria.* . . . Gabriele D'Annunzio. We young men who derive from him and find in him the herald of our lives, we can, even without mentioning his name, celebrate every one of his lofty victories, showing in [our] actions the life his dream foresees.

For Taddei, the poet was the voice of the fatherland. He knew what the masses only felt. "The poet has ascended the mountain before us . . . [and] now, on the mountain, he is no longer Gabriele D'Annunzio, he no longer has a name we know. His figure is identified with the ideal figure of the poet, of all the poets." He is—now that "we know a race can have a voice"—the "prophet of the race." He had at last returned to his fatherland, to his sisters and his "immortal mother." Now his father, anxious over his "name and that of his forefathers," cedes "his place to the son" and goes "to sleep in peace. . . . The son ascend[s] the mountain; divine prophecy swell[s] his breast . . . the song of light [arises] from his soul, and he summon[s] the sons of the land; he utter[s] the heroic pronouncement; he salute[s] Mother Italy." [7]

Hermes became a rallying point for the poet-pilgrims who sought in D'Annunzio's pagan "neoclassicism" the resurrection of Italy. Croce himself had consecrated the effort by his hymn to D'Annunzio as well as by his praise for the efforts of Borgese. Moreover, Croce not only allowed Borgese to write in *La critica,* but Croce wrote in *Hermes.*

In *Hermes* (and in the D'Annunzian *Marzocco,* the apparent "standard bearer of the Crocean *Estetica*"), [8] there was the culmination of the battle waged by De Sanctis and Croce to free art from the clutches of the Hegelian Vichian *Weltgeist.* Art's liberation and exaltation became, in an age bored with the confining determinism of positivism, a crusade that inevitably spilled over into other aspects of life. Croce did not note that if, in the abstract, D'Annunzio could be conceived as *l'art pour l'art,* in Borgese, in *Hermes,* and elsewhere, he was having a much wider effect.

The revolt of the D'Annunziani was also a revolt against the bourgeoisie of Italy, the complacent, narrow-minded men, oblivious to art and culture, content to see Italy remain in every respect a second-rate state while they scurried after the material furnishings of life. It was a revolt that found wide support among intellectuals and young people throughout Italy, and no two men have received more attention in this respect than Giuseppe Prezzolini and Giovanni Papini. And with good reason, for even if they were mere symptoms of this age of restlessness, their names were intertwined for more than a quarter of a century with nearly every significant cultural phenomenon in Italy, from idealism to futurism, from modernism to fascism.

Hermes collapsed after a mere two years. The magazine of Papini and Prezzolini, on the other hand, endured for nearly five years. And if, in the crude measure of time, that seems unimpressive, it ought also to be pointed out that during those five years, it occasionally drew the rather startled attention of men like Henri Bergson, Georges Sorel, William James, Charles Saunders Peirce, as well as of Croce and Gentile, and that when it ceased publication—"committed suicide," as its directors put it—it had, again according to its directors, in addition to its Italian audience, readers in "France, England, America, Germany, even in Tien-tsin and Cairo."[9] Even if that last be a little inflated, *Leonardo* certainly caused a sensation between 1903 and 1907 and has arrested nearly every Italian historian ever since. The journal's allure lies partly in its eerie prescience. Papini, wrote Angelo Crespi, "is representative of thousands and tens of thousands in having begun, even before the Great War, to feel the noisy and pretentious emptiness of so much of what we call modern civilization." Papini, he said, "may only have been our great common forerunner."[10] And Garin, in the early pages of his great work on Italian culture, picked out Papini as well, for Papini had "sensed that it was not only a particular edifice that was in danger, but everything seemed about to crumble; it was not a question of a particular episode, but an entire drama. . . . [Papini] sensed that all mankind, in every dimension, was in crisis."[11]

There is more, however, to *Leonardo* than its perception of our imminent demise. Its significance lay in its total and unabashed reliance upon the power of man alone to stave off collapse by construction of a radically new and totally free society. And it was here that Papini and Prezzolini felt they differed with Borgese. Though they wrote in Borgese's magazine, their interests were not aesthetic but philosophic. They regarded aesthetics as a force that liberated man from corrupt society, but as an insufficient foundation for the construction of a new one. Thus, Prezzolini wrote to Angelo Conti, one of the prime movers of the D'Annunzian *Marzocco,* "I am grateful to you, for your word has been opium and hashish for me; you have made me dream and rise above and outside the present miseries." But it is "philosophy . . . [which] is an efficient means of liberation that removes us from the chain of natural forces . . . [which] gives us dominion over things, makes us creators, . . . and makes of the future a marvelous rising of indeterminate and most novel events."[12] It was the desire of the *Leonardiani* to free man from the bourgeois decadence of modern society by providing a philosophical basis for a new order of things. Their "philosophy" in reality was philosophy aestheticized, freed from the confining rigor of logic and transformed into a personal statement, a personal protest.

Thus, the opening "Synthetic Program" of *Leonardo:*

A group of *young men,* yearning for liberation, wishing for universality, eager for a superior intellectual life, have gathered in Florence under the symbolic augural name of *Leonardo* in order to intensify individual existence, elevate individual thought, exalt individual art. In LIFE they are *pagans* and *individualists. . . .* In THOUGHT they are *personalists* and *idealists,* that is, superior to any system and to every limit, convinced that every philosophy is only a personal code of life. . . . In ART they love the ideal transfiguration of life. . . . They aspire to beauty as the suggestive configuration of a revelation of a profound and serene life.[13]

Leonardo passed through three stages in its quest after "life," "thought," and "art": an initial mystical phase, which turned quickly into a "pragmatist" phase, which in turn passed into the culminating crescendo of "the occult." Reacting against positivism, against the laws that masked the real, the *Leonardiani* longed for a liberty unconfined by natural laws, a life more intimate and profound; and immediately they seized upon men like Maeterlinck, Meyers, Remacle, and James. The early *Leonardo* was thus filled with passionate hymns to the mystics, to Böhme, and to Paracelsus, and to Prezzolini's discovery of Novalis. It was filled, too, as it passed from mysticism to "pragmatism," with passionate praise for what Prezzolini called the "God-Man," created by Croce's *Estetica.*

Art, as opposed to the vulgar, petty, and almost savage criterion of exact reproduction of things, is always affirmed as a personal vision—the nascent consciousness of the ideal transformation of these forms in the artist, the always stronger desire for unreal worlds and fantastic creations. Whence the aesthetic, beyond an absolute relativism, comes to be seen as the fundamental autonomy of the imagination, and classifications, the old rhetorical and stylistic classifications, are thrown away. *Thus reads the last philosophical essay of B. Croce.*[14]

The *Estetica* of Croce, like the hashish of *Marzocco,* provided *Leonardo* with the basis for a movement into the "philosophy" of pragmatism. Moving from God-Man to pragmatism—one aspect of pragmatism anyway—did not constitute, however, much of a change in perspective for the *Leonardiani.* In fact, it merely provided philosophical justification for the God-Man idea. Having praised Croce's aesthetics, Prezzolini went on, in the next paragraph, to attack science ("this adversary of the marvellous that wants to show us a future synonymous with the past and to ostracize every future novelty") as nothing more than "an improverishment of real life and an instrument created for practical ends."[15] He did not cite Croce, who was coming to the same conclusion, but rather Poincaré, Milhaud, Bergson, Le Roy, and Mach. "Mach says 'all theoretical conceptions of physics—caloric, electricity, molecules, atoms, and energy —must be considered pure expedients and aids to facilitate our knowledge of things.'" Geometry, too, Prezzolini learned from reading Poincaré, was merely a series "of conventions posited by the spirit." Hence "science is not imposed upon us by facts, but we impose these upon science."[16] From the idea that men imposed facts upon science, that science and geometry were mere conventions useful to the men who created them, Prezzolini moved easily to the idea that truth was man-made and its value lay not in its validity, but in its acceptability to the individual who proposed it. If *he* accepted it, then it was valuable to him; if others accepted it, then it became valuable to them. Prezzolini's aim, in other words, was to separate, as James had separated, the mere existence of a thing—or the nonexistence of a thing, for that matter—from its value, the dull reality from the extraordinary possibility. Many facts existed, were true, but value came from those facts that were believed, that inspired action. "According to James," Prezzolini explained,

> American and English pragmatism . . . [makes] individual utility . . . the supreme criterion in, not only conduct, but the truth of things. James . . . clearly distinguished existential judgments from evaluative [judgments]; that a thing exists or not belongs to the first, its value to the second. Thus, value is independent of the existence of things; that Napoleon was an epileptic, Savonarola, a monomaniac, or even that Christ never existed; what has all this to do with their value?"[17]

For Prezzolini, as for Sorel, an idea was valuable if a man believed it so, and if, in believing it so, he acted upon it.

There was here a slight misunderstanding, however, for a convention is not, by definition, an individual belief nor is it, except perhaps at the higher reaches of science, the product of men simply sitting down in the full light of the sun to say, "Let us agree that the moon shall be Diana's and the sun Apollo's." It is too artificial. That geometry is a convention does not mean that Euclid thought it conventional. Moreover, some beliefs appear to be more likely to gain acceptance as truths—even if conventional truths. They are the truths that, in science, allow us to move from one step to another. In Vico, in Peirce, a hypothesis was tested in the doing; indeed, one might say it grew from the doing and was confirmed not only by surrounding reality, but by the completion of the task to be accomplished. In Prezzolini, intoxicated with the God-Man idea, the notion acquired a novel guise, for as an "idealist" he found no reason to test his hypothesis in nature. Instead, the hypothesis itself became the reality. Since he envisioned no particular task to be accomplished, he had no way of knowing if his hypothesis served him well or ill and no way of judging if he had completed his "task." It is not surprising. Prezzolini sought to make of pragmatism not an instrument of science by which one could proceed from one step to another, but a religion to replace the shattered certainties and questioned truths that surrounded him. He did not see that truth had been shattered because it had been exposed as convention and hence artifice, and so he sought another artificial convention to replace it. "The Categorical Imperative is *our* law, no longer given by God." [18] The desperation of the attempt—conscious or not—is its most striking and sympathetic characteristic.

Within a year of their discovery of James, pragmatism became the "official" philosophy of *Leonardo*. A new writer joined the journal, too: Ferdinand Canning Scott Schiller, an English pragmatist educated in Germany, and one who shared with the *Leonardiani* the view that man could, as it were, create his own world. This "David of English Philosophy" as Prezzolini called him, "proposes to us a way in which we can cut and sew our metaphysical wardrobes." [19] Shortly thereafter Prezzolini began to call himself the "spiritual tailor" as he constructed his own wardrobe, his own reality, and went on to explain Schiller's insight that "universal" or "necessary" truths were simply postulates in the last stage of "evolution." If these truths were accepted, then they were universals. Some were accepted, he added, and others were not. Thus, "life is experimentation and these absolutes were mere means to our ends: they were the last act of a Will to Believe that had dared to postulate and had been recompensed by the world." [20]

At the same time that Prezzolini lauded Schiller, Papini revealed another important aspect of this new pragmatism: it was a philosophy of action rather than contemplation. Too much energy was directed toward thought *about* action rather than to action itself. "Our aim now is to [develop] . . . that mode of magical action which consists in making real the world of the idea, in rendering external and concrete what is internal and in the word." [21]

In an article of 1906 entitled "The Campaign for the Compulsory Reawakening," Papini elaborated his "program with respect to Italy."

> I want to awaken the drowsy ones, but I do not, at least right now, want to say what they must do when they awaken. It is enough for me that they no longer lie about on the beds of habit and the grass of mediocrity. . . . A few men who know and feel what I want is enough. With their contagion they will change the moral atmosphere of a nation, [and] the contagion of the nation will be able to change the world. In culture as in politics, the few lead the many. . . . What is the most important thing to be accomplished? A new ideal renaissance in Italy. Make Italy a great center of culture and [make] some Italians again generals in the conquest of spirit. . . . *Dare to be crazy!* . . . *All rhetoric must die.* . . . *Let us seek out terrible problems!* This, in brief, is the first proclamation for the compulsory reawakening. [22]

For both Papini and Prezzolini, pragmatism was the equivalent of emancipation from reality and therefore a step into a world where action did not suffer the "determinism" of logic or reality, of nature. Thus, Papini explained, "We are *philosophers that wish escape from philosophy,* philosophers that have surpassed or are surpassing philosophy."[23] Philosophy was the last external, abstract limit barring the way to the free construction of reality.[24]

The first mention Croce made of *Leonardo* was in a review in *La critica* of July 20, 1893, in which he examined the early issues of *Leonardo.* The review was and is a most curious affair, coming as it did midway between Croce's praise for Carducci and D'Annunzio, and in the midst of Croce's attack upon science. Croce began by welcoming "these lively and caustic . . . idealists from the fine Bergsonian school." They were "antiprofessorial" and "antischolastic," "men of culture": "This cannot but strongly attract our sympathy." He mentioned several articles that especially pleased him, one of which was Prezzolini's "God-Man." Croce then turned to certain problems he felt the *Leonardiani* had encountered, certain excesses into which they had fallen: their hostility toward science and practical life, their exaltation of idealism at the expense of daily affairs, and their construction of private worlds removed from reality.

> The revelation that idealism makes, by pointing out in spirit the liberty, the reality in its fullness, and the consequent limitation on empirical reality and the materialist sciences, exalts souls easily to the point where they forget that that revelation itself has its limits, an inferior limit if you wish, but nonetheless a limit.

And Croce further added,

> Idealism, in overcoming intellectually empiricism and naturalism, cannot abolish them; otherwise it would abolish itself. It, in other words, is turned toward understanding life, and not of course to fashion a life different from the real.[25]

It was an indication, but only an indication, that something was amiss between Croce and his supposed followers. After this reproof, Croce said nothing critical of the *Leonardiani* for the next four years. In fact, for all intents and purposes Croce lent them every support: after all, they had the same enemies. Thus, Garin concluded that in *Leonardo* Croce had found his "guerrilla forces" in the battle against Freemasonry and positivism.

> Croce was pleased by the destructive criticism even if, perhaps, it seemed to him at times excessive and unjust. True, those stones hurled against the academic windows, those violent diatribes against positivists and spiritualists . . . would not have been welcome in the very composed pages of *La critica.* [But] they did not seem to him very different from the disoriented, but useful, attacks [carried out] by bands of irregulars.[26]

A few months after his article on *Leonardo,* Croce wrote again in *La critica:* "We applaud the many things said and said rather well by Prezzolini, and I have no desire to expose here and now the few things from which we dissent." [27] The programs of *Leonardo* and *La critica* were in fact so close that Croce himself described them as "competitive collaboration." [28] So it would seem. Thus, when Croce wrote "Concerning Italian Positivism" in the second issue of *La critica* in 1905, *Leonardo* was so enthusiastic that it reviewed the essay lavishly in its next issue. In fact, it was more of a reprint than a review. Similarly, when, in the third issue of *La critica* in 1904, Croce wrote a particularly scathing attack on Filippo Masci, professor of philosophy at the University of Naples, *Leonardo* reprinted the article in the February issue of 1905. [29]

Throughout the years of "magical pragmatism" and "mysticism," Croce remained content with *Leonardo.* One is not, for example, surprised to read the endorsement of mysticism written by Croce in honor of the publication by *Leonardo* of the edited works of Madame Guyon, Meister Eckhart, and others.

> I think a combination of the *aesthetic spirit* and the mystical disposition is entirely useful to the daily progress of philosophical studies, it seeming to me that this is a rather efficacious way to liberate oneself from the superstitions of the naturalisitic method. [30]

Nor, for that matter, is one surprised to find that many, including a Pisan professor, were convinced that *Leonardo* was secretly directed and written by Croce himself. [31]

"It must not be forgotten," wrote Frigessi, "that Croce followed *Leonardo* from its beginning with benevolence and sympathy and waited until it had reached the extreme limit of magical pragmatism [and the] occult, before he assumed a position of moral and critical separation" from the journal. [32]

Whatever doubts Croce may have had about the usefulness or even the sanity of much of *Leonardo* may have been assuaged by Giovanni Papini, who wrote to reassure Croce that they did not intend to leap right out of reality, that they intended in fact to concern themselves with "practical" struggle against materialism and positivism.

> I do not build another life, but I enjoy all at once all the lives already existing: and I make them succeed one another and I use them; and all this is the game. . . . Thus, I could respond that my desire for the practical life is only the expression of another me . . . and *I could tell you that there is another me that is also worried about action and it will soon give you some proof, fighting precisely those socialists* that are, in social life, the most influential representatives of vulgar, economic, and philosophical materialism. [33]

That struggle against "vulgar" socialism, socialism born of economic materialism and positivist slogans, was one in which the *Leonardiani* and Croce shared a
good deal of common ground. Whatever their differences, *Leonardo* and Croce
together constituted an attack upon the society of modern Italy, and instead of
finding in socialism an ally in that attack, they found an enemy, for the reformist socialists were not opposed to the ideas of the ruling class but to the fact that
they were not of that class. As to its revolutionary nature, then, Italian socialism was a sheep in wolf's clothing. Croce had long since broken with Labriola—
not because Labriola was too revolutionary, but because he was, at least as
Croce understood him, too tame and too narrow to appeal to the proletariat's
sense of duty and idealism. In the socialism of the Italian Socialist party Croce
found something even more insipid: evolutionary positivism, Enlightenment
sentimentalism, and crass materialism.

The fin de siècle discontent that produced at the beginning of the new century that D'Annunzian desire for liberation and direct action came, more or
less coincidentally, at the same time as the rise of the Italian Socialist party (PSI).
Had the theoreticians of socialism been more mature, it is possible that they
might in fact have capitalized upon this discontent. Instead, quite unwittingly,
they set themselves upon a collision course—suicidal in the long run—with the
forces unleashed by the idealists, magical pragmatists, and D'Annunziani. Dis-
tilled and coalesced down to its fundamentals, the revolt of the aesthetes constituted no less a revolt against the bourgeoisie than did socialism. The socialists
at this juncture, however, chose—for good enough reasons— to ally with the
bourgeois parliamentary state. Socialism chose, too, to accept as its ideology the
increasingly unfashionable positivism then being assailed by the aesthetes.

Since the 1870s a number of "socialist" theories in Italy had begun to make
converts among many variously inclined politicians and intellectuals. Mazzinians
and positivists, anarchists and Hegelians, materialists and idealists combined
and collided in a maelstrom that, after twenty years, left the positivists in tenuous
control. In 1892 these theoreticians expelled the anarchists and constituted
themselves as the Italian Socialist party. It was a "transfigured Marxism, combined eclectically with positivistic ideas of various origins, and not rarely in
a rather bizarre guise." [34] The best-known early form of this Marxism was an
extreme economic determinist version of Marx put forth by Achille Loria.
Loria and others of a more or less similar persuasion, such as Saverio Merlino and
Carlo Ferraris, were widely accepted by Marxist politicians and intellectuals
alike. Their theories combined Spencerian evolutionary history, rigid economic
determinism, and an abiding faith that positivist science would reveal the laws
of history. No space was given in this tidy world for human creativity, spontaneity,

or, for that matter, revolution. In the words of one bitter opponent, "The social-ism of Merlino ceased to be the idea of a class and became the aspiration of all humanity for greater well-being and a greater culture: the class war did not exist because of socialism, but despite it." [35]

Nonetheless, it was during this period of ideological confusion that socialism began to be more and more widely accepted in Italy, owing to the efforts of a Milanese lawyer of (more or less) positivist persuasion, Filippo Turati. [36] In 1891, Turati, with Claudio Treves, began the socialist journal *Critica sociale,* and in 1892 Turati became the leader of the Italian Socialist party, founded in that year. Socialism, Croce noted, had attracted by the late 1890s "all or almost all the elect of the younger generation." [37] The Marxist thought that attracted this gen-eration, however, remained a curious mixture of Lorian positivism, Mazzinian anarchic sentimentalism (often funneled through the ideas of Bakunin), and, out-side the party, Antonio Labriola's revolutionary antideterminism. Labriola re-mained aloof from official socialism and even refused to attend its founding congress. A "philosopher of socialism," as he liked to call himself, Labriola re-mained "outside," hurling invectives at the leadership of the neophyte party. To Labriola the ascendent Turatians were amateurish thinkers who had smoth-ered the Labriolan dialectic in a morass of Spencerian optimisim. Labriola pre-ferred to see socialism grounded in revolution and not metaphysical positivism.

In the strictly political arena, however, Turati still remained dominant. He cared little for the ideological squabbles and little understood the puritanical zeal of Labriola. A flexible pragmatist who saw the triumph of socialism as a by-product of the maturation of economic conditions, Turati was dedicated to making life tolerable for the masses until history took its course. "There was in Turati a fundamental coherence," wrote Lelio Basso, "especially in his general vision of life and of the world, which remained always, at base, an evolutionary positivism." [38]

To Turati and Treves at *Critica sociale,* to Leonida Bissolati, the first editor of the party's daily, *Avanti!,* the struggle for socialism had to be preceded by a struggle for democracy. In those years following the 1896 disaster at Adowa, Italy had slipped closer and closer to military dictatorship. Months and months of rioting and civil unrest, culminating in the *fatti di Milano,* in which some eighty civilians had been shot down by the army, had polarized Italy into two factions: those who would have ended constitutional government in favor of the army, and those who sought to preserve it. [39] To Turati, who had been ar-rested and sentenced to twelve years in prison for "spreading socialist propa-ganda," [40] it was more important to preserve democracy than to press forward claims so radical they would only assure continued turmoil and repression. No course save that of alliance with other groups committed to constitutional government seemed possible, and under the prevailing circumstances, revolution seemed suicidal. Released from prison after less than a year, Turati cautioned his party to work to save the only viable means by which they could eventually come to power: the ballot.

> Up to a certain point . . . the development of socialism can do without a free press, free speech, and freedom of association. . . . But there is one thing without which this development absolutely cannot proceed in civilized ways; without which the problem cannot but be in Italy for a very long time, [reduced to] complete paralysis or bloody sedition: it is the right to vote. . . . So, this we say to whomever finds us, so to speak, insufficiently socialist; what we are doing . . . what our newspapers, with *Avanti!* in the lead, are doing, what our party for years has been doing, is defending liberty; it is a generous protest, it is a necessary democratic battle; it has, if you wish, nothing to do with socialism. We will begin to be socialists in action the day when, out of necessity, we need not be, as we are today, simply democrats. [41]

The danger in this "generous protest," of course, was that of compromising one's integrity. The more the revolutionary tactic receded, the more the Socialist leadership became indistinguishable from the parliament it supposedly opposed, indistinguishable from Bernsteinian revisionism. In fact, by 1906 Turati concluded in *Critica sociale,* "All our propaganda is penetrated by a more or less Bernsteinian revisionism; and if we remain in some way Marxist, it is but in the wide direction, in the general spirit of the doctrine, in the concept and practice of the class struggle and of economic materialism." [42]

This tendency toward revisionism had been evident from the turn of the century and was to prevail throughout most of the years in which the liberal prime minister Giovanni Giolitti ruled (1900-15). The near collapse of Italian democracy under Crispi, Di Rudinì, and Pelloux had left an indelible imprint upon the minds of the socialist leadership. Thus, Claudio Treves, while separating himself—not too clearly—from Giolitti, would say in August of 1899 that if only Giolitti would create "an open and widely productive regime, reinvigorate industry [while] giving assurances to capital, save the humble by increased taxation of the mighty, create the proletariat by creating the bourgeoisie—why then how much glory would be due him." [43]

The difficulty with this drift into Bernsteinian parliamentary democracy was not only that the Socialists seemed to many to be no different from existing parties, but that it was out of fashion with the avant-garde aesthetes who had come increasingly to detest the bourgeoisie and its moderate institutions. A more successful course might have prevailed had socialism's alliance with bourgeois institutions been explicit and coupled with a joint attack upon this discontent. The Socialists too, however, were prisoners of their own rhetoric, and so they remained, right down to the critical days of 1922. To ally themselves any more explicitly with the state than they already had, to join with the state in a joint attack upon the nationalists and antipositivists, would have divided the party even more dangerously. The Socialists chose instead not to notice the looming battle. The result was, at first, a halfhearted and divisive tolerance of the parliamentary system and, later, the collapse of moderate socialism along with parliament under the weight of Mussolini.

As moderate Socialists became more and more committed to the government, antipositivists, nationalists, and mystics came more and more to denounce both socialism and the bourgeois state. That flaccid and decadent class, insensitive to art and impervious to idealism, had lost its former sense of duty and mission, the determined intransigence with which it had brought down the feudal regime. Seduced by Enlightenment slogans of brotherhood and equality, it had lost its right to rule. It amazed Croce that the Socialists, the leaders of the proletariat, who could have ushered in a new era, who could have instituted a kind of national resurgence with a new humanist culture and a new sense of purpose, should instead have made themselves indistinguishable from Enlightenment humanitarianism and sentimentalism. Looking again through Croce's Socialist writings, looking at his "Socialist period," one is inclined to say that it was not socialism at all. Despite his later remark that he too had been captivated by socialism, one finds the "captivation" lukewarm. It was not proletarian socialism that Croce sought, but a kind of Vichian *ricorso* which would give Italians— Italians of every class—a sense of direction and duty. His journey into socialism was a kind of quest, his writings too analytical to be taken as Socialist, too dispassionate to be partisan. Croce's essays were concerned with Italy, not the proletariat. It was not a revolution he sought, but a Risorgimento, and if that meant a clear separation, a clear departure, from the bourgeois state of Giolittian Italy, it did not mean socialism nor did it mean, in any narrow or chauvinist sense, nationalism.

This is not by any means to imply that Croce's early influence was not revolutionary or his as yet half-formed doctrine not explosive. On the contrary, its revolutionary force came from the fact that it cut through all the abstract creeds and social institutions that society had erected to protect itself against humanity and exposed them as "superstructure," the thin tissue covering the naked skeleton of man. Moreover, because the doctrine venerated history, it was ever anxious to consign the present to the past so as to unveil those new historical forces that were to advance humanity another step. Those new forces needed new doctrines, and Croce saw in the Socialist's aping of the "decadent bourgeoisie" the surest indication that the proletarian movement would fail. The authentic bourgeoisie, Croce noted in 1907, had not been the spokesmen of Enlightenment sentimentalism but a revolutionary force. The Socialists' desire "to liquidate the bourgeoisie" ought also to be revolutionary. The "bourgeoisie [had] liquidated the feudal regime," Croce observed, "but [that old] bourgeoisie . . . knew how to organize itself, to struggle and rest; it knew how to sacrifice entire generations to assure the victory for its sons and grandsons." Look, he said, at the Italian Risorgimento, one of "the most recent bourgeois movements" and one that was "widely illustrative." There one did not have collaboration, but a "Mazzinian education to intransigence." If the "rulers and rebels had come to agreement . . . Italy would not have been accomplished." Therefore, if the "proletariat wishes to emulate the bourgeoisie in the destruction of an old society, it must have the fortitude to imitate it also in the harsh methods of destruction and reeducation. Such conditions are imposed by history, and by observing them, socialism is no more frightening [*è tanto poco pauroso*] to the thinking man than what is necessary."[44]

Comparing Croce's analysis of the bourgeoisie with the analyses of Papini, Prezzolini, and even Enrico Corradini, one finds a remarkable convergence, which led many in that era to see them all as a united force. Each agreed upon the heroism of the old bourgeoisie that had made Italy; and each now agreed in pinpointing the Italian "crisis" in the decadence of what Croce called "the old society," the ruling bourgeoisie.

The difference between Croce and the others, however, was that while Croce hoped to find a true revolutionary force capable of moving men, a kind of post-Christian religion which would catapult the society out of its torpor, Prezzolini, Corradini, and their associates hoped to revivify the old bourgeoisie.

"If only the bourgeoisie were as the Socialists paint it," lamented Prezzolini. If only "they would adopt the forces of genius, the shrewdness, and the subtlety of the dialectic . . . the audacious oratory," if only "they would defend and maintain in their own hands the riches that heredity, privilege, tenacious savings" had given them, "then the bourgeoisie would not be corrupt." If only they would really use the "army," the "priests," and the "servility of the magistracy . . . to exclude from wealth, power, and honor the proletarian class," if only they really did constitute a "closed and arrogant . . . caste . . . then I would take their part and aid them in the struggle." Instead, said Prezzolini, the bourgeoisie's defense against the proletarians was "concessions," and the "bourgeoisie

... infiltrated with Socialist ideas ... aids and applauds its own ruin. ... Nothing is more apocryphal than the bourgeois reaction, a myth created by democrats to spur on the pleb and give it the illusion it fights something forceful and mighty." The only resistance the bourgeoisie offered, he concluded, was "its sloth and inertia."[45]

The despair over the bourgeoisie's loss of initiative was evident also in Corradini's *Il regno* as the editor outlined his "sole task: to be a voice among all those others who despair and lament the vileness of the present national hour." Corradini meant "to disgrace those who demonstrate that they have done everything possible to be defeated, to disgrace the Italian bourgeoisie."

> I'm not speaking of its fear, which creates the audacity of the aggressors, nor of its retreating as rapidly as they advance; I'm speaking, amidst nausea and rage, of what wrenches the heart with laughter: its making itself their accomplice in its own demise. ... The Italian bourgeoisie obstinately insists upon feeling compassion for the doctrines of liberty and internationalism. It has become the sinkhole of sentimental socialism. ... All the worst signs of putrid decrepitude of degenerate men are present in the contemplative life of the Italian bourgeoisie.[46]

The despair over what Papini called "the rule of impersonalness," the feeling that no one, no class, was in charge of the state or had responsibility for it, was widespread. There was the official country and the real country, the *pays réal* and the *pays legal,* and the task was to bring them together. Thus, Corradini reviled the languid bourgeoisie who occupied the seat of government but did not govern. "In other words, it is always necessary for someone to say, after the French king, '*L'état c'est moi*'; if it is not a king it must be a class of citizens. For a state to exist as a true and proper organism these words must be spoken by someone with a full and ruthless consciousness. ... [But] the Italian bourgeoisie has lost this consciousness."[47]

Similarly, Croce separated himself from the bourgeois official state, but he did not call for an infusion of new blood for the bourgeois rulers but for a new sense of purpose, of ethicalness, which would come from outside the state.

> The point is to find out where the true state is in the actual world ... where the ethical force really is. Now, if the state is concrete ethicalness [*eticità*], it is not said that this [ethicalness] must always be incarnate in the government, in the sovereign, the ministers, the Chambers, rather than in those who do not directly participate in the government, in the adversaries and enemies of a particular state, in the revolutionaries. ... It is not rare for

a man of thought to be forced to exclaim, before actual states, *"L'état c'est moi,"* and he can be perfectly right in this.[48]

And Croce added a few pages later, "Let us remember that we are the real state ... [that] the philosophical revival of Italy must be the work of the laity and not of the universities," that is, of the official institutions.[49]

The rising tide of antibourgeois sentiment chose as its first target the Socialist party, which had, to save democracy, allied itself with the regime. The bourgeoisie and the PSI became in the minds of the avant-garde synonymous, but the Socialists were the more despicable because of their masquerade as a revolutionary force. It was a sentiment expressed at length by Papini in 1903. "Socialism is the doctrine of the poor," he wrote, and "in keeping with its character," it had begun by borrowing, "borrowing that is, the doctrine of the bourgeoisie" with its "preoccupation with material well-being." The classic prototype "of the 'fat bourgeois'" which appeared in all democratic propaganda was a man "concerned with filling his belly and his wallet." Papini saw no difference between this and Turatian socialism: "The Socialists completely accept this view; they, too, desire above all and before all an increase in material welfare. Their sociologists have made the question of the belly the foundation of history under the significant name of historical materialism." Papini went on to say that the Socialists hated the ruling classes not because they were well-to-do, but because they were more well-to-do than the Socialists; the Socialists wanted merely to make everyone bourgeois. "Socialism, if one looks carefully, does not aim, at base, to be anything different than its enemy." The Socialists wanted what the bourgeoisie already had and brought nothing new, no new ideology, no new desires, to the cause of renewing Italy. "Liberty, equality, justice are not proletarian creations" but merely the old bourgeois ideals. They merely want to add to the rights of man, "the right to work, which is, parenthetically, the stupidest of all." Like Nietzsche, Papini saw in socialism "the egoism of the weak" bound "together in order to be strong," a desire for nothing more than equality: "juridical equality ... economic equality, and who knows, intellectual equality."

In philosophy the Socialists had no originality either, for they had merely elevated themselves to "the summits of positivism, to this timid doctrine of hod carriers" which they held in common with "a good part of the bourgeoisie." And it was not only in philosophy and in the desire for material well-being that Papini saw the convergence of the bourgeoisie and the Socialists. He and the rest of the *Leonardiani* who desired the emancipation of the individual from all constraints saw that both the oppressed and the oppressor "hate and fear the individual. Bourgeois society hates all that tries to elevate itself over the dominant mediocrity." The bourgeois ideal of government, which treated each man alike under "common programs, uniform rules, is an essentially anti-individualistic ideal," a "bureaucratic and misoneistic coalition." Socialism has merely accepted this ideal, exaggerated it into "the most perfect expression of itself," which is "collectivist society . . . the Leviathan state." [50]

Croce also sneered at "socialism, which could do no more than borrow from the bourgeoisie its materialistic philosophy and its [notion] of the class struggle and has succeeded so well in this that now, exchanging roles, it passes for the inventor of what it simply found attractive and completed and before whose power it now kneels." [51] For Croce, who condemned the bourgeoisie for its acceptance of eighteenth-century ideals of liberty, equality, and natural law, the idea that socialism would now accept these ideals too meant the end of socialism. To Croce and to the *Leonardiani,* the revolt against bourgeois sentimentalism was essential to their Risorgimento, and their movement could not coalesce with socialism, for it had become indistinguishable from the opposition.

Turatian socialism was, therefore, too tame for Croce. It was "contemplation" rather than "action," and the real Marx had been immobilized in that Turatian contemplation. The essence of Marxism, Croce said, lay not in its philosophy, which he felt he had already demolished in his debate with Labriola, but in its action. Marx's standing Hegel right side up did not mean replacing one philosophy with another, replacing "the speculative dialectical method" with "naturalistic" method, "subject with object, or spirit with matter." As the *Theses on Feuerbach* indicated, Marx destroyed all philosophy and replaced it with action.

> Is that clear? *Standing Hegel right side up* consisted in replacing philosophy with practice, philosophy with revolution. . . . Marx not only overturned Hegelian philosophy but philosophy in general, every sort of philosophy, and supplanted philosophizing with practical activity . . . the revolutionary activity of the proletariat. [52]

The agreement of Croce with Papini, Prezzolini, and Corradini, as well as with many collaborators in their journals, was, then, based upon a common rejection of the bourgeois state, as well as upon a rejection of "official" socialism as an alternative to that state. From that point on, however, Croce took a different course than the others—at least for a time. Corradini, for all his vituperation of the decadent bourgeois state, felt that only through its resurrection and revivification could Italy be saved. The *Leonardiani,* in part, shared this feeling, but with their individualism, their mysticism, their occultism, they muddied any clear decision as to the course to be taken. It was this which caused Croce to break with them. Initially attracted to *Leonardo* if for no other reason than its antipositivism and antiestablishment crusade, Croce eventually came to feel that as an alternative, it had little to offer.[53] His condemnation was explicit. In the spring of 1907 Croce denounced the *Leonardiani's* empty rhetoric, which offended his sense of concreteness and practicality.

> You want to conceive a philosophy quite different from those that have appeared in history . . . [and you invent] new methods of science and art [and proclaim] knowledge through the will or logic through fantasy . . . but we have never aimed at effects such as these that tend toward the marvelous. We are simple workers who wish to defend, according to our abilities, speculative idealism; to apply it to historical problems; to write with as great an exactness as possible the history of literature and philosophy and of the contemporary Italian culture . . . ; to distinguish ourselves from the positivists, the spiritualists, and the mystics; and this we say in our program and this we have done and this we are doing.[54]

This condemnation did not by any means end Croce's relationship with Prezzolini or even, for that matter, with Papini. Within a year they would again be collaborating, this time in another journal, however, for *Leonardo* collapsed in the fall of 1907.[55]

A few months after Croce's reproval of *Leonardo,* D'Annunzio and his clique received the same treatment. In a dramatic article in which Croce broke off his examination of the history of Italian literature, Croce condemned contemporary writing, seeing for the first time that aesthetics, at least the aesthetics of one like D'Annunzio, could not remain a mere expression of an intuition, that it, in fact, had become a way of life.[56]

The article compared the period 1865 to 1885 with the period in which Croce was then writing. The latter period, dominated, he said, by D'Annunzio, Fogazzaro, and Pascoli, was not equal to the "heroic paganism" of Carducci in the earlier period. This present period, he said, was *"imperialist, mystic, and foppish."* This was a period of "the greatest industry: the great industry of *the void [del vuoto]*."[57] Croce ended, nevertheless, by blaming positivism for causing D'Annunzio and all that went with him. As soon as it became clear that positivism had claimed to be more than it was, as soon as it became clear that positivism was "insufficient, what had to happen, happened: reality revealed itself as an ineffable beyond, an unknowable, a mystery; and positivism generated from its own breast mysticism and renewed religious forms." Thus, mysticism was seen to be "the legitimate son of [positivism]." In that sense, however, so too was Croce the son of positivism, for no one more than he pointed out the need for a religious consciousness and aesthetic awareness. That Croce had come to blows with D'Annunzio should not obscure that initial, if rash, approval. The article ended, however, on an optimistic note in which Croce said that the young people then being educated in Italy would not succumb to D'Annunzianism. They knew "how to take care of themselves." [58]

Croce was not often to be so wrong. The star of D'Annunzio had only begun to rise, the arc it was to describe coinciding later on with the arc that the young generation of Italians nurtured on D'Annunzian ecstasy was itself to describe. The anxious, the troubled, the bored looked to D'Annunzio as the fulfillment of the prophecy of the Crocean aesthetic of 1902. And yet D'Annunzio in a sense was insufficient. No one perhaps in the history of man was so intoxicated with himself as D'Annunzio, and yet even he, in the end, had to make of himself more than himself, had to play out his final drama at Fiume not as the narcissistic artist that he was, but rather as a poet-outlaw who, for all his perverted egoism, still had to see his mission not as personal but as the fulfillment of an Italian nationalist. If it was counterfeit nationalism, it was still only as nationalism that it could inspire followers. D'Annunzio as a man was insufficient.

Croce's philosophy too celebrated man, the resurgence of man, but for most of his contemporaries, man was insufficient and derived his meaning from something outside himself. Nietzsche and De Sanctis had imagined that man could self-consciously pose goals for himself and, attaining them, become great himself. But the conscious posing of the goal makes it artificial, as if for mere man to propose it makes it unworthy of that hot pursuit which alone will achieve it. The goals that inspire are those that arise naturally and are felt, so to speak, before they are articulated. It is the religious orientation of which Croce had spoken that moved men.

Croce himself had sought that meaning in Marxism. He had criticized, in 1907, those who sought to find meaning in mysticism and the void. Concreteness, he counseled, was essential to a lay religion that had dispensed with transcendence. The meaning had to be found in man, in his society, and his nation.

It was inevitable, one feels, rather than intentional, that the idealist revival of Italy should have slid over into a kind of nationalism. "The problem that torments us today," observed the historian Anzilotti in 1911, "brings us back to its origins when the modern state created the dualism between the individual and the state. Today we feel a kind of nostalgia for that social fabric, for that organic unity which helped and absorbed individuals in the old regime." [59]

Separating itself from French positivism and Anglo-Saxon empiricism, call-

ing for the spiritual revival of an Italian soul while condemning divisive political
parties, searching for a national culture and a national orientation, it was only a
matter of time before a certain narrowness should appear in Italian idealism, a
certain longing for a unity to overcome the years of division. It is a familiar irony
that individual spiritual emancipation, egoistic exaltation that vents its wrath
upon a free and tolerant society, so often finds contentment and peace in a rigid
and omnipresent society. Only in that kind of social milieu, it seems, could
these men find meaning. Papini's road from Fichtean egoism to Catholicism was
already well trodden when he made the journey, and comparing a list of later
fascist eminences with a list of these early rebels makes one wonder if fascism
did not bring them a sigh of relief rather like that given after a long journey
upon one's arrival home. The difficulty with so many of these poet rebels was
that they had confused liberty and the void; not only did they deplore a society
without a sense of direction, they deplored as well a society that did not enforce
a sense of direction on everyone, thus giving society a purpose at the expense
of freedom.

Underlying much of this period was a kind of spiritual disorientation which
tended to coalesce around impatient nationalism. This nationalism is one, but
only one, of the more salient characteristics of the journal *La voce,* which Prezzolini had begun in 1908. True, many, like Salvemini, could not tolerate the
more militant aspects of that nationalism; others, like Prezzolini, found cause
to quarrel with Corradini over whose nationalism was the more genuine.[60]
Still, it is not without sensing that he had hit the mark, even if in an exaggerated
way, that one reads Prezzolini's later remarks:

> Notwithstanding the serious differences of method, I could say that in a
> certain sense Mussolini appeared as the realization of the ideals of *La voce.*
> ... Willingly or not, we had prepared the formation of fascism.[61]

The stand taken by Croce and the idealists, aesthetes, and antisocialists with
respect to nationalism was all the more ambivalent because the nationalists had
adopted more and more of the rhetoric of idealism and the language of antipositivism. Even after the expiration of *Leonardo* and *Il regno* there was a continuation of that earlier campaign waged by *Il regno* against Freemasonry, socialism,
and positivism. In fact, many of the *Vociani* (writers in *La voce*), such as Th. Neal,
Papini, Prezzolini, as well as other intellectuals associated with Croce, such as
G. A. Borgese, had participated earlier in the century in the nationalist magazine
of Corradini.

This link with nationalism is apparent in the problem of Alfredo Oriani.

Born to a wealthy family in the violent Romagna, Oriani dedicated himself at an early age to "literature," writing a series of obscure and generally vulgar novels and leading, right up to his death, a life of precious little significance.

A friend of Angelo Camillo De Meis, Oriani developed a fashionable, if lighthearted, taste for Hegelianism of the right, and in later years he turned to composing histories of Italy, which were violently and enthusiastically attacked by the positivists. A "republican" like Carducci, Oriani saw in the Italian monarchy only an interim stage to be "overcome" through a final synthesis of man and state. His major work, *The Political Struggle in Italy: Origins of the Contemporary Struggle,* was a modern version of Cuoco's "passive revolution," in which Oriani pointed out the failure of the Risorgimento, the cowardice of Italy's leadership, and the general disinterest of the masses in the success of the unification process. As with Carducci, Oriani's hero was Crispi and Italy's mission was revenge for Adowa and Dogali. The second part of the work, the examination of the origins of the "present struggle," was never written, almost as if the author, overcome with disgust, could not continue.

Calling for a renewal of the Italian state, a rebirth of ancient Roman power and the end of the positivist hegemony, it is not surprising that Oriani should be chosen by the nationalists as another of their literary heroes. With his constant references to imperial destiny, his use of Roman symbolism, and his glorification of war, Oriani had from the beginning been the darling of the nationalists and was later hailed by Mussolini as a prophet of fascism. Outside nationalist circles, however, Oriani was not well known until after his death. "Oriani's novels never achieved any success in his lifetime" Thayer has said; and his attempts at history were widely criticized. [62] But in 1909, the year he died, the Oriani revival was proclaimed by Croce, who wrote a reappraisal of his works and urged them upon Italian readers.

In Oriani, Croce did not claim to see a political viewpoint, for Oriani was an "historian" and a "poet." His Hegelianism had protected him "from positivism, Darwinism, evolutionary materialism [*evoluzionismo naturalistico*]," and yet "being as acute as he was" he refused to accept Hegel's "philosophy of history. ... In sum, Oriani's philosophy of history is quite empirical. ... It is not born, as in Hegel, from the very depths of the logos; or at least it is presented as independent of a determined metaphysic." For Croce, Oriani had departed from "orthodox Hegelianism" and perhaps "philosophical coherence," but it was a victory for "the historian, who must have an open soul to accept all the variety of facts and a ready eye to follow their crooked path." In short, "Oriani possessed the uncommon ability to 'look at the facts from on high,' as De Sanctis used to say, an essential gift of the historian."

Turning to *The Political Struggle in Italy,* Croce found that it was "a history above political parties, governed by that impartiality that comes from the choice of an elevated point of view. . . . One feels that [Oriani] has observed and re-counted with a ready and sympathetic spirit but with an unprejudiced mind and total honesty; *sine ira et studio,* a rather common phrase [but] rather rare in reality." [63]

It was an important essay both for its praise of Oriani and for the publicity it gave him. If Oriani had not been very well received before this, now Croce's publisher friend, Giovanni Laterza, began a republication of his works. There can be little question that Croce played an important role in Laterza's decision; [64] many years later, in 1934, a quite different Croce acknowledged, "It is a fact that the rise of [Oriani's] reputation came from my essay and from Laterza's republication of his works." [65] But, Croce added in 1935, Oriani (and Croce's first essay) had been misunderstood. Oriani had not in fact been against Giolitti, against democracy and Parliament; in fact, at the time of his death he had gone so far as to accept these things he had always opposed. [66] That, however, had not been entirely clear in the earlier period, and even if Oriani had changed, it was certainly not the "changed" Oriani that began to gain fame after 1909. As with D'Annunzio, Croce had begun by defending the very persons he would later be forced to condemn, his search for a religion that moved and inspired leading him to measure too often only the strength of the inspiration rather than its direction.

The year the essay was published, Oriani died, and Croce's praise for the man was echoed in a eulogy written by Prezzolini in *La voce.* He too had now dis-covered this "cavalier" who was "never so full of himself that he did not feel humanity and never so swollen with humanity that he lost sight of himself." For the *Vociani,* Oriani's death was a sad occasion. Oriani "today is dead [but] he will be read. . . . His strength of character came to him from his almost religious convictions, in fact, in the formal sense of the word, from his absolutely religious [convictions]." [67] Prezzolini was quite right later to say, "We were at base also nationalists. Papini had opened *La voce* with a beautiful piece called 'Italy Re-sponds' in which vibrated that sentiment held by many after 1900 for an Italy that was slowly being brought to the highest of nations." [68]

It was in pointing out those "religious convictions" of Oriani that Prezzolini had come closest to what had also impressed Croce. It was not important that Oriani's histories were anthems rather than analyses, because for Croce Italy had suffered too long from analysis. Analyses, Croce quite rightly saw, had no point of view, no religious convictions within which to fit the facts.

In 1907 Croce had found another social observer who knew the importance of belief over mere facts, one who also appreciated the need for a religious faith and a sense of conviction, and Croce meant to make him known in Italy. He was Georges Sorel.

6 SOREL AND CROCE: MYTH AND FAITH

Georges Sorel was, of course, no stranger to Croce when in 1903, in a series of essay reviews, Croce began to popularize the French syndicalist's works in Italy. They had become acquainted nearly ten years earlier, before Sorel had become a syndicalist, through the medium of Antonio Labriola. The young Sorel had attracted Labriola's attention because of their shared interest in antipositivist theories of Marxism as well as their common devotion to revolution. It was through Labriola that Sorel made the acquaintance of the then largely unknown Benedetto Croce. From early 1895 to the fall of 1897, Croce and Sorel had worked with Labriola to perfect an antievolutionary theory of Marxism. Then, with the publication of Croce's *"Per l'interpretazione e la critica di alcuni concetti del marxismo,"* a breach had opened between Croce and Labriola, a breach that would prove fatal to their friendship and in many ways fatal to Italian Marxism. On the other hand, it was to open a partnership between Croce and Sorel that was to become the basis for a dual attack upon the left Hegelian ideas of Labriola on the one hand and the evolutionary gradualism of the Italian Socialist party on the other. The publication of Croce's essay had, as we have seen, reduced Marxism à la Labriola to but a single aspect of man's behavior, the economic. Sorel had no idea at that time that Croce would follow through in the *Estetica* with a complete picture of man, but he did see almost at once that Croce shared a good many of his own views about human nature. In fact, as early as May 1898 Sorel had abandoned Labriola for "the best commentator on Marx," Benedetto Croce.[1] Sorel and Croce had come to extraordinarily similar views about man in general and Marxism in particular.

For a graduate of the Ecole polytechnique and a civil engineer, Georges Sorel had a singular appreciation for the emotional, irrational, and daffier aspects of human nature. A brilliant social psychologist with an unswerving devotion to a revolution that would create a never very precisely defined worker's society, Sorel gave all his attention to the discovery of those forces that he felt would move men to create the new society. Every bit the product of the age that produced Freud and Le Bon, Sorel was unimpressed with notions, like positivism, which proclaimed the rationality of man and the society in which he lived.

Sorel's contribution to Marxism lay, first, in his belief that Marxism had much more in common with the religious movements of the ancient and medieval world than its anti-Christian leadership was prepared to admit and, second, in his conviction that struggle, violence, and self-sacrifice were intrinsically necessary for proletarian victory. Sorel saw in the early Christian determination to evangelize and appropriate the ancient world the prototype for Socialist victory. Those ancient believers, moved by an unswerving faith in their own righteousness and the righteousness of their cause, had converted the mightiest empire on earth and all of Western society.

> The Christian . . . awaits the glorious second coming of Christ, who will destroy the rule of Satan and call his comrades in the fight to the heavenly Jerusalem. The Christian life of that time was dominated by the necessity of membership in the holy army, which was constantly exposed to the ambuscades set by the accomplices of Satan; this conception produced many heroic acts, engendered a courageous propaganda, and was the cause of considerable moral progress. The deliverance did not take place, but we know by innumerable testimonies from that time what great things the march toward deliverance can bring about.[2]

For the ancient Christians and those of the Reformation, for the participants in the French Revolution of 1789 and the followers of Mazzini,[3] faith in the final victory had produced the final victory. Zeal and enthusiasm counted far more than being right. For Sorel it mattered not that the ideals that produced the actions of the early Christians were "myths," but only that they had produced the action. It is this catalytic aspect of the ideal, whether true or false, that he recommended to the leadership of the Socialist parties. "The myth must be judged as a means of acting on the present; any attempt to discuss how far it can be taken literally as a future history is devoid of sense. *It is the myth in its entirety which is alone important.*"[4]

Yet sometimes, Sorel recognized, myths do fail. They fail when the course they chart, the goal they envision, proves—not too difficult—but too easy. Like Luther's condemnation of the Catholic sacraments for being too easy to acquire and therefore too unlikely to inspire, Sorel believed that unless the proletariat were forced to do battle, suffer martyrdom and setbacks, they would become bored with the struggle, and victory would vanish. Thus, he envisioned every fresh concession of material comfort won from the bourgeoisie as a sop to neutralize the revolutionary myth and urged his followers to

> repay with *black ingratitude* the *benevolence* of those who would protect the workers, to meet with insults the homilies of the defenders of human fraternity, and to reply by blows to the advances of the propagators of social peace. . . . It is a very practical way of indicating to the middle class that they must mind their own business and only that.[5]

To Croce, intent upon his own notion of social regeneration, the ideas of Sorel seemed especially important. Croce, too, believed at that point that the essence of practical socialism, the essence of any action, lay in philosophy, a word he used, significantly, interchangeably with ideology and religion.[6] For Croce, a philosophy that was merely contemplative and lacked the inspiration of ideology and religion was an abstraction unworthy of notice. German idealism for Croce meant the primacy of the idea as impetus to action.[7] Thus, Croce concluded that the essence of Marxism lay not in Labriola's antiphilosophy, his destruction of faith and abstract barriers to action. That was only half the journey, and to halt there would leave man exactly where Croce had found him at the turn of the century: without faith, not knowing which way to turn, the victim of a scientific destruction of all that he had held sacred. The destruction of religion would leave man suspended in midair unless it was replaced by another religion. "Without religion, or rather without this orientation, one does not live, or one lives with a soul divided and perplexed, [one lives] unhappily."[8] Labriola's Marxism could demystify, could smash icons, but it could do nothing, Croce felt, to ignite the spark of human action. Men, like mountains, are moved by faith, and faiths, to Croce as to Sorel, were held sacred only when they required self-sacrifice, duty, and struggle. The real Marx for Croce, therefore, was the Marx who had disputed and refuted the gospel of the bourgeoisie, had thereby torn down the abstract barriers—philosophy, religion, liberalism—to the proletarian conquest of power. This was the Marx who preached revolution, conquest, victory through battle, and this was the Marx who could inspire followers. Thus, Marx recalled to Croce, as he tried in 1917 to explain what had attracted him to Marxism two decades earlier, the teachings of Machiavelli, whose realism had cut through the medieval barriers to Italian patriotism and counseled Italians to struggle, whatever the cost, whatever the necessity, for Italian unification. Hence, to Marx "I proposed to give . . . a title of honor, the 'Machiavelli of the proletariat.'"[9] Marx recalled to Croce "the best traditions of Italian political science, thanks to his firm principles of strength, struggle, power, and the satirical caustic opposition to the insipidities of antihistorical and democratic natural law and to the so-called ideals of 1789."[10]

This notion, that socialism was a faith that the more tenaciously it was held, the more severely tested, the more likely it was to succeed, led Croce and Sorel to turn first upon Labriola and then upon the democratic socialists. The "crisis of Marxism," to use Masaryk's expression, began with Croce's essay reducing Labriolan historical materialism to a single economic aspect of human nature. Labriolan Marxism was not a religion but a mere "canon of historical interpretation," therefore passive and not active. The essay was, of course, not at all what Labriola had in mind, and Labriola "could scarcely believe," wrote Croce, "that I, I myself, had participated in overturning and putting in mortal danger the doctrine to which he had introduced me."[11]

In the evolutionary positivism of *Critica sociale* Croce found precisely what he and Sorel had most feared. Turati had so persuaded himself and his followers that victory was assured that there no longer appeared to be any reason to struggle. For Sorel and Croce, the masses had to be told that victory was certain not because history would produce it, but because men must produce it. Turati, instead of being a revolutionary, had become for Croce a priest counseling pacifism and renunciation of the present world and its problems.[12]

Reading through *Critica sociale* of this period gives the impression that historical circumstances forced the party into a steady progress toward Bernsteinian revisionism. Yet even though that be true, what troubles one in these long analyses of contemporary trends and political personages, these open-minded reviews of books whose authors represented all that socialism opposed, is the ideological innocence of the journal. It was so open-minded that it represented the opposite tendency of Croce's *La critica,* with its "determinate point of view." No coherent perspective, right or wrong, was set out against which events could be measured or within which circumstances could be placed. It is almost as if Bernstein were discovered as an afterthought after the drift had been completed. In a journal that represented evolutionary positivism of men like Turati and Treves an appreciation of the catalytic or motivating potential of thought would hardly play a very large role. But what arrests even the casual reader was the editors' failure to understand the debate that circled closer and closer around them. In the arena of ideology, the PSI leadership were the vestal virgins of socialism. An article in the April 16, 1898, *Critica sociale* on the "Recentissima letteratura marxista"—only six months after Croce had written his most important critique of Marxism, reducing Marxism to an emotional urge and a canon of historical interpretation—lists as "followers of Marxism": Antonio Labriola, Benedetto Croce, Sorel, along with Kautsky, Sombart, and Bernstein. No attempt is made to differentiate among them; all are followers of Marxism. In fact, the author praises Croce and Sombart and goes so far as to repeat Croce's warning to all Socialists that they should avoid metaphysical speculation. He concludes: "Into this *metaphysical danger* even Labriola has fallen. . . . [In fact] in historical materialism there is no determinate conception of life or of the world; it is simply a canon of historical interpretation." [13]

With perception, the Marxist Giuseppe Petronio wrote, "Turati's magazine reflects, as is natural, the character of Italian socialism at the end of the last century and at the beginning of this one, a socialism without firm Marxist foundations, made [up] of humanitarianism and good-will more than of ideological preparation, moved more by the heart than the intellect, [the] work of the bourgeoisie stirred by a popular cause." [14] Turati seems in fact not to have noticed that the views of Croce were diametrically opposed to his own, to Lafargue's, and to Loria's, let alone Labriola's. Thus, when Croce wrote his attack upon Lafargue (whose works at that time were being serialized in *Critica sociale*), Turati then incredibly added that "between the thought of Croce and that of Lafargue it does not seem to us that there are truly grave and substantial doctrinal differences." [15]

To counter this ideological naïveté, this positivism, Croce began to popularize the works of Sorel and what Croce called "Marxist socialism," heir to German classical thought. It separated Croce from the Reformists—and from democracy as well.

My horror of positivism . . . became so violent that it suffocated for many years my democratic instincts. . . . For Italian democracy was, it is not known why (except, perhaps, because of . . . its popularity, an almost inevitable liability of all democracies) positivistic and my stomach refused to digest it until it was seasoned with Marxist socialism, which, as is very well known, has imbibed classical German philosophy. Even today [1905] the positivistic phraseology of certain Italian democrats arouses my conservative instincts. [16]

In classical German philosophy, according to Croce, there was the idea, the motivating force, the "myth," which activated man. It was not the childish myth of 1789 and the ideals of natural law, but the struggle against that myth. To move men required not the coherence of eighteenth-century thought, but the inspiration of religion, the Marx of Sorel.

Croce had been drawn to Sorel more than Labriola from the beginning of his acquaintance with the Frenchmen. In September 1899 he wrote to Gentile of Sorel:

He is a man of powerful and lucid genius, yet he has done it by himself;
he has never had regular philosophical studies, and he doesn't know a word
of German. I am amazed at how he has seen many questions so accurately
since he is so little (formally) prepared. You compared him quite unfavor-
ably with Labriola. In truth Sorel, who is not a philosopher by profession
like Labriola, always has a clear and determined thought and does not get
muddled in words nor make [logical] leaps as Labriola unfortunately does.
Moreover, he is a man of great intellectual loyalty—better, of morality. [17]

Recommending Sorel as "a true Marxist, perhaps the only Marxist worthy
of the name," Croce turned his attention, in the second issue of *La critica*, [18]
to the Italian translation of some of Sorel's critical essays on Marxism. [19] These
essays confirmed Croce's own earlier work on Marxism: Marxism was not a
philosophy and had nothing to do with Labriola's historical materialism. True
Marxism was that of the class war, and Sorel, like Croce, had glimpsed the
truth. In Sorel there is the "condemnation of all the principal theories of Marx
when taken in a rigorous or philosophical sense," and Sorel's ideas were therefore of great practical rather than theoretical use. [20] The practical significance
of Sorel was in his recommendation of the general strike. Croce noted the great
importance Sorel assigned to the general strike and praised him because

instead of being disturbed, as is usual, by the dangers and damage that [the
general strike] occasions, he sees in that instinctive proletarian violence "the
salvation of humanity." It makes no difference that [the strike] produces
no immediate effects. . . . The general strike, which causes the ideal of an
emancipated work to dance before the eyes of the workers, is the only image
able to excite enthusiasm for the task. . . . These practical conclusions [of
Sorel's] highlight an entire life of observations, thoughts, and studies moved
by the thirst for truth and justice. [21]

Although, Croce said, one could not set out any formulae or program of action
sufficiently inclusive to guarantee success to the proletariat, or sufficiently concrete to take account of every particular in "countries, times, and conditions
of the most varying nature and among continuous changes, dangers, and unexpected events," this book of Sorel's supplied much-needed advice. "I do not
know which or how many [other] books might offer [as much] good advice
to the practical man as these of Sorel. It is rare that social reality is so ardently
brought to light in its multiple and fleeting aspects." [22]

What especially interested Croce, caught up as he was in the desire to re-
juvenate Italian society, was Sorel's teachings on Christianity, his comparison of

socialism with Christianity. Thus, in 1907 Croce wrote a long review of Sorel's recently published *Le système historique de Renan.*[23]

In socialism Croce saw not the improved material life of the proletariat, but moral regeneration for all society. To increase material comforts, to simply share more of the same decadent bourgeois values with the proletariat, would not advance civilization one whit.

> It must be said that Sorel has grasped the essential problem. The proletarian movement excites interest not certainly insofar as it is a simple search for improved material benefits, of a more comfortable life . . . but insofar as it augurs the formation of a further form of human society by virtue of a new social class entering society. The theoreticians of socialism usually affirm that the proletariat wants to imitate the bourgeoisie.[24]

Sorel did not. He went back to the real model of socialism: Christianity.

> The study of the proletarian movement has led Sorel to turn his attention . . . to the origins of Christianity [not simply to point out the superficial similarities in] the ideas of brotherhood, justice, and property relationships. The relationship studied by Sorel is far more important and real. Christianity was precisely an infusion of new life [a "singular and instructive case of the regeneration of society" reads Croce's revised edition in *Conversazione critiche*]; it was a beginning. Ancient civilization presented . . . a general decadence of internal life. . . . Christianity began a truly new era. One could say that it carried to the Aryan populations a rebirth.[25]

This rebirth recalled to Croce, as it did to Sorel, the *ricorsi* of Vico, during which civilizations, having fallen, arise again to take "the course the nations run."[26] Such an agreeable analysis of the past and such a profound understanding of the course to take in the present led Croce to assert that Sorel's book itself was "a *ricorso,* that is, it brings back history in its internal nature: as the research of past life that is also present life and a clarification of those parts of the past which, depending on the various historical periods, arouse greatest and most lively interest."[27] The review so pleased Croce that he used it for the introduction to Sorel's *Reflections on Violence,* which Croce caused to be printed in Italy in 1909.[28] And the introduction so pleased Mussolini that he reviewed the book favorably in *Il popolo* of Trent,[29] linking Croce and Sorel, for "both are opposed to superficial positivism as also to metaphysical nebulousness; both teach man that life is struggle, sacrifice, conquest, and continuous overcoming of the self."[30]

When in the next year, 1908, Sorel published his new work, *The Illusion of*

Progress, [31] Croce again pointed out the similarity between his own doctrine and that of Sorel, a similarity so striking as to shatter any notion that Croce in those years was an ally of Prime Minister Giolitti. [32] Referring again to Sorel's attraction to realism, his refusal to propound or accept political dogma in a world so fleeting that no dogma could be effective, Croce lauded Sorel's assault upon "bourgeois philosophy," notions of progress and other "Cartesian-Encyclopedist" ideas. The bourgeois concept of progress is "not so much a concept as a recipe for inebriating the spiritual and moral forces of men." [33] Lest anyone feel these ideas applied only to France and not to Giolittian Italy, Croce advised his compatriots that the Italian bourgeoisie too had been as corrupted by Enlightenment slogans as the French: "French democracy has produced a great effect also in Italy and now regains vigor among us from beyond the Alps ... [therefore] the book that we have discussed has contemporary value also for Italy." [34]

As Gramsci has noted, the effect of Croce's "revision" of socialism was to detach it from historical materialism, certainly historical materialism à la Labriola, [35] and this separation certainly contributed "to the loss of faith by Italian socialists in the scientific content of Marxism." [36] The same may be said for Croce's separation of socialism from reformist positivism. What does not seem to be appreciated, however, is that this was not, certainly in the first decade of this century, meant as a conservative reaction against Marxism but quite the opposite.

Sorel represented a resurgence, an assault against bourgeois morality and decadence. It was "the affirmation of an austere, serious morality, divested of pomposity and chitchat, a combative morality, acting to preserve the life of the forces that move history and impede those that stagnate and corrupt it." [37]

This "quasi-Kantian" morality urged workers to develop moral character and steel themselves for the fight. Sorel never ceased to admonish the proletariat for their loose morals, addiction to alcohol, and general laziness. Adherence to the counsel of Sorel was far more likely to produce revolt than the notions of Labriola and Turati, which promised only material comforts. For Croce and Sorel it would be a revolution not like that of 1789 or even 1917; rather, its nearest kin was the Revolution of the Saints in 1640, an apocalyptic upheaval to restore moral passion and zeal to society. Croce felt both Labriola and Turati were incapable of inspiring this change. Too much can be made of the fact that Croce ceased in 1904 his collaboration with *Avanti!* and began to write in Sidney Sonnino's *Giornale d'Italia.* [38] This does not mean that he became a conservative but that he could no longer support the tepid revisionism of *Avanti!*. Since for the next ten years he popularized Sorel's doctrine of revolution against the state, it is obvious that he could not, or would not, do this in Prime Minister

Giolitti's own *Tribuno.* Hence, he began to write in his friend and fellow southerner Sonnino's *Giornale d'Italia*–as, for that matter, did Labriola. [39]

It was Croce himself who explained his real feelings about Marxism and about the course of history at that time. As Croce saw it, the history of modern socialism had begun with the demise of the utopian socialists at the hands of Marx in 1849 and the 1850s: not "Marx the economist and Marx the philosopher . . . but Marx the agitator and *politico,* who is the true Marx of socialism." As to Marx the "economist" and Marx the "philosopher," that was so much "fantasy of dreams and poetry," for Marx as a thinker was *also* a utopian. [40] Marx's economy and his historical materialism were simply fantasies, abstractions having nothing to do with reality and containing no scientific truth whatever. The true Marx is the Marx of agitation, violence, class war, and class hatred. And yet the true Marx, the violent agitator, did not last in socialism. Instead, he was replaced by reformism. Socialism thus "degenerated into reformism and the loudmouthed [*parolaio*] integralism of [Enrico] Ferri." True Marxism was only to be reborn in "syndicalism," which was "pure Marxist socialism. . . . I admired Sorel; I recognized that socialism, if it was to be, had to be of that variety and none other." [41] In his own way, then, Croce helped to make Sorelian voluntarism respectable and at the same time inserted himself into Marxist circles.

This is the period of the first real revisionism in Italy. Enzo Santarelli has argued that a good part of the revisionism in this period was not in ideas but in politics–that is, in the politics of Turatian and Bernsteinian pragmatism. [42] Yet while it is true that this nonrevolutionary revisionism also contributed to the ideological troubles of Marxism, it would be a mistake—especially in the light of later events in Italy—to underrate the significance of issues raised by Croce. Positivism, pragmatism, and reformism did not in fact win favor throughout the Italian Socialist party. A large portion of that party (and of the nation) succumbed to a form of syndicalist voluntarism. "The [Socialist] party's function" as a guide, wrote Giuseppe Mammarella, "was diminished before the growing tide of the syndicalist movement." [43] One reason for this was certainly Croce's authorization of such a view of Marxism. "*Critica sociale* seemed to shrink before *La critica,*" wrote Santarelli. "Croce had connections with the most daring and resourceful intellectual groups in the country," and all the young men who might otherwise have entered reformist socialism "directly or indirectly [fell under] the vast orbit of Crocean thought." [44] Croce suddenly found himself at the head of that longed-for cultural renewal.

It was not only outside the party that Croce attracted so much attention. In 1905 no less a figure than Giuseppe Rensi began to take account of this

"Rebirth of Idealism." His article appeared in Turati's *Critica sociale.* [45] Rensi began with what at first appeared a traditional Crocean-Labriolan attack upon any deterministic interpretations of historical materialism and a plea for the reacquisition of the "autonomy and efficacy of political action." But Rensi's intentions were rather more than this. To him historical materialism itself was unworthy of socialism and would have to be jettisoned. "Historical materialism deludes itself," he wrote, in thinking that it has discovered the "laws" of society. The "real content" of society "entirely escapes it. . . . Therefore the conclusions of historical materialism are a blind alley." [46]

Rensi therefore proposed that the socialists (and everyone else) adopt the world view of Crocean and Gentilean idealism, because it "regives to us the autonomy of the human spirit." Thus, he concluded, "for us the idealist movement . . . gives . . . new sustenance and new comfort." [47] It was the habit, as Petronio noted, of the editors of *Critica sociale* to append a note to articles with which they disagreed. Here, however, there was nothing. Since it is impossible to believe that Turati had become an idealist, one can only conclude that he thought the issue irrelevant.

In 1909, writing in the pages of Turati's *Critica sociale,* Ettore Marchiolli, another "socialist," recommended the adoption of Croce's idealism. He began his essay with a comment that indicates the general ignorance of the Socialists about the important ideological rift between Croce and Labriola. To Marchiolli, Croce's 1898 essay "on historical materialism, next to those of Labriola, remains the best that has been written in Italy on the argument." It is again emblematic of the acceptance of Croceanism with Socialist party ranks. Marchiolli then went on to suggest the great advantage of adopting an idealist Crocean socialism.

> After having been retarded for so long on the beaches of sensistic positivism, [modern thought had now set out on] the sunlit bank where the idea has built its serene temple. . . . [Croce] is not only the literary critic and the formidable erudite whom you can admire every two months in the magazine he directs, but is happily gifted with dialectical power and with that *rara mens philosophica* that knows how to combine in systematic synthesis the multiplicity and the particular. . . . Here we behold . . . a true and proper reconciliation of theory and practice. [48]

Oddly there was again no word of disagreement from the positivist editors.

What made the new idealism of Croce (and Gentile) so appealing was that it seemed to offer the best of all possible worlds to discontented intellectuals. To those discontent with determinism, idealism offered spontaneity; to those discontent with materialism, idealism offered art and creativity; and finally, to those discontent with Labriola, the idealists offered proof that man was not a mere material creature. It is no wonder that many Marxists wished to infuse their historical materialism with Croce rather than remain grounded in Labriola's system. Croce offered so much more!

Speaking of the "grave" philosophical conditions elsewhere in Europe, of the "hunger" for a philosophical "system," Giuseppe Prezzolini, editor of *Leonardo,* compared Italy with the wasteland to the north.

> In Italy! This is our fortune: to have Croce. His merit . . . is precisely in the fact that he has a system. See how he is right, how his figure dominates. See how he could do what Bergson could not do. . . . Croce [has given] . . . *a total impulse* to our culture and to our nation. . . . I am a Crocean. Many are more Crocean than I, but they do not wish to confess because they do not know how to give the world even a part of what that world, through Croce, has given them. . . . It is the security, it is the certainty, it is the substance of faith, that I find in Croce that matters to me.[49]

In 1914 Angelo Crespi wrote a long article in *Critica sociale* in which he too defended idealism.

> In a time when socialism seemed to be finished and its philosophical bases shaken, the minds of most people, and especially of the young . . . , drew from historical idealism and its philosophy and from the concept of the nation an antithesis to both individualistic atomism and class anarchism. . . . It would be a grave error to be, to become, or to continue to be, let's say, positivists, just because the nationalists are of the contrary view.[50]

It was at this point that Claudio Treves chose to add a footnote in which he defended positivism; but, he added, typically, that Crespi and others "exaggerate . . . the practical efficacy of philosophy on the action of men. . . . Nevertheless the noble wishful words of Angelo Crespi have all our approval."[51] That was in April 1914. The July issue of *Critica sociale* came out three days after Germany had declared war on Russia. In that issue Agostino Lanzillo wrote a long paean to Alfredo Oriani,[52] the nationalist darling of the then Socialist Mussolini and to Oriani's recently published new book *La lotta politica.* Oriani had died in 1909 without achieving much success, but discovered by Croce in 1909, Oriani now appeared in, of all places, *Critica sociale,* praised by Lanzillo, who saw Oriani as nationalizing socialism.

This time, however, some interesting remarks followed Lanzillo's article on Oriani. These condemned Oriani and the nationalists, concluding: "The proletariat is alone; the bourgeoisie is reunited; Senator Croce pontificates."[53]

By 1914 socialism as a theoretical system had suffered severe and prolonged attacks. These, perhaps, did not jostle the faith of men like Treves, who acknowledged that ideas and their effects can be exaggerated, nor perhaps did the jostling disturb the rank and file in any direct way; but among the intellectuals seeking to justify and rationalize their own ideas and to prepare a defense against syndicalism and Mussolini, the assault of the idealists was difficult to cope with. One such figure was Tullio Collucci. Summing up the era in a long article in *Critica sociale,* he observed: "The present moment is called skepticism. . . . Truths have become garments that one puts on or takes off at will." And yet, he did not call for a return to Marx, to Labriola, for he too had seen that historical materialism was a mere canon of historical interpretation unrelated to practical socialism. Instead, Collucci ended his article with what was to be the anxious plea not only of a man but of a party. He ended, in short, with a question: "Socialism . . . implores, who will give me a faith?" [54] The faith was to be supplied by the idealists, nationalists, and radicals on the right, who, with the receding of socialism, arose and gained strength after 1910.

7 BENEDETTO CROCE:
THE OTHERWORLDLINESS OF
ABSOLUTE HISTORICISM

Between the years 1902 and 1907 Croce was to make two major revisions of his Philosophy of Spirit, adding to the *Estetica* two new volumes. These revisions allow one to see, if not the details of the final form of the Philosophy of Spirit, at least its general configuration. It is through an understanding of these revisions that we shall see the reasons for Croce's declining popularity on the eve of World War I.

The first major revision involved the removal of science from the category of philosophy-science and its demotion to a mere practical activity governed by the spirit as a whole—quite as De Sanctis and Spaventa had envisioned. The second revision involved the removal of history from the aesthetic category and its placement in the philosophical category. Indeed, in the final scheme of things, history exhausted the philosophical category.

In its original conception, the *Estetica* of 1902 was designed, as Croce pointed out, to be a complete statement of the Philosophy of Spirit.[1] Yet,

> On reading the galley proofs for that volume, two things became evident; first, that I could not leave it without certain further developments, applications, exemplifications, and related discussions and polemics; second, that the book into which it seemed to me I had emptied my mind of all its accumulated thought, had instead left me filled again with philosophy, or rather with doubts and problems, especially about the other forms of spirit.[2]

Croce's views on science and philosophy began to undergo a change just after the founding of *La critica*. Since his 1893 essay he had maintained that science, like philosophy, dealt with universals or concepts. The equation was maintained in the *Estetica* of 1902[3] but had become somewhat forced. Science meant, not only to Croce but to most persons at that time, positivism, and Croce's antipathy to positivism, combined with his admiration for philosophy, which he equated with the Italian tradition of "idealism," forced him after the turn of the century into separating "science" from philosophy. Croce saw positivism as an outgrowth of the Enlightenment and, as such, nothing but a series of universal statements devoid of particular references. Like Vico, De Sanctis, and Spaventa before him, Croce could not abide what seemed never to deal with particularity. It was only that in the first three men particularity meant concreteness, while in Croce this had been lost. The *Estetica,* with its constant stress upon the individual work of art, its defiance of systems and schemes of classifying "types" of art, emphasized particularity at the expense of abstract definitions; but it also, through its reliance upon intuition, its blurring of the distinction between the real and the imaginary, emphasized particularity at the expense of concreteness, at the expense of reality. For Croce the need to avoid abstraction took precedence over all other needs and hence his growing hostility toward science or positivism.

> Like any man, even I have done or at least written some foolish things [but] . . . I have never been a positivist. It was not easy to remain immune to positivism . . . [but I have always had] an invincible repugnance against positivism and now that I look for the reasons for this I notice without doubt that the first of these [came from reading the] celebrated positivists and [finding only] an incoherent hoard of trivial facts.[4]

When the positivists like Tarozzi and Marchesini, yearning for a taste of liberty promised by idealism, broke with Ardigò's rigid determinism and sought to incorporate idealism into positivism, Croce erupted in anger.

> Why do hints and words of blame against professorial habits and universities occur so often amongst our pages? . . . You, in good faith, do you really propound a determinate order of ideas? . . . Does idealism seem to prevail? And so the positivists make themselves into idealists and offer their *positivismo idealistico* to the market. Does pragmatism require a little attention? And so the Thomists become pragmatists. . . . In the universities adventurers without conscience proceed, ready to defend any thesis, because they are supported by men who are deficient, if not mentally, at least practically.[5]

In May of 1903 Croce wrote to Vossler that he intended to make a thorough investigation of science, and in July that he had decided to "devalue" science and make it "practical" rather than "theoretic."[6] This removal of science from the realm of conceptual thought to that of practice,[7] elaborated at length in the

Philosophy of the Practical of 1908 and the *Logic* of 1909, remained Croce's final thought on the matter.[8] The most logical explanation for Croce's demotion of science seems to be that which Croce himself had set out in the *Estetica:* empirical distinctions were arbitrary and had no philosophical justification or pertinence. His hostility toward a division of literature into epic, tragic, comic, and so forth was carried over into his judgments about science; its distinctions and evaluations, its division of life into genus, species, family, and so forth were arbitrary. Thus, in his polemic with Francesco De Sarlo,[9] who wished to reconcile the "science" of psychology with philosophy, Croce wrote that the classifications of science are arbitrary. "To be able to *choose* this or that basis of division (the organs of nutrition, or reproduction, etc. or this or that particular part of the organs or functions) is precisely the arbitrary element and hence the extraneous [element] that is introduced. In philosophy, choice is excluded."[10]

It was Bernardo Varisco, that erratic "positivist" later transformed into a "Thomist,"[11] who responded to Croce in a long article entitled, with self-conscious irony, "The End of Positivism." "Positivism, they say, is dying," he wrote, citing Croce, but "in fact the number of those who work to raise it from the grave grows every day."[12] He went on to warn Croce that philosophy had to take account of the findings of science. Croce, with his notion that "the philosopher need only consider his own reflections without introducing to them any element provided by science, without worrying whether the results arrived at are compatible with what the sciences have asserted," would lead philosophy "back to the Middle Ages."[13]

Varisco's voice, like that of De Sarlo and even of Vossler,[14] was lost in the rising tide of idealism. "The idealist philosophical currents [Croce and Gentile]," noted Gramsci, "have brought about a first step [*un primo processo*] in the isolation of the scientists [natural and exact science] from the world of culture. Philosophy and science were separated and the scientists have lost much of their prestige."[15]

Having removed science from the theoretical realm, Croce now turned his attention back to theory to see what remained. He began the investigation by coming to grips with Hegel. Naples had long been regarded as the Italian center of Hegelianism, and in fact Croce and his young colleague Gentile have long been regarded as the modern celebrants of a Hegelian tradition that stretched back to De Sanctis and Spaventa. By the beginning of the twentieth century, however, the term Hegelian had become so broad and illusive that it did little more than earmark its participants as "antipositivists," and men as disparate as Vera, Labriola, De Meis, Spaventa, and De Sanctis were accommodated within its ranks. By 1904, Croce had decided that Hegel deserved a

"Christian burial." Croce did not mean by this that Hegel had to be abandoned or forgotten but rather that the vital part of Hegel had to be separated from the moribund. Hegel had been the "principal representative of the idealist movement" set in motion by Kant. He had liberated the Kantian synthetic a priori from "the *caput mortuum* of the thing-in-itself and the other *caput mortuum* of practical reason." Hegel had recognized that "where man was unable to know everything . . . he was unable to know anything." It was therefore necessary, Croce said, after Spaventa, to struggle back to Hegel, for after him the world had again been separated into appearance and reality, matter and spirit, and the "priests in the laboratory" along with the "priests upon the altar" had rent the world into two unknowns.[16]

To return to the vital aspects of Hegelian thought required a critical examination of Hegel so that the rest might be entombed. In 1906 Croce published his *What is Living and What is Dead in the Philosophy of Hegel.*[17] As an aspect of Croce's own thought the book on Hegel represented a further investigation of the category of philosophy. With the placement of science in the world of practice and the will, philosophy was purged, in Croce, of its purely practical aspects. Philosophy became, therefore, the method by which one examined the real. In this respect Croce felt that, at least where Hegel was consistent, one could glean a good deal from Hegelian philosophy. The first part of the text dealt therefore with the "living" part of Hegel, his philosophy as explanation of the real, as *historical* explanation. Hegel's had been an all-encompassing philosophy aimed at closing the gaps in knowledge opened by Kant's practical reason, the thing-in-itself, and the Enlightenment insistence upon placing the ideal above the historical flux. In Hegel, by contrast, the real and the rational coincided and so, for Croce, Hegel appeared as the opponent of all abstraction. The philosophy of Hegel did not deal with anything but the real, with history. It was, in short, an exposition of and an explanation of the fact that the "process" of thought is the same as the "process" of events. Mind and the world are of the same rationality, and hence all dualism is banished in a history that makes the real and the possible synonymous. For Hegel and for Croce, *"all history becomes sacred history."*[18]

Hegel was thus "the great enemy of the discontented with life, of those sensitive souls who perpetually declaim and agitate in the name of a reason and virtue"[19] outside the real. He was therefore the "enemy of *encyclopedic humanitarianism*" and "*Kantian abstractness.*"[20] Hegel "hates the *Sollen,* the 'ought to be,'" and "the destiny of that 'ought to be' is to become wearisome, as do all the most beautiful words (justice, virtue, duty, morality, liberty, etc.)."[21]

Croce did not mean here, any more than Hegel did, that life was passive and man was to remain an observer of the real rather than a participant in the possible. Croce, perhaps, here drew upon not only his reading of Hegel but his reading of Sorel. The world moved forward because of passion. The *Sollen,* the ideal, was banished from philosophy but not from practical life; rather, it was the most fiery aspect of that life. For purposes of philosophy, however, Croce divided the past from the present: the former was the realm of philosophy; the latter, the realm of passion and the will. History would reconcile the two worlds at twilight. In the present man must act, for ideals did not sit in repose above the cause of events. The "ought to be" was not an ideal above the fray but one that worked itself out in the concrete course of events. Men must "not fear soiling the purity of the idea by translating it into deed."[22] This translation into deed was done through the will, through passion—not through philosophy. "Nothing can be achieved if it does not become a passion of man: Nothing great can be done without passion."[23] It was a continuation of the theme Croce had found in Marx—not Marx the philosopher, but Marx the Machiavelli of the proletariat. This notion had come to fruition in Sorel. The myth stirred men's passions and forced them to labor in this world. An ideal needed to be catalytic and was always in danger of becoming soporific when men devoted their energy to working out the details of action rather than in implementing it.

The will operated independently from philosophy then, and Croce noted that in Hegel himself this was true. There was a "historical individual, the Hegel who took part, under certain determinate conditions, in the social and political problems of his time and of his nation," and there was "the philosopher Hegel" whose "conception of life was so philosophical that conservation, revolution, and restoration, each in turn, finds its justification in it."[24]

Croce noted, too, that Hegel, like Vico before him, had seen that the sacred aspect of history meant that individual wills were often frustrated by the greater will of history. Thus, Hegel's *List der Vernunft,* cunning of reason, and Vico's providence, became, like Mandeville's idea in the *Fable of the Bees: Private Vices, Public Benefits,* the force which—as we *reflect back upon it*—alone was rational. "What does it matter that men are unconscious of what they do?" asked Croce. "The fact is not therefore less rational."[25]

Croce then turned to what he considered "dead" in Hegel, and, as it turned out, far more was dead than alive. Hegel had gone wrong because he had taken the dialectic of opposites, adequate for explaining opposing concepts such as being and nothing, true and false, good and evil, and extended it to distinct concepts such as art and philosophy, religion and ethics. For Hegel, the march of spirit was the march of philosophy as it absorbed art, science, religion, and other inferior forms of reason. But art and philosophy were not opposites like being and nothing.

> Our thought finds itself . . . face to face not only with opposite but distinct concepts. . . . The logical category of distinction is one theory; the category of opposition is another. . . . Two distinct concepts unite with one another, although they are distinct; but two opposite concepts seem to exclude each other. Where one enters, the other totally disappears. A distinct concept is presupposed by and lived in its other. . . . An opposite concept is slain by its opposite.[26]

Hegel, it appeared to Croce, had gone wrong from the very beginning of his *Logic* when he set out the two notions of being and nothing and resolved them into becoming. The two concepts of being and nothing were abstractions which, if preserved at all, were preserved only metaphysically in becoming.[27] Croce began his own *Logic* not with two abstract opposites but with two concrete distincts: art and philosophy. The spirit begins by intuiting particulars, and finding this dissatisfying or inadequate, it passes on to philosophy.[28] This did not, as we have seen, resolve forever the inferior into the superior mode of thought. On the contrary, Croce said man can and continually does return to intuition, to art. Artistic intuition remains throughout time a distinct and uncancelable "moment" in man's spiritual activity. The reason Hegel had been misled, then, was that he had not taken two distincts as the basics of his dialectic, but two opposites.

> Hegel did not make this most important distinction . . . between the theory of opposites and the theory of distincts. *He conceived the connection of these* [distincts] *in the manner of the dialectic of opposites.* The theory of distincts and the theory of opposites became for him one and the same.[29]

Thus Croce separated himself from Hegel over the issue of the dialectic and especially over the implications of the Hegelian dialectical synthesis.[30] In a way it is testimony to Croce's consistency. He had rejected Labriola's Marx because it had seemed unilateral in its resolution of every human aspect into economics. He now rejected Hegel's thought because it, too, was unilateral, resolving man's particular activities into philosophy. For Croce, especially the Croce before 1928, each human activity, though related, had its own raison d'être and its own logic. As art had to be preserved from ethics, economics, and so forth, so too did philosophy. Even though Croce was not, in 1906, entirely certain about the exact role played by philosophy, he was certain of its independence from morality, art, and from practical life. Vico and Hegel had been wrong in regarding art as an inferior mode of thought destined to be overcome in time. "This is *the first case of that abuse of the triadic form* which has offended and still offends so seriously all who approach the system of Hegel."[31]

From this first abuse, Croce said, a second great abuse followed. The first abuse had been to resolve art into philosophy. The second abuse was to force nature and man's history into the triadic dialectic. Hegel's logic, Croce said, was replete with the arbitrary imposition of the thesis-antithesis-synthesis formula upon events that little felt the effect of that formula. Historical judgments dealt with facts and could not, as Croce said to Labriola, be forced into a philosophy of history, for that would inevitably lead to raising the philosophy over and above the events. For Croce history, at this point, was therefore autonomous from philosophy.

> The idea of a philosophy of history is the nonrecognition of the autonomy of historiography to the advantage of abstract philosophy. Whenever such a claim is made, one seems to hear the bells tolling for the death of the history of the historians. The historians . . . rebel with violence when anyone talks to them of a philosophy of history, of some sort of speculative method of knowing history, or when the attempt is made to persuade them to consign [their] labor . . . to the hands of philosophers who are not historians, to revise and complete it. . . . Before Hegel seeks the data of facts, he knows what they must be; he knows them in anticipation.[32]

Let us not enter into the dispute over whether Hegel discovered the way events worked before he discovered his logic or vice versa. It is enough here to note that in Hegel Croce had found the same nemesis he had found in Labriola: a "philosophy of history," and he rejected it as he would for the rest of his life. A human providence, a human *List der Vernunft,* very well; but no one, in Croce's view, could impose any pattern or end upon that cunning of providence.

Croce then went on to dispute both Hegel and Schelling's attempt to resolve nature and science into philosophy. Science, Croce had already decided, was practical, not, like art or religion, an inferior mode of reasoning awaiting resolution in philosophy but an autonomous activity.[33] Croce here disputed Hegel's whole concept of a philosophy of nature. For Hegel nature had no history, and this is why it was susceptible to a greater or lesser extent to the study of physics. Yet since in Hegel no knowledge could stand outside the dialectic, physics had to be conceived, like art and religion, as an inferior form of reasoning awaiting resolution in philosophy. But this, according to Croce, was to make the same error Hegel had made before: to have philosophy absorb art, he had had to conceive of art as the opposite of philosophy rather than as its distinct. Here, in his philosophy of nature, Hegel now made science appear as the opposite of philosophy rather than as distinct. Once this had been done, science, like art and religion, disappeared into philosophy. The only way, said Croce, to make nature the opposite of philosophy was to conceive "nature as constructed and mummified into abstract classes and concepts."[34] That is to say, nature had no history, no development. How could nature then be a form of knowledge? asked Croce.

"If all reality be movement and development, how can a part of reality ever be conceived which is not . . . in the process of becoming?"[35] Croce's answer had been to place nature, or our conception of nature, science, in an autonomous spiritual category that was distinct from philosophy—the practical. This severe circumscription of science to the realm of mere technique reflected Croce's determination to eclipse science and positivism as all-encompassing "philosophies."

Hence "the second great abuse" of Hegel was his unwillingness to recognize the autonomy of history and science from the triadic dialectic, in other words, his determination to include these two categories which have their own logic, as art had its own logic, in the category of the dialectic of opposites. On this issue then Croce parted company with Hegel and with Vico as well. For in Vico nature, being made by God, was beyond the ken of man. Croce's idealism here reached its zenith, including within it not only man and his history, but nature as it was understood by man. Yet there is no panlogism in Croce, for the panlogism of Hegel is replaced by spiritual functions which preserve their own distinct spheres, spheres which Croce would later connect, but never eliminate.

Hegel's determination to extend the dialectic of opposites into areas where it did not apply constituted for Croce the supreme satirization of the triadic method. "The Hegelian dialectic has often been satirized, but no satire can compare with that which the author himself unconsciously gives when he tries to think of Africa, Asia, and Europe, or the hand, the nose, and the ear, or family, patrimony, paternal authority and the last will and testament with the same rhythm with which he had thought of being, nothing, and becoming."[36] It was Hegel's theological devotion to his system that bothered Croce, as it had bothered De Sanctis, for the devotion to the triad was a subtraction from the devotion that ought to have been given to the worldly life of man.[37]

In the final analysis, however, Croce felt that Hegel failed because he had fallen back into dualism, and his philosophy was therefore rent into two factions: those who accepted the physics and materialism of the philosophy of nature and made of it an immanent materialism, and those who accepted the philosophy of the Logos and made of it a transcendent God. This is the

> reason for the division of the Hegelian school into a right and left and for the eventual extensions of the latter to an extreme left. The right wing interpreted Hegel theistically. The subject, the Logos of Hegel, was the personal God. . . . The left wing [Labriola] was opposed to all transcendence and to the whole

conception of a personal God. It emphasized the character of immanence in
the system, and finally came to sympathize with philosophical materialism
insofar as this has, in its own way, an immanent rather than a transcendent
character. It would be impossible to decide which of these two interpretations
was more faithful to the thought of Hegel; for both were opposed and hostile
to each other precisely because contradictory.[38]

The central purpose of Croce's mature thought was to overcome this dualism
by finding room within the spirit for the distinct forms of science, art, philosophy,
history, practice, and ethics while avoiding the transcendent Logos and the built-
in *corsi* and *ricorsi* of Vico. This is the subject of two works that appeared in 1908
and 1909: *The Philosophy of the Practical: Economic and Ethic* and *Logic as
Science of the Pure Concept.*

The *Logic* had as its primary purpose the explanation of one aspect of man's
activity: philosophical judgment. It was the first of Croce's investigations of the
theoretical realm after science had been made a practical activity, and its point
was to establish a new concept of philosophy, a philosophy that explained
the past but because of its hostility to philosophy of history, made no observations about either the present or the future. Indeed, one of its primary purposes
was to deny the possibility of making a meaningful statement about the future,
about something that did not yet exist. Nevertheless, despite this rejection of one
aspect of Hegel and Vico, Croce returned to precisely the dilemma raised by
Vico two hundred years earlier: philosophy was, or had always been, one-sided.
It yielded up judgments that were either synthetic or a priori. Mathematics, for
example, was abstract, analytic, and deductive. Its propositions were universal and
necessary, but they lacked concreteness. Empirical knowledge, on the other
hand, was inductive and synthetic, but its propositions were neither necessary nor
universal. Mathematical knowledge paid no attention to sense experience, and
empiricism paid attention to it alone.

A new form of knowledge was therefore required, a form not based upon
fragmentary truths or abstractions but one that dealt with concrete reality and
yielded absolute and universal truths, for a true philosophy would not separate
the universal and the concrete. The task of the *Logic* was to show that the hiatus
between the a priori and the a posteriori did not exist, that "spirit is nothing
but the synthesis a priori."[39] Croce argued that concrete judgments implied
or presupposed universal judgments and that, similarly, universal judgments
implied or presupposed concrete judgments. As Croce put it, the universal
and the concrete judgments were the same thing.

The statement of fact, or the "individual judgment" as Croce called it, was
distinguished from the analytic or definitional and universal statement because

it contained *something more than a mere definition;* it contained an "individual or representative element, which in being transformed into a logical fact does not lose that individuality but rather reaffirms it with more clear distinction."[40] Croce then suggested that this individual factual judgment presupposed a definitive judgment.[41] The factual statement that the man Peter exists, he said, presupposed a definition of man;[42] and so Croce arrived at the conclusion that *every* statement of fact presupposed a definitional and universal statement.[43] Similarly, "if . . . one considers the definition in its concrete reality, one will always find there . . . the representative element and the individual judgment." Croce based this conclusion on what was to be regarded as one of his most important ideas: "Every definition is the response to a question, the solution to a problem," a problem existing in the real, concrete world. A "definition," he asserted, did "not exist in the air," was not to be abstracted from "the where, the when, the individual and the other circumstances of fact."[44] It existed in history. History dealt with the particular event, the single event. Thus, a question elicited a response or, as Croce called it, a definition; but since the question arose under definite historical conditions, it was concrete, synthetic. Thus, Croce wrote:

> The nature of the question colors by itself the response, and . . . a definition, considered in its concreteness, *appears determined by the problem that makes it arise.* Varying the problem, one varies the definitive act. But the question, the problem, the doubt is always individually conditioned: the doubt of the child is not that of the adult; the doubt of the uncultivated man, not that of the cultivated; the doubt of an Italian is not that of a German; and the doubt of a German of 1800 is not that of a German of 1900; *that is to say that the doubt formulated by an individual in a determinate moment is not that which the same individual will formulate a moment later.* To simplify, it is usually said that a single question has been moved as such by many men in various countries and in various times; but by saying this one oversimplifies, one makes an abstraction. *In reality every question is different from every other, and every definition, however constant it sounds and however circumscribed by determinate words, in reality is different from the others,* because even the words, when they seem materially to be the same, are effectively different according to the spiritual diversity of those that pronounce them, for those are individuals and find themselves therefore always in individual and new circumstances.[45]

Thus, he came to the general conclusion that it was impossible to maintain the distinction between the a priori and the a posteriori, that to establish the definition of man required the existence of Peter, and Peter required the definition of man in order to be recognized; and so the two things presupposed each other and were the same.

It seems that there is only one path open to us in these difficulties; and that would seem to be the one of maintaining the conclusion [earlier] adopted; that is, the necessity of the definitive judgment as presupposition of the individual judgment, but also of affirming the necessity of the individual judgment as the presupposition of the definitive.[46]

And so, "every definition is at the same time an individual judgment."[47]

Thus, Croce concluded that there was no distinction between truths of the mind and truths of fact. The only form of truth was the synthetic a priori. The true act of thought, he said,

will be a synthetic analysis, an analytic synthesis, an a posteriori-a priori or, if you please, a synthetic a priori. In such a way the identity established by us between the definitive judgment and the individual judgment ends by assuming a name celebrated in the annals of modern philosophy.[48]

One is reminded of Burke's common law. It is impossible to state the law apart from examples of the law. One cannot explain or even state the "law of equity" apart from its examples, examples that tie it to history and the concrete. Croce was thus an absolute historicist. Where Hegel had reduced history to philosophy, Croce had reduced philosophy to history.

It can be said that with the criticism of transcendental philosophy, philosophy itself, in its autonomy, is dead, because its pretext of autonomy was founded precisely in the character of its metaphysic. What has taken its place is no longer philosophy, but history, or what is the same thing, philosophy insofar as it is history, and history insofar as it is philosophy.[49]

For Croce this was the final separation of "modern philosophy" from Hegelian "theology," the celebration of the abstract at the expense of the concrete. The empty forms of categories of truth, beauty, good, and utility were equated with specific activities of man, and they enjoyed no independent existence.

Every concept exists only insofar as it is thought and enclosed in words, or rather insofar as it is defined, and if the definitions vary, the concept varies also . . . [for the definitions] are the life of the concept.[50]

The nature of truth, beauty, the good, and utility therefore change with our definitions of them; and our definitions are conditioned by time and circumstance, are "always historically conditioned." Thus, as history or reality changes, so the definitions of the concepts change. "By changing history, philosophy also changes; and since history changes at every instant, philosophy is at every instant new."[51]

Croce felt here that he had at last resolved the dilemma of the *Estetica,* for now history could no longer be confused with aesthetics, for it had a category of its own. Moreover, history was no longer purely fancy; it was logical, conceptual, or synthetic a priori. The maze of undifferentiated intuitions, some real, some imaginary, now began to separate for Croce. True intuitions of historical reality were distinguished from the imaginary intuitions of the aesthetic category by synthetic a priori knowledge.

Thus did the *Logic* begin with an attack upon those who had read into the *Estetica* (and who could blame them?) a complete form of knowledge. The intuition, the particular, was, Croce now said, an incomplete form of knowledge of no use in action or life. For that matter, knowledge even in its complete form, since it was of the past, since it could not predict, was of no use in action. Even more disappointing to the aesthetes was the seeming serenity of this historical knowledge, the dispassionate, almost resigned manner in which it contemplated the twilight while ignoring the present.

It was Croce's view that by historicizing the activities of man, by grounding them in the concrete, he had not only avoided the problem of those who lived constantly in the abstract, but that he had also preserved the sanctity of the values, the *bonum, verum, pulchrum.* No longer did they float just out of reach upon the horizon, nor were they to be dismissed as "myths" as the positivists chose to do. They were concrete aspects of life and history, aspects that changed with history, that developed and were enriched by human experience.

> The eternity of every philosophical principle is to be affirmed against those that consider all the propositions as deprived of value and transient . . . because philosophical principles, even though historically conditioned, are not determined effects produced by such conditions, but rather creations of thought that continue to be in and for themselves.[52]

It was not an idea that Croce would ever abandon. Thirty years later in *La storia come pensiero e come azione*—translated for some reason as *History as the Story of Liberty*—Croce explained that the error of the "old" transcendental philosophy was not in its attempt to preserve the spiritual values of the good, the true, and the beautiful from the historical flux but rather in its attempt to separate those values "from the flux and put them in safety in a superior sphere transcending reality, a fantastic solution."[53]

With values preserved, the problem of skepticism vanished, said Croce. Croce derived this conclusion from his earlier observation that every definition was a response to a particular historical problem, was the solution to that problem. There was, he said, an intimate connection between a problem and its solution, for to formulate a problem was to formulate at the same time its solution.

Thus, in his 1919 essay "Sulla filosofia teologizzante," Croce argued that a problem acquired the nature of being a problem only at the point in which it was resolved. He gave the example of whether or not Gemma Donati was a good wife to Dante Alighieri and said that although this was a matter of great interest and debate, it was not a problem because we did not have any correspondence between the two persons which would allow the question to be resolved.[54]

Thus, for Croce skepticism was rejected because one could only be skeptical about what one felt one could not know, and for Croce there was nothing that was real that was not known. This is the converse of Hegel's historicism, for in Hegel the transcendent Logos was outside the world, using man as its instrument and gaining consciousness in the process. In Croce's immanentism, spirit was life *and* absolute consciousness of life. Outside there was nothing, for to avoid the problem of transcendence, Croce conceived the absolute as already realized, or rather as constant absolute realization. Croce's philosophy was, thus, a variation of Voltaire's theme that all that was not susceptible to reason was chimerical. Thus, Cecil Sprigge has argued that Croce was the "spokesman of an anti-metaphysical and anti-utopian Humanism."[55] He celebrated man alone—concrete, historical man. Man defined the nature of the true, the beautiful, the good, and the useful at every instant, according to the historical situation with which he was faced. "The philosopher of our times, like it or not, cannot leap out of the historical conditions in which he lives, or prevent what has happened before him from having happened."[56]

The result of Croce's absolute historicism was a kind of otherworldliness, a kind of indifference which for all its concern with man made man nonetheless isolated and lonely. It was, perhaps, a perfect perspective for a historian but, as Croce maintained, of no use in practical life.

Even turning to that "companion" of the *Logic, The Philosophy of the Practical: Economic and Ethic,* with its return to the theme of passion and the will, with its long reminders that nothing can be done without passion and that reflection is the enemy of action, there, too, one finds a kind of lofty dispassion.

The Philosophy of the Practical[57] was regarded by Croce as one of his greatest philosophical insights. To the historic triad of the true, the good, and the beautiful, Croce added the merely useful.[58]

The conclusions that Croce drew with respect to the connection between the will and the intellect were already implied in the discussion of the *Logic,* the most important of which was that there was only *one* logical category and that that category yielded judgments that were historical.

> It is not enough to say that history is historical judgment but it must be added that *every judgment is historical judgment* or simply history.... The historical

judgment is not only an order of knowledge, but it is knowledge itself, the form that *entirely fills and exhausts* the cognitive field.[59]

All knowledge therefore was of what *had* happened, for that "which is not, is not an object of knowledge," and the future "is" not. Hence "all knowledge of the action and of the deed follows and does not precede the action and the deed."[60]

Croce was quick to draw the appropriate corollary. Our knowledge of history was (obviously) of no use in the present. Man "remembers judgments" which he has made in the past, "which are afterwards collected into abstract formulae," but these "formulae do not possess any absolute value in the single concrete situation: in fact, they can even be exchanged or substituted for formulae that affirm their opposite."[61]

Since knowledge, which can only be historical, cannot guide man in his actions, Croce concluded that man's actions were responses to particular historical situations, responses shaped by man but tied to history, for "action is necessitated or always conditioned by a situation and precisely by that situation in which it arises."[62] It was an individual's passion, his religion, which shaped the manner in which he perceived the situation and responded to it. Thus, Croce concluded, as De Sanctis concluded, that it was always necessary to have a conception of life and a faith.

We remain inert if something does not intervene that rouses [us] to action, something analogous to the inspiration that makes a shiver of joy and of voluptuousness through the veins of the artist. If the will be not engaged, every argument, however plausible it may seem, every situation, however clear, remains pure theory.[63]

Although the title of the work alluded to some resolution of man's ethical life, the work itself, by tying every response to a historical situation while stressing the uniqueness of that situation, did little to assuage the doubts and fears of that new generation of men born after the eclipse of religion, nature, and metaphysics in general. Far from proving a guide, the work shifted from the individual perspective of the *Estetica* to a kind of cosmic indifference to the individual.

Croce's whole perspective at this point was to shift emphasis away from ethics and metaphysics. Art, philosophy-history, the useful and the ethical, each had its own logic and its own spheres, and an infusion of ethics into the other realm was specifically denounced. The result was that ethics proved to be a merely formal category placed in the practical, one is tempted to say, for purposes of pure symmetry rather than—as an ethic must be—as a guide, a limit, to one's activities in general. But Croce was so much the child of Machiavelli and so much the enemy of eighteenth-century humanitarianism that he rejected any limits at all. This was the opposite of the idea that ethics are to be adhered to except on those rare occasions when because of a unique situation or some political necessity, they must be suspended. Here Croce said instead that every situation was unique, and hence a general morality can never apply. Morality was, instead, a cosmic justification given ex post facto to the acts of a man, or better, of an age.

> From the cosmic point of view from which we now speak. . . . [The] web of history is composed of labors to which all collaborate; but it is not the work and cannot be the purpose of any one of them in particular, because each one is exclusively intent on his own particular work, and only in *rem suam agere,* does he also do the business of the world. History is happening and as has been seen . . . it always transcends individuals. . . . [Yet] the supreme rationality that guides the course of history should not . . . be conceived as the work of a transcendent intelligence or providence, as is the case in religious or semifanciful thought. [For] if history be rationality, the providence certainly directs it; but of such a kind as becomes actual in individuals, and acts not on them but in them.[64]

One might well wonder, however, at the meaning of this "rationality" that could not be tested against anything rational, that avoided philosophy of history as well as any transcendent constant above the fray. How was one to know it was rational? In Vico and Hegel rationality had meant conformity with the universal, a conformity evident only to the historian—but at least evident. In Croce history seemed to mean only movement, the idea of "progress" being supported only by Croce's faith. This faith in reason, in a progress that conformed to no law of progress, cut Croce off from the men of action who insisted upon inserting themselves into daily life. It appeared to them that Croce had assumed a kind of otherworldliness, a kind of condescension which the historian might conceivably feel toward men of another era, but which was distinctly out of place when directed at one's own. Those men of action believed that philosophy ought to shed light on this world. Croce saw philosophy[65] not as clarifying this world, but as arising from the lack of clarity in the world. It did not clarify the practical; it originated in the practical, and as such it could only tell us where we had been and why we were where we were. To those in search of a faith this was no comfort. "Life," Croce was fond of saying, "is not worth living if, when at the rendering of accounts, one does not present an account of work accomplished for the enrichment, elevation, and splendor of the society to which one belongs: a job of any sort, worker or manager, farmer or scientist, industrialist or poet (because all are of equal importance and equal prestige, one does not stand without another)."[66] Equal? Yes, of course, but there was in Croce's egalitarianism a sort of, well, Brobdingnagianism which made ordinary mortals at best a bit weary and at worst a bit—enraged. Yes, said Croce, he too understood the problems of the young, torn between one course and another, one truth and another, but "there has been injustice and villainy ever since the world was a world." Even, alas, knowing the secret of life was no help, for, as Goethe observed, "What is inherited from the father it is necessary to earn again with one's own efforts. So to the young there is nothing to say except, Go and suffer, you, as those that were young before you, and earn your truth. We would give it to you, but we cannot."[67]

Like De Sanctis before him, Croce found himself urging action and involvement upon persons while at the same time telling them that whatever they did, it would all be for the best. In De Sanctis the message had not been quite so clear, but where it was clear, De Sanctis became not the inspiration for action, not the remedy for a situation, but rather "the conscience of the nation," raised above partisan politics into a kind of loftiness. As had happened to Vico in the eighteenth century, Croce's thought had to be brought back to earth, for ironically it now suffered from the same problem that Croce had found in Labriola: an inability to inspire action. It needed to be historicized, politicized, before it could become anything more than a canon of historical interpretation. This was one of the things that Gramsci had in mind when he wrote out those famous lines in his book *On Historical Materialism and Benedetto Croce*.

> It is necessary to make of the philosophical conception of Croce the very same reduction that the first [Marxist] theorists did for the Hegelian conception. This is the only historical possibility which will permit an adequate rebirth of Marxism. . . . For we Italians, to be the heirs of classical German philosophy means to be the heirs of Crocean philosophy, which is the contemporary world moment of classical German philosophy.[68]

The philosophy of humanism thus described a circle in its development from Vico to Croce, for if Vico had described a philosophy of history and Croce had denied it, the two men joined hands over the centuries in setting out a philosophy that described rather than prescribed; however much the one might have accepted the transcendence the other abhorred, both still surrendered human autonomy to the inevitability of history. And could it be any other way? To make history, with its ceaseless movement, whether cyclical or no, with its inevitable "this too shall pass," the basis of action was to expect the sand to build the castle. Only by grafting onto the Vichian *corsi e ricorsi* or onto the Crocean ceaseless progress the myth of a philosophy of history which had no *ricorsi* but was a *progressus ad infinitum,* and a *progressus* whose final destiny could be envisioned, could history be made to serve the ends, the practical ends, of men, of a certain group of men. "Without religion, or at least without this perspective, man cannot live."

8 THE PROPHET WHO FAILED

"I, as a philosopher and critic," said Croce to his biographer, "do not retreat before any thought however radical and destructive it might seem; and as a man, I accept and promote any elevation of human society even if it pass it through the most dire tests. . . . And yet, when I catch myself dreaming, do you know what aspiration I find deep in my soul? . . . A seventeenth-century Neapolitan convent with its white cells and cloisters and in the middle an orange and lemon grove, and outside the tumult of pompous life beating in vain against the high walls."[1]

Most earlier followers of Croce refused asylum in that Neapolitan cloister. They remembered an earlier Croce, a Croce who had been impassioned with a zeal for a new Italy; and they were determined to break with any system that forced them into the role of mere observers.

The effect of Croce's historicism had been to connect theory and practice only in the past, leaving man in the present with a lay religion that celebrated the past and watched with curiosity, an evidently painless curiosity, the "present tumult of pompous life." Croce had indeed escaped the *corsi* of Vico and the *Weltgeist* of Hegel, had escaped as well the Marxian philosophy of history. The irony was that in escaping abstract philosophy because it took away man's freedom, Croce ended by giving man freedom and no choice as to how he might use it. For Croce man goes through life backwards, the only thing visible to him being the wake of his ship. Unable and unwilling to end his "dialogue with a myth," Croce had ended it with truth. Antonio Gramsci, even as he contemplated another myth, saw the effect.

> Where does all this restless anxiety come from: because action is "blind" and one acts [only] in order to act. Moreover, it is not true that the anxiety is

154

only of the blind "activists"; it happens that the restlessness leads to immo-
bility. . . . It can be said that the anxiety is due to the fact that there is no
connection between theory and practice.[2]

It was a rejection of Croce's Olympianism, of Croce's "betrayal." Positivism
had imprisoned man within inexorable laws; Croce imprisoned man within
history. Croce's early followers found themselves driven now to reject Croce.

Perhaps the first indication of a turning away from Croce was an article by
one of his close associates, Renato Serra, in which, as Croce's biographer quickly
saw, there was "implicit anti-Croceanism." (How many terrible things "Croce
pardoned in Serra and not in others," wrote Nicolini.)[3] The article appeared in
La voce,[4] and it sought, rather clumsily, to make a comparison between Croce
and Carducci. "Let us suppose we have [Croce and Carducci] before us and that
we ask our conscience what can be expected from each." With Croce, he said,
"I could entirely confess my virtues and my faults with absolute sincerity because
his mind is open to everything in the world." And yet Croce was detached.
"What I tell him would not grieve him, but would [arouse his] curiosity." The
mood would be strange to him, simply "a little problem." He would accept it
"with curiosity [and dismiss it] with perhaps a smile." With Croce he could
speak of anything, "and yet if I think about it, I received no satisfaction." "But
with Carducci things would be different. . . . Carducci has anxieties that Croce
does not understand. . . . He [Carducci] knows he is a man, not immortal" while
Croce "is pure thought and you cannot imitate him." Carducci did "not pose as
a hero or a prophet; he confessed humanly his charming passion."[5]

Serra was one of the first to see that Croce, although he listened to these
younger men, to their problems, and had urged them forward, was "pure thought"
untroubled by life outside the cloister. The article by Serra caused somewhat
of a sensation. It was so stunning an event and Serra was so embarrassed that he
wrote quickly to Croce to apologize: "Certainly there was something lacking
in the article—the clear expression of my reverence and affection for you," and
he promised to do "better in another article."[6]

But the article by Serra in December 1910 had provided an example; and in
the next year there came a more dramatic break. In it one sees the very beginning
of Croce's realization that the revolution against positivism was becoming
dangerous, was being translated into action, and had become an end in itself.
The break came with Giuseppe Antonio Borgese.

Borgese, as we have seen, had taken part in that early enthusiasm for the
Crocean *Estetica*. In 1904 he had founded the Florentine journal *Hermes*, which
was, through its director,[7] an expression of the Crocean *Estetica*. Croce had first

discovered Borgese's writing in *Leonardo* and had singled him out as especially acute in aesthetics. *Hermes* was primarily a literary magazine, but with its nationalism[8] and mysticism, its articles on "The Prophets of Race"[9] and "The Religion of Beauty,"[10] it too may be said to have taken part in the cultural revival led by *Leonardo*, *Il regno*, and Croce. An editorial in *Hermes* of 1904 made the connection between *Hermes* and the two other Florentine journals. "Between *Hermes*, *Leonardo*, and *Il regno* there will be an exchange of collaborators. *Leonardo* in a more strictly philosophical area, *Il regno* in a more strictly political area, will pursue ends not far from nor dissimilar to those of *Hermes*."[11]

A close relationship, then, had developed between Croce and Borgese, and Borgese's prestige, as that of his magazine, was helped by the Crocean patronage. A break with Borgese was a serious matter; and it came when Borgese began to see that after the break with positivism, he was still the prisoner of another system—that of Croce. Borgese was one of the first to wish to carry the revolution beyond the point where Croce had stopped. Borgese's "revisionism" became evident in 1911 when he printed a review of Croce's *La filosofia di Giambattista Vico* in the Turin newspaper *La stampa*.[12] "Borgese," Nicolini would write, "felt he had 'arrived' . . . [and so] without having read a single line of the *New Science*, he published a . . . sharp review of Croce's monograph . . . counterposing an imaginary Vico."[13] Croce's response was also sharp. Croce saw, in Borgese, "the prototype" of a dangerous form of youth, one in constant rebellion, continually trying to overcome what was stable and necessary. Borgese was "representative of the spiritual conditions of many young men in our days," men who have "lost sight of the simple search for the true" and replaced it with "a certain turgid phraseological grandioseness."[14] "I know very well what Borgese feels is lacking in my book: what is today called 'style' and is [really] the swollen and pompous jargon made fashionable by D'Annunzio."[15]

The review was directed only in part to Borgese, "prototype"; it was really a warning to all that things had gone far enough, that a little more balance was required.

> I would like the young to know (and Borgese with them) that [although] the life of honest industrious work seems prosaic to those that throb with the feverish life of Monte Carlo, the world moves forward on account of the work of the prosaic and not because of the "passionate" anxieties of these poets.[16]

Before this, it seemed to Borgese, Croce had been untroubled by the "feverish life"; and Borgese, not surprisingly, was angered at this sudden transformation in Croce. "*You have dressed me in this miserable flesh*," he declared,

"and now you undress me." In Croce, "between 1902 and 1910," he had found
a "liberator and an educator," but now Croce's "system" no longer satisfied
him. Croce's "first essays were opposition; this [your system] is domination. In
the *Estetica* there was promise, unlimited like any promise; in the system there
is [only] conclusion." It is "limited and closed" and "therefore an instigator of
new anxieties."[17]

Serra and Borgese had inaugurated a general reaction against Croce and his
system, a desperate effort to break out of the Crocean hegemony. In a few
months another article appeared in *La voce* written by Giovanni Boine under the
pseudonym *Un ignoto,* or "An Unknown."[18] Its purpose was to draw up an
aesthetic emancipated from Croceanism. Croce's response was heated: "I have
seen," he wrote bitterly of Boine's ideas,

> that for some time young Italians have trifled with these trivialities and
> [that they] . . . do not recognize that they are only trivialities. . . . They
> caress their mental immaturity and they believe they have embraced
> the cosmos, they celebrate the mysteries of the absolute, they have glimpsed
> the face of God invisible to the profane. . . . This is not the way to proceed.[19]

Boine, angry, was quick to respond:

> I have had no visions. I have tried as honestly as possible to order myself
> from within. I tell you that the thought of Croce has helped me. [But]
> I say all thought is not in the three volumes of Croce—and not all honesty
> either.[20]

At the same time that Boine, Serra, and Borgese were reacting against Croce,
the important Florentine journal *La voce* began to break up into various factions
and groups, many of which were opposed to Croce and his suggested role of
detachment for the intellectual. In 1911, Papini and Amendola formed their
own magazine *Anima (Soul)* and in the first issue keynoted the beginning
of a new era of despair:

> Today we would willingly give up ten polemics for a single truth. . . . There
> is no longer about us the gay atmosphere of the twenty-year-old. We do
> not believe that thought or courage will snatch the secret of the universe.[21]

In the same year in which *Anima* was born, Salvemini left *La voce* to
form his own journal, *L'unità,* dedicated essentially to the political problems of
southern Italy. Both *Anima* and *L'unità* indicated a certain restlessness and
dissatisfaction with a life of detached historical investigation. This was the height
of the Libyan crisis, and it was necessary to take sides. Salvemini explained to
Prezzolini exactly the reason he had to leave *La voce:*

The [Libyan crisis] is only the most salient of the general crises of *La voce.*
Yes, you are right; there are not two groups in *La voce* but ten, twenty.
We are all persons at the edge of groups. *But this armed vigil cannot continue.*
We all feel, *after two or three years of nonsense, the need* to conclude, *to move into action.*[22]

Throughout most of the intellectual community the sentiment that the time for action had come prevailed. What was the use of all the preparation, of all the investigation, if nothing could come of it? *L'unità* and *Anima* were only the first, and for that matter the mildest, of expressions of hostility toward idle thought. The most violent was yet to come. *Anima* failed after less than two years, but during that time others had left *La voce.* Then, in 1913 they all came together to launch the futurist journal *Lacerba.* The magazine was an apocalypse of bitterness. The present situation required action. All thought must go!

We know too much! We understand too much; we are at a crossroads. Either to kill ourselves—or to fight, to laugh, to sing. We choose the latter way— for now. Life is tremendous. Long live life.[23]

Lacerba was explicitly anti-Crocean. Croce and his system had replaced positivism as the enemy of freedom. To those of *Lacerba* (Papini, Soffici, Marinetti, Palazzeschi), to affirm life meant precisely to overcome Croce. In Croce, wrote an almost hysterical Papini, there is *nothing;* "Tautologies, affirmations without proof. [Croce says] : 'You never escape from reality or from history.' Thanks a lot!"

An outraged Croce answered: "Papini has, for some time, had a big mouth, posing in newspapers, books, and lectures at being a poetic genius, a revolutionary philosopher, and an apostle of the new life."

But then Papini had found his mark.

Here is what bothers you, Senator. You too have a big mouth, and for some time have posed at being a poetic genius, a revolutionary philosopher, and an apostle of the new life. You want to be the only pope, the only messiah, the only dictator of Italian culture. You are upset because your disciples are leaving, that few now take you seriously, and that someone has broken the professional and journalistic chorus of eulogies. Senator, I understand you perfectly.[24]

Papini, in his own immoderate way, had come close to the truth—but he did not understand Croce "perfectly." Croce had hoped to inaugurate a new culture, and it appeared that now he had turned suddenly against it. But Croce probably had never intended to have the cultural revolution go as far as Papini wished. He had not taken sides against it before because he had concentrated so long on the other enemy, positivism. He now began to see his "guerrilla forces" in a quite different light; and indeed, they began to see Croce in a different light. The result was, as Papini had stated, that the "disciples were leaving." In vain did Croce now begin to emphasize that man was unable to "escape from reality or from history," that the will acted only in response to certain given concrete situations and was determined by those situations. For these men, that meant not the affirmation of life but the rejection of life. "This philosophy," wrote an exasperated Piero Marucchi in 1911, "has overcome death, but truly it has also overcome life."[25]

Just after Papini's exchange with Croce, Papini had gone to Rome to deliver a speech entitled "Against Rome and Benedetto Croce" in which he urged his listeners to abandon the Crocean prison:

> The Italian culture is tremendously decrepit and professional: we must get out of this dead sea of contemplation, adoration, and imitation of the past or we will become the most imbecile people in the world.[26]

The men of *Lacerba* became the most vocal element in a desperate attempt to overcome history and leap out of reality. To overcome Croce meant to them that *everything* had to be destroyed. In April of 1911 they at last embraced the apocalypse:

> That the spirit of *Lacerba* is revolutionary . . . all by now understand. . . . We of *Lacerba* wish to contribute, with our negative propaganda, to the coming of that day of perfect destruction, which will be followed by a tomorrow of perfect creation.[27]

From that point on, *Lacerba* and its writers conducted an unending campaign against Croce. In magazines and in speeches Croce was ridiculed and spurned: "The philosophy of Benedetto Croce: the body of a good bourgeois with a pure concept for a head."[28] Croce was now bourgeois, conservative, a defender of "what was stable and necessary." His philosophy appeared complicated but was simplicity and complacency:

> *Benedetto Croce*: Half of sixteen previously divided by the double of one is equal to the product of the sum of two ones multiplied by the result of the addition of four halfs.
> *The superficial man:* You mean $2 \times 2 = 4$, right?[29]

Many were finding that what had attracted them in Croce had been, as Borgese put it, "promise." But there had been no fulfillment. They had been misled by the promise, by the appearance. Here is the analogy of the former *Vocean* Ardengò Soffici, as he compared the southern Neapolitan "artichoke" to the northern Florentine "artichoke."

The Neapolitan is clear, round, and blooms like a beautiful rose; pregnant
and full of promise [but as you peel it, it seems] a little woolly, and without
taste. Patience! There are many leaves. . . . Let's peel some more . . . and
more and more! [But] I find only a whitewashed hole surrounded by soft
white hair! In fact there is little substance. [Now in the northern artichoke]
even the very first leaves are fat and tasty. . . . I don't intend, of course, to
make anything [of this] , but doesn't it seem to you that these two artichokes,
that this contrast, these appearances and substances, suggest to the mind
analogies . . . analogies . . . how shall I put it . . . of a superior order?[30]

Soffici highlighted the foremost sentiment of the *Lacerba* group. They felt
betrayed. Guido Marpurgo-Tagliabue has said it rather well: "Croce was the
master that had deluded and *betrayed* his disciples. Croce was the heir of idealistic
lay thought who had not wished to develop that laicism into an effective *political* religion."[31] Now the disciples felt lost. "Goodbye to reason, morality, and
tradition," wrote Soffici, "goodbye to you who were most dear of all; goodbye
to art. . . . Toward greatness or imbecility, what's the difference? Let's go."[32]

It was not only against Croce himself, however, that these youths rebelled.
It was rather that Croceanism had become a school of thought, a life-style, a
culture all its own. As such, it claimed to answer all things and include all questions. To those *ortodossi* who were content to accept those answers, Croce's
three volumes *did* contain all thought. Where Croce himself was flexible, articulate, and perceptive, the *ortodossi,* or many of them, were simply "scholastics."
Piero Gobetti wrote that he admired Croce,

> but I hate the *Crociani*. They are empty blabbermouths just like the *anti-
> crociani.* I despise them as much as I admire Croce. . . . [They are] the
> professors deprived of originality, pedants, mechanics that have memorized
> the *Estetica* and made it the new Gospel.[33]

It was something Prezzolini had already noticed in 1906: "In the first disciples one feels already that the system has lost its vitality and become an
occasion for pedantry, limitation."[34] Renato Serra could tolerate it no longer.
To Ambrosini he wrote, "I am going to break with Croce and his whole intoler-
able sect. Auff!"[35] To Serra, Croce had become "pure thought" and cared
nothing for him or his problems.

> Oh, so you want to talk of Croce . . . who deigns to console our anxieties
> from the heights of his philosophy, sure that in the end all will be and
> cannot but be good, advantage, and progress.[36]

This "otherworldliness" and Olympianism was in truth the cause of much
of the discontent and bitterness. Croce now spoke about the problems of

life, even the serious problems, as if they did not concern *him*, but only those beneath him. The Sicilian philosopher Vladimiro Arango-Ruiz, caught up in the Crocean idealist system, remembered his rejection of it in the following terms: first he praised the active side of Croce, the attacking Croce, the Croce who was against metaphysics and concerned with the affairs of men, but then,

> Did I say Croce? Croce, the most mundane and antimetaphysical? But Croce, alas, also ends by becoming a metaphysician and a theologian. . . . In sum, another world, "otherworldliness" in Croce too. And this "other-worldliness" causes his disinterest in this world, that indifference, that doubt that makes him, willingly or not, a conservative.[37]

Croce had encouraged these men and had given them hope. He had directed them on the road to the cultural revolution, yet when it was to be carried into political terms, into action, he had abandoned them. At the beginning there was the "promise"; at the end, the despair. Croce's philosophy, they found, was suited to tearing down the abstractions but useless for building the conventions necessary for life. "In depth, when you analyze the content of this work," wrote Aliotta back in 1906, "you find there an unbridled criticism, in fact a demolition of traditional and formalistic logic . . . but little or nothing . . . of positive construction."[38] In the end, for those who had followed him, Croce's philosophy was simply the personal ethic of an uncommon man, a man who in the long run had more in common with the muses than with his fellows. That Olympianism accounted for the bitterness of so many of his former admirers. "It is the insufficiency, the sense of insufficiency, that I want to express" wrote Giovanni Boine.[39] "I am free, but empty," wrote Serra. "I remain suspended and [ready] to taste my liberty . . . [but] in me there is nothing but the void." Unlike Boine, however, Serra suggested an answer, grim, frightening, almost as if given by a prophetic vision. The void began to dissipate and "Now I seem to be full of men just like myself. [They are] filled with my anxiety, setting out on my road, ready, if the time comes, to support each other, to live or to die together without knowing why."[40]

Indeed many, including Serra, were to be killed in the war; and few did know why.

When the first war came, Croce's influence over Italian intellectuals had ebbed.[41] It was replaced by the influence of Giovanni Gentile, with his idea of the ethical state. All transcendent faiths having been crushed, man having been found inadequate, the state became the new god, the collectivity replaced the individual. Some came to this new god out of fear; others, only after long philosophical reflection; still others, the majority, out of a sense of relief at finding an alternative to the void. This new state, born before the war, strengthened by the war, was an awesome thing. It had to be. It had to take the place of all those faiths, customs, traditions, and conventions that had perished with man's "emancipation." Free at last, man sought safety in numbers.

In Croce, too, the state began to assume a larger role, poetry a lesser one. Against the aesthetes, futurists, and D'Annunziani, Croce began a lengthy polemic. Clearly, he was by now quite aware of the violence of poetry. The young people today, he would write,

> wish to change their natural weaknesses and immaturities into conscious forces . . . to turn them against the old and the no longer young . . . to constitute themselves as a sort of corporation with rights but without duties; they lack respect for others . . . ; [they have] declared war against their elders. . . . What does one do with a young man who knows only how to be young and pretends to be a man of purpose and mission? . . . [They are a] caricature and [they only say] "We are the young—here we are."[42]

Clearly that was not the same Croce who once thought that mysticism was a useful way to liberate men from positivism. To hold these young rebels in check, Croce, too, began to give a new emphasis to the role of the state, began, in fact, to politicize his lay religion. The state in this period became in Croce the incarnation of the power (*potenza*); and increasingly in the pages of *La critica* there were long hymns to Treitschke,[43] to *Realpolitik*,[44] and long lamentations about increasing

> social atomism which is revealed . . . in these dispositions of the soul and which lives . . . in those that wish to bring Italy to a higher destiny. [This] cannot but generate fallacious programs . . . or really programs with a beautiful but inanimate appearance. Inanimate because the spirit which should move them is absent and there is present . . . the spirit of individualism, materialism which should be corrected and overcome.[45]

Thus the philosopher of immanentism, like his nineteenth-century predecessor Spaventa, had to condemn individualism and atomism. Things had come full circle. Now the enemy was "this weakening of the consciousness of social unity, this diffuse indiscipline." And what was it that had demolished those conventions necessary for social unity? Looking beyond the Alps Croce found the antidote to Italian disunity in the German state of the Kaiser. The discovery, however, was ill-timed. Italy was about to go to war with the very nation that had come to symbolize to Croce social discipline and the absence of atomism. The more Croce exalted Germanic discipline, *Machtpolitik*, and the state, the more Croce seemed only to echo Gentile. With the entry of Italy

into the war in the spring of 1915, Croce found himself torn between his belief
in the superiority of German *Kultur* and his patriotism. In the Senate he voted
for the declaration of war against Austria. Privately he wrote to Giuseppe
Lombardo-Radice,

> I confess to you that I would have been very content if Italy had found
> herself ready in body and spirit to fight alongside of her allies [Germany
> and Austria]. Austria does not worry me and Germany . . . is still the people
> who represent the state and the social discipline and the ideal ends that no
> longer exist in the Western democracies.[46]

This fear of social atomism and admiration for Germanic discipline was
paralleled by a revision in Croce's hopes for Marxism. No longer did Marx the
agitator and Sorel's syndicalism appear as the highest form of Marxism. "At
one time," he wrote,

> I was impassioned by the socialism of Marx and then by the syndicalist
> socialism of Sorel; I hoped to find in one and the other a regeneration of
> present social life. . . . But now there is aflame in me the desire for a
> proletarian movement enclosed and resolved into historical tradition, a state
> or nationalist socialism; and I think perhaps Germany will do this [and]
> give an example and a model to other peoples, [while] the demagogues of
> France, England, and Italy will not do it, or will do it badly.[47]

It was for this reason that Croce praised the German socialists who

> have rigorously interpreted the principles of their [Marxist] political doc-
> trine, and [so] have placed themselves openly on the side of the Germanic
> state, and for this they deserve praise for coherence and seriousness.[48]

Croce's use of the words "national socialism" and his admiration for Germanic discipline, of course, did not have the same meaning then that they have
today, and I recall them here only to establish again that pattern we have seen
earlier in Cuoco, Spaventa, and De Sanctis. In each of them, as in Croce, the initial revolutionary idea that man could create and alter his history at will came
in the end to rest on a conservative plateau. In Croce this plateau was reached on
the eve of World War I and came as a result of his shock and amazement at the
excesses of vitalists, who still dreamed of ex nihilo creation. The irony, of course,
lay in Croce's earlier publication of the *Estetica*, which, along with his support
of Sorelianism, had contributed to the very excess he sought now to curb.

In the final analysis, however, there seems little use in searching in Croce for
any political theory. Politics, of course, requires a theory, and because Croce
rejected even the existence of anything outside of history, his philosophy is not

political. Indeed, Croce does not even permit man consciousness of anything save the past. Thus, in Croce—as in Vico and Hegel—history has a life of its own. It is just that in Croce history is aimless, because man, its author, is also aimless.

In the end Croceanism reduces itself to stoicism, to commitment to Voltaire's garden, while retaining full knowledge that life is something best not thought about too deeply. Most persons, however, have rejected that counsel. Those that consider themselves Croceans and still want to theorize about the meaning of it all therefore have had to couple their Croceanism with some constant faith outside of history. Thus, one finds Crocean Marxists, Crocean liberals, Crocean fascists, Crocean conservatives—even Crocean Catholics—but rarely Crocean Croceans, for the creed on its own is useful only, to be perfectly precise, as a canon of historical investigation. It is, in fact, a question whether *any* culture, *any* lay religion, that historicizes can be political, can provide that impetus to action that previously religion or natural law provided. Certainly a historicist culture that sees "philosophy of history" as a myth cannot provide that impetus, for it faces always the danger of immobilizing *skepticism* or, alternatively, of ignoring the void that has been exposed. By the time of Croce a fundamental tension lay at the base of historicism, a tension between the effort to construct and impose a new culture and common sense upon modern life, a new basis for purposeful action, and the absolute historicist perspective, which regarded with Olympian placidity the unfolding drama, the unfolding absurdity, of history, which in seeing nothing outside the historical dialectic ran the risk of depriving that common sense of any inspiration for action.

The Greeks, too, valued "culture," calling it instead "opinion." They stressed the importance of having good opinions strengthened through dialectic and made eloquent by rhetoric. They saw, too, that opinion is the foundation upon which society rests, but unlike the modern humanist, they believed, or they may have had the good sense to say that they believed, that this opinion was not formed by history, but informed by eternal principles, principles that endured beyond the life of man, that stood outside the dialectic, and were therefore more important than man. The danger in making man the measure is the present fear and trembling, which was allayed by the Greeks.

Glaucon: Yes, the rewards are splendid and sure.
Socrates: These, however, are as nothing in number or in greatness, when compared with the recompense awaiting the just and the unjust after death. This must now be told, in order that each may be paid in full what the argument shows to be his due.
Glaucon: Go on, there are not many things I would sooner hear about.

NOTES

CHAPTER 1

1. Any Vico scholar, but especially those restricted to English, owes a great debt to Max H. Fisch and Thomas G. Bergin for their excellent translations and commentaries on Vico. I have used the translations extensively and, on the whole, in an unaltered form. They are cited as follows: Giambattista Vico, *The Autobiography of Giambattista Vico,* trans. Fisch and Bergin (Ithaca, 1963), hereafter Vico, *Autobiography;* Giambattista Vico, *The New Science of Giambattista Vico,* abridged, revised, and trans. Fisch and Bergin (New York, 1961), hereafter Vico, *New Science.* The standard Italian is Nicolini's of the Laterza Press at Bari. I have cited them as follows: Giambattista Vico, *La scienza nuova seconda,* ed. Fausto Nicolini (Bari, 1953), 2 vols., hereafter Vico, *Scienza nuova* 1 or 2; Giambattista Vico, *L'autobiografia, il carteggio, e le poesie varie,* ed. Benedetto Croce and Fausto Nicolini (Bari, 1911), hereafter *L'autobiografia;* Giambattista Vico, *Le orazioni inaugurali, il de Italorum sapientia, e le polemiche,* ed. Giovanni Gentile and Fausto Nicolini (Bari, 1914), hereafter *Le orazioni* followed by the title of the *orazione.*

2. René Descartes, *Philosophical Writings,* ed. and trans. Norman Kemp Smith (New York, 1958), pp. 99–100. See, too, Fisch and Bergin, introduction to *Autobiography,* p. 29. "This early anti-historical bent appears most clearly in Descartes' remarks on the necessary imperfection of whatever has been slow of growth: buildings, cities, laws, religions, sciences, even the mind of an adult!"

3. Nearly countless anyway. The official judicial census of 1735 listed the number of urban thieves at 30,000. "The beggars were, of course, much more numerous" (Robert Flint, *Vico* [Edinburgh and London, 1884?], p. 10).

4. Ibid., pp. 26–27.

5. Vico was born in Naples in 1668. In his *Autobiography,* where through-out the work, he referred to himself in the third person—a "reaction to the ubiquitous 'I' of the *Discourse,*" noted Fisch and Bergin—Vico gave the date as 1670, but no matter; if Vico's knowledge of his early life was hazy, the haziness may stem from an incident he recounted in his autobiography.

At the age of seven he fell head first from the top of a ladder to the floor below and remained a good five hours without motion or consciousness. The right side of the cranium was fractured, but the skin was not broken. The fracture gave rise to a large tumor, and the child suffered much loss of blood from the many deep lancings. The surgeon, indeed, observing the broken cranium and considering the long period of unconsciousness, predicted that he would either die of it or grow up an idiot. However, by God's mercy neither part of his prediction came true, but as a result of this mischance he grew up with a melancholy and irritable temperament such as belongs to men of ingenuity and depth who, thanks to the one, are quick as lightning in perception, and thanks to the other, take no pleasure in shallow witticisms or falsehoods. (*Autobiography*, p. 111)

6. Fisch and Bergin, introduction to *Autobiography*, pp. 46–47.

7. There seems little question that Vico exaggerated the abstractness of many of the philosophes or, at any rate, that he attributed to all a fault of only some. Yvon Beleval questions, persuasively, whether Vico had in fact actually read Descartes.

Did he read him? He quotes the titles of the *Discours,* the *Méditations,* the *Principes,* the *Traité des passions de l'âme.* On the other hand, since he consistently [refused to learn French] in what language did he read the *Discours?* He believes the *Discours* to be later in date than the *Méditations* and most often associates it with the *Logique* of Arnauld. . . . Ultimately, Vico's statements seem constantly to be the products of second hand information. (Yvon Beleval, "Vico and Anti-cartesianism," in *Giambattista Vico: An International Symposium,* ed. Giorgio Tagliacozzo, coeditor Hayden V. White [Baltimore, 1969], p. 78, hereafter *Symposium*)

Nevertheless, Vico remains devastating to the Cartesian approach when that approach is turned upon the world of events.

8. It is not known if Vico was familiar with Hobbes's remarks in his famous *Six Lessons to the Professors of Mathematics:*

Of arts, some are demonstrable, other indemonstrable; and demonstrable are those the construction of the subject whereof is in the power of the artist himself, who, in his demonstration, does no more but deduce the consequences of his own operation. The reason whereof is this, that the science of every subject is derived from a precognition of the causes, generation, and construction of the same; and consequently where the causes are known, there is place for demonstration, but not where the causes are to seek for. Geometry therefore is demonstrable, for the lines and figures from which we reason are drawn and described by ourselves; and civil philosophy is demonstrable, because we make the commonwealth ourselves. But because of natural bodies we know not the construction, but seek it from the effects, there lies no demonstration of what the causes be we seek for, but only of what they may be. (Thomas Hobbes, *The English Works of Thomas Hobbes,* vol. 7, ed. Sir William Molesworth [London, 1845], pp. 183–84)

9. Vico, *Le orazioni,* "De nostri temporis studiorum ratione," p. 85. The "De nostri" has been translated. See G. Vico, *On the Study Methods of Our Time,* trans. Elio Gianturco (Indianapolis, 1965), p. 23, hereafter *Study Methods.* And see, too, R. G. Collingwood, *The Idea of History* (New York, 1956):

> Mathematics is intelligible to man, because the objects of mathematical thought are fictions or hypotheses which the mathematician has constructed. Any piece of mathematical thinkings begins with a *fiat: Let* ABC be a triangle and *let* AB = AC. It is because by this act of will the mathematician makes the triangle, because it is in his *factum,* that he can have true knowledge of it. (p. 64)

The "De nostri" was delivered as an address (*prolusione*) to the students and faculty but, needless to say, it did not alter the Cartesian atmosphere at the University of Naples. In a letter of 12 January 1729, Vico wrote to the lawyer Francesco Saverio Estevan:

> The moral philosophies, which the Greeks alone understood through [their] endlesss study of poets, historians, and orators, and the Greek and Latin languages, which are necessary to understand them well, have been quite abandoned. And they have been abandoned principally upon the authority of René Descartes and his method. . . . He has gathered a great following on account of that weakness of human nature which would know everything in a very brief time and with very little effort. That is the reason why today books other than new methods and abridgements are not produced. (Giambattista Vico, *Opere,* ed. Paolo Rossi [Milan, 1959], pp. 232–33)

10. Vico, *L'autobiografia,* p. 227; *Autobiography,* p. 29.

11. "At philosophiae genus Empiricum placita magis deformia et monstrosa educit, quam Sophisticum aut rationale genus; quia non in luce notionum vulgarium . . . sed in paucorum experimentorum angustiis et obscuritate fundamentum est" (*Novum organum,* in Francis Bacon, *Works of Francis Bacon,* ed. James Spedding, Robert Leslie Ellis, and Douglas Denon Heath [London, 1889], 1:174–75).

12. "The spider spinning his web . . . produces cobwebs of learning, admirable for the fineness of thread and work, but trifling and empty as to use" [Arenea texans telam . . . parit certe telas quasdam doctrinae tenuitate fili operisque admirabiles, sed quoad usum frivolas et inanes] " (*De augmentis scientiarum,* in *Works,* 1:453).

13. [Unde] homines abduxere se a contemplatione naturae atque ab experientia, in propiis meditationibus et ingenii commentis susque deque voluntates." And, citing the "just censure" of Heraclitus, he added *"Homines . . . quaerunt veritatem in microcosmis suis, non in mundo majori."* See *De augmentis,* in *Works,* 1:460.

14. "Contemplatio et actio arctiore quam ad hoc vinculo copularentur" (*De augmentis,* in *Works,* 1:462–63.

15. Vico, *L'autobiografia,* p. 27; *Autobiography,* p. 139.

16. Vico, *Le orazioni,* "De antiquissima Italorum sapientia," p. 206.

17. Vico, *Scienza nuova,* 1:115; *New Science,* p. 50.
18. *Le orazioni,* "De antiquissima," p. 208. And see, too, Collingwood, p. 64: "That I think my ideas clear and distinct only proves that I believe them, not that they are true." Not seeing that this anticipation of the *verum-factum* might cut in two directions, the Jesuits—in hot pursuit of Descartes—reviewed Vico favorably:

> Le seigneur Jean Baptiste de Vico, professeur d'eloquence . . . est un de ces génies singuliers qui s'ouvrent de nouvelles route. Les deux ouvrages qu'il vient de donner au public sont plens d'idées neuves et originales. . . . [Vico montre que, parce que le but de la méthode cartesienne] est de tendre à la certitude et d'écarter non seulement le faux et le douteux, mais encore le vraisemblable, l'étude de la critique preoccupe les jeunes gens contre toutes les sciences qui ont le vraisemblable pour objet, elle les dégoûte des beaux arts, de l'histoire de la jurisprudence. Poussée trop loin, elle va jusqu'à compter pour rien la certitude morale, dont tous les articles, toutes les maxims n'ont pas une évidence metaphysique. (Anonymous review in the Jesuit *Memoires pour l'histoire des sciences et des beaux arts,* February 1712, in Vico, *Le orazioni,* p. 243)

19. The *New Science* was issued initially in 1725, was revised and reissued in 1730, and was put in its final form in 1744. Its first formulations were received, in that age of Cartesian orthodoxy, with a resounding yawn. "The book appeared," Vico wrote in a letter of 1726, "in an age that, to use the expression of Tacitus as he reflected upon his own times—times so very similar to our own—*corrumpere et corrumpi 'saeculum vocatur,* and therefore, being a book that dismays or disturbs the multitude, cannot receive universal applause." *L'autobiografia,* p. 185. Letter to the Abbé Giuseppe Luigi Esperti.
20. *Scienza nuova,* 1:128–29; *New Science,* p. 63; Max H. Fisch, "Vico and Pragmatism," *Symposium,* p. 412.
21. In fact Vico himself had suggested in the "De antiquissima" that man, through experimentation—which he then believed to be a kind of creation—could gain an approximate knowledge of the physical world.
22. *Factum* has nothing to do with "fact" but with the Latin verb *facere,* or the Italian *fare* (French *faire*): to do, to make. It is an active verb whose meaning is quite lost when rendered as the abstract "fact." See A. Robert Caponigri, *Time and Idea: The Theory of History in Giambattista Vico* (London, 1953), p. 148.
23. *Scienza nuova,* 1:117–18; *New Science,* pp. 52–53.
24. In Max Fisch's words, "Yes, to be is to be one, true, good—*ens = unum = verum = bonum;* but, since all but God that in any way is, is made, since *ens = factum;* and, as I shall now argue, it is only as *factum* that it is *verum,* only as made that it is true or intelligible—and intelligible only to its maker." Fisch continues, "Similarly in Greek philosophy, craftsmanship is a standing paradigm both of creation and of knowledge. . . . [e.g., in the *Timaeus*] Later periods yield other hints, on down to Bacon's ringing equation of knowl-

edge and power: 'What in working is most useful, that in knowing is most true'"
(*Symposium*, p. 403).

25. Maria Goretti, "Vico's Pedagogic Thought and That of Today," *Symposium*, p. 556.

26. James M. Edie, "Vico and Existential Philosophy," *Symposium*, p. 491.

27. *Scienza nuova*, 1:28; *New Science*, p. 5.

28. *Scienza nuova*, 1:214–15; *New Science*, pp. 125–26.

29. Fisch and Bergin, introduction to *Autobiography*, p. 63.

30. Yet, Croce added, Vico's intention was hardly anti-Catholic: "All Vico's writings show the Catholic religion established in his heart, grave, solid and immovable." Perhaps. See Benedetto Croce, *The Philosophy of Giambattista Vico*, trans. R. G. Collingwood (New York, 1913), pp. 247–48.

31. *Scienza nuova*, 1:113; *New Science*, p. 48.

32. *Scienza nuova*, 1:146; *New Science*, p. 75.

33. *Scienza nuova*, 1:140; *New Science*, pp. 72–73.

34. Fisch and Bergin, introduction to *Autobiography*, p. 43.

35. *Scienza nuova*, 1:112; *New Science*, p. 48.

36. The phrase is, more or less, Professor Becker's. See *The Heavenly City of the Eighteenth-Century Philosophers* (New Haven, 1970), p. 47.

37. Ernesto Grassi, "Critical Philosophy or Topical Philosophy? Meditations on *De nostri temporis studiorum ratione*," *Symposium*, p. 39.

38. Goretti, *Symposium*, pp. 562–63.

39. "De nostri," p. 92; *Study Methods*, p. 35.

40. Aristotle, *The Works of Aristotle Translated into English*, ed. W. D. Ross (London, 1955), vol. 1, *Topica*, book 1, chapter 1, hereafter Aristotle, *Works*, followed by volume number and title of work. Grassi, *Symposium*, p. 45.

41. Aristotle, *Works*, vol. 9, *Etica Nicomachea*, book 1, chapter 3.

42. It was concrete reasoning; it dealt with things closest to man. For Aristotle it enabled man to discuss the "ultimate basis of the principles used in the several sciences . . . [because] it is impossible to discuss [the sciences] at all from the principles proper to the particular science in hand, seeing that the principles are the *prius* of everything else: it is through the opinions generally held on the particular points that these have to be discussed, and this task belongs properly, or most appropriately, to dialectic: for dialectic is a process of criticism wherein lies the path to the principles of all inquiry" (Aristotle, *Works*, vol. 1, *Topica*, book 1, chapter 2). Given that first principles lie in opinion, Aristotle recognized, we cannot submit them to the test of logic. Yet since these principles are the core of society, its morals, politics, customs, traditions, and even its science, we cannot leave them to whim either. We must settle for something less than certainty and more than whimsy. "We shall be in perfect possession of the way to proceed when we are in a position like that which we occupy with regard to rhetoric and medicine and faculties of that kind" (ibid., chapter 3). And Plato too acknowledged that "knowledge and opinion [have] distinct powers [and] have also distinct spheres or subject matters." Knowledge deals with the world of "being" and opinion with the world of "becoming" (*The Republic of Plato*, trans. F. M. Cornford, book 5, paragraphs 474–84).

43. *Scienza nuova,* 1:77; *New Science,* p. 21; common sense, as Aristotle noted (book 1, chapter 2) in the *Ethics,* dictated even to the scientific community, for it constituted the *prius* of science, that is, it dictated what counted as science. Thomas S. Kuhn in his *Structure of Scientific Revolutions* (Chicago, 1970) carried the notion to its logical conclusion.

> Perhaps science does not develop by the accumulation of individual discoveries and inventions. . . . The more carefully [we] study, say, Aristotelian dynamics, phlogistic chemistry, or caloric thermodynamics, the more certain [we] feel that those once current views of nature were, as a whole, neither less scientific nor more the product of human idiosyncrasy than those current today. If these out-of-date beliefs are to be called myths, then myths can be produced by the same sorts of methods and held for the same sorts of reasons that now lead to scientific knowledge. If, on the other hand, they are to be called science, then science has included bodies of belief quite incompatible with the ones we hold today." (P. 2)

Perhaps, Kuhn says, science does not "progress" toward truth but merely changes its "common sense," or "paradigm" as he calls it. Why, he asks, should science be any different than art, political theory, or philosophy? Why should we believe that science moves "steadily ahead as say art, political theory, or philosophy do not? . . . Why should progress . . . be the apparently universal concomitant of scientific revolutions? . . . We may . . . [in fact] have to relinquish the notion, explicit or implicit, that changes of paradigm carry scientists and those who learn from them closer and closer to the truth" (ibid., pp. 159–69).

44. *Scienza nuova,* 1:77; *New Science,* p. 21.

45. Caponigri, *Time and Idea,* p. 151.

46. Descartes, *Writings,* p. 100.

47. *Scienza nuova,* 2:55; *New Science,* p. 288. And compare the words of Bertrando Spaventa on Oriental (i.e., Indian) philosophy, in which man was unable to distinguish between object and subject. Bertrando Spaventa, *La filosofia italiana nelle sue relazioni con la filosofia europea,* in *Opere,* ed. Giovanni Gentile (Florence, 1972), 1:449–57.

48. See Hayden White, "What Is Living and What Is Dead in Croce's Criticism of Vico," *Symposium,* p. 388: "The death of a person before puberty does not invalidate the 'physiological law of development' governing the pubertial phase; it merely requires . . . that we invoke other laws . . . to explain why the prediction that puberty would *normally* occur was not borne out." Collingwood says: "Certain periods of history had a general character, colouring every detail, which reappeared in other periods, so that two different periods might have the same general character, and it was possible to argue analogically from one to another." For Vico, Collingwood indicated, it was not that history was cyclical: "It is not a circle but a spiral; for history never repeats itself but comes round to each new phase in a form differentiated by what has gone before. Thus, the Christian barbarism of the Middle Ages is differentiated from the pagan barbarism of the Homeric age by everything that makes it distinctively an expression of the Christian mind." And yet the similarities of the Homeric and the Middle Ages were

plain: "government by a warrior aristocracy, an agricultural economy, a ballad literature, a morality based upon personal prowess and loyalty and so forth." The "spiral," however, is horizontal, not vertical. See R. G. Collingwood, *The Idea of History* (New York, 1956), pp. 64-68.

49. Thus, Vico noted the origins of such things as marriage, civil institutions, and liberty evolved against the private ends of man. "Men mean to gratify their brutal lust and abandon their offspring and they inaugurate the chastity of marriage"; fathers "mean to exercise without restraint their paternal power over their clients, and they subject them to the civil powers from which the cities arise." The "nobles mean to abuse their lordly freedom over the plebians and they are obliged to submit to the laws which establish popular liberty." See *Scienza nuova*, 2:164; *New Science*, pp. 382-83.

50. *Scienza nuova*, 2:164; *New Science*, pp. 382-83.

51. *Scienza nuova*, 1:113; *New Science*, p. 48.

52. Pietro Piovani, in an article significantly entitled "Vico without Hegel," argues:

When all has been said, the Vichian Providence, however much it is explained in history and with history, retains its traditional function, by which its rationality, while being of a "legislative mind," remains unscrutable. Undoubtedly, the *New Science,* as a demonstration of Providence is, before all else, a bold and unprejudiced scrutiny of the inscrutable; however, between the ordering divinity and human actions, voluntary and involuntary, conscious and unconscious, there remains, in Vico, a gap which is filled now by the traditional workings of the all-seeing Providence, now by the work of the responsible men of history. (*Symposium,* p. 121)

53. A. William Salomone, "Pluralism and Universality in Vico's *Scienza nuova,*" *Symposium,* p. 529.

54. The dean of this Vichian school in the mid eighteenth century was the Abbé Antonio Genovesi, a promoter of Montesquieu and D'Alembert and a noted lecturer on political economy, the supreme importance of science, the "reform of agriculture and [the] redistribution of property" (Harold Acton, *The Bourbons of Naples* [Northampton, Great Britain, 1963], pp. 97-100). In all of this he seemed to feel himself still a Vichian. So apparently did many others—at least for a while. Thus, Vincenzo Cuoco (who would later give quite a different account of the social implications of Vico) announced, "In Italy, the school of Genovesi, who was Vico's disciple, held him always in greatest esteem; and in proportion as the influence of Genovesi's school spread through the other regions of Italy, Vico's reputation has grown. This indicates two things: (1) the fact that the school of Genovesi coincides with that of Vico; (2) the intellectual continuity between Vico and Genovesi." They are words that Cuoco would learn to forget. (Enrico De Mas, "Vico and Italian Thought," *Symposium,* pp. 149n-150n.) In the years of the French Revolution the leading Vichian figures were Ferdinando Galiani, Emanuele Duni, Mario Pagano, and Vincenzo Cuoco. Cuoco and Pagano were, doubtless, the most famous of these Vichians and will be discussed in the text; but a note on Galiani and Duni will give the

flavor of this eighteenth-century Vichianism. Galiani (the nephew of the great reformer of the University of Naples, Monsignor Celestino Galiani) was the author, at the age of twenty-two, of a treatise, "On Money," which attracted royal attention. Patronized by both the king and Benedict XIV, he led a comfortable, scholarly, and political life, serving for ten years as the secretary to the Neapolitan ambassador to France. There, at home in the home of the Enlightenment, he became the constant companion of Mme. Epinay, and when, through a bit of court intrigue, he was forced to return to Naples, he brought with him a full measure of the heavenly city of the philosophes. Harmonizing Vico with the thought of France, Galiani introduced Vico's providence in a new garb, the texture of which is revealed in a didactic fable Galiani aimed at the materialist circle of Baron d'Holbach.

> Please suppose, gentlemen, that one of you, who is quite convinced that this world is the result of chance, is playing at dice, not in a gambling den but in one of the best houses in Paris. His opponent, casting one, two, three, four, many times, always throws number six. After the game has continued a while my friend Diderot, let us say, who is losing money, will be sure to call out: "The dice are cogged! This is some swindler's den!" What ho, Master Philosopher! Because you lose half a dozen francs after ten or twelve throws of the dice, you are positive that this is the result of some clever plan, an artificial combination, an elaborate trick; and yet, seeing in the world innumerable combinations a thousand times more difficult, more complicated, and more useful, do you not suspect that Nature's dice are also cogged and that above there is a great Arranger? (Acton, *Bourbons,* pp. 109–10)

For Galiani, Vico's providence had become again Providence, the Great Arranger of the laws of nature. Emanuele Duni is similar:

> A professor . . . at the Sapienza of Rome, [he] elaborated an *Essay on Universal Jurisprudence,* where, endeavoring to investigate the common features of the "customs constantly practiced by the most civilized nations," he utilizes, in a cosmopolitan sense, the connection established by Vico between philosophy and philology, and ends by emphatically reasserting the concept of Providence. It is Providence, in Duni's view, which, starting at the deepest core of historical development, takes care of translating into the universal terms of "natural" law all those "barbaric legal practices," springing from coarse, rough, materialistic ideas, which, as time went on, gradually became less gross, and drew closer to the refinements of "natural equity." (De Mas, *Symposium,* pp. 155–56)

55. De Mas, *Symposium,* p. 155.

56. Where to lay the blame? It is not clear. For years the middle class had worked with the Bourbon regime to effect reforms that had "won the recognition of the most enlightened and advanced sectors of European opinion" (A. Robert Caponigri, *History and Liberty: The Historical Writings of Benedetto Croce* [London, 1955], p. 29), when suddenly it had been transformed into a Jacobin elite unsatisfied with mere reform and quite out of touch with the population.

Croce noted that for years the *ceto medio* had worked together with the monarchy when suddenly the regime, not wishing to be stampeded into reform or play a secondary role to the bourgeois reformers, became reactionary. On the other side the reformers became radicals, and the partnership ended. "It would be difficult to say," Croce observed, "on which part of the two groups the hostility began. . . . The hostility of the two groups began at the same time." They had apparently been tempted by the seeming ease with which the monarchy had been toppled in France. Benedetto Croce, *Storia del regno di Napoli* (Bari, 1967), pp. 204–5.

57. Acton, *Bourbons,* p. 381.

58. As the author of the celebrated *Processo criminale* and enjoying an international reputation in jurisprudence, Pagano had been, before 1789, advisor to the crown on matters of criminal reform (Croce, *Napoli,* p. 200). From that high level he had fallen after the French Revolution, and in 1794 he was imprisoned for four years for his spirited defense of three Neapolitan Jacobins. Pagano had been released from prison just prior to the arrival of the French and, catapulted into power upon the flight of the king, he meant to rid southern Italy of all the royal-aristocratic claptrap, which, he believed, was the only obstacle to the acceptance of the Enlightenment in his country.

59. Luigi Salvatorelli, *A Concise History of Italy,* trans. Bernard Maill (New York, 1940), p. 497.

60. Acton, *Bourbons,* pp. 349–51.

61. Vincenzo Cuoco, *Saggio storico sulla rivoluzione napoletana del 1799 seguito dal rapporto al cittadino Carnot di Francesco Lomonaco,* ed. Fausto Nicolini (Bari, 1913), p. 222.

62. Machiavelli, advising on the conquest of a republic: "But in the case of republics there is greater life, greater hatred, more desire for revenge; the memory of their ancient liberty will not and cannot allow them to rest; so the surest way is to destroy them or to take up residence there" (*The Prince,* trans. Mark Musa [New York, 1964], p. 39). For Cuoco this memory existed even under Bourbon absolutism.

63. Cuoco, *Saggio,* pp. 220–21.

64. For a fuller account of the revolution see, among others, Croce, *Napoli,* pp. 191–255; Croce, *La rivoluzione napoletana del 1799,* 5th ed. (Bari, 1948); Acton, *Bourbons;* Cuoco, *Saggio;* George Martin, *The Red Shirt and the Cross of Savoy* (New York, 1969), pp. 101–31.

65. The first edition of his history was a bitter denunciation of monarchy coupled, however, with a shrewd analysis of why the revolution had failed. See *Saggio.* The second edition of 1806 was published under the dictatorship of Murat and deleted the cruder remarks about monarchy. For the parts deleted— and they are worth reading—see Fausto Nicolini's appendix in *Saggio,* pp. 265–85; for his trouble Cuoco was made, along with many other "veterans of '99," a responsible official in Murat's government. See Oldrini, *La cultura filosofica napoletana dell'ottocento* (Bari, 1973), p. 9.

66. "Philosophy," warned Vico, "considers man as he should be and so can be of service to but very few. . . . Legislation considers man as he is in order

to turn him to good uses in human society" (Vico, *Scienza nuova*, 2:75; *New Science*, p. 20).

67. Cuoco, *Saggio*, p. 87.

68. Croce, "Due conversazioni," in *Cultura e vita morale*, 3rd ed. (Bari, 1955), p. 145.

69. It is not an unambiguous word. "Patriot," footnoted Cuoco. "What is a patriot? This name ought to refer to one who loves his country. In the last decade it was synonymous with republican, though certainly not all republicans were patriots." And did not the peasantry love their country? In fact, Cuoco was none too sure of the "patriots." Later on in the text he remarks:

> Among our patriots . . . very many had the republic on their lips, very many in their heads, very few in their hearts. For many the revolution was a fashionable thing and they were republicans only because the French were republicans; some were republican because of a longing of the spirit, others for want of religion. . . . Some confused liberty with license and believed that with the revolution they had gained the right to insult public authority with impunity. (Cuoco, *Saggio*, p. 94)

70. Ibid., p. 90; the notion recalled De Maistre's view that the "tenants" of a nation ought not to tamper lightly with what has been built up over the centuries. There is evidence, too, said De Mas, that Cuoco had taken De Maistre as his "guide in his studies of Vico's works" (De Mas, *Symposium*, p. 160). On the other hand, there appears to be evidence, too, that Vico played a major role in the development of De Maistre's thought, that, as Alain Pons observed in his analysis of the impact of Vico in France, "De Maistre's whole work presupposes that of the Neapolitan philosopher" (Alain Pons, "Vico in French Thought," *Symposium*, pp. 176, 165-85).

71. "Cuoco's Vico is pre-eminently, the author of the sociology of the two peoples, a thinker for whom history is never the creation of the lowest stratum of the population (the plebians), but is instead the work of a minority" (De Mas, *Symposium*, p. 159). In Vico the difference between the pleb and the cultured elite, as De Mas noted, appears as the difference between the *famuli* and the heroes. According to Vico, the gulf between those moved by the "senses" and those moved by "reason," between the *"popolo sensiente"* and the *"popolo raziocinante,"* occurred when the *famuli*, the simplest, weakest men living terror-stricken in the state of nature, sought and were granted asylum among the heroes. See Vico, *Scienza nuova*, 2: 250-51. These *famuli*, "these refugees were received by the heroes under the just law of protection by which they sustained their natural lives under the obligation of serving the heroes as day laborers. . . . To distinguish the sons of the heroes from those of the *famuli*, the former were called *liberi*, free. . . . The word *liberi* meant also noble so that the *artes liberes* are noble arts and *liberalis* kept the meaning wellborn and *liberalitatis* that of gentility" (Vico, *Scienza nuova*, 2:252-53).

72. In Napoleon and in Napoleon's colorful brother-in-law Murat, that amiable despot installed by the French upon the Neapolitan throne, Cuoco saw "a popular monarchy, the immediate expression of the people, the supreme

magistracy of the state and therefore a responsible power. . . . The legislature and the executive, whose disassociation produce inertia and caprice, [are in him] fused into one" (Guido De Ruggiero, *The History of European Liberalism,* trans. R. G. Collingwood [Boston, 1959], p. 259). Murat's shrewd and flamboyant behavior made him the darling of those elements of the kingdom the Parthenopean republicans had alienated. Not only was he supported by the feudal lords but he owned too the support of the masses, who might otherwise have unloosed upon him another *sanfedisti* bloodbath. The monarchy of Murat, as one Englishwoman noted, was supported by the *sans culottes.* See Croce, *Napoli,* pp. 216–17.

73. De Ruggiero, p. 259.

74. Dina Bertoni Jovine, *La scuola italiana dal 1870 ai giorni nostri* (Rome, 1967), p. 206.

75. Vincenzo Cuoco, *Scritti vari,* ed. Fausto Nicolini and Nino Cortese, *Parte seconda, periodo napoletano 1806-1815 e carteggio* (Bari, 1924), "Rapporto al re Gioacchino Murat e progetto di decreto per l'organizzazione della pubblica istruzione (1809)," p. 4 (hereafter "Rapporto").

76. Ibid., p. 55.

77. Ibid., p. 36.

78. Ibid.

79. Ibid., p. 7.

80. Ibid., p. 8.

81. In Cuoco the integrity of the individual is sacrificed to the good of the whole. See, for instance, Lamberto Borghi, *Educazione e autorità nell'Italia moderna* (Florence, 1950): "Vincenzo Cuoco was one of many links in this long chain of political and historical thinkers who employed the theory of the organic development of the people in the defense of the principle of authority against the corrosive work of criticism and popular action. His concept . . . has been considered as an early anticipation of fascist ideology" (p. 60).

82. To overcome the hostility of the masses to education of any kind, Cuoco proposed to offer all manner of inducements to lure the population into the schools (prizes, contests, public recognition, etc.).

It is said of Pythagoras that, upon his return from Egypt, he wished to open a school of geometry at Samos, his homeland. He had no students. What was to be done? Instead of insisting upon a salary, he promised a prize to the one who, among the students, should gain the greatest benefit. The hope of the prize motivated those that had not been motivated by curiosity for geometry. A great number attended; in all of them there was a very great desire to study. In the middle of the lessons, Pythagoras suspended the course and declared that he would not continue without being paid. The knowledge of a portion of geometry had generated the need to know it all, and everyone was pleased to pay. This, be it true or false, provides us with a model. (Cuoco, "Rapporto," p. 18).

83. Ibid.

84. Not, that is, unless one is a specialist in the area—in which case one is

inundated with material, material, however, of a highly polemical and controversial nature. To cite here only some of the basic literature on the subject: Giovanni Gentile, *Opere complete*, Fondazione Giovanni Gentile per gli studi filosofici (Florence, 1955), 27:1–65 and vols. 31–34; Santino Caramella, "Il liberalismo hegeliano del Mezzogiorno. I. Bertrando Spaventa," *Rivoluzione liberale* 1 (28 September 1922): 105; Guido De Ruggiero, *Il pensiero politico meridionale nei secoli XVIII e XIX* (Bari, 1922); Luigi Russo, *Francesco De Sanctis e la cultura napoletana* (Venice, 1928. All references are to the 3rd edition [Florence, 1958]); *Gli hegeliani d'Italia: Vera, Spaventa, Jaja, Maturi, Gentile*, ed. A. Guzzo and A. Plebe (Turin, 1953); Giuseppe Berti, "Bertrando Spaventa, Antonio Labriola e l'hegelismo napoletano," *Società* 10 (1954): 406–30, 583–607, 764–91; Italo Cubeddù, "Bertrando Spaventa pubblicista (giugno–dicembre 1851)," *Giornale critico della filosofia italiana* 42 (1963): 46–65; Italo Cubeddù, *Bertrando Spaventa* (Florence, 1964); S. Landucci, "Il giovane Spaventa fra hegelismo e socialismo," *Annali dell'Istituto Giangiacomo Feltrinelli* 6 (1963): 647–707; Guido Oldrini, *Gli hegeliani di Napoli: Augusto Vera e la corrente ortodosso* (Milan, 1964); S. Landucci, "L'hegelismo in Italia nell'età del Risorgimento," *Studi storici* 7 (1965): 597–628; S. Onufrio, "Lo 'stato etico' e gli hegeliani di Napoli," *Nuovi quaderni del meridione* 5 (1967): 76–90, 171–88, 436–57; Giuseppe Vacca, *Politica e filosofia in Bertrando Spaventa* (Bari, 1967); Guido Oldrini, *La cultura filosofica napoletana dell' ottocento* (Bari, 1973).

85. Quoted by Berti, "Bertrando Spaventa," p. 409.

86. Thus, 1851 marked the end of the Hegelian alliance with the republican–Mazzinian!–youth of Naples. In the Mazzinian *Il dovere*, for example, there appeared a letter of 27 May 1865 in which one Pier Vicenzo de Luca pointed out the sudden collapse of the Mazzinian-Hegelian "alliance." The youths of Naples "until now have had as their guides Hegel in philosophy and Mazzini in politics. Now in his last letter to the students of Palermo Mazzini has launched a brave accusation against the philosophy of Hegel and against the University of Naples. He has produced a tumult among the young Hegelian and republican youth." De Luca, therefore, took it upon himself to heal the breach and restore that natural alliance of Hegelians and Mazzinians. Thus, he wrote to *Il dovere:*

> Until now only priests and followers of theological philosophy raised the cross against Hegelianism. Inauspiciously, the authoritative voice of Mazzini also thunders now against Hegel. . . . I think I ought to write a few words for the student body who have always joined in sacred love [the names of] Hegel and Mazzini, following the first in science and the second in politics. I exhort them to continue to hold both in the greatest affection, because Hegel will always be the robust castle of absolute liberty as Mazzini will always be the Atlas of Italian liberty. (Alessandro Casati, "Mazzini e gli hegeliani di Napoli," *La critica* 9 (1912): 78)

87. Translating German into French, especially the German of Hegel with its untranslatable *Deutscheit*, is a thankless task at best. "Hegel est," wrote Willm in the 1840s, "dans son langage et dans toute sa manière d'être et de

sentir, le plus allemand des penseurs de l'Allemagne. Il est par cela même le plus intraduisible des écrivains. Il se sert d'une foule de mots arbitrairement composés, qui se refusent a toute version directe, et qui le plus souvent ne peuvent être rendus en français par des circonlocutions qu'aux dépens de la précision, et quelquefois de la clarté et de la fidélité" (quoted by Oldrini, *La cultura filoso-fica napoletana,* p. 397). Vera's translations have received therefore near universal criticism. See, e.g., Oldrini, *Gli hegeliani di Napoli,* and Benedetto Croce, "L'Enciclopedia di Hegel e i suoi traduttori," in *Aneddoti di varia letteratura* (Bari, 1954), 4:261–65.

88. Guido Oldrini, "Introduzione," in *La cultura: il primo hegelismo italiano,* ed. Guido Oldrini (Florence, 1969), pp. 64–65, hereafter *Primo hegel-ismo.*

89. Giovanni Gentile, *Bertrando Spaventa* (Florence, [1924]), now in Bertrando Spaventa, *Opere,* ed. Giovanni Gentile (Florence, 1972), 1:5, here-after *Opere* followed by volume number and title of work. See, too, Eugenio Garin, *Cronache di filosofia italiana* (Bari, 1966), 1:18.

90. Gentile, *Opere,* vol. 1, *Spaventa,* p. 155.

91. Vacca, "Recenti studi sull'hegelismo napoletano," *Studi storici* 7 (1966); and Berti, "Bertrando Spaventa."

92. Berti, "Bertrando Spaventa," p. 427.

93. Ibid.

94. See Cubeddù, "Bertrando Spaventa pubblicista."

95. The political and intellectual were, according to Gentile, separate realms in Spaventa. "Bertrando was not born to do, but to think" (*Opere,* vol. 1, *Spaventa,* p. 21). Gentile completely ignored the social conditions under which Spaventa labored, treating his thought as one thing and his politics as another, so this philosophy appeared as a "happy historiographical-speculative insight, interesting for the specialist and not at all what it really was, the axis of homo-geneous cultural politics and a determined interpretation of the Risorgimento as a revolution to be oriented according to the 'highest points' of European bour-geois society" (i.e., according to Gramsci's view of the Risorgimento as the "failed revolution," *la rivoluzione mancata*). See Vacca, "Recenti studi," p. 194. See, too, Hervé A. Cavallera, "Sviluppo e significato del concetto di religione in Giovanni Gentile," *Giornale critico della filosofia italiana* 53 (January 1974); 61–137, who clarified Gentile's orientation very well: "Hegel is really the Old Testa-ment of modern philosophy in which is attempted an accord between man and God, an accord that his rebellious sons, Marx, Kierkegaard, refute. . . . Gentile received Hegel from Spaventa through Jaja, and it is the gnosiological problem which most concerns him." It was through Spaventa, too, that Gentile saw Rosmini and Gioberti: "Spaventa had made Gioberti the Italian Hegel: to the pure thought of the German corresponded the *intuito* of the Italian" (p. 66).

96. Gentile, *Opere,* vol. 1, *Spaventa,* p. 11.

97. See Vacca, *Politica in Spaventa,* chapter 1.

98. Like his brother Silvio, about whom a great deal more is known, Bertrando fell under the sway of Hegelianism shortly after his arrival at Naples. The closeness of their relationship has never been questioned, so the general

drift of Bertrando's thought may be supposed as similar to that of Silvio's. On the intimate relationship between Silvio and Bertrando, see S. Spaventa, *Dal 1848 al 1861, lettere, scritti, documenti,* ed. Benedetto Croce, 2nd. ed. rev. (Bari, 1923), pp. 103, 141.

99. Spaventa, *Opere,* vol. 3, *Logica e metafisica,* p. 19.

100. S. Spaventa, "Il fine ultimo delle rivoluzioni e il fine proprio della rivoluzione italiana," in *Dal 1848 al 1860, lettere, scritti, documenti,* p. 36. "In every revolution" he continued,

> it is necessary to distinguish three things: the idea, the men, and the form. The idea is the rationality of the revolution. . . . The men are the means which the revolution uses in order to proceed, and at the same time they are the matter of this execution. The means then and the matter are in men of passion, [their] ends and particular interests such as desire for wealth, glory, love of power and similar things. The form then is the way the revolution becomes a fact, a concrete existence. (Ibid)

Men thus were the means by which the idea realized itself. See, too, Vacca, *Politica in Spaventa,* pp. 36-37.

101. Harold Acton, *The Last Bourbons* (London, 1961), pp. 219-65; even given Acton's point of view, there seems little reason to dispute the population's general boredom with the success—though not the excitement—of the revolution.

102. The articles have been reprinted in *Primo hegelismo,* pp. 297-345. In fact, the articles are quoted later on by Spaventa himself in 1867 in the preface to *Logica e metafisica.* Here Spaventa attempted, unsuccessfully it seems to me, to prove that he thought in 1867 what he thought earlier in 1850: "I cite this, my first work, only as documentation for what I thought then and which in part I also believe now" (Spaventa, *Opere,* 3:23).

103. It was Rousseauian, Rousseauian even before Spaventa had encountered—and misunderstood—Rousseau. See below, p. 40.

104. Spaventa, "Introduzione a Hegel," in *Primo hegelismo,* pp. 309-11, 343.

105. Spaventa, *Opere,* vol. 3, *Libertà d'insegnamento,* pp. 674-76.

106. Ibid., p. 676.

107. Ibid., p. 723.

108. Analyzing the "marvelous drama of the French Revolution" of 1789, Spaventa noted that "before the revolution, the state, or the supreme power, was founded on a right or on a will superior to the right of the popular will . . . : the privilege of the noble and clerical order. The right of birth was in absolute contradiction to the principle of equality. The revolution had to begin by struggling against and destroying the political order" (Vacca, *Politica in Spaventa* p. 89). The success of the 1789 Revolution, Spaventa said, had established a new criterion for social class: property. "With property was born the bourgeoisie. . . . On account of property, society was newly divided into two classes, the propertied and the unpropertied." This had given rise to the "social movement" manifested in "St. Simon, Fourier, and socialism in general. And thus was prepared the principle of the new French revolution, which was to be only a wider application of the principle that produced the first." Thus, in early 1851,

before Napoleon III's coup d'etat, Spaventa explained of the 1848 revolution: "The new French revolution has marked the end of all purely political movements and the beginning of the social movements" (ibid., p. 90). The articles in which Spaventa sets out these judgments were unknown to Gentile and have only recently been published by Italo Cubeddù in *Giornale critico della filosofia italiana*. It is, in part, on the basis of these articles that Spaventa has attracted so much attention among Marxist scholars. For Cubeddù, it was through a reading of Lorez von Stein's *Der Socialismus und Communismus des heutigen Frankreichs* that Spaventa drew his revolutionary ideas. "The reading of Stein allows us therefore to reassemble in a sufficiently clear picture many ideas, hints, and accents of the young Spaventa." The ideas may have come from Stein, but they seem to have been remolded to Spaventa's primary purpose, which was not the classless and stateless society of Marx, but the creation of the Italian state. See "Bertrando Spaventa pubblicista," *Giornale critico della filosofia italiana* 42 (1963):62, and the following articles. Actually at the time Spaventa was accused by his contemporaries of being a Utopian, and he responded:

> "Utopia": it is the sacred word with which the pedants of journalism condemn every thought which surpasses the limits set out by their infallible authority, their long experience, their moderation. The use of the word, adopted so generally and without distinction, is very dangerous and an obstacle to the diffusion of the truth, and often covers a great misery of reasons, so that it is worthwhile determining the concept in order to see if it can always be reasonably applied to every new idea and every thought that contradicts the present conditions of society and the state and has less concern with the present than the future of people. (Vacca, *Politica in Spaventa*, p. 98)

109. Cubeddù, "Bertrando Spaventa pubblicista," p. 63 as well as the articles from *Il progresso* reprinted here, especially p. 83.

110. The revolution, moreover, did not mean the "destruction of property, family, and society." It meant, rather, "finding the foundation for a new order of things which will cause all those social inequalities to disappear. . . . It is not to be a destruction and an absolute negation but a truly Christian and rational organization of property, family, and society" (Vacca, *Politica in Spaventa*, p. 91). That "Christian" (but not Roman Catholic) and "rational" order could be provided only by the state and within the state.

111. Spaventa, *Opere*, 8:851–52.

112. And the criticism continues down to this day. Thus, Vacca laments that Spaventa "passes in fact from ideological polemics which have determined and concrete political content, to theoretical battles on principles and even in defense of the great conquests of bourgeois society" (*Politica in Spaventa*, p. 160).

113. Spaventa, *Opere*, 3:849.

114. Indeed, for years after the unification the South was torn apart by civil war between southern brigands and the new government. "A civil war is the cruelest thing that can happen to a country and the Risorgimento had been a succession of civil wars of which this [struggle in the South] was the most cruel, the most protracted and costly. . . . More people perished in it than were

killed in all the other wars of the Risorgimento put together" (Dennis Mack Smith, *Italy: A Modern History*, 2nd ed. rev. [Ann Arbor, 1969], p. 25).

115. It need scarcely be noted that this is a peculiar reading of Rousseau. Rousseau, in fact, argues—as clearly as Rousseau ever argues—nearly the same thing Spaventa found in Hegel.

116. Spaventa, *Opere*, vol. 2, *Sopra alcuni giudizi di Niccolò Tommaseo*, pp. 191–97.

117. Russo, *Francesco De Sanctis*, pp. 26–27.

118. Ibid.

119. Letter of 21 February 1862, in Bertrando Spaventa, *La filosofia italiana nelle sue relazioni con la filosofia europea con note e appendici di documenti*, ed. Giovanni Gentile, 3rd ed. (Bari, 1926), hereafter *La filosofia italiana*.

120. Ibid., p. 284; and ever was it so. In Croce's *History of Naples*, for instance, are recorded the impressions of those who came to Naples and were astounded. "This kingdom is supposed to belong to the Holy Church," wrote a fifteenth-century Italian, "but I say it belongs to the Holy Devil. Don't you see that all the lords are demons who seek nothing but war?" Right down to the time of Spaventa Naples retained its reputation as a "paradise, but one peopled by devils," men who are "malicious, evil, endowed with little talent and traitorous to the bone" (ibid., pp. 74–75). After two years Spaventa began to wonder whether or not the new state could ever prosper, whether or not it could turn the pleb into citizen. After new funds had been sent to Naples, Bertrando lamented to Silvio that nothing could please the Neapolitans.

> The discontent has multiplied to infinity. The government isn't aware of anything; to satisfy the Neapolitans requires more than the standard of general and public interest; . . . what it requires is as many standards as there are single individuals. You have to satisfy each one individually: to one a pension or a job, or a trial, or something else. I believe San Gennaro himself [the patron saint of Naples] is discontent with the donations of I don't know how much money . . . and even he wants a pension. Why not hire San Gennaro? . . . The people—sovereign—don't understand anything. While the Bourbons on one side and the *azionisti* [the followers of Mazzini's Action party] on the other huff and puff so much there is nothing to do but joke [*non ci è da scherzare*]. It will end in collapse one way or another. Even the followers of Murat . . . have arisen again and they too huff and puff. Even the Madonna—the hundreds and thousands of Madonnas—from the environs of Naples have been shaken from their torpor and begin to perform miracles. As you see, [Silvio], in two years we have made great progress at Naples: the press is free, opinions are free, and the asses and pigs are more free than ever. (Spaventa, *La filosofia italiana*, p. 292)

121. Spaventa, "Introduzione a Hegel," in *Primo hegelismo*, pp. 311–12.

122. Spaventa, *Opere*, vol. 2, *La filosofia italiana dal secolo XVI al nostro tempo*, p. 609. Having arrived late, however, meant that drastic measures had now to be taken to make up for lost time and to abolish the false idols installed in the interim.

It is necessary to release the natural Italian genius and, without destroying it, set it on the way to the modern idea. . . . The Italian mind has been torn violently from its natural development, separated from the life of the universal spirit, and its natural form has begun to turn false and stagnant. It is therefore necessary to regrasp the interrupted course of that truly national tradition, undo the work of three centuries which attempted the destruction of even the vestiges of the Italian intellect, develop the seeds of a new civilization which in those years was suffocated, welcome as our heredity those that have flourished in freer lands and which now form the substance and the beginning of intellectual, political, and religious life of other nations. (Spaventa, *Opere*, vol. 3, *Logica e metafisica*, p. 25)

123. *La filosofia italiana*, pp. 274–75.

124. Ibid., p. 292.

125. It is odd today to refer to Vera so obliquely, for in the 1860s—and indeed before and after that critical decade—Augusto Vera was, among intellectuals in France and Italy at any rate, nearly a household word. On Vera, see Oldrini, *Gli hegeliani di Napoli;* Giovanni Gentile, *Le origini della filosofia contemporanea in Italia* (Naples, 1903), 3:271–387. Born at Amelia in Umbria in 1813, Vera left Italy at the age of twenty-two to take up his studies in Switzerland and France. There he encountered Hegel and there he set about the translation of Hegel's works into French. As Oldrini put it, Hegel was then "virgin territory," protected by the impenetrability of the German language. After Vera, and to a large extent because of Vera (and Michelet), Hegel—even if a badly translated Hegel—became an international commodity.

126. Spaventa, *La filosofia italiana*, p. 233.

127. Ibid., p. 122.

128. Ibid., pp. 20–21.

129. "The true Unity, the true One, the Only, is development; development of itself: from itself, for itself, to itself: that is truly and totally Itself. This is the new concept which, more or less explicitly, consciously and unconsciously, is the soul of the *New Science*: is the great value of Vico" (ibid., p. 122).

130. Berti, "Bertrando Spaventa." See above, pp. 33–34.

131. Nonetheless, there is in Spaventa little appreciation of that subtle dialectical interplay of theory and practice seen in Marx and Vico. This is not surprising, for the mature Spaventa saw the locus of historical reason in the state, a state guarded and guided by an elite that had custody of the truth. If one must have an analogy with Marxism then, it is not Marx that is appropriate, but Lenin, for Marx and Spaventa were at opposite ends of the political spectrum, unfamiliar with each other because they would not even have noticed each other. Marx, on the whole, ignored nineteenth-century nationalism, utterly misunderstanding the power of that ideology to conquer every so-called proletarian movement. Spaventa, on the other hand, was the apotheosis of nationalism, the prophet of a state whose purpose was revolt against the masses.

132. Spaventa, *Opere*, vol. 1, *Principi di etica*, p. 733.

133. Ibid., p. 774.

134. Ibid., pp. 774, 756–57. That a state with such awesome responsibilities might fall into the wrong hands did not occur to Spaventa. It occurred to Adolfo Omodeo, writing too late in a review of Luigi Russo's extraordinary book, *Francesco De Sanctis*. See *La critica* 27 (1928): 335–60. And see, too, Santino Caramella, who, summing up the "travail" of Spaventa's unsuccessful attempt to mediate between the "sovereign of the idea and the autonomy of the individual," concluded that Spaventa "does not succeed in reconciling the two terms, and remains firm in the conclusion that the individual finds in the state higher values than those in his practical spirit, and in his adhesion to the state recognizes in it *naturaliter* his higher self. . . . The question did not have and would not have from Spaventa a direct response" (quoted by Italo Cubbedù in Spaventa, *Opere*, 3:977–78).

135. Landucci, as quoted by Vacca, "Recenti studi," p. 189.

136. For Spaventa that dualism of subject and object opened again the chasm that modern philosophy sought to close. "In such a way the so much vaunted difference between the two worlds posed by Vico was not only a step forward, [but] was really a step backward" (*La filosofia italiana*, p. 130). The emergence in ancient Greece of subject and object after the monism of Eastern religious-philosophical thought led to the dualism inherent in modern thought, a division of the universe into that part which was nature's or God's and that part which was man's. Various branches of thought had been traded back and forth between these two realms, but the dualism remained. The Romans had shown the way out, Spaventa said, for they had made law the product of the human will. It was the task of modern thought to further this anthropological perspective. "Only the modern spirit . . . only this spirit was able to conceive the true self and say it was not being . . . but creator" (ibid). Vico, said Spaventa, had overcome Descartes's staticism by the introduction of historical thought, but Vico had not really understood the *cogito ergo sum*, which humanized all reality, made both God and nature products of human thought.

> Vico is obscure. . . . Vico lacks the expressed, speculative, metaphysical concept of the new unity. . . . Vico lacks . . . the new *cogito ergo sum*: the new thought which is not the immediate position but the absolute mediation and therefore transparency of being. Vico, himself, confessed the obscure point of the *New Science*, insisting upon a new metaphysic: that of the mind. Did he provide it? No. He was not content with Descartes and he was right; Cartesian dogmatism cannot comprehend the historical (critical) process of the spirit. But had he, metaphysically, understood thought any better? Did he respond to its demands?" (Spaventa, *Opere*, vol. 2, *La filosofia italiana dal secolo XVI al nostro tempo*, pp. 546–47).

137. Spaventa, *Opere*, vol. 1, *Un luogo di Galilei*, p. 851.

138. Russo, *Francesco De Sanctis*, pp. 318–19.

139. Ibid., p. 343.

140. Quoted by Guido Macera, *Francesco De Sanctis: Restauro critico* (Naples, 1968), p. 37.

141. Croce left, in three places, his often contradictory remarks upon his

predecessor. See "Le lezioni del De Sanctis nella prima scuola e la sua filosofia," *Una famiglia di patrioti e altri saggi storici e critici* (Bari, 1949), pp. 369–
86. Here Croce noted in De Sanctis a "repudiation" and a "revision of the
mental positions of Hegel," that is an "abandonment" on the part of De Sanctis
of Hegelianism. The article was of 1913. Also in 1913 in the *Saggio sullo Hegel*
(Bari, 1913), however, Croce had noted, "The change of De Sanctis was anything
but an abandonment of philosophy and Hegelianism; it was a definitive liberation from certain erroneous concepts of the Hegelian dialectic. . . . It was not
anti-Hegelianism, but an attempt, however unconscious, to disentangle genuine
Hegelianism from abstract scholastic Hegelianism" (p. 375). For this, see Oldrini,
La cultura filosofica napoletana, p. 365n.

142. See Croce's remarks in the preface to Silvio Spaventa, *Lettere politiche*,
ed. Giovanni Castellano (Bari, 1926). An objective reading of De Sanctis makes
Gentile's claim that De Sanctis was an opponent of abstract intellectualism (which
he was) and therefore signaled an endorsement of some mystical vitalism (which
he did not) difficult to maintain. For Gentile's remarks on the context in which,
according to Gentile, De Sanctis operated, see "La tradizione liberale Italiana,"
in Giovanni Gentile, *Chè cosa è il fascismo* (Florence, 1924), pp. 125–35 and "Il
liberalismo di B. Croce," in ibid., pp. 153–61. "I wish that all young fascists
would read De Sanctis, the great critic, but also a greater educator. . . . A great
liberal, De Sanctis, but political liberty he himself says is an *instrument of
work* which, before adopting it, requires that men be made free; to make them so
he pointed the way through the *restoration of limits on liberty*" (ibid., pp. 157–
58).

143. Russo, *Francesco De Sanctis*, p. 339.

144. Croce, *Storia d'Italia* (Bari, 1928).

145. On the present conflict between the Crociani and the Marxists, see
the famous—or infamous, with its article on "Humanism in Stalin"—issue of
Società 9 (1953), which is devoted to De Sanctis. Especially enlightening on this
is V. Gerratana, "Introduzione all'estetica desanctisiana," pp. 114–41. See also
V. Gerratana, "De Sanctis—Croce o De Sanctis—Gramsci?" *Società* 8 (1952):
41–69; S. Landucci, *Cultura e ideologia in Francesco De Sanctis* (Milan, 1964);
and the review of the latter: Alda Croce, review of S. Landucci, *Cultura e
ideologia* . . . in *Giornale storico della letteratura italiana* 91 (1964): 620. For
the Crocean view: Elena and Alda Croce, *Francesco De Sanctis* (Turin, 1964).
With respect to Gerratana but with reference to the whole Marxist school beginning with Gramsci, see V. De Caprariis, "Il ritorno a De Sanctis," *Nord e sud*,
2 (November 1955): 29–36. De Caprariis here refers to Gerratana's "De Sanctis—
Croce o De Sanctis—Gramsci?": "It must not be forgotten that [Gramsci] was,
above all else, a political Marxist (to say this is not meant to offend anyone but
merely to recognize the true nature of his ideology) and therefore tended to
instrumentalize everything for political ends; for him, as for the majority of his
followers today, De Sanctis was nothing more than a new weapon in the struggle
against the so-called *bourgeoisie*" (p. 33). De Caprariis, again in *Nord e sud*,
2 (December 1955): 16–39, the next month addressed Gerratana's 1953
article "Introduzione," refuting the author's efforts to find a materialist-realist

aesthetic in De Sanctis and "restoring" as well the picture of De Sanctis as an Italian advocate of *le juste-milieu* (of Thiers, however, not of Guizot). Fundamental for an understanding of De Sanctis and the contemporary polemic is Guido Macera, *Francesco De Sanctis: Restauro critico* (Naples, 1968), though Macera has too modestly acknowledged that a history of "De Sanctis in the political and parliamentary life of the new Italy . . . remains to be written" (p. 17). As to the work of Croce's daughters, he noted, it suffers from "excessive discretion," from the "limits [imposed by] the paternal research," while the efforts of the Marxists (Landucci, in particular) "are not worth the effort of a point-by-point refutation since they derive in a direct line from the greatest error of . . . post-war Marxist historiography: the hypostasis of a socialist movement at the beginning of our unification" (p. 14).

146. See Croce, "De Sanctis–Gramsci," now in *Terze pagine sparse* (Bari, 1955), 2:166–68. Croce found also a danger to the legacy he had left of De Sanctis in the fact that Franco Laterza, editor of the large publishing firm, had enlisted Luigi Russo, author of that 1928 work that had initially set out a new De Sanctis, to edit the complete works of De Sanctis. Russo, who since 1928 had moved dramatically to the left, could not, Croce felt, present an objective De Sanctis.

> My dear Franco, it would grieve me if . . . your editions should succumb to what you fear will happen in those of [the Marxist press of] Einaudi. You ought not hide from yourself [the fact] that the director of your [De Sanctis] series [Russo] is a man of brisk temperament who has recently been to Russia and has made Italy laugh through his account of the investigation conducted in Russia to ascertain whether or not that people enjoys liberty and of the positive assurances of it that he received from the people he stopped to ask . . . in the street. . . . To [this sort] the political pages of De Sanctis are to be entrusted!

See Croce, "Per due edizione delle opere complete di Francesco De Sanctis," (lettera aperta a Franco Laterza), *Terze pagine sparse*, 2:282–85.

147. Somewhat more of the young De Sanctis is known than of that enigma, the young Spaventa, but even in De Sanctis there are gaps. On the early years of his life De Sanctis himself has given the reader the *Giovinezza*, which next to the *Storia della letteratura italiana* is probably the best known, certainly the most widely read, of his works. Dictated, on account of De Sanctis's ailing eyes, to his friend Pasquale Villari, the *Giovinezza* details the early formation of De Sanctis from the perspective of a man now sixty-four and in failing health. The work tells us a great deal, but it is occasionally contradicted by other mature works of De Sanctis, and it tends to anticipate the development of the author's thoughts by years, occasionally decades (Macera, *Francesco De Sanctis*, p. 12). On De Sanctis's early life, see Nicola Gaetani-Tamburini, *Francesco De Sanctis* in *Scritti varii, inediti, o rari di Francesco De Sanctis*, ed. B. Croce (Naples, 1898), 2:268–287; Jacopo Moleschott, *Francesco De Sanctis*, in ibid., pp. 287–90; Gerardo Laurini, *Francesco De Sanctis*, in ibid., pp. 291–99; B. Croce, *Francesco De Sanctis*, in *Letteratura della nuova Italia* (Bari, 1914), 1:121–67; Alda and Elena

Croce, *Francesco De Sanctis* (Turin, 1964); in English, Louis Anthony Beglio, *Life and Criticism of Francesco De Sanctis* (New York, 1941).

148. "I . . . was entirely [involved] in grammar and language" (*Giovinezza,* p. 194).

149. Francesco De Sanctis, *Opere,* ed. Nino Cortese, vol. 18. *Un viaggio elettorale seguito da discorsi biografici, dal Taccuino parlamentare e da scritti politici vari* (Turin, 1968), "Adolfo Thiers," p. 542. Hereafter *Opere* (Cortese) followed by volume number, title and article.

150. *Giovinezza,* p. 188.

151. Later, in 1860, Mazzini wrote, "We saw each other quite amicably at Zurich, where I learned to esteem you as a loyal patriot as before I esteemed you for your intellect" (Alessandro Casati, "Mazzini e gli Hegeliani di Napoli," *La critica* [1912,] p. 77). See also Mario Mirri, *Francesco De Sanctis politico e storico della civiltà* (Messina and Florence, 1961); for De Sanctis's later (but it is 1865), none too flattering opinion of Mazzini, "the Prophet," see among others De Sanctis, *Opere* (Cortese), vol. 18, "Un Viaggio," pp. 452-53.

152. Francesco De Sanctis, *Scritti politici di Francesco De Sanctis,* ed. Giuseppe Ferrarelli (Naples, 1900), pp. 203-18.

153. A celebrated and angry discourse dedicated to La Vista urging the youths of Italy to dedicate themselves to the renewal of the patria is in *Memorie e scritti giovanile* (Naples, 1930), ed. Nino Cortese.

154. See "La Prigione," in Francesco De Sanctis, *Scritti varii,* 1:161-71; the preface to the manuscript bears the date 24 February 1850, but that cannot be, for De Sanctis was not imprisoned until December 1850. Croce changed the date to 24 February 1851, which seems to apply to the verses but not the preface, which must have been written later, in Turin, in 1853. See Macera, *Francesco De Sanctis,* p. 20.

155. *Scritti varii,* 1:162.

156. Benedetto Croce, *L'estetica come scienza dell'espressione e linguistica generale,* 3rd ed. (Bari, 1908), p. 415.

157. Ibid.

158. *Scritti politici,* pp. 20-26, "Torino l'unificatrice," 22 December 1865.

159. Francesco De Sanctis, *Opere,* ed. Niccolò Gallo (Millan, 1961), p. 1089. Hereafter *Opere* (Gallo).

160. As quoted by Berti, "Bertrando Spaventa," p. 412.

161. Only to have them shortly disappear again into the Philosophies of Gentile and later Gramsci.

162. *Opere* (Gallo), pp. 1091-92.

163. Ibid., p. 1094.

164. Ibid. The Hegelians, however, had taken away all independence and liberty from form: "Now what is the point of talking to me of indissoluble, indestructible unity when you destroy it at the same time you affirm it, distinguishing the two terms and making one serve to demonstrate the other" (Ibid., p. 1095).

165. Ibid., p. 1096. And elsewhere, "I hear it often said—the poet created such an individual to show such an example or such a character in order to show

such an idea—that is the result of this criticism, falsifier of art. The poet shows the individual as individual for itself" (*Opere* [Gallo], p. 1102). And see Croce, *Estetica*, p. 423. "For De Sanctis, the concept of form was identical with that of imagination, the faculty of expression, or representation, artistic vision." Art was thus not to be judged according to whether it was in conformity with logic, morality, and other matters unrelated to art. "This idea of art as art and not willful and purposeful propaganda," asked a concerned Antonio Gramsci, "is it, in itself, an obstacle to the formation of determinate cultural currents that are the reflection of their time and contribute to the reinforcement of certain political currents? . . . No, it doesn't seem so," he wrote, relieved, "for what is excluded [according to this mode of criticism] is only that a work of art not be [deemed] beautiful because of its moral or political content. . . . If the cultural world for which [the artist] struggles is a living and necessary fact, its effusiveness will be irresistible; it will find its artists." See Antonio Gramsci, *Letteratura e vita nazionale* (Rome, 1971), pp. 26–28. In De Sanctis's concept of the lay religion, in fact, Gramsci was to find yet another example of the "hegemony" he hoped to create as preparation for the proletarian revolution. See below, pp. 52–53, on Machiavelli.

166. *Scritti politici*, p. 34.

167. "Savonarola was the last ray of a past sun that was settling behind the horizon; Machiavelli was the early sunrise of modern times: the former the last prototype of the old medieval man; the latter the first prototype of the modern man." See *Machiavelli conferenze*, in *Scritti varii*, 2:15.

168. *Opere* (Gallo), p. 486.

169. Ibid., p. 489.

170. Ibid., pp. 487–88.

171. Ibid., pp. 488–89.

172. Many others had suggested the task, of course, but few knew how it might be accomplished. "Guicciardini, although only a few years younger than Machiavelli and Michelangelo, hardly seems in the same generation. . . . He had the same aspirations as Machiavelli. He hated priests. He hated the foreigner. He desired a united Italy. . . . But they were simply desires, and he could never lift a finger to achieve them" *Opere* (Gallo), p. 528.

173. Ibid., p. 497.

174. *Scritti politici*, "La misura dell'ideale," pp. 150–51.

175. *Opere* (Gallo), p. 1049.

176. Ibid., p. 1052.

177. Ibid., p. 641.

178. Ibid., p. 1045.

179. *Scritti politici*, "La cultura politica," pp. 71–72.

180. Ibid., pp. 73–74.

181. Here are the words of the editors of *La voce* in 1911 as they founded a journal whose aim was to insert the intellectuals into the culture:

If a group of shopkeepers, or any other group of producers . . . or a federation of workers decide to put Italy on a certain road there is some possibility that they will succeed in their desire. . . . But the educated Italians, those who know where Italy came from and how it came to be constituted as a modern state and who sometimes see the immediate circumstances more clearly, not only do not succeed in imposing a direction on the historical life of their country, but they do not even know how to make their voice heard.

La voce meant to change that. See Giuseppe Prezzolini, "La politica della Voce," *La voce* 3 (30 November 1911): 697–99. Similarly, Antonio Gramsci: "The contact between intellectuals and simple men is not aimed at limiting scientific activity in order to maintain contact with the low level of the masses, but precisely to construct an intellectual-moral base to render politically possible an intellectual progress of the masses rather than of isolated intellectual groups" (*Il materialismo storico e la filosofia di Benedetto Croce* [Rome, 1971], p. 12). See also by Gramsci the entire *Gli intellettuali e l'organizzazione della cultura* (*The Intellectuals and the Organization of the Culture*) (Rome, 1971).

182. *Letteratura e vita nazionale*, p. 20.

CHAPTER 2

1. Croce, *Contributo alla critica di me stesso* in *Etica e politica* (Bari, 1967), p. 316. Hereafter, *Contributo*.
2. Ibid.
3. Ibid., p. 320.
4. Ibid., p. 322.
5. Ibid., p. 321.
6. Eugenio Garin, *Intellettuali italiani del XX secolo* (Rome, 1974), p. 5. Hereafter, *Intellettuali*.
7. *Contributo*, p. 323.
8. Garin, *Intellettuali*, pp. 10-11.
9. *Contributo*, p. 341.
10. For instance, *Rivoluzione napoletana del 1799; Teatri di Napoli dal Rinascimento alla fine del secolo decimottavo.*
11. And see, too, R. Franchini, *La teoria della storia di Benedetto Croce* (Naples, 1966). Croce, said Franchini, had read and cited Droysen, Dilthey, and Simmel before 1892, but his early work seems to reject the idea that anything more needed to be done with "the speculative questions" (p. 37).
12. Garin, *Intellettuali*, p. 5.
13. Pietro Rossi, "Benedetto Croce e lo storicismo assoluto," *Il mulino* (1957), pp. 327-29; H. Stuart Hughes, *Consciousness and Society* (New York, 1958), pp. 190-95.
14. Antonio Rotondò, "Lo storicismo assoluto e la tradizione vichiana." *Società* 2, no. 19 (1955): 1018.
15. *Contributo*, p. 326.
16. Anyone who looks at these early writings of Croce, wrote Eugenio Garin, "will notice immediately the painful voyage made by Croce in order to see clearly the proper concept of philosophy," his troublesome attempts to reconcile

the distinctions between "the moral sciences" and the "mathematical and natural sciences" and their relation with history; "it was a long voyage" (Eugenio Garin, *Cronache di filosofia italiana* [Bari, 1966], 1:244).

17. Garin, *Intellettuali*, p. 6.

18. *Contributo*, p. 343.

19. Garin, *Intellettuali*, p. 11.

20. Ibid., p. 56, n. 13.

21. Ibid., pp. 146–48. Jaja, a convinced Hegelian or, as Eugenio Garin put it, convinced of being a Hegelian, was the student of Spaventa and an associate of De Meis. Reaching maturity in the heyday of positivism, his influence was necessarily circumscribed by the anti-idealist cultural atmosphere. Nevertheless, his influence was substantial in the sense that his students, Ernesto Codignola and Giovanni Gentile to mention only the most famous, were in a later period to become some of the leading spokesmen for a cultural rebirth of humanism.

Jaja was concerned with what, in a matter of weeks, was to be Croce's central concern: the relationship between science and history. Like De Sanctis and Spaventa before him, he was not opposed to science itself, but rather to its inflation into an independent metaphysic. "For Jaja," Garin explained, "the problem was precisely to define science and its tasks . . . and to determine the relationship between science and philosophy" (*Intellettuali*, p. 145).

Writing in *La nazione* from Pisa on 7 May 1892, Jaja explained that there are two sciences: one is of the laboratory and treats the knowable, "which grasps things as they come to it one after another, one next to another"; the other deals with the totality of human history with all its contradictions. Without this latter science "what would be the value of history? . . . This science excludes nothing and denies nothing . . . [but] kneels reverently before the indefinite multiplicity and contradictory aspirations of life" (*Intellettuali*, p. 145). To restrict "science" to the science of the laboratory excluded, therefore, the study of all that was human, and science had therefore to be a wider category. Croce did not listen.

22. Pasquale Villari, "La storia è una scienza?" *Nuova antologia* (16 February, 16 April, 16, July, 1891). The articles of Villari were inconclusive.

23. *La storia ridotta sotto il concetto generale dell'art*, now in *Primi saggi*, 3rd ed. (Bari, 1951), pp. 3–41. Hereafter *Storia ridotta*.

24. This appeared to Mario Vinciguerra to make "the narration of history" more important than "the facts of history" (*Croce: Ricordi e pensiero* [Naples, 1957], pp. 81–85). But Vinciguerra seemed not to notice that Croce here referred not to "narration" but to the idea that history dealt with facts, not philosophy; that history in other words did not conform to any ideal pattern.

25. *Storia ridotta*, p. 23.

26. *Benedetto Croce ed il pensiero contemporaneo* (Milan, 1963), p. 410, passim. Parallel to the difficulties of distinguishing the companion forms history and art, there was another problem of which Croce was as yet unaware: distinguishing the nature of the two elements he had opposed to art and history. The very claim that science and philosophy were in the same category and that they classified particular facts under general concepts led to the same problem Croce had encountered in the assertion that art and history were alike: hav-

ing brought science and philosophy together, how were they to be distinguished? At the very outset, then, Croce had, through his initial inquiry into the nature of history, raised equally puzzling questions about the nature of art, science, and philosophy. And see, too, A. Caracciolo, *L'estetica di B. Croce nel suo svolgimento e nei suoi limite* (Turin, 1948), p. 28.

27. *Storia ridotta*, p. 9. To Francesco De Sarlo, Croce wrote on 1 March 1898: "I was able to see with great satisfaction that you understand and deeply feel the moral problem. It is truly consoling that students and thinkers like you are emerging [!] after the period that has passed when it was, especially in Italy, absolutely forbidden to pronounce the words *moral ideas, absolute value, duty,* etc. One risked being taken for an innocent or being sent to Berlin by the so-called positivists!" See "Un'inedita lettera di Croce a De Sarlo su marxismo e vita morale," *Rivista di studi crociani* 5 (1968): 76. See, too, Emilio Agazzi, *Il giovane Croce e il marxismo* (Turin, 1962), pp. 75–76; Francesco Olgiati, *Benedetto Croce e lo storicismo* (Milan, 1953), pp. 87–90.

28. Croce, "Come nacque e come morì il marxismo teorico in Italia (1895–1900)," *Materialismo storico ed economia marxistica* (Bari, 1968), pp. 254–56. Hereafter *MSEM*. The following account of Croce's involvement with Marxism is based on my article "Labriola, Croce, and Italian Marxism," *Journal of the History of Ideas* 36 (April–May 1975):297–318.

29. G. Arfè, *Storia del socialismo italiano* (1892–1926) (Turin, 1965), pp. 9–21.

30. Ibid., p. 83.

31. Labriola, *Socialism and Philosophy,* trans. E. Unterman (Chicago, 1918), p. 41.

32. Ibid., p. 60.

33. Ibid., p. 67.

34. Ibid.

35. Labriola, *Essays on the Materialistic Conception of History,* trans. Charles H. Kerr (Chicago, 1908), pp. 135–36.

36. Ibid., p. 203.

37. Ibid., p. 200.

38. In short, it taught that "the proletariat as a necessary result of modern society, has for its mission to succeed the bourgeoisie, and to succeed it as the producing force of a new social order in which class antagonism shall disappear" (ibid., p. 27).

39. Labriola, *Socialism and Philosophy,* p. 65.

40. Ibid., p. 66.

41. Ibid., p. 76.

42. Ibid.

43. Ibid., p. 8.

44. Ibid., p. 43.

45. "Sulla storiografia socialistica: il communismo di Tomaseo Campanella," *MSEM*, p. 171. Lafargue was discredited both by Croce and by Engels's preface to the third volume of *Das Kapital.*

46. Rotondò, "Lo storicismo assoluto," p. 1023.

47. "Sulla forma scientifica del materialismo storico," now in *MSEM*, pp. 1–21; esp. p. 1.

48. Ibid., p. 2.

49. Ibid. And to Gentile he wrote, "I am a bad interpreter of Labriola's books because, besides the books, I have read . . . the author, and so in the books I see often more and [often] less than what the words say." See "Lettere di Benedetto Croce a Giovanni Gentile (dal 27 Giugno 1896 al Dicembre 1899)," *Giornale critico della filosofia italiana* 48 (1969): 8.

50. Ibid.

51. This was something Croce had concluded in an essay two years earlier in 1893 and which he retained even after his encounter with Labriola and Marx. See "La storia ridotta sotto il concetto generale dell'arte," now in *Primi saggi*, 2nd ed. rev. (Bari, 1927), pp. 3–41.

52. "Sulla forma scientifica del materialismo storico," now in *MSEM*, p. 3.

53. Ibid., p. 4.

54. Ibid., p. 9.

55. Ibid., p. 15.

56. As the Marxist Antonio Lovecchio observed, Labriola had indeed purified Marxism of positivism and theology, but he had also thereby removed the impetus to action. See Lovecchio, *Il marxismo in Italia* (Milan, 1962), pp. 75–82.

57. Georges Sorel, *Reflections on Violence,* trans. J. Roth and T. E. Hulme (New York, 1961), pp. 41–42.

58. Labriola, *Socialism and Philosophy,* p. 66.

59. Ibid., p. 10.

60. Georgi Plekhanov, "Review of *Materialismo storico* by Croce," reprinted in Italian in *Cultura sovietica* 2 (Rome, 1945): 108.

61. Giovanni Mastroianni, "I principi del Croce," *Società* 17 (May–June 1961): 291.

62. Letter of 15 January 1897, "Lettere di Benedetto Croce," p. 6.

63. Croce, "Come nacque e come morì il marxismo teorico in Italia (1895–1900)," in *MSEM*, p. 276.

64. Ibid., p. 279.

65. Ibid., p. 276.

66. Ibid., p. 283.

67. Ibid., p. 271.

68. "Per l'interpretazione e la critica di alcuni concetti del marxismo," now in *MSEM*, pp. 53–105.

69. Ibid., pp. 63–75.

70. See Rotondò, "Lo storicismo assoluto," p. 1023: "The *Weltanschauung* . . . affirmed and defended by Labriola was denied by the identification of the innovative and merely subsidiary value of it within the ambit of only the economic sphere."

71. Now in *MSEM*, p. 103.

72. Ibid., p. 75.

73. Ibid., pp. 103–4.

74. Jacobitti, "Labriola, Croce, and Italian Marxism."

75. See Agazzi, *Il giovane Croce*, pp. 76–79, who cites numerous occasions where Croce is seen as an official spokesman for Marxism.

76. Croce, "Come nacque e come morì il marxismo teorico in Italia (1895–1900)," *MSEM*, p. 286.

77. Ibid.

78. Ibid., pp. 286–87. (Emphasis added.)

79. Ibid., p. 274.

80. Reprinted in *Socialism and Philosophy*, p. 165.

81. Giuseppe Petronio, "Problemi della cultura," in Mario Spinella et al., eds., *Critica sociale* 1 (Milan, 1959): 145.

82. P. xi and pp. 78, 81, 101.

83. Agazzi, *Il giovane Croce*, pp. 234–43, 269–83; Henry Stilton Harris, introduction to G. Gentile, *Genesis and Structure of Society* (Urbana and London, 1966), p. 2.

84. "Sulla forma scientifica del materialismo storico," now in *MSEM*, p. 15.

85. Ugo Spirito, *L'idealismo italiano e i suoi critici* (Florence, 1930), p. 41.

86. *Contributo*, p. 330.

87. "Una critica del materialismo storico," *Studi storici* 3 (1897): 372–423, and now in *La filosofia di Marx* (Pisa, 1899), pp. 1–47.

88. Garin, *Intellettuali*, p. 16, n. 19; Agazzi, *Il giovane croce*, pp. 241–42; Garin, *Cronache*, 1:213.

89. Aldo Lo Schiavo, *Gentile* (Bari, 1974), p. 15. It was a Hegelianization of Marx which, as Garin pointed out, also transported Hegel on to a "metaphysical level, from which Feuerbach's criticism had attempted to remove him" (*Cronache*, 1:214, n. 46).

90. Gentile, as quoted by Garin in *Cronache* 1:213–15; and see, too, Gentile, *Genesis*, pp. 73–77; Agazzi, *Il giovane Croce*, pp. 269–83; Ugo Spirito, *La filosofia del communismo* (Florence, 1948), pp. 121–32; M. Rossi, "Lo storicismo 'mistificato' della fenomenologia hegeliana," *Società* 4 (1957): 639–84.

91. S. Alberghi, "Su l'attualismo gentiliano e la filosofia della prassi," *Fatti e teorie* 9 (1948): 1–37; Garin, *Cronache* 1:213–14. Spirito, however, disagrees.

92. Letter 39, *Giornale critico della filosofia italiana* 1 (1969): 48–49.

93. Garin, *Intellettuali*, p. 16.

94. Harris, introduction to G. Gentile, *Genesis*, p. 2. "It seems now to be agreed by those who have access to their correspondence that in this formative period Gentile's influence on Croce was more fundamental than Croce's upon Gentile. The increasingly 'Hegelian' character of the successive volumes of [Croce's] Philosophy of Spirit was apparent to observers from the beginning." Croce himself came close to acknowledging this when he recalled these years at the end of the century when "I began my collaboration with Gentile, whom I had known when very young, still a student at the University of Pisa, and who had published reviews of my books on the theory and practice of Marxism. With Gentile, aside from an ordinary [*pratiche*] friendship, I received an affinity

of mental and cultural development [*mi stringevano affinità di svolgimento mentale e di cultura*] " (*Contributo*, p. 330). And Spirito, "Gentile e Croce: Lettera aperta a B. Croce," *Giornale critico della filosofia italiana* 29 (June–March 1950): 1–11. "You know that the thought of Gentile had a decisive influence upon you, from back in 1896 when Gentile, at the age of twenty-one, still a university student, began to awaken in you an initial philosophical interest" (p. 2). And later, "You are the first disciple of Gentile" (p. 6); and Garin, *Cronache* 1:260. And see, too, Henry Stilton Harris, *The Social Philosophy of Giovanni Gentile* (Urbana, 1960), pp. 19–20, 245n, 259n.

95. Gian Orsini, *Benedetto Croce* (Carbondale, 1961), p. 173.

96. Now in *Una famiglia di patrioti ed altri saggi storici e critici* (Bari, 1919), pp. 189–236.

97. Ibid., pp. 194–95.

98. Ibid., p. 198.

99. Ibid., p. 232.

100. *Conversazione critiche,* 2nd ed. rev. (Bari, 1951), 4:33.

101. Croce's life from that point on was a constant struggle to affect, with his ideas, the world about him. His histories were political statements as much as factual history. Consider only the antifascist *History of Italy from 1870 to 1915*, written, significantly, in 1928, after Croce had condemned fascism. It was one of Croce's primary theses that "research and historical investigation arise only from the present and contemporary struggle . . . from the need which is in each of us to follow the path of his duty." All history is contemporary history. This hiatus between Croce's own theory and his practice remains an inexplicable contradiction which, however, when accepted, serves to explain a good deal of the period in question. Croce's Philosophy of Spirit said one thing; Croce another. "Fortunately, no one," said Garin, "was less Crocean than Croce" (*Intellettuali*, pp. 61–62).

CHAPTER 3

1. Benedetto Croce, "Per la rinascita dell'idealismo," now in *Cultura e vita morale,* 3rd ed. (Bari, 1955), pp. 33–37.

2. Maria Donizelli, "Interpretazioni e assimilazioni del pensiero vichiano in Francesco Fiorentino," *Rivista di studi crociani* 4 (1967): 333.

3. *Contributo alla critica di me stesso,* in *Etica e politica* (Bari, 1967), pp. 342–43. Hereafter, *Contributo.* Spaventa was dismissed as a theologian: "Spaventa came from the Church and from theology; and the most important and nearly sole problem for him was always that of the connection between being and thought" (*Contributo,* p. 342). There was here, however, a slight misreading of Spaventa, for if his sole problem was that of being and thought, his sole nightmare, spelled out in page after page of his works, was that of being left alone with a thought that was unconnectable, "unverifiable" as the empiricists say, in the real world. This kind of idealism was what Croce set out in his *Estetica* of 1902, and later he would regret it.

4. "The point at which Croce had most clearly begun his work as a scholar

had been [his] entirely new vision of art and language," explained Parente as
he examined the dramatic rise after 1902 of Croce's prestige. See Alfredo
Parente, *La "Critica" e il tempo della cultura crociana* (Bari, 1953), pp. 22–23.
The text of this work was originally a lecture solicited by the Italian state radio,
RAI, and heard, on the third program, 7 December 1952, just after Croce's
death.

5. Vinciguerra, "Il primo e l'ultimo Croce," in *Croce: Ricordi e pensieri*
(Naples, 1957), p. 72.

6. Eugenio Garin, *Cronache di filosofia italiana* (Bari, 1966), 1:226. Hereafter, *Cronache* followed by volume number.

7. Ibid.

8. Raffaelo Piccoli, *Benedetto Croce: An Introduction to his Philosophy*
(New York, 1927), p. 140.

9. *Estetica come scienza dell'espressione e linguistica generale,* 3rd ed.
rev. (Bari, 1908), pp. 58–59.

10. The exclusion of technique from the artistic activity has led some
critics to call Croce's aesthetics the aesthetics of the unpainted picture, *il quadro
non dipinto.* See p. 50 of the excellent introduction to Giovanni Gentile, *The
Philosophy of Art* (Ithaca, 1972), by Giovanni Gullace, who is also translator. To
Angelo Crespi, the kind of art authorized by Croce's aesthetics was not so placid.
For him it seemed to lead to short staccato explosions beginning when the
artist first felt them and ending when he lost them or had expelled them. Thus,
he cited as examples of art forms set in motion by Croce the *Fragments* of
Ardengò Soffici or the rantings of Giovanni Papini. See Angelo Crespi, *Con-
temporary Thought in Italy* (New York, 1926), p. 34.

11. *Estetica,* pp. 59–61.

12. Ibid., p. 133.

13. Ibid., p. 78.

14. Ibid., p. 63.

15. Ibid., preface to 2nd ed., p. x of 3rd ed.

16. Ibid., p. 11.

17. Ibid.

18. Ibid., p. 60. And see Gentile's objections in Gentile, *The Philosophy of
Art,* p. 289.

19. *Estetica,* p. 113.

20. Most positivists, in fact, simply ignored art altogether. Thus, Tarozzi:
"Ardigò, the most representative and most vigorous man of positivism in Italy,
maintained an almost complete estrangement from . . . historical-literary
studies; . . . there is in all his works no true and proper aesthetic doctrine"
(Giuseppe Tarozzi, "Per la libertà filosofica," *Rivista di psicologia* 16 [January–
March 1920] : 108–14).

21. *Estetica,* p. 30.

22. Delia Frigessi, "Introduzione," in *La cultura italiana del '900 attraverso
le riviste,* vol. 1, *Leonardo, Hermes, Il Regno* (Turin, 1960), p. 41.

23. Ferdinando Albeggiani, "Il messaggio laico di Benedetto Croce,"
Belfagor 8 (30 November 1953): 713.

24. *Estetica,* p. 16.
25. Ibid., p. 17.
26. Ibid., pp. 169–70.
27. Ibid., p. 151.
28. Vico, *Scienza nuova,* 1:146.
29. *Estetica,* pp. 346–47.
30. Ibid. What Hegel *really* had to say about art had caused trouble for De Sanctis, Croce, Marx, and a host of others. Perhaps it will always be so. It is said that upon the occasion of his death, Hegel uttered this last lament: "Only one man has ever understood me. . . . And he never understood me." Did Hegel condemn art to death, asked Bernard Bosanquet? "Croce mistranslates and misreads Hegel's historical judgement upon the dissolution of art. . . . The phrase the 'death of art,' which Croce reiterates as if a verbal quotation, does not occur in the sixteen hundred pages of Hegel's Lectures on Aesthetics and I do not believe that it occurs anywhere in his works" (Bosanquet, "Appendix on Croce's Conception of the 'Death of Art' in Hegel," *Proceedings of the British Academy* [10 December, 1919], p. 21).
31. According to Bernard Bosanquet, it was in his equation of language with creation that Croce had gone wrong. To the English critic, Croce's "doctrine is sound, it does justice to the essential qualities of the beautiful; to its spirituality and its simplicity" (ibid., p. 1), but "Croce's propensity to sweeping and unmodified conclusions" to "exaggerations and distortions" had led him astray. Croce's assertion that all expression is language, is "perpetual creation," never to mean again what it had meant when first uttered, meant that any "conceptual or conventional meaning must necessarily be banished from our language" (p. 5). Language thus loses its "fine capacity for significance . . . [and has] become a gesture or a tune." Language, Croce said, had not arisen (as it had for Vico) through trial and error and the progress of certain utterances into conventional meanings. For Croce language predated convention, predated thought itself. "But it cannot be so. The whole conception of antedating intuition and language by comparison with the logical affirmation and the concept or category is a nest of contradictions. . . . It is a complete absurdity. . . . Language, in short, is not language without its conceptual side" (p. 9).

For Antonio Aliotta, editor of the positivist *Logos,* the Crocean conception of art was not a concept of art but of life and had the effect of making literally everything into art. If history was art, then so too was life. Aliotta was a staunch opponent of Croce. His writings on Croce's philosophy appeared, largely in *Logos* and in various colloquia over a fifteen-year period, and were collected in 1920 into *L'estetica del Croce e la crisi dell'idealismo moderno* (Naples, 1920). On the significance of Aliotta's critique, see Luigi Pareyson, "Antonio Aliotta: L'estetica di Kant e degl'idealisti romantici," *Filosofia* 2 (January 1951): 141–49; for Croce's denunciation of Aliotta, see Croce, "Conoscenza intuitiva ed attività estetica," in G. A. Borgese's *Hermes* 1 (March–April 1903): 142–46.
32. *Estetica,* p. 6.
33. Ibid., p. 34.
34. In an original formulation of the *Estetica* called the *Tesi fondamentali*

di un'estetica come scienza dell'espressione e linguistica generale read to the Accademia Pontaniana 18 February, 18 March, and 6 May 1900, later published: Adelchi Attisani, ed., *La prima forma dell'estetica e della logica* (Rome and Messina, 1924), Croce had relied not upon memory but upon faith to distinguish the real from the unreal: "With historicity one adds to pure aestheticism an element of faith" (quoted by Francesco Olgiati, *Benedetto Croce e lo storicismo* [Milan, 1953], p. 86). See also Nicola Petruzzellis, *Il problema della storia nell' idealismo moderno,* 2nd ed. rev. (Florence, 1940), pp. 208–10.

35. *Estetica,* p. 33.

36. "Art here meant," as Nicola Petruzzellis pointed out, "knowledge of the individual" fact. See *Il problema della storia,* pp. 208–48.

37. *Estetica,* p. 263.

38. Ibid., p. 262.

39. Ibid., p. 265.

40. Boileau de Malherbe, as quoted by Sergio Solmi, "Croce e noi," *La rassegna d'Italia* 1 (February–March 1946): 262.

41. "Lettera privata per un'omaggio," *La rassegna d'Italia* 1 (February–March 1946): 226.

42. Vinciguerra, "Il grande solitario," in *Croce: ricordi,* p. 43.

43. Giovanni Scirocco, *Croce: La religione della libertà* (Milan, 1973), p. 187.

44. Edmund E. Jacobitti, "Hegemony before Gramsci: The Case of Benedetto Croce," *Journal of Modern History* 52 (March 1980): 66–83.

CHAPTER 4

1. "Il risveglio filosofico e la cultura italiana," *Cultura e vita morale* (Bari, 1955), pp. 22–23.

2. Delia Frigessi, "Introduzione," in *La cultura italiana del '900 attraverso le riviste,* vol. 1, *Leonardo, Hermes, Il Regno* (Turin, 1960), pp. 18–20. On Croce's *opposition* to Giolittian Italy, see Ernesto Ragionieri, *Politica e amministrazione nella storia dell'Italia unita* (Bari, 1967) and Giuseppe Galasso, *Croce, Gramsci e altri storici* (Milan, 1970).

3. *Contributo critica di me stesso,* in *Etica e politica* (Bari, 1967), pp. 334–35. Hereafter, *Contributo.*

4. *Scritti politici di Francesco De Sanctis,* ed. Giuseppe Ferrarelli (Naples, 1900), pp. 73–74.

5. See letter of 24 July 1902, in R. Colapietra, "Lettere inedite di Benedetto Croce a Giuseppe Lombardo Radice," *Il ponte* 24 (31 August 1968): 977–78.

6. "Rejecting the prudence of *divide et impera,* he struck out simultaneously in every direction; and in this way solicited the most reluctant and hesitant spirits" (Alfredo Parente, *La "Critica" e il tempo della cultura crociana* [Bari, 1953], pp. 205–12).

7. Mario Vinciguerra, "Il grande solitario," *Croce: Ricordi e pensieri* (Naples, 1957), p. 11.

8. Attilio Momigliano, "La Critica," *La rassegna d'Italia* 1 (February–March 1946): 235. And see Alfredo Parente's description of *La critica:* "An original movement, in fact, in its thought . . . with a disconcerting novelty in its historical and critical methodology, with the richness of its investigations" (*La "Critica" e il tempo,* p. 9). See also Armando Carlini: "There has been a reform in Italy," he wrote in 1922, and "the decisive beginning of it was signaled by the appearance of Croce's *La critica* in 1903 " ("Benedetto Croce e il fascismo," *La nuova politica liberale* 2 [February 1924] : 34).

9. "Conversazioni con Benedetto Croce," *Belfagor* 8 (31 January 1953):1.

10. Renato Serra, *Epistolario di Renato Serra,* ed. Luigi Ambrosini, Giuseppe De Robertis, and Alfredo Grilli, 2nd ed. (Florence, 1953), p. 310; Fausto Nicolini, *Benedetto Croce* (Turin, 1962), pp. 205–10.

11. Croce, "Ho letto ...," *Cultura e vita morale,* p. 125.

12. Prezzolini, "La critica," *Leonardo* 4 (October–December 1906): 362.

13. Inasmuch as the magazine came out every two months and contained several long articles by the founders in addition to the long detailed reviews and polemics, it is no wonder that many have commented on Croce's perseverance and indefatigability. See, for example, N. Matteucci's somewhat backhanded praise of Croce's industriousness in "Un commento a Croce," *Il mulino* 4 (June 1955): 516–19; and Parente's reply, "Chi sono i fedeli di Croce?" *Il mulino* 4 (November 1955): 894–903. A general idea of the difficulty involved in keeping the journal going and in securing articles for it can be gained from reading the correspondence of the erratic Renato Serra, *Epistolario di Renato Serra.* Of interest, too, are Prezzolini's accounts of his own attempts to publish a journal in *L'italiano inutile* (Florence, 1964), e.g., pp. 171–80; and in *Il tempo della Voce* (Milan and Florence, 1960), pp. 1–20.

14. Edmondo Cione, *Benedetto Croce ed il pensiero contemporaneo* (Milan, 1963), pp. 96–97.

15. Thus, Armando Carlini later taunted the positivists in Marchesini's *Rivista di filosofia,* where one does not hear "even an echo of the name B. Croce. I said Croce: and look, everyone turns around, everyone looks intently, half with a smile (the other half not smiling). Well do they read *La critica*? Of course they read it" ("Le riviste italiane di filosofia," *La voce* 6, no. 12 (28 June 1914): 43.

16. "Due conversazioni," *Cultura e vita morale,* p. 145.

17. Ibid., pp. 145–46.

18. Carducci was also, however, a Freemason impressed with positivism. "Dear Croce," wrote F. Agnoletti, a Freemason, "the historical method of your [previous remarks] on Freemasonry stinks. Garibaldi, Mazzini, and Carducci [were Freemasons]. You use only three insignificant documents" ("Pro e contro la massoneria," *La voce* 2 [11 August 1910] : 374.

19. The publisher Zanichelli at Bologna published, in 1900, all of Carducci's poetry in a single 1,100-page volume. His attempt to contain all of Carducci's prose in a companion volume in 1904 proved unsuccessful owing to its quantity. In any case, it satisfied Carducci, who called it the "definitive edition" and, as he said in a letter published at the beginning of the volume, was "moved by

the love that others have shown my works" to help in the selection of these writings which "because of their quantity and quality" did not lend themselves to easy selection. I have used the 25th ed. published in 1963. They are cited as Carducci, *Prose* and Carducci, *Poesia*.

20. William Roscoe Thayer, *Italica: Studies in Italian Life and Letters* (Freeport, N.Y., 1969), p. 349.

21. Giuseppe Basilone, *Guida allo studio dell'opera letteraria di Carducci* (Naples, 1953), p. 7.

22. Carducci, *Prose,* p. 983.

23. John Thayer, *Italy and the Great War* (Madison, 1964), pp. 10–12.

24. Carducci, *Prose,* pp. 932–34.

25. Carducci's enthusiasm for Crispi was boundless. One evening, it is said, when Carducci was dining at an inn, a certain Policarpo Petrocchi began to criticize the prime minister. Carducci seized a knife from the table and exclaimed, "If you don't stop, I'll kill you" (Giuseppe Basilone, *Guida allo studio,* p. 2).

26. And when 8,000 Italians lost their lives at Adowa in the first defeat of a European army by primitive natives, Carducci urged Crispi—even as he was driven from office—to return with still another army. Gioacchino Volpe, *L'italia in cammino,* as quoted by A. W. Salomone, ed., in *Italy from the Risorgimento to Fascism* (Garden City, N.Y., 1970), p. 345; and Dennis Mack Smith, *Italy: A Modern History,* 2nd ed. rev. (Ann Arbor, 1969), pp. 186–87.

27. Carducci, *Poesia,* p. 385.

28. John Bailey, *Carducci* (Oxford, 1926), p. 12.

29. Basilone, *Guida allo studio,* p. 47.

30. Ibid.

31. Of the "Hymn to Satan," Bailey wrote, "It gave, and no doubt was meant to give, great offense to Catholics: and indeed to all Christians: and still does: offense which in his later years Carducci regretted. We must admit that he was always definitely a pagan: and often, especially in the first half of his life, not merely a pagan but an anti-Christian" (Bailey, *Carducci,* p. 12).

32. Ibid.

33. Luigi Russo, *Francesco De Sanctis e la cultura napoletana,* 3rd ed. (Florence, 1958), p. 259.

34. Angelo Crespi, *Contemporary Thought in Italy* (New York, 1926), p. 24.

35. Vittorio Vettori, *Riviste italiane del novecento* (Rome, 1958), p. 11.

36. Giovanni Spadolini, "Croce e il mondo Carducciano," *Rivista di studi crociani* 3 (1969): 79.

37. The conclusion drawn by Antonio Rotondò, "Lo storicismo assoluto e la tradizione vichiana," *Società* 2 (1955): 1011–47, that Croce had abandoned his notion of revolution-regeneration and was only interested in the destruction of Marxism and the pursuit of philosophy is true only of a later Croce. Left Hegelianism and Jacobinism were rejected because Croce felt they could not achieve the goal, not because the goal was abandoned.

38. Benedetto Croce, "Note sulla letterature italiana: Giosuè Carducci, I," *La critica* 1 (1903): 9.

39. Ibid., p. 11.
40. Ibid., pp. 13–14.
41. Ibid., p. 21.
42. Ibid., p. 15.
43. Ibid., p. 16.
44. Ibid., p. 27.
45. Carducci, *Poesia*, p. 483.
46. It is unlikely that we shall find out what Carducci meant to convey in those lines. Was he referring to the Kant of the synthetic a priori or to the Kant of natural law? Had he merely picked up a phrase by then common among intellectuals? Croce implied that the phrase linked Kant to the abstract thought of the eighteenth century and not to the later Kant. Carducci, he said, picked up the idea from a reading of Heinrich Heine's *Zur Geschichte der Religion und Philosophie in Deutschland*. But the idea was, Croce went on, not original with Heine either. It occurred in one of Hegel's letters to Schelling (21 July 1795) and in a letter of 1791 from Baggesen to Reinheld and in many other places. It was, as Croce pointed out, a notion that was "in the air." But we need not concern ourselves with what Carducci meant. The issue is what Croce thought of it, and to him Kant meant the synthetic a priori and obviously not "natural law." See Croce, *Conversazioni critiche*, 4th ed. rev. (1950), pp. 292–94.
47. How to translate the one language into the other, wondered Gramsci, even as he languished in one of Mussolini's prisons. From Carducci to the *Holy Family*, to the *Theses on Feuerbach* took Gramsci less than a page. "The philosophers," Gramsci quoted Marx, "have only interpreted the world, in various ways; the point, however, is to change it." Gramsci, *Materialismo storico*, pp. 78–79.
48. In 1903 the essay had ended:

> Carducci . . . is not material for the refined, for little coteries, nor does it rove in a limited circle of sentimental complications. It resounds in the national soul and in all cultivated spirits: everyone of us can remember how as a young man he awaited and welcomed every new ode of Carducci; how he stirred and inebriated the heart, and how Carducci seemed a brother, the perpetuator of the great Italian poets transmitted to us in school. (Croce, "Note sulla letterature italiana: Giosue Carducci," p. 30)

In the *Storia d'Italia dal 1871 al 1915*, 15th ed. (Bari, 1967):

> Only one man in those days had the wings of an eagle and drew us young men after him. He was not a thinker but a poet, Giosue Carducci, who, living on the confines of two ages, seized the inner spirit of the one, transmitted it, and planted it in the heart of the other. Carducci was a romantic, in that he shared through his imagination in the life and history of the past, thus joining hands with the immanentist beliefs of the idealists. He was an Italian or Latin romantic in his worship of liberty and of the new life, inexhaustible in its creative force, which dwells within human reason. (p. 136)

49. *Storia d'Italia*, p. 99.
50. *Contributo*, p. 342.

51. Benedetto Croce, "Note sulla letteratura italiana: Gabriele D'Annunzio," *La critica* 2 (1904): 1.

52. See Enrico Alpino, "La poesia di Giosue Carducci nell'interpretazione di Benedetto Croce," *Rivista di studi crociani* 1 (1964): 17; Basilone, *Guida allo studio*, pp. 101–05.

53. Some critics are thus wont, and one is inclined to agree, to make a continuum Carducci–D'Annunzio which, if not apparent in style, is often apparent in theme; see Domenico Petrini: "Given the *Barbarian Odes*, Pascoli and D'Annunzio are in sight." As quoted, reluctantly, by Alpino, "La poesia di Carducci," p. 179; see, too, M. Fubini, "L'ultimo Carducci," in *Romanticismo italiano* (Bari, 1960), p. 258; Garin, *Cronache* 1: 180n–81n; G. Bertacchi, *Dalle Odi Barbare carducciane alle Laudi dannunziane* (Rome, 1963).

54. By the 1890s Carducci was being hooted in his own classroom. On 11 March 1891, for example, having already spent the night whooping beneath Carducci's window, a group of students invaded his classroom, shouting, "Buffoon! Coward! Down with Carducci!" The old man remained unmoved and, when the din had sufficiently moderated, solemnly intoned, "It is useless of you to shout 'Down' when nature has placed me so high. You ought to shout 'Death!'" (Basilone, *Guida allo studio*, p. 14).

55. D'Annunzio, as is known, had the morality of a satyr, which he nevertheless self-consciously puffed up into an "ethic" worthy of only the chosen few, those artists who because of their mission to lesser mortals were relieved of the obligations everyday life imposes upon the rest of us. A glimpse into the "secret" of his life may be had from his secretary's book, Tommaseo Antongini, *Vita segreta di Gabriele D'Annunzio* (Milan, 1958). For an unvarnished hymn to this "modern Italian spirit," see A. Bruers *Gabriele D'Annunzio e il moderno spirito italiano* (Rome, 1921); Bruers, *Gabriele D'Annunzio–il pensiero e l'azione* (Bologna, 1934); Bruers, *Nuovi saggi D'Annunziane* (Bologna, 1938). Bruers, incidentally, was D'Annunzio's librarian and ended as editor of a fascist journal. See too C. A. Traversi, *D'Annunzio nella vita e nelle opere: documenti inediti e rari* (Rome, 1934).

56. Gerhard Masur, *Prophets of Yesterday* (New York, 1966), p. 137.

57. Croce, "D'Annunzio," p. 1.

58. Ibid., pp. 2–3.

59. Ibid., p. 5.

60. Ibid., p. 3.

61. Ibid., p. 21.

62. Ibid., p. 2.

63. Ibid., p. 5.

64. Ibid., p. 6.

65. "Note sulla letteratura italiana: Gabriele D'Annunzio II," *La critica* 2 (1904): 110.

CHAPTER 5

1. Delia Frigessi, "Introduzione," in *La cultura italiana del'900 attraverso*

le riviste, vol 1, *Leonardo, Hermes, Il Regno* (Turin, 1960), pp. 11–12. Hereafter, *La cultura* followed by the volume number and page.

2. Borgese, "Il vascella fantasma," *Hermes* 2 (1904): 100–04; *La cultura*, 1: 379.

3. Maffio Maffi (1881–1957), also a graduate of the Istituto di Studi Superiori of Florence, later director and founder of *Il giornale* of Vicenza, vice-director of Rome's *Tribuna* (1910–24), director of Turin's *Gazetta del popolo* (1926–27), director of *Corriere della sera* (1928–29), director of *La nazione* of Florence (1932–43), and a writer in numerous other newspapers and journals; Emilio Cecchi (1884–19??), a collaborator of *La voce*, author of various critical literary works and a prominent writer in Piero Gobetti's *Baretti*; a member of Salvemini's Lega Democratica per il Rinnovamento della Politica Nazionale; Giovanni Calò, later a senator and undersecretary of public instruction; Nello Tarchiani; and several others.

4. Croce, "Leonardo," *La critica* 1 (1903): 1n.

5. "Prefazione," *Hermes* 1 (1904): 1–3; *La cultura*, 1: 370.

6. "Congedo," *Hermes* 12 (1906): 266; *La cultura*, 1: 436–37.

7. Marcello Taddei, "I profeti della stirpe," *Hermes* 3 (1904):117–27; *La cultura*, 1: 380–92.

8. *La cultura*, 1:14.

9. Giovanni Papini and Giuseppe Prezzolini, "La fine," *Leonardo* 5 (August 1907): 257–63; *La cultura*, 1: 362.

10. Crespi, *Contemporary Thought in Italy* (New York, 1926), pp. 22–24.

11. Eugenio Garin, *Cronache di filosofia italiana 1900–1943* (Bari, 1966), 1: 25.

12. Giuliano il Sofista [Prezzolini], "Vita trionfante," *Leonardo* 1 (4 January 1903): 4–5; *La cultura*, 1: 97–98.

13. "Programa sintetico," *Leonardo* 1 (4 January 1903): 1; *La cultura*, 1:89.

14. Prezzolini, "L'uomo-Dio," *Leonardo* 1 (27 January 1903): 3–4 (emphasis added); *La cultura*, 1: 117.

15. Prezzolini, "L'uomo-Dio," *Leonardo* 1 (27 January 1903): 4.

16. Ibid., pp. 4, 118.

17. Ibid.

18. Ibid. *"Leonardo,"* remarked Carlo Martini, "was principally mystical even when it was the organ of Italian pragmatism because it always appealed to the inner forces of the personality against reason; it was the organ, truly, of romanticism" (*La voce: storica e bibliografia* [Pisa, 1956], pp. 10–11). And see, too, Vittorio Vettori: *Leonardo* was "generic mysticism" (*Riviste italiane del novecento* [Rome, 1958], p. 22).

19. Giuliano il Sofista [G. Prezzolini], "Un compagno di scavi, (F. C. S. Schiller," *Leonardo* 2 (June 1904): 4–7; *La cultura*, 1:154.

20. Giuliano il Sofista, "Un compagno di scavi," p. 4; *La cultura*, 1:155.

21. Gian Falco [G. Papini], "Marta e Maria," *Leonardo* 2 (March 1904): 7; and see also Gian Falco [G. Papini], "Athena e Faust," *Leonardo* 3 (February 1905): 8–14; *La cultura*, 1:198–212.

22. Gian Falco [G. Papini], "Campagna per il forzato risveglio," *Leonardo*
4 (August 1906): 193–99; *La cultura,* 1:312–16. Not all the Italian pragmatist
movement, of course, accepted these ideas, not even all the *Leonardiani.*
Another wing of the movement had been drawn to Charles Sanders Peirce's
articles, such as "Illustrations of the Logic of Science" in the November 1877
issue of the *Popular Science Monthly.* There Peirce suggested that in the case
of opinions which are as yet untested, one should choose the opinion most likely
to lead to the desired result. In order to clarify an idea, one must pay attention
to *the sensible result of that idea* rather than to the idea itself, for an idea is
tested in reality and not in the mind. Peirce's idea was sustained by two other
Leonardiani, Mario Calderoni and Giovanni Vailati, both of whom opposed any
type of mysticism and soon came into conflict with the mystical wing of pragmatism sponsored by Papini and Prezzolini. To Calderoni, Vailati, and Peirce,
an idea was merely provisory, awaiting confirmation in external reality; and barring such confirmation, the idea would be regarded as unfounded. One could
subscribe, of course, to any idea one chose, but the test of the truth of the idea
was in reality; as Peirce said to James, choose to believe what you will, but
"will nature honor the check?" See Aurelia Bobbio, *Le riviste fiorentine del
principio del secolo 1903–11* (Florence, 1936), p. 41.

Calderoni objected to Prezzolini's world of magic, for it seemed to take no
account of consequences in reality.

> If in fact we did not have beliefs about *consequences,* about things and
> facts, all would be, or we would at least believe ourselves to be, omnipotent.
> But precisely because our beliefs are the base of every rule and action, it
> is not in any way legitimate to vary our beliefs for some caprice. *Precisely
> because* believing modifies our mode of acting, believing a false thing is a
> very serious thing for us. ("La varietà del pragmatismo," *Leonardo* 2 [No-
> vember 1904]: 3; emphasis added)

Calderoni went on to show that true pragmatism had never intended that we
make assertions about areas that were unverifiable in experiences; that the pragmatists were in fact the most fiery adversaries of such ideas. Pragmatism, said
Calderoni, had nothing to do with morality. It had "never attempted a justification of ethical or sentimental needs" because they were empirically unverifiable.
Prezzolini replied:

> There are two varieties of pragmatism, one of which operates in science and
> is represented by Peirce in logic, by Mach and others in physics; the other,
> which operates in morality, is represented by James, Schiller, Caldwell, and others.
> Both fabricate or accept for their own needs [propositions] already fabricated
> by metaphysics, but for the first it is best to prefer impartiality, for the sec-
> ond, such is not necessary . . . since the first rest in the natural world, the
> others in the supernatural. Thus, the two types of pragmatism vary according
> to the types of things to which they are applied." (Ibid., pp. 175–76)

On the whole pragmatist movement in Italy, see Luigi Pedrazzi, "Il pragmatismo
in Italia: 1903–1911," *Il mulino* 2 (August 1952): 495–520.

23. Gian Falco [G. Papini], "Cosa vogliamo?" *Leonardo* 2 (November 1904): 9–19; *La cultura*, 1: 181. The difficulty with Papini's notion of action, and Prezzolini's as well, was that they sought to liberate action from thought, to make, in other words, action into impulse and at the same time make thought "retroactive." It was a notion derived from a passage dealing with hypnotism in James's *Principles of Psychology*, a passage to which Prezzolini returned again and again through the life of his journal. A patient who had been hypnotized may be given a post-hypnotic suggestion and when the patient carries out the suggestion, Prezzolini quoted James, he "forgets the circumstance of the impulse having been suggested to him in a previous trance; regards it as arising within himself; and often improvises, as he yields to it, some more or less plausible or ingenious motive by which to justify it to the lookers-on" (Giuliano il Sofista [G. Prezzolini], "La miseria dei logici," *Leonardo* 1 [1903]: 7). Prezzolini then went on to draw from this the view that "all our reasonings are like those the hypnotized subject invents; and if those who believe themselves to be more than others with respect to reason and followers of logic in [this] action, they are only more able inventors of sophisms to justify action" (ibid). Prezzolini could not forget the passage and his conclusions from it. Two years later, challenged to explain his notion of liberty, he again referred to the passage in James. See Giuliano il Sofista [G. Prezzolini], "Risposta a Calderoni," *Leonardo* 2 (1904): 7.

Yet James, only five pages before those lines Prezzolini singled out, had said too: "It is unfair, however, to say that in those cases the subject is a pure puppet with no spontaneity. . . . If the thing suggested be too intimately repugnant, the subject may strenuously resist. . . . The subject surrenders himself good-naturedly to the performance, stabs the pasteboard dagger you give him because he knows what it is, and fires off the pistol because he knows it has no ball; but for a real murder he would not be your man" (William James, *Principles of Psychology* [Chicago, 1952], p. 843).

24. "Miracles," explained Papini, "are only extraordinary results obtained by an intense will." See Gian Falco [G. Papini], "Cosa vogliamo?", p. 11; *La cultura*, 1: 188.

25. Croce, "Leonardo," *La critica* 1 (1903): 287.

26. Eugenio Garin, "Note sul pensiero italiano del'900," *Leonardo* 15 (February 1946): 22–32; ibid. (April 1946): 78–86; ibid. (August–October 1946): 201–10.

27. Croce, "Review of *Il linguaggio come cause d'errore*–H. Bergson by G. Prezzolini," *La critica* 2 (1904): 150.

28. Ibid.

29. Croce had reviewed Masci's *Psicologia* in *La critica* and concluded that the book was worthless, eclectic, and confusing. Aiming to discredit Masci before his students, Croce concluded:

How could a book be well written when the author does not know what he means? . . . The book is not understood, not because abstruse, but because the author does not understand himself. . . . Professor Masci should try this cure: Not to read any books for many years and to settle accounts with himself in order to *clarify his ideas,* before again taking up the pen. (Croce, "Review of *Psicologia* by Filippo Masci," *La critica* 2 [1904]: 195)

Masci, unhumbled, again took up the pen, however, and so Croce was forced to write again of Masci. This time Croce told Masci that he, Croce, had written a great many books that had had a considerable impact on Italy, as had his magazine, *La critica,* and that during all that time he, unlike Masci, had never felt it necessary to make himself understood by professors or to convince established professors of his point of view. The professors were without hope, he said:

> I well know [that the professors] need a certain vulgar and dimwitted [*maccheronica*] philosophy made from rehashes of other books badly sewn together and eclectic, which hold the middle ground between what is fashionable and what is traditional, as clear in appearance as they are obscure, rather impenetrable, at base, and reasoned out to the first, second, third, fourth, and tenth degree. (*La critica* 2 [1904]: 520)

Croce wrote, he said, only to the few, for the majority of professors, "were they in a position for an instant to comprehend the gravity of the charges such as those that I have made against them, would no longer deserve them" (ibid).

30. Quoted in Garin, "Note sul pensiero italiano del'900," p. 85.

31. See Fausto Nicolini, *Benedetto Croce* (Turin, 1962), p. 439, passim, and the letter by Croce of 31 May 1909, in Prezzolini, *Il tempo della Voce* (Milan, 1960), pp. 229–32. And see also Prezzolini, *L'italiano inutile* (Florence, 1964), p. 199.

32. *La cultura,* 1:18–19. In fact, during the pragmatist phase Croce assaulted not the magical pragmatists but Mario Calderoni, leader of the moderate and realistic brand of Italian pragmatism. It was an attack on Calderoni's empiricism which took the form of a review blasting Calderoni's denigration of the Kantian categorical imperative. In his book *Disarmonie economiche e disarmonie morali* Calderoni had ridiculed Kant's moral theory.

> In an overloaded boat the opportunity to seat oneself on one side or the other depends on the number of persons seated on the opposite side; if one here followed any Kantian imperative, the capsizing of the boat would put an end to the advice of the pilot and the good will of the passengers. (Mario Calderoni, *Disarmonie* [Florence, 1906], p. 66)

Croce had responded that Calderoni had not understood Kant or the nature of the moral problem, for Calderoni did not see that the

> Kantian imperative is merely formal. . . . Calderoni imagines that absoluteness of moral activity is in contrast to the relativity of moral actions; when instead that absoluteness does not exclude, but rather includes, the variety of moral acts not only of epoch after epoch, and of people after people, but of individual after individual. (Croce, "Review of *Disarmonie,*" *La critica* 4 [1906]: 132–34)

It was, as we shall see, an idea that Croce would always maintain and that would later be developed to its high point in the *Philosophy of the Practical*. Calderoni, not surprisingly, was somewhat astonished at this view of Kant ("that this is a faithful interpretation of Kant seems to me more than contestable") and retorted that Croce had personalized the imperative and made it meaningless. See Calderoni, "L'imperativo categorico," *Leonardo* 4 (April–June 1906): 144. To which Croce responded, "If Kant had ever really thought what Calderoni attributes to him he would have been a cretin; and to reduce a great philosopher to a cretin does not seem to me to be the best point of departure for a criticism" ("Mario Calderoni: l'imperativo categorico," *La critica* 4 [1906] : 316).

33. Gian Falco [G. Papini], "Risposta a Benedetto Croce," *Leonardo* 1 (10 November 1903): 10–11. (Emphasis added.)

34. E. Agazzi, *Il giovane Croce e il marxismo* (Turin, 1962), p. 104.

35. Ibid., p. 149.

36. Turati's "positivism" is also a matter of some debate within Marxist circles. See, e.g., Lelio Basso, "Turati, il reformismo e la via democratica," *Problemi del socialismo* 1 (February 1958): 90–110; Luigi Cortese, "La giovanezza di Filippo Turati," *Rivista storica del socialismo* 1 (January–June 1958): 3–40; Roberto Ardigò, "Sei lettere di F. Turati ad Anna Kulischioff," ibid., pp. 41–43; Antonio Labriola, "Undici lettere a F. Turati," ibid., pp. 44–52; S. Massimo Ganci, "La formazione positivista di Filippo Turati," ibid., pp. 56–68; Gaetano Arfè, "Guidizi e pregiudizi su Filippo Turati," ibid., pp. 98–104.

37. *Storia d'Italia*, p. 142.

38. Lelio Basso, "Turati, il riformismo e la via democratica," *Problemi del socialismo* 1 (February 1958): 88. Basso approved Turati's gradualism up to 1900. After that Turati failed to see the "new requirements, new tasks, that were before the proletariat, and his evolutionary positivism gained the upper hand over the Marxist superstructure of his thought" (ibid., p. 90).

39. Dennis Mack Smith, *Italy: A Modern History*, 2nd ed. rev. (Ann Arbor, 1969): "Violence smoldered throughout 1897. Riots in January 1898 led to Rome's being put for several days in a state of siege. . . . A government circular of May 1898 complained that everywhere the local authorities were invoking the aid of the army. . . . Socialist deputies were camping in the parliament buildings so as to avoid arrest" (p. 192).

40. Ibid., p. 192. It was during Turati's imprisonment that F. S. Merlino, an anarchist, inserted himself into Marxism by beginning his *Rivista critica del socialismo*. The journal popularized several forms of revisionism from Bernstein to Sorel and even Luigi Einaudi. See Arfè, "Guidizi e pregiudizi," pp. 86–87.

41. Noi, pseud. [Turati], "La sinistra alla prova," [response to Ivanoe Bonomi], *Critica sociale* 8 (1 August 1899): 182. In the next issue of *Critica sociale* Claudio Treves expounded, with a vaguely disapproving air, the ideas of Antonio Grazeadei, "optimist," whose "apology for capitalism" had just then been published (*La produzione capitalista* [Turin, 1899]). Grazeadei, said Treves, believed he had shown ("correctly, it seems to me") that Marx's predictions were wrong. The salaries of the proletariat would not fall but would rise because "the increase in salary . . . is in the self-interest of capitalism"; increased industrialization would lead not to more unemployment and more routinization of

labor, but to "completely the opposite results." Hard pressed to find anything which he could actually dispute, Treves was forced to dismiss Grazeadei's "unfriendliness to Karl Marx . . . as mere words," words which, because of their optimism, Treves thought he would present as an antidote to the present "sadness" brought on by the "crisi del marxismo." Perhaps from this would come a "great socialist palingenesis." (See Claudio Treves, "Socialismo ottimista," *Critica sociale* 8 (16 August 1899): 199–201. See also Lamberto Borghi, *Educazione e autorità nell'Italia moderna* [Florence, 1950], p. 199.) Evidently Professor Grazeadei later lost his optimism, for in 1921, with Amadeo Bordiga and Giuseppe Tuntar, Grazeadei helped to organize the Italian Communist party.

It was not, however, only the problem of preserving democracy which troubled Italian socialists after 1900. Equally serious was the problem of where to base the party. For Turati, Marxism was a phenomenon reserved to the industrialized sectors of Europe, and at least a full half of Italy was, and to a large extent remains today, outside the modern world of industry. *Il problema del mezzogiorno*, the problem of the South, was and is an agonizing one for Italian Marxists (and everyone else, too, for that matter). To Turati only time, not socialism, could cure the South: "In the South . . . there is no industrial proletariat, no possibility of Marxist socialism because there agriculture is feudal, the Camorra rules, illiteracy is triumphant, and only one struggle is possible, the democratic struggle for the abolition of the medieval era" (quoted in Basso, "Turati," p. 96). In Turati's mind, and in the minds of many others, therefore, socialism had to be restricted to the North. This "abandonment" of the South goes a long way toward explaining why many intellectuals from the South like Giustino Fortunato, Antonio Labriola, and Gaetano Salvemini have had such difficulty in accepting Italian socialism. Roberto Garibbo, in fact, argued that the only reason Croce allied himself with "extremist elements" (Sorel) was that he felt the South might somehow benefit from the alliance. It is an interesting hypothesis. See Garibbo, "Le alleanze politico-culturali di Benedetto Croce nel periodo precedente la prima guerra mondiale," *Rivista di studi crociani* 6 (1969): 38–49; see also pp. 193–204 (esp. pp. 196–99).

42. As quoted by Basso, "Turati," p. 91.

43. Claudio Treves, "Giolitti," *Critica sociale* 8 (1 August 1899): 184.

44. Croce, "Cristianesimo, socialismo e metodo storico," *La critica* 5 (1907): 321–22.

45. Giuliano il Sofista [G. Prezzolini], "Decadenza borghese," *Leonardo* 1 (1903): 7–8; *La cultura*, 1: 129–31.

46. Enrico Corradini, "Per coloro che risorgono," *Il regno* 1 (1903): 1–2; *La cultura*, 1: 441–43.

47. Enrico Corradini, "Tornando sul nostro programma. II La liberta," *Il regno* 1 (1904): 1–3; *La cultura*, 1: 515.

48. Croce, "Il risveglio filosofico e la cultura italiana," in *Cultura e vita morale*, 3rd ed. (Bari, 1955), pp. 24–28.

49. Ibid., p. 28.

50. Gian Falco [G. Papini], "Chi sono i socialisti," *Leonardo* 1 (1903): 1–4; *La cultura*, 1:120–28.

51. "Note sulla letteratura italiana: Gabriele D'Annunzio," *La critica* 2 (1904): 5.

52. Croce, "Socialismo e filosofia," now in *Conversazioni critiche,* 4th ed. rev. (Bari, 1950): 297–99.

53. As "guerrilla forces," as Garin called them, they were useful, but in the construction of an alternative, "mere fireworks." Renato Serra, writing again to Ambrosini, aptly summed up the differences between *Leonardo* and Croce's *La critica.* In March 1910, he wrote of *La critica,* "all substance . . . supported by calm thought," and of *Leonardo* that, although it had "great merit . . . in moving stagnant water," its authors, "all those of *Leonardo* . . . [were] mere fireworks. . . . The magazine was without structure. It knew what it was necessary to destroy and knock down, but it did not know what it was necessary to substitute." To the enemies of materialism and positivism "it opposed an uncertain and scattered program, internally poor in constructive force." See Renato Serra, *Epistolario di Renato Serra,* ed. Luigi Ambrosini, Giuseppe De Robertis, and Alfredo Grilli, 2nd ed. (Florence, 1953), pp. 310–13. See too Alfredo Parente, *La "Critica" e il tempo della cultura crociana* (Bari, 1953), pp. 18–19.

54. Croce, "Leonardo, rivista d'idee," *La critica* 5 (1907): 68.

55. The new journal was *La voce,* far more popular than *Leonardo.* Its life may be divided into three (or four) distinct periods. The first lasted until 1911, when Gaetano Salvemini, one of the most important figures in the magazine, withdrew to form his own journal, *L'unità.* The second period lasted until March of 1912, when Prezzolini, director of the magazine, departed and turned the magazine over to Papini. The third period was from November 1912, when Prezzolini returned, until his final departure in November 1914. After this *La voce* continued under the directorship of the literary critic Giuseppe De Robertis, but it was then a magazine devoted almost entirely to literature. On *La voce* see: Giuseppe Prezzolini, *Il tempo della Voce* (Milan and Florence, 1960) and *L'italiano inutile* (Florence, 1964); Eugenio Garin, *Cronache di filosofia italiana* (Bari, 1966), esp. 2:302–12; Eugenio Garin, "Un secolo di cultura a Firenze," *Ponte* 15 (November 1959): 1408–25; Wolfgang Rossini, "L'esperienza della Voce," *La rassegna d'Italia* 3 (January and February 1948): 36–47, 140–49; Aurelia Bobio, *Le riviste fiorentine del principio del secolo, 1903–16* (Florence, 1936); Vittorio Vettori, *Riviste italiane del novecento* (Rome, 1958); Carlo Martini, *La voce, storia e bibliografia* (Pisa, 1956); Cesare Vasoli, "Considerazioni su La Voce," *Ponte* 13 (March 1957): 390–401; and Angelo Romanò, "Introduzione," in *La cultura italiana del'900 attraverso le reviste,* vol. 3, *La Voce 1908–1914* (Turin, 1960). All of these works contain useful information on the writers in *La voce.* I have listed below articles concerning some individual collaborators, but important information on *La voce* will also be found in those. On Giovanni Boine, see Giuliano Manacorda, "Giovanni Boine," *Belfagor* 5 (31 May 1950): 308–17; and Camillo Pellizzi, *Gli spiriti della vigilia* (Florence, 1924), pp. 89–160. On Giovanni Amendola, see Piero Gobetti, "Amendola," *Rivoluzione liberale* 4 (31 May 1925): 6–8; see also the references of Prezzolini in *Il tempo della Voce* and those of Garin in *Cronache.*

Amendola was both philosopher and politician, and for his writings one should see, in addition to those in *La voce*, the works in the 1911 magazine *Anima*, which was directed by Amendola and Papini. On Scipio Slataper, see Delia Frigessi, "Ideologia de S. Slataper," *Lo spettatore italiano* (June 1950): 221-29.

56. At this point Croce began to rethink his aesthetics, giving more and more attention over the years to the "content" of art rather than its mere form or intuitive purity. By 1928, that most significant date for Croce, intuition has been replaced as the content of art by "morality": "the foundation of all poetry is, therefore, the human personality, and since the human personality fulfills itself morally, the foundation of all poetry is the moral conscience." See Croce, "Estetica in nuce," in *Philosophy, Poetry, History: An Anthology of Essays,* trans. Cecil Sprigge (London, 1966), p. 221. On Croce's gradual change, see Gian N. G. Orsini, *Benedetto Croce* (Carbondale, 1961), pp. 202, 221-22, 275.

57. Croce, "Di un carattere della più recente letteratura italiana," *La critica* 5 (1907): 182.

58. Ibid., p. 190.

59. Antonio Anzilotti, "Il problema della democrazia," *La voce* 3 (2 November 1911): 240-41.

60. In December 1910, the year of the birth of the Nationalist party, Prezzolini celebrated the seventh anniversary of the birth of *Il regno* (and the first anniversary of its death) by claiming that *"Leonardo,* with articles by G. Papini and G. Prezzolini, contained in essence all the ideas later developed, enlarged, and deduced in *Il regno"* and that he and Papini had produced all that was worthy in nationalism, while Corradini had produced all that was corrupt. Prezzolini, "Nel VII anniversario della nascita del *Regno,"* *La voce* 2 (1 December 1910): 445.

61. Prezzolini, *L'italiano inutile*, p. 250.

62. John Thayer, *Italy and the Great War* (Madison, 1964), pp. 36-38.

63. Croce, "Note sulla letteratura italiana: Alfredo Oriani," *La critica* 8 (1909): 14-15. Croce found, too, in Oriani's history the mark of the poet, for "Oriani had created . . . the world of his dream; a society of most noble spirits, women of high intellect and sensitive soul, men who are philosophers, artists, explorers, scientists" (p. 22).

64. On Croce and the Laterza press, see: Tullio Gregory, "Per i sessant'anni della casa Laterza," *Belfagor* 17 (30 November 1962): 702; Ricardo Zagaria, "Bari," *La voce* 4 (15 February 1912): 757-58. A thoroughly displeased Antonio Gramsci noted the significance of Croce's "hegemony" over Giovanni Laterza: "In the South there exists [only] the publishing house of Laterza and the magazine *La critica;* there exist academies and cultural groups of great erudition," but there were no small or medium-sized magazines, no publishers "around which southern middle-class intellectuals are gathered"; if they sought to escape this, they must find "hospitality" in magazines published outside the South. See "La questione meridionale," *Rinascita* 2 (February 1945): 41 (published posthumously).

65. Croce, "Notizie ed osservazioni," *La critica* 32 (1934): 80.

66. Croce, "Ripresa di vecchi giudizzi: Oriani postumo," *La critica* 33(1934): 181-88.

67. Prezzolini, "Alfredo Oriani," *La voce* 45 (21 October 1908): 187. In fact, his convictions, or at any rate his histories, seem to have come rather less from religion "in the formal sense of the word" than was supposed. The next year, in 1910, Luigi Ambrosini pointed out in a letter to Croce (and later in a series of articles) that Oriani's famous political history *La lotta politica* had been plagiarized, to which Croce responded in a letter to Ambrosini: "If I ever collect my essays into a volume I will have to redo, in part, the one on Oriani because of your demonstrations" (quoted by Prezzolini in *Il tempo della Voce*, p. 359).

68. Prezzolini, *L'italiano inutile*, p. 177.

CHAPTER 6

1. Georges Sorel, "La crisi del socialismo scientifico," *Critica sociale* 8 (May 1898): 135.

2. Sorel, *Reflections on Violence*, trans. J. Roth and T. E. Hulme (New York, 1961), p. 35.

3. Ibid., pp. 42, 126.

4. Ibid., p. 126.

5. Ibid., p. 91.

6. "The ideal of philosophy which we have delineated, is distinct from natural and mathematical views, tied to religion." See "Il risveglio filosofico e la cultura italiana," now in *Cultura e vita morale*, 3rd ed. (Bari, 1955), p. 17 and pp. 35–40; see too Gramsci, *Gli intellettuali e l'organizzazione della cultura* (Rome, 1971), pp. 64–65.

7. Gramsci, *Gli intellettuali*, pp. 64–65.

8. Croce, "Per la rinascita dell'idealismo," now in *Cultura e vita morale*, pp. 35–40.

9. *Materialismo storico ed economia marxistica* (Bari, 1968), p. 104. Hereafter, *MSEM*.

10. Ibid., p. xiii.

11. Croce, "Come nacqui e come morì il marxismo teorico in Italia," now in *MSEM*, p. 284.

12. In fact, he "preached socialism" so assiduously that much later when Croce's young friend Luigi Russo was about to set off from Naples to meet Turati, Croce cautioned him: "Watch out! He is a Jesuit." To which Russo replied, "But you have defended Jesuitism . . . and you too have delivered a eulogy to intolerance" (Russo, "Nuove conversazioni con Benedetto Croce," *Belfagor* 8 [31 March 1953] : 162).

13. Ille Ego, "La recentissima letteratura marxistica," *Critica sociale* 8 (April 1898): 126–27. See, too, Enzo Santarelli, "La revisione del marxismo in Italia," *Rivista storica del socialismo* 1 (October–December 1958): 390–91.

14. Giuseppe Petronio, "Problemi della cultura," in Mario Spinella et al., eds., *Critica sociale* (Milan, 1959), 1: 135.

15. "Nota," *Critica sociale* 6 (April 1896): 110–11.

16. Croce, "A proposito del positivismo italiano," now in *Cultura e vita morale,* p. 45.

17. Letter of 15 September 1899 in "Lettere di Benedetto Croce a Giovanni Gentile," *Giornale critico della filosofia italiana* 1 (1969): 85.

18. It is significant, too, that Croce permitted Sorel to write in *La critica,* with its "restricted collaboration" and its "determinate point of view." See, e.g., G. Sorel review of G. Amadori-Virgili, *L'istituto familiare dell società primordiale* in *La critica* 1 (20 May 1903); G. Sorel, review of Alessandro Levi, *Delitto e pena nel pensiero dei Greci* in *La critica* 1 (20 September 1903); etc.

19. Georges Sorel, *Saggi di critici del marxismo,* ed. Vittorio Racca (Palermo, 1903).

20. See *La critica* 1 (20 March 1903): 226-29 and in *Conversazioni critiche,* 4th ed. rev. (Bari, 1950), 1:282-85. Those interested in boning up on the philosophical significance of Marx were referred to Gentile, who explained what Marx ought to have said: see Gentile, *Filosofia di Marx* (Pisa, 1899).

21. *Conversazioni critiche,* 1:311-12.

22. Ibid., p. 285.

23. Paris, 1906.

24. Croce, "Cristianiesimo, socialismo e metodo storico," *La critica* 5 (1907): 321.

25. Ibid., p. 322; *Conversazioni critiche,* 1:313.

26. Sorel, *Reflections,* p. 97; Croce, "Cristianiesimo," p. 326.

27. Croce, "Cristianiesimo," p. 326.

28. *Considerazioni sulla violenza* (Bari, 1909); see Borgese, *Goliath: The March of Fascism* (New York, 1938): "Croce delighted in Sorel because of the moral value he supported in the latter's opposition to optimism, pacifism, humanitarianism, and all the other trashy ideas of the 'eighteenth-century mentality' which he ever and wholeheartedly abhorred." Croce published the *Reflections,* "accompanying it with a very flattering preface and pushing its diffusion with all the power of publicity at his disposal." The book, "a classic of intellectual and moral disorder," tried to remove from socialism all the humanitarian and rational aspects and make of it a "Wagnerian twilight" (p. 199).

29. Laura Fermi, *Mussolini* (Chicago, 1966), p. 75.

30. Mussolini, as quoted by Max H. Fisch, "Vico e Croce," *Rivista di studi crociani* 5 (1968): 22.

31. Georges Sorel, *Les illusions du progrès* (Paris, 1908).

32. Croce's admiration for Sorel endured in fact beyond the Giolittian period. Thus, Croce was to urge Luigi Russo in 1921-22 to abandon Turati in favor of Sorel. See Russo, "Nuove conversazioni con Benedetto Croce," p. 162. The impact of Sorel in Italy is probably incalculable, for it spread into theories of religion, the family, and even law. See, e.g., works of Sergio Panunzio, *Il diritto e l'autorità* (Turin, 1912); *Diritto, forza violenza* (Bologna, 1921). Panunzio remained a syndicalist right up to the last—when he became a friend of Mussolini, seeing in fascism rather than Marxism the new "church": "This association of minds is not a party, but ecclesiastical in nature; we might even say the missionary nature is the first character of the Fascist state" (Panunzio,

Il sentimento dello stato, as quoted by Herman Finer, *Mussolini's Italy* [London, 1965], pp. 339–40).

33. Croce, *Conversazioni critiche,* 1:287.

34. Ibid.

35. Gramsci, *Il materialismo storico* (Rome, 1971), pp. 228–29.

36. Enzo Santarelli, "La revisione del marxismo in Italia," p. 394.

37. *Conversazioni critiche,* 1:309.

38. Michele Abbate, *La filosofia di Benedetto Croce e la crisi della società italiana* (Turin, 1966), p. 105.

39. Roberto Garibbo, "Le alleanze politico-culturale di Benedetto Croce nel periodo precente la prima guerra mondiale," *Rivista di studi crociani* 6 (January–March 1969): 227.

40. Ten years earlier, in a letter to Gentile, it had been the opposite. "Modern socialism would never be utopian, because it would rest on an assessment of social forces [which] really exist either in fact or in formation. The utopian calculated nonexistent or fantastically exaggerated forces" (Croce, "Lettere di Benedetto Croce a Giovanni Gentile," *Giornale critico della filosofia italiana* 1 (January 1969): 7–8).

41. Marxism produced a "fervor and enthusiasm which burned in the breasts of many and (why should I deny it?) I was also captured by it" ("Due conversazioni," *Cultura e vita morale,* p. 157. Some of this material is based on my article, "Labriola, Croce, and Italian Socialism," *Journal of the History of Ideas* 36 (April–May 1975): 279–318.

42. Santarelli, "La revisione del marxismo in Italia," p. 371.

43. Giuseppe Mammarella, *Riformisti e rivoluzionare PSI 1900–1912* (Florence, 1968), p. 85.

44. Santarelli, "La revisione del marxismo in Italia," p. 399.

45. Giuseppe Rensi, editor of *Coenobium* during the first decade of the present century, was an important figure in various, often contradictory, intellectual movements. His spiritual itinerary included positivism, idealism, socialism, and fascism. Nineteen years after he had written this hymn to idealism, Rensi would find himself writing another hymn—the second to be antidote to the first. We now live, he would say, "in an age of unreflective, capricious impulse," of "tumultuous violence," and "*Sturm und Drang* romanticism. . . . The idealist philosophy is the full expression of this present abnormality, convulsiveness, *elatie gestiens* of spirits and is the factor which by three quarters has created it." And a month later he would add, "Idealism is, in its substantive nature, the philosophy of absolute liberty and, more precisely, of anarchy" (Rensi, "Le colpe delle filosofia," *Critica sociale* 34 (July 1924): 205 and (August 1924): 237. In *The Philosophy of Authority* (Milan, [1920]) Rensi prescribed the cure: "In the present moment, in the political and economic sphere, as well as in the spiritual, the most profound need and the most live thirst is for authority" (p. 243).

46. Rensi, "La rinascita dell'idealismo," in Spinella, *Critica sociale,* 2: 629–43, esp. p. 639.

47. Ibid., pp. 642–43.

48. Ettore Marchiolli, "La filosofia della pratica," *Critica sociale* 19 (October 1909): 301.

49. Giuseppe Prezzolini, "Io devo...," *La voce* 4 (February 1912): 756. (Emphasis added.)

50. Angelo Crespi, "Socialismo, idealismo, nazionalismo," *Critica sociale* 24 (April 1914): 121.

51. C[laudio] T[reves], "Postilla," *Critica sociale* 24 (April 1914): 123–24.

52. Agostino Lanzillo, "Alfredo Oriani," *Critica sociale* 24 (July 1914): 223–24. Lanzillo lamented the poor sales of the work and blamed this on the positivists and politicians who could not accept Oriani's "impartial and severe" conclusions. Oriani's greatest fault, according to Lanzillo, was his impartiality.

53. Il Vice, "Postilla," *Critica sociale* 24 (July 1914): 223.

54. Collucci, "Scetticismo," *Critica sociale* 23 (July 1913): 221–24.

CHAPTER 7

1. "The three volumes were not conceived and written simultaneously; if they had been, some details would have been differently arranged. When I wrote the *Estetica* I had no idea of giving it, as I have now done, two such companions; and I therefore designed it to be, as I say, complete in itself" (Benedetto Croce, *Estetica*, 3rd ed. rev. (Bari, 1909), pp. ix–x.

2. *Contributo alla critica di me stesso*, in *Etica e politica* (Bari, 1967), p. 333. Hereafter, *Contributo*.

3. *Estetica*, pp. 55–69.

4. Perhaps, but according to Olgiati's well-researched polemic against Croce, the Neapolitan had been, at first, as much taken with positivism as anyone else in his generation. Thus, Olgiati explained that upon Croce's first reading of Villari's articles in *Nuova antologia*, asking if history was a science, Croce at first responded that indeed it was. "Having breathed the air of the positivists," Croce wrote an article saying history categorically was a science. Then, having second thoughts, he withdrew the article just before publication and set to work on the "Storia ridotta" (Olgiati, *Benedetto Croce e lo storicismo* [Milan, 1953], p. 83). Nevertheless, from the time he came "of age" his antipositivism remained unalterable. This consistency was, doubtless, aided by the effort of some positivists to prove the "inferiority" of southerners. See Roberto Garibbo, "Le alleanze politico-culturale di Benedetto Croce nel periodo precente la prima guerra mondiale," *Rivista di studi crociani* 6 (January–March 1969): 42.

5. Croce, "Scienza e università," now in *Cultura e vita morale*, 3rd ed. (Bari, 1955), p. 72.

6. Eugenio Garin, *Cronache di filosofia italiana* (Bari, 1966), 1:244–45.

7. Garin suggested (ibid.) that this devaluation of science came from the influence of American and English pragmatism then being elaborated by Giovanni Papini and Giuseppe Prezzolini in *Leonardo*. It is possible. The beginning of the pragmatist phase of *Leonardo* came at the same time as Croce's devaluation. This was also the moment when the ideas of Mach, Poincaré, Le Roy, etc. reached Italy. It led Croce to the conclusion that scientific concepts were "pseudoconcepts," arbitrary and "empirical," having nothing to do with philosophy. (See Croce's article in *Giornale d'Italia*, 7 May 1905.) "The naturalistic disciplines and philosophical research are quite different things" (quoted

by Bernardo Varisco, "La fine del positivismo," *Rivista filosofica* 7 (1905): 327).

8. Science qua science never interested Croce, and after having worked out his placement of it in the practical sphere, it almost never concerned him. The ramifications of Croce's notions of science were worked out by others, notably Francesco Albergamo, who remained for nearly all his life a convinced Crocean. See *La critica della scienza del novecento*, 2nd ed. (Florence, 1941), pp. 75-107; *Storia della logica delle scienze esatte* (Bari, 1947), pp. 290-322. Then suddenly in the year in which Croce died, Albergamo's Croceanism died as well, and he published *Storia della logica delle scienze empiriche* (Bari, 1952) and "overcame" Croce (see p. 365, e.g.), becoming as devoted to Marxism as he had before been to Croceanism.

9. Francesco De Sarlo (1854-1937) was from 1900 to 1933 professor of theoretical philosophy at the prestigious Istituto di Studi Superiori in Florence, founder in 1903 of the Gabinetto di Psicologia Sperimentale, and founder in 1907 of the journal *La cultura filosofica*, which he edited until 1917. De Sarlo had been, though it is not widely known, a sometime friend of Croce (see, e.g., Domenice Pesce, "Un'inedita lettera di Croce a De Sarlo su marxismo e vita morale," *Rivista di studi crociani* 5 [1968]: 73-83) and was an important thinker in Florence who between 1905 and 1915 enjoyed a small but devoted following, including Antonio Aliotta, editor of *Logos,* senator and under-secretary of public instruction; Giovanni Calò; Guido della Valle; and others. He and his school were opponents of both positivism and idealism, attempting instead to reconcile philosophy with the "science" of psychology. On De Sarlo's view of Croce and Gentile, see De Sarlo, *Gentile e Croce: Lettere filosofiche di un superato* (Florence, 1925); for a taste of Croce and Gentile on De Sarlo, try Croce, "Il professore De Sarlo e il problema della logica filosofica," *La critica* 4 (1907): 165-69; and "Una seconda risposta al professore De Sarlo," *La critica* 4 (1907): 243-47.

10. Croce, "Il professore De Sarlo," p. 165.

11. Bernardo Varisco (1850-1933) was a figure both emblematic and symptomatic of the period 1900-29, that is, from the rise of idealism to its demise. A professor at the University of Rome, later a senator of the realm appointed by Mussolini, Varisco evidently began his "philosophical itinerary" as some kind of "positivist"—though Michele Federico Sciacca (*Il Secolo XX* [Milan, 1942], p. 241) disagrees—only to abandon that viewpoint for some kind of "idealism"; finally, as the title of his last work announced, he went *From Man to God* (Padua, 1939, published posthumously, edited by E. Castelli and G. Alliney). On Varisco, see *Il pensiero vissuto* (Rome, 1935), which is an essay by Enrico Castelli, one of Varisco's followers though hardly a slavish one; for the viewpoint of the Gentileans, see Guido Calogero, *La filosofia di Bernardo Varisco* (Messina and Florence, 1950); and Ugo Spirito, *L'idealismo italiano e i suoi critici* (Florence, 1930). Naturally, in the latter Varisco is criticized for his dualism.

12. Bernardo Varisco, "La fine del positivismo," *Rivista filosofica* 7 (1905): 324.

13. Ibid., p. 328.

14. Garin, *Cronache,* 1:244–45.

15. Antonio Gramsci, *Gli intellettuali e l'organizzazione della cultura* (Rome, 1971), pp. 64–65.

16. Croce, "Siamo noi hegeliani?", now in *Cultura e vita morale,* pp. 48–49.

17. Benedetto Croce, *Ciò che è vivo e ciò che è morto nella filosofia di Hegel* (Bari, 1907).

18. Ibid., p. 67.

19. Ibid., p. 59.

20. Ibid., p. 60.

21. Ibid.

22. Ibid.

23. Ibid., p. 62.

24. Ibid., p. 64.

25. Ibid., p. 73.

26. Ibid., pp. 9–10.

27. Ibid., p. 90.

28. Ibid., pp. 92–93.

29. Ibid., p. 93.

30. The distincts, however, appear even before he read Hegel.

31. Croce, *Ciò che è vivo,* p. 95.

32. Ibid., pp. 132–35.

33. Ibid., pp. 148–59.

34. Ibid., p. 154.

35. Ibid.

36. Ibid., p. 184.

37. Garin, *Cronache,* 1:210.

38. Croce, *Ciò che è vivo,* p. 194 (printed mistakenly in the text as 94).

39. Croce, *Logica come scienza del concetto puro* (Bari, 1967), p. 133.

40. Ibid., pp. 92–93.

41. Ibid., p. 121.

42. Ibid.

43. Ibid., pp. 121–22.

44. Ibid., p. 126.

45. Ibid., pp. 126–29. (Emphasis added.)

46. Ibid., p. 124.

47. Ibid., p. 128.

48. Ibid., p. 132.

49. Croce, "La conoscenza storica come tutta la conoscenza," *La storia come pensiero e come azione* (Bari, 1966), pp. 25–26.

50. Croce, *Logica come scienze,* pp. 127–28.

51. Ibid., p. 187.

52. Ibid., pp. 189–90.

53. *La storia come pensiero,* p. 29. And see also *History as the Story of Liberty,* trans. Sylvia Sprigge (Chicago, 1970), p. 38.

54. Croce, "Sulla filosofia teologizzante," *Nuovi saggi di estetica,* 6th ed. (Bari, 1955), pp. 60–63.

55. Sprigge, *History,* p. 54.

56. Croce, *Logica come scienza,* p. 185.

57. On the philosophy of the Practical, see the following: Carlo Antoni, "La scoperta dell'ùtile," *Il mondo* (24 November 1951); Carlo Antoni, *Commento a Croce,* 2nd ed. (Venice, 1964), pp. 227–36; Edmondo Cione, *Benedetto Croce ed il pensiero contemporaneo* (Milan, 1963), pp. 218–64; Manlio Ciardo, "Il vitale e la dialettica dei distinti," *Lo spettatore italiano* 6 (1953): 166–68; Raffaelo Franchini, *Esperienza dello storicismo* (Naples, 1953), pp. 124–33; L. Mossini, *La categoria dell'utilità nel pensiero di Benedetto Croce* (Milan, 1959); F. Olgiati, *Benedetto Croce e lo storicismo* (Milan, 1953), pp. 163–266; Antonello Gerbi, "La filosofia della pratica," *Omaggio a Benedetto Croce* (Edizione Radio Italiano, ILTE, 1953), pp. 67–79; and Giulio F. Pagallo, "La filosofia della prassi e la formazione dello storicismo crociano," *Giornale critico della filosofia italiano* 31 (April–June 1952): 218–40.

58. It was an element he felt had been slighted by the classics, although Francesco Olgiati protested:

> There was here a slight error. The *verum, bonum* and *pulchrum* of which Croce speaks were concepts with respect to ontology. It was a question of *verum ontologicum,* not of logical truth for classical philosophy; . . . And it was for this reason that the concept of the useful was not placed alongside of these others, because it did not belong to ontology. (Olgiati, *Benedetto Croce e lo storicismo,* p. 125)

But to Croce, who had already taken the classical virtues out of their transcendent abode and placed them in human activity, as *factum,* this was not a difficulty. Croce felt that he had discovered a new element in human activity:

> Now I have tried to show, and it seems to me that I have succeeded, how we can conceive of men quite economical in the conduct of their lives, men who are deprived, or have a scarce sense, of ethics. In the *Tesi dell'estetica* I cited Iago in art and Cesar Borgia in history. . . . I confess that, since I do not see that this had been done by others, I give no little importance to have brought out this role of the useful [*utilità*] . . . . The useful has been reputed until now by philosophers to be either a secondary or confused act of a simple case of moral deviation [*egoismo*]. It is, instead, in my view, a distinct and autonomous moment in the life of the spirit: the moment in which the will is will. (Croce, "Il giudizio economico e il giudizio tecnico," *Materialismo storico ed economia marxistica* (Bari, 1968), pp. 238–39)

Croce distinguished the two spheres of will and intellectual activity rather graphically: "Intellectual light is cold; the will is hot. When we pass from theoretical contemplation to action and the practical, we have almost the feeling of procreation, and sons are not generated with thoughts and words" (*Filosofia della pratica* [Bari, 1955], p. 7).

59. *Storia come pensiero,* pp. 23–24. (Emphasis added.) And see Alfredo

Parente, *Il tramonto della logica antica e il problema della storia* (Bari, 1952), p. 35: "Whoever says 'history' in the Crocean sense of the word says not only the universe in the totality of its being and of its relations, and in the inexhaustibility of its appearances and creatures, but he says knowledge, or the knowability of the universe in all its aspects, with shadows and without inaccessible depths." But, complained Norberto Bobbio:

> When one realizes (and it is not difficult to do so, given the number of times Croce repeated it) that the service philosophy should render to historiography consists in the elaborations of some very wide concepts that, as opposed to the infinite other concepts formulated by the human mind, have the singular and strange privilege of permitting the formation of the historical judgment as the only cognitive judgment and these concepts are the four forms of the universal spirit, one is forced to ask oneself if the discovery could not have been a little more fruitful. ("Benedetto Croce a dieci anni dalla morte," *Belfagor* 17 [30 November 1962]: 638)

60. Croce, *Filosofia della pratica*, pp. 35-39, passim.
61. Ibid., p. 36.
62. Ibid., pp. 176-77.
63. Ibid., p. 71.
64. Ibid., pp. 173-78.
65. See Giovanni Gulacce, introduction to Giovanni Gentile, *The Philosophy of Art*, trans. Giovanni Gulacce (Ithaca, 1972).
66. Croce, "L'aristocrazia e i giovani," now in *Cultura e vita morale*, p. 176.
67. Ibid., pp. 180-81.
68. Gramsci, *Il materialismo storico e la filosofia di Benedetto Croce* (Turin, 1948), pp. 199-200.

CHAPTER 8

1. Fausto Nicolini, *Benedetto Croce, vita intellettuale, l'erudito* (Naples, 1944), p. 82.
2. Antonio Gramsci, *Passato e presente* (Turin, 1951), p. 5.
3. Fausto Nicolini, *Benedetto Croce* (Turin, 1962), p. 451. Hereafter, *Croce*.
4. Renato Serra, "Croce e Carducci," *La voce* 2 (22 December 1910): 465-68.
5. Ibid.
6. Letter of Serra to Croce, 22 December 1910, *Epistolario di Renato Serra*, ed. Luigi Ambrosini, Giuseppe De Robertis, and Alfredo Grilli, 2nd ed. (Florence, 1953), p. 352.
7. Gian N. G. Orsini, *Benedetto Croce* (Carbondale, 1961), p. 215.
8. For instance, G. A. Borgese, "Le sette lampede d'oro del Corradini," *Hermes* 1 (March-April 1904): 168-70; as well as M. M. (Maffio Maffi?), "Il regno," *Hermes* 1 (January 1904): 3; and the very precise comments of Sergio Bertelli: "*Leonardo, Hermes, Il regno*. Three magazines, but in substance, a

single group that had its political spokesman in *Il regno,* and in the other two
. . . [its] philosophical and literary [spokesman] " ("Incunabile del nazionalismo,"
Nord e sud 8 [April 1961] : 78).

9. Marcello Taddei, "I profeti della stirpe," *Hermes* 1 (March–April
1904): 117–27.

10. Maffio Maffi, "La religione della bellezza," *Hermes* 2 (May 1904):
42–46.

11. "Leonardo," *Hermes* 1 (January 1904): 59.

12. *La stampa* (Turin), 10 April 1911; and also in *Il mattino* (Naples),
13–14 April 1911.

13. Nicolini, *Croce,* p. 217.

14. "Pretese a bella letteratura nella storia della filosofia," *La critica* 8
(1911): 223.

15. Ibid., p. 228.

16. Ibid., p. 229.

17. Borgese, "Croce e Vico e Croce e i giovani," *La cultura contemporanea*
4 (March–April 1912): 125–75.

18. *La voce* 4(8 February 1912): 750–52.

19. Croce, "Amori con le nuvole," *La voce* 4 (4 April 1912): 789.

20. Boine, "Amori con l'onestà," *La voce* 4 (11 April 1912): 793.

21. "Avvertimento," *Anima* (January 1911): 1.

22. As quoted by Angelo Romanò, "Introduzione," in *La cultura italiana
del'900 attraverso le riviste,* vol. 3, *La voce, 1908-1914,* 2nd ed. (Turin, 1960),
p. 58. (Emphasis added.)

23. "Introibo," *Lacerba* 1 (1 January 1913): 1.

24. The entire exchange is in Papini, "I miei conti con Croce," *Lacerba* 1
(1 June 1913): 116–19.

25. Piero Marucchi, "Il punto morto nel sistema di Benedetto Croce," *La
voce* 3 (12 January 1911): 486.

26. Papini, *Esperienze futuriste* (Florence, 1927), p. 65, passim. And
see, too, Eugenio Garin, *Cronache di filosofia italiana* (Bari, 1966), 2:295.

27. Papini, "La necessità della rivoluzione," *Lacerba* 1 (15 April 1913):
73–77.

28. Ardengò Soffici, *Giornale di bordo* (Florence, 1915), p. 124.

29. Ibid., p. 97.

30. "Giornale di bordo," *Lacerba* 1 (1 May 1913): 9; and in *Giornale di
bordo,* pp. 76–78.

31. Guido Marpurgo-Tagliabue, "Gramsci tra Croce e Marx," *Ponte* 4 (May
1948): 429. (Emphasis added.)

32. Soffici, *Giornale di bordo,* p. 272.

33. Piero Gobetti, untitled note in *Energie nove* 1 (1–15 January 1919): 80.

34. Giuliano il Sofista [G. Prezzolini], "La critica," *Leonardo* 4 (October–
December 1906): 362.

35. Letter from Serra to Luigi Ambrosini of 8 July 1911, *Epistolario di
Renato Serra,* p. 399.

36. Renato Serra, *Esame di coscienza di un letterato seguito da ultime*

lettere dal campo, ed. Giuseppe De Robertis and Luigi Ambrosini (Milan, 1915); Renato Serra, *Le lettere,* ed. Giuseppe De Robertis and Antonio Grilli (Florence, 1948), p. 354.

37. Vladimiro Arango-Ruiz, "Otherworldliness," *La rassegna d'Italia* 1 (June 1946): 81.

38. Antonio Aliotta, "La reazione al positivismo," *Rivista filosofica* (May–June 1906): 381.

39. Boine, "Amori con l'onestà," p. 793.

40. Serra, *Esame,* pp. 60–61, 81.

41. John Thayer, *Italy and the Great War* (Madison, 1964), p. 381.

42. "I giovani," *La critica* 7 (1915): 401–2.

43. Croce, "Un nome abominato," *L'italia dal 1914 al 1918: Pagine sulla Guerra,* 3rd ed. (Bari, 1967), pp. 79–81.

44. "Lo stato come potenza" and "L'entrata dell'Italia in guerra e i doveri degli studiosi," in *Pagine sulla Guerra,* pp. 51–55, 74–89.

45. "Fede e programmi," *Cultura e vita morale,* 3rd ed. (Bari, 1955), p. 166.

46. Raffaele Colapietra, "Lettere inedite di Benedetto Croce ad Giuseppe Lombardo-Radice," *Ponte* 24 (31 August 1968): 976–77.

47. Croce, "Cultura tedesca e politica italiana," *Pagine sulla Guerra,* p. 22.

48. "Tre socialismi," *Pagine sulla Guerra,* p. 284.

SELECTED BIBLIOGRAPHY

BOOKS

Abbate, Michele. *La filosofia di Benedetto Croce e la crisi della società italiana.* New ed. Turin, 1966.

Acton, Harold. *The Last Bourbons.* London, 1961.

Agazzi, Emilio. *Il giovane Croce e il marxismo.* Turin, 1962.

Albergamo, Francesco. *La critica della scienza del novecento.* 2nd ed. Florence, 1941.

Aliotta, Antonio. *L'estetica de Croce e la crisi dell'idealismo italiano.* Rome, 1951.

——. *L'estetica di Kant e degli idealisti romantici.* Rome, 1951.

——. *Storia della logica delle scienze empiriche.* Bari, 1952.

——. *Storia della logica della scienze esatte.* Bari, 1947.

Antongini, Tommaseo. *Vita segreta di Gabriele d'Annunzio.* Milan, 1958.

Antoni, Carlo. *Commento a Croce.* 2nd ed. Venice, 1964.

——. *La lotta contro la ragione.* Florence, 1942.

——. *Lo storicismo.* Turin, 1957.

Arfè, Gaetano. *Storia del socialismo italiano (1892-1926).* Turin, 1965.

Attisani, Adelchi. *La prima forma dell'estetica e della logica.* Rome and Messina, 1924.

Bailey, John. *Carducci.* Oxford, 1926.

Basilone, Giuseppe. *Guida allo studio dell'opera letterarea di Carducci.* Naples, 1953.

Beglio, Louis Anthony. *Life and Criticism of Francesco De Sanctis.* New York, 1941.

Benedetti, Ulisse. *Croce e il fascismo.* Rome, 1967.

Bertacchi, G. *Dalle Odi Barbare carducciane alle Laudi dannunziane.* Rome, 1963.

Bianchi Bandinelli, Ranuccio. *Dal diario di un Borghese e altri scritti.* Verona, 1948.

Bobbio, Aurelia. *Le riviste fiorentine del principio del secolo 1903-16.* Florence, 1936.

Bobbio, Norberto. *Politica e cultura.* Turin, 1955.

Boine, Giovanni. *Frantumi seguita da plause e botte.* Florence, 1918.

Borgese, Giuseppe Antonio. *Goliath: The March of Fascism.* New York, 1938.

Borghi, Lamberto. *Educazione e authorità nell'Italia moderna.* Florence, 1950.

Bruers, A. *Gabriele D'Annunzio e il moderno spirito italiano.* Rome, 1921.

——. *Gabriele D'Annunzio—il pensiero e l'azione.* Bologna, 1934.

——. *Nuovi saggi D'Annunziane.* Bologna, 1938.

Calderoni, Mario. *Disarmonie economiche e disarmonie morali.* Florence, 1906.

Calogero, Guido. *La filosofia di Bernardo Varisco.* Messina and Florence, 1950.

Caponigri, A. Robert. *History and Liberty: The Historical Writings of Benedetto Croce.* London, 1955.

——. *Time and Idea: The Theory of History in Giambattista Vico.* London, 1953.

Caracciolo, Alberto. *L'estetica di B. Croce nel suo svolgimento e nei suoi limite.* Turin, 1948.

Carducci, Giosuè. *Poesia.* 25th ed. Bologna, 1963.

——. *Prose.* 25th ed. Bologna, 1963.

Carlini, Armando. *Filosofia e religione nel pensiero di Mussolini.* Rome, 1934.

Castellano, Giovanni. *Benedetto Croce, il filosofo, il critico, lo storico.* 2nd ed. Bari, 1936.

Castelli, Enrico. *Il pensiero vissuto.* Rome, 1935.

Child Arthur. *Making and Knowing in Hobbes, Vico, and Dewey.* Berkeley, 1953.

Ciardo, Manlio. *Le quattro epoche dello storicismo: Vico, Kant, Hegel, Croce.* Bari, 1947.

Cione, Edmondo. *Benedetto Croce ed il pensiero contemporaneo.* Milan, 1963.

Collingwood, R. G. *The Idea of History.* New York, 1956.

Contini, Gianfranco. *L'influenza culturale di Benedetto Croce.* Milan, 1967.

Crespi, Angelo. *Contemporary Thought in Italy.* New York, 1926.

Croce, Benedetto. *Aesthetics as Science of Expression and General Linguistics.* Translated by Douglas Ainslie. 9th ed. Bari, 1950.

——. *Aneddotti de varia letteratura,* vol. 4. Bari, 1954.

——. *Carteggio Croce-Vossler.* Bari, 1951.

——. *Conversazioni critiche,* vol. 1. 2nd ed. Bari, 1950.

——. *Cultura e vita morale.* 3rd ed. Bari, 1955.

——. *Etica e politica.* Bari, 1967.

——. *Filosofia della pratica.* 7th ed. Bari, 1957.

——. *History as the Story of Liberty.* Translated by Sylvia Sprigge. Chicago, 1970.

——. *La letteratura della nuova Italia,* vol. 4. 5th ed. Bari, 1947.

——. *La prima forma dell'estetica e della logica.* Edited by Adelchi Attisani. Messina, 1924.

——. *La rivoluzione napoletana del 1799.* 5th ed. Bari, 1948.

——. *La storia come pensiero ed azione.* Bari, 1966.

——. *Letteratura della nuova Italia,* vol. 1. Bari, 1914.

——. *L'italia dal 1914 al 1918: Pagine sulla Guerra.* 3rd ed. Bari, 1967.
——. *Logica come scienza del concetto puro.* Bari, 1967.
——. *Materialismo storico ed economia marxistica.* Bari, 1968.
——. *Nuovi saggi di estetica.* 6th ed. Bari, 1955.
——. *The Philosophy of Giambattista Vico.* Translated by R. G. Collingwood. New York, 1913.
——. *Philosophy of the Practical.* Translated by Douglas Ainslie. London, 1913.
——. *Primi saggi.* 3rd ed. Bari, 1951.
——. *Scritti e discorsi politici 1943–47,* vol. 1. Bari, 1963.
——. *Storia del regno di Napoli.* Bari, 1967.
——. *Storia d'italia (1871–1915).* Bari, 1928.
——. *Storiografia e idealità morale.* Bari, 1967.
——. *Una famiglia di patrioti e altri saggi storici e critici.* Bari, 1948.
Croce, Elena, and Croce, Alda. *Francesco De Sanctis.* Turin, 1964.
Cuoco, Vincenzo. *Saggio storico sulla rivoluzione napoletana del 1799 seguito dal rapporto al cittadino Carnot di Francesco Lomonaco.* Edited by Fausto Nicolini. Bari, 1913.
——. *Scritti vari.* Edited by Fausto Nicolini and Nino Cortese. Bari, 1924.
De Felice, Renzo. *Interpretazioni del fascismo.* Bari, 1969.
De Gennaro, Angelo A. *The Philosophy of Benedetto Croce.* New York, 1961.
De Sanctis, Francesco. *Giovinezza.* Florence, 1947.
——. *Memorie e scritti giovanile.* Edited by Nino Cortese. Naples, 1930.
——. *Opere.* Edited by Nino Cortese. Turin, 1968.
——. *Opere.* Edited by Niccolò Gallo. Milan, 1961.
——. *Scritti politici di Francesco De Sanctis.* Edited by Giuseppe Ferrarelli. Naples, 1900.
——. *Scritti varii, inediti, o rari di Francesco De Sanctis,* vols. 1–2. Edited by Benedetto Croce. Naples, 1898.
De Sarlo, Francesco. *Gentile e Croce: Lettere filosofiche di un superato.* Florence, 1925.
Descartes, René. *Philosophical Writings.* Edited and translated by Norman Kemp Smith. New York, 1958.
Fermi, Laura. *Mussolini.* Chicago, 1966.
Finer, Herman. *Mussolini's Italy.* London, 1965.
Flint, Robert. *Vico.* Edinburgh and London, 1884.
Focher, Ferruccio. *Profilo del opera di Benedetto Croce.* Cremona, 1963.
Franchini, Raffaello. *Esperienza dello storicismo.* Naples, 1953.
——. *La teoria della storia di Benedetto Croce.* Naples, 1966.
——. *Note biografiche di Benedetto Croce.* Bari, 1957.
Frigessi, Delia, ed. *La cultura italiana del'900 attraverse le riviste.* Vol. 1, *Leonardo, Hermes, Il Regno.* Turin, 1960.
Galasso, Giuseppe. *Croce, Gramsci e altri storici.* Milan, 1970.
Garin, Eugenio. *Cronache di filosofia italiana, 1900–1943,* vols. 1–2. Bari, 1966.
——. *Intellettuali italiani del XX Secolo.* Rome, 1974.
——. *La cultura italiano tra'800 e '900.* 2nd ed. Bari, 1962.
Gentile, Giovanni. *Che cosa è il facismo.* Florence, 1924.

——. *Filosofia di Marx*. Pisa, 1899.
——. *Genesis and Structure of Society*. Translated by Henry Stilton Harris. Urbana and London, 1966.
——. *Le origini della filosofia contemporanea in Italia*, vol. 3. Naples, 1903.
——. *The Philosophy of Art*. Translated by Giovanni Gullace. Ithaca, 1972.
Gramsci, Antonio. *Gli intellettuali e l'organizzazione della cultura*. Turin, 1949.
——. *Il materialismo storico e la filosofia di Benedetto Croce*. Turin, 1960.
——. *Letteratura e vita nazionale*. Rome, 1971.
——. *Passato e presente*. Turin, 1951.
——. *Scritti giovanile (1914-1918)*. Turin, 1958.
Grazeadei, Antonio. *La produzione capitalista*. Turin, 1899.
Guzzo, Augusto. *Dieci anni dopo (1952-1962)*. Turin, 1962.
Harris, Henry Stilton. *The Social Philosophy of Giovanni Gentile*. Urbana, 1960.
Hobbes, Thomas. *The English Works of Thomas Hobbes*, vol. 7. Edited by Sir William Molesworth. London, 1845.
Hughes, H. Stuart. *Consciousness and Society: The Reorientation of European Social Thought, 1890-1930*. New York, 1958.
Jovine, Dina Bertoni. *La scuola italiana dal 1870 ai giorni nostri*. Rome, 1967.
Kuhn, Thomas S. *The Structure of Scientific Revolutions*. 2nd ed. Chicago, 1970.
Labriola, Antonio. *Essays on the Materialistic Conception of History*. Translated by Charles H. Kerr. Chicago, 1908.
——. *Socialism and Philosophy*. Translated by E. Unterman. Chicago, 1918.
Landucci, Sergio. *Cultura e ideologia in Francesco De Sanctis*. Turin, 1964.
Lo Schiavo, Aldo. *Gentile*. Bari, 1974.
Lovecchio, Antonino. *Il marxismo in Italia*. Milan, 1952.
Macera, Guido. *Francesco De Sanctis: Restauro critico*. Naples, 1968.
Machiavelli, Niccolò. *The Prince*. Translated by Mark Musa. New York, 1964.
Mack Smith, Dennis. *Italy: A Modern History*. 2nd ed., rev. Ann Arbor, 1969.
Mammarella, Giuseppe. *Riformisti e rivoluzionari PSI 1900-1912*. Florence, 1968.
Martin, George. *The Red Shirt and the Cross of Savoy*. New York, 1969.
Martini, Carlo. *La Voce, storia e bibliografia*. Pisa, 1956.
Masur, Gerhard. *Prophets of Yesterday*. New York, 1966.
Mautino, Aldo. *La formazione della filosofia politica di Benedetto Croce*. Edited by Norberto Bobbio. 3rd ed. Bari, 1953.
Mirri, Mario. *Francesco De Sanctis politico e storico della civiltà*. Messina and Florence, 1961.
Mosca, Gaetano. *La classe politica*. Bari, 1966.
Mossini, Lanfranco. *La categoria dell'utilità nel pensiero di Benedetto Croce*. Milan, 1956.
Nicolini, Fausto. *Benedetto Croce*. Turin, 1962.
——. *Benedetto Croce, vita intellettuale, l'erudito*. Naples, 1944.
Oldrini, Guido. *Gli hegeliani di Napoli: Augusto Vera e la corrente ortodossa*. Milan, 1964.
——. *La cultura filosofica napoletana dell'ottocento*. Bari, 1973.
——, ed. *La cultura: Il primo hegelismo italiano*. Florence, 1969.

Olgiati, Francesco. *Benedetto Croce e lo storicismo*. Milan, 1953.

Orsini, Gian N. G. *Benedetto Croce*. Carbondale, 1961.

Panunzio, Sergio. *Diritto, forza, violenza*. Bologna, 1921.

——. *Il diritto e l'autorità*. Turin, 1912.

Papini, Giovanni. *Esperienze futuriste*. Florence, 1927.

Parente, Alfredo. *Il pensiero politico di Benedetto Croce e il nuovo liberalismo*. Naples, 1944.

——. *Il tramonto della logica antica e il problema della storia*. Bari, 1952.

——. *La "Critica" e il tempo della cultura crociana*. Bari, 1953.

Pellizzi, Camillo. *Gli spiriti della vigilia*. Florence, 1924.

Petruzzellis, Nicola. *Il problema della storia nell'idealismo moderno*. 2nd ed., rev. Florence, 1940.

Piccoli, Raffaelo. *Benedetto Croce: An Introduction to his Philosophy*. New York, 1927.

Prezzolini, Giuseppe. *Il tempo della Voce*. Milan and Florence, 1960.

——. *L'italiano inutile*. Florence, 1964.

——. *Quattro scoperte: Croce, Papini, Mussolini, Amendola*. Rome, 1964.

——. *Saggio sulla libertà mistica, studi e capricci sui mistici tedeschi*. Florence, 1922.

Ragionieri, Ernesto. *Politica e amministrazione nella storia dell'Italia unita*. Bari, 1967.

Rensi, Giuseppe. *La filosofia dell'autorità*. Milan, 1920.

Romanò, Angelo, ed. *La cultura italiana del'900 attraverso le riviste*. Vol. 3, *La Voce, 1908-1914*. Turin, 1960.

Romano, Francesco Salvatore. *Il concetto della storia nella filosofia di Benedetto Croce*. Palermo, 1933.

Russo, Luigi. *Elogia della polemica*. Bari, 1933.

——. *Francesco De Sanctis e la cultura napoletana*. 3rd ed. Florence, 1958.

Salomone, William. *Italy in the Giolittian Era*. Philadelphia, 1960.

Salvadori, Massimo S. *Gaetano Salvemini*. 2nd ed. Turin, 1963.

Salvatorelli, Luigi. *A Concise History of Italy*. Translated by Bernard Miall. New York, 1940.

Saragat, Giuseppe. *Nel primo centenario della nascita di Benedetto Croce*. Naples, 1966.

Sartori, Giovanni. *Stato e politica nel pensiero di Benedetto Croce*. Naples, 1966.

Sciacca, Michele Federico. *Il secolo XX*. Milan, 1942.

Scirocco, Giovanni. *Croce: La religione della libertà*. Milan, 1973.

Serra, Renato. *Epistolario di Renato Serra*. Edited by Luigi Ambrosini, Giuseppe De Robertis, and Alfredo Grilli. 2nd ed. Florence, 1953.

——. *Esame di coscienza di un letterato seguito da ultime lettere dal campo*. Edited by Giuseppe De Robertis and Luigi Ambrosini. Milan, 1915.

——. *Le lettere*. Edited by Giuseppe De Robertis and Antonio Grilli. Florence, 1948.

Soffici, Ardengò. *Battaglia fra due vittorie*. Florence, 1923.

Sorel, Georges. *Reflections on Violence*. Translated by J. Roth and T. E. Hulme. New York, 1961.

Spaventa, Bertrando. *La filosofia italiana nelle sue relazioni con la filosofia europea con note e appendici di documenti.* Edited by Giovanni Gentile. 34th ed. Bari, 1926.

——. *Opere,* vols. 1–3. Edited by Giovanni Gentile. Florence, 1972.

Spaventa, Silvio. *Dal 1848 al 1861, lettere, scritti, documenti.* Edited by Benedetto Croce. 2nd ed., rev. Bari, 1923.

Spinella, Mario et al., eds. *Critica sociale.* Milan, 1959.

Spirito, Ugo. *La filosofia del communismo.* Florence, 1948.

——. *L'idealismo italiano e i suoi critici.* Florence, 1930.

Sprigge, Cecil. *Benedetto Croce, Man and Thinker.* New Haven, 1952.

Strauss, Leo. *Persecution and the Art of Writing.* Glencoe, 1952.

Tagliacozzo, Giorgio, ed. *Giambattista Vico: An International Symposium.* Baltimore, 1969.

Thayer, John. *Italy and the Great War.* Madison, 1964.

Thayer, William Roscoe. *Italica: Studies in Italian Life and Letters.* Freeport, N.Y., 1969.

Vaughn, Frederick. *The Political Philosophy of Giambattista Vico: An Introduction to La Scienza Nuova.* The Hague, 1972.

Vettori, Vittorio. *Riviste italiane del novecento.* Rome, 1958.

Vico, Giambattista. *The Autobiography of Giambattista Vico.* Translated by Max Harold Fisch and Thomas Goddard Bergin. Ithaca, 1963.

——. *L'Autobiographia, il carteggio, e le poesie varie.* Edited by Benedetto Croce and Fausto Nicolini. Bari, 1911.

——. *La scienza nuova seconda,* vols. 1–2. Edited by Fausto Nicolini. Bari, 1953.

——. *Le orazioni inaugurali, il de Italorum sapientia e le polemiche.* Edited by Giovanni Gentile and Fausto Nicolini. Bari, 1914.

——. *The New Science.* Abridged, revised, and translated by Max H. Fisch and Thomas G. Bergin. New York, 1961.

——. *On the Study Methods of Our Time.* Translated by Elio Gianturco. Indianapolis, 1965.

——. *Opere.* Edited by Paolo Rossi. Milan, 1959.

Vinciguerra, Mario. *Croce: Ricordi e pensieri.* Naples, 1957.

Wellek, René. *A History of Modern Criticism: 1750–1950.* Vol. 2, *The Romantic Age.* New Haven, 1955.

Zuccalà, Salvatore. *Croce, Mussolini e il fascismo.* Lecce, 1966.

ARTICLES

Agazzi, Emilio. "Introduzione al problema." *Passato e presente* 1 (May–June, 1958): 295–307.

Agnoletti, Francesco. "Pro e contro la massoneria." *La voce* 2 (11 August 1910): 374.

Ainslie, Douglas. "The Philosopher of Aesthetic: Benedetto Croce." *Fortnightly* 86 (July–December 1909): 679–88.

Albeggiani, Ferdinando. "Il messaggio laico di Benedetto Croce." *Belfagor* 8 (30 November 1953): 705–15.

Alfieri, Vittorio Enzo. "Croce e i giovani." *Rivista di studi crociani* 1 (January–March 1964): 58–72.

Alicata, Mario, "Gramsci e l'Ordine Nuovo." *Società* 11 (April 1955): 197–204.

Aliotta, Antonio. "La reazione al positivismo." *Rivista filosofica* 9 (May–June, 1906): 376–88.

Anaceschi, Luciano. "Lettera privata per un'omaggio." *La rassegna d'Italia* 1 (February–March 1946): 260–63.

Ansaldo, Giovanni. "Il caso Soffici." *Rivoluzione liberale* 1 (20 November 1923): 147–48.

Antoni, Carlo. "La scoperta dell'ùtile." *Il mondo* (Florence), 24 November 1951.

Anzilotti, Antonio. "Il problema della democrazia." *La voce* 3 (2 November 1911): 679.

Arango-Ruiz, Vladimiro. "Otherworldliness." *La rassegna d'Italia* 1 (June 1946): 80–88.

Ardigò, Roberto. "Sei lettere a Filippo Turati e ad Anna Kulischioff." *Problemi del socialismo* 1 (February 1958): 41–43.

Arfè, Gaetano. "Guidizi e pregiudizi su Filippo Turati." *Rivista storica del socialismo* 1 (January–June 1958): 98–104.

Ascoli, Max. "Il gentiluomo liberale." *Rivoluzione liberale* 1 (19 June 1923): 80.

"Attorno al materialismo storico." *Rivista popolare di politica, lettere e scienze sociale,* 15 February 1897, pp. 295–96.

"Avvertimento." *Anima* 2 (January 1911): 1.

Bachelli, Ricardo. "Benedetto Croce, libero spirito." *La rassegna d'Italia* 1 (February–March 1946): 17–26.

Bartolini, Luigi. "Omaggio a Benedetto Croce." *La rassegna d'Italia* 1 (February–March 1946): 265–67.

Basso, Lelio. "Turati, il reformismo e la via democratica." *Problemi del socialismo* 1 (February 1958): 85–97.

"Benito Mussolini alla Direzione." *Polemica* 1 (February 1922): 1.

Berlin, Isiah. Review of *My Philosophy* by Benedetto Croce. *Mind* 61 (October 1952): 574–78.

Berti, Giuseppi. "Bertrando Spaventa, Antonio Labriola e l'hegelismo napoletano." *Società* 10 (1954): 406–30, 583–607, 764–91.

Bertelli, Sergio. "Incunabili del nazionalismo." *Nord e sud* 8 (April 1961): 75–94.

Biscione, Michele. "Croce e Meinecke." *Rivista di studi crociani* 2 (April–June 1965): 129–39.

Bobbio, Norberto. "Benedetto Croce a dieci anni dalla morte." *Belfagor* 17 (November 1962): 622–38.

———. "Cultura vecchia e politica nuova." *Il mulino* 4 (July 1955): 575–87.

———. "Liberalism Old and New." *Confluence* 5 (Fall 1956): 239–51.

Boine, Giovanni. "Un ignoto." *La voce* 4 (8 February 1912): 750.

———. "Amori con l'onestà." *La voce* 4 (11 April 1912): 793.

Borgese, Giuseppe Antonio. "Croce e Vico, Croce e i giovani." *La cultura contemporanea,* March–April, 1912, 125–75.

———. "Il vascella fantasma." *Hermes* 2 (February 1904): 100–04.

——. "Le sette lampade d'oro del Corradini." *Hermes* 1 (March-April 1904): 168–70.
——. "Prefazione." *Hermes* 1 (January 1904): 1.
——. Review of *La filosofia di Giambattista Vico* by Benedetto Croce. *La stampa* (Turin), 10 April 1911.
Bosanquet, Bernard. "Appendix on Croce's Conception of the 'Death of Art' in Hegel." *Proceedings of the British Academy* (10 December 1919): 1–28.
Bottai, Giuseppe. "Il fascismo e la crisi spirituale italiana." *Polemica* 1 (March 1922): 354–71.
Brunelli, Bruno. "Il liberalismo di Benedetto Croce." *Vita nova* 4 (June 1930): 490–93.
Burzio, Filippo. "Croce e gli italiani durante il fascismo." *La rassegna d'Italia* 1 (February–March 1946): 135–44.
Calderoni, Mario. "L'imperativo categorico." *Leonardo* 2 (November 1904): 3–7.
Capanna, Francesco. "Attualità dello storicismo crociano." *Nuova rivista storica* 46 (May–August 1962): 344–68.
——. "Croce di fronte al fascismo." *Nuova rivista storica* 48 (September–December 1964): 579–605.
Caramella, Santino. "Croce politico." *Rivoluzione liberale* 1 (9 April 1922): 31.
Carli, Mario. "L'alcova d'accacio di F. T. Marinetti." *Polemica* 1 (March 1922): 141–46.
Carlini, Armando. "Benedetto Croce e il fascismo." *Nuova politica liberale* 2 (February 1924): 33–45.
——. "Filosofia." *Vita nova* 7 (November 1931): 993–95.
——. "Le riviste italiane di filosofia." *La voce* 6 (28 June 1914): 40–47.
——. "Trapassato remoto." *Il saggiatore* 4 (April 1933): 85–90.
Carocci, Giampiero. "Un intellettuale fra Lenin e Croce." *Belfagor* 3 (31 July 1948): 435–45.
Carritt, E. F. "Croce and His Aesthetic." *Mind* 43 (1953): 452–64.
Casati, Alessandro. "Mazzini e gli Hegeliani di Napoli." *La critica* 9 (1912): 78.
Casotti, Mario. Review of *Lineamenti di filosofia scetica* by Giuseppe Rensi. *Giornale critico di filosofia italiana* 1 (January 1920): 108–16.
Castellano, Giovanni. "Dopo i pieni poteri." *Polemica* 3 (February 1924): 112–15.
——. "Una parola chiara." *Polemica* 3 (June–July 1924): 331–33.
Cavallera, Herve A. "Sviluppo e significato del concetto di religione in Giovanni Gentile." *Giornale critico della filosofia italiana* 1 (1974): 61–137.
Ciardo, Manlio. "Il vitale e la dialettica dei distinti." *Lo spettatore italiano* 6 (1953): 166–68.
Cione, Edmondo. "Bilancio del pro e del contro." *La fiera letteraria* (23 December 1962): 3.
"Coerenza." *Il saggiatore* 4 (December 1933): 458–60.
Colapietra, Raffaele. "Lettere inedite di Benedetto Croce a Giuseppe Lombardo-Radice." *Il ponte* 24 (31 August 1968): 976–97.
Collucci, Tullio. "Scetticismo." *Critica sociale* 23 (16–31 July 1913): 221–24.
Corradini, Enrico. "Per coloro che risorgono." *Il regno* 1 (29 November 1903): 1.
——. "Tornando sul nostro programma: la libertà." *Il regno* 2 (9 October 1904): 1–3.

Cortese, Luigi. "La giovinezza di Filippo Turati." *Problemi del socialismo* 1 (February 1958): 3–40.

——. "Socialismo, idealismo, nazionalismo." *Critica sociale* 24 (16–30 April 1914): 123–24.

Croce, Alda. Review of S. Landucci, *Cultura e ideologia. . . . Giornale storico della letteratura italiana* 141 (1964): 620.

Croce, Benedetto. "Amori con le nuvole." *La voce* 4 (4 April 1912): 789.

——. "Congedo." *Hermes* 12 (July 1906): 266.

——. "Conoscenza intuitiva ed attività estetica." *Hermes* 1 (March–April 1903): 142–47.

——. "Cristianesimo, socialismo e metodo storico." *La critica* 5 (1907): 317–30.

——. "De Sanctis-Gramsci." *Terze pagine sparse* 2 (1955): 166–68.

——. "Di un carattere della più recente letterature italiana." *La critica* 33 (1935): 179–90.

——. "Giovanni Bovio e la poesia della filosofia." *La critica* 5 (1907): 340–47.

——. "I giovani." *La critica* 7 (1915): 401–02.

——. "Il professore De Sarlo e i problemi della logica filosofica." *La critica* 4 (1907): 165–69.

——. "Leonardo." *La critica* 2 (1903): 287.

——. "Lettere di Benedetto Croce a Giovanni Gentile (dal 27 giugno 1896 al dicembre 1899)." *Giornale critico della filosofia italiana* 48 (January 1969): 1–100.

——. "Lettere di Benedetto Croce sulla reforma Gentile." *La nuovo politica liberale* 2 (December 1923): 432–34.

——. "Mario Calderoni: l'imperativo categorico." *La critica* 4 (1906): 144.

——. "Nota." *La critica* 21 (1924): 192.

——. "Note sulla letterature italiana: Alredo Oriani." *La critica* 7 (1909): 1–28.

——. "Note sulla letterature italiana: Gabriele D'Annunzio." *La critica* 2 (1904): 1–28, 85–110.

——. "Note sulla letterature italiana: Giosuè Carducci I." *La critica* 1 (1903): 7–31.

——. "Notizie ed osservazioni." *La critica* 32 (1934): 80.

——. "Per due edizione delle opere complete di Francesco De Sanctis." *Terze pagine sparse* 2 (1955): 282–85.

——. "Postilla." *La critica* 22 (1924): 189–92.

——. "Postille politiche." *Politica* 1 (19 January 1919): 202–12.

——. "Postille politiche." *Politica* 1 (24 April 1919): 48–59.

——. "Prefazione." *Hermes* 1 (January 1904): 1–4.

——. "Pretese a bella letteratura nella storia della filosofia." *La critica* 8 (1911): 223.

——. Review of *Disarmonie economiche e disarmonie morali* by M. Calderoni. *La critica* 4 (1906): 132–34.

——. Review of *Il linguaggio come cause d'errore–H. Bergson* by G. Prezzolini. *La critica* 2 (1904): 150.

——. Review of *Psicologia* by Filippo Masci. *La critica* 2 (1904): 321–23.

——. "Ripressa di vecchi giudizzi: Oriano postumo." *La critica* 33 (1935): 181–88.

——. "Roots of Liberty." In *Freedom and Its Meaning*. Edited by Ruth Nanda Anshen. Translated by Arthur Livingston. New York, 1940.

——. "Una seconda riposta a Professore De Sarlo." *La critica* 4 (1907): 243–47.

——. "Una tranquilla revoluzione filosofica." *Il mondo,* 17 February 1951.

Cubeddù, Italo. "Bertrando Spaventa pubblicista: guigno-dicembre 1851." *Giornale critico della filosofia italiana* 1 (1974): 46–65.

D'Andrea, Antonio. "Senso olimpico della vita o angosciato isolamento nel diario di Benedetto Croce." *Belfagor* 4 (31 March 1949): 222–26.

De Caprariis, Vittorio. "Il ritorno a De Sanctis." *Nord e sud* 2 (November 1955): 29–36; (December 1955); 16–39.

——. "Vecchia sociologia in Italia." *Nord e sud* 5 (October 1958): 56–59.

Del Secolo, Floriano. "Croce e la sua casa nel ventennio." *La rassegna d'Italia* 1 (February–March 1946): 274–80.

De Ruggiero, Guido. "Croce e il marxismo." *La rassegna d'Italia* 2 (February–March 1946): 114–17.

Destler, Chester. "Benedetto Croce and Italian Fascism." *Journal of Modern History* 24 (December 1952): 382–90.

Donizelli, Maria. "Interpretazioni e assimilazioni del pensiero vichiano in Francesco Fiorentino." *Rivista di studi crociani* 4 (July–September 1967); 331–37.

Ego, Ille. "La recentissima letterature marxista." *Critica sociale* 8 (16 April 1898): 126–27.

Falco, Gian, pseud. [Giovanni Papini.] "Marta e Maria." *Leonardo* 2 (March 1904): 3–8.

——. "Athena e Faust." *Leonardo* 3 (February 1905): 8–15.

——. "Risposta a Benedetto Croce." *Leonardo* 1 (10 November 1903): 10.

——. "Chi sono i socialisti." *Leonardo* 1 (February 1903): 1–4.

——. "Chi sono i socialisti." *Leonardo* 2 (March 1903): 1–3.

Fisch, Max. "Vico e Croce." *Rivista di studi crociani* 5 (January–March 1968): 5–30; (March–April and April–June 1968): 151–71.

——. "The Theory of History in Giambattista Vico." *Journal of Philosophy* 54 (1957): 648–52.

Flora, Francesco. "Viaggio nel tempo crociano." *La rassegna d'Italia* 1 (February–March 1946): 3–16.

Franchini, Raffaello. "La 'metodologia dell'azione' di A. Gramsci." *Lo spettatore italiano* 1 (June 1948): 88–90.

Gaeta, Franco. "Note su Croce storiografo." *Rivista di studi crociani* 1 (April–June 1964); 153–67.

Ganci, S. Massimo. "Dieci anni di cultura democratica in Italia." *Problemi del socialismo* 1 (January 1958): 37–52.

——. "La formazione positivista di Filippo Turati." *Rivista storica del socialismo* 1 (January–June 1958): 56–68.

Garibbo, Roberto. "Le alleanze politico-culturale di Benedetto Croce nel periodo precente la prima guerra mondiale." *Rivista di studi crociani* 6 (January–March 1969): 38–49; (April–June 1969): 193–204.

Garin, Eugenio. "Cronache di filosofia." *Il ponte* 13 (July 1957): 1056–63.

——. "Gramsci nella cultura italiana." *Nuovi argomenti* 1 (January–February 1958): 154–80.

——. "Guido De Ruggiero." *Belfagor* 13 (30 November 1958): 722–28.

——. "Note sul pensiero italiano dell'900." Part 1: "Una rivista, 'Leonardo.'" *Leonardo* 15 (February 1946): 22–23. Part 2: "Attorno a 'Leonardo.'" *Leonardo* 15 (April 1946): 78–86. Part 3: "Il pragmatismo." *Leonardo* 15 (August–October 1946): 201–10.

——. "Un secolo di cultura a Firenze." *Il ponte* 15 (November 1959): 1408–26.

Gemelli, Agostino. "Per il programma del nostro lavoro." *Rivista di filosofia neo-scolastica* 11 (28 February 1919): 1–4.

Gentile, Giovanni. "Il concetto della storia." *Studi storici del Crivellucci* 8 (1899): 76–94.

——. "Il mio liberalismo." *La nuova politica liberale* 1 (23 January 1923): 9–11.

——. "Proemio." *Giornale critico della filosofia italiana* 1 (January 1920): 2–5.

Gerrantano, Valentino. "Antonio Gramsci, scritti giovanile." *Rinascita* 15 (August 1958): 537–39.

Ginzberg, Leone. "Croce e Valery." *La rassegna d'Italia* 1 (February–March 1946): 226–27.

Giusso, Lorenzo. "Il fascismo e Benedetto Croce." *Gerarchia* 3 (1924): 634–36.

Gobetti, Piero. "Croce oppositore." *Rivoluzione liberale* 4 (6 September 1926): 125.

——. "Amendola." *Rivoluzione liberale* 4 (31 May 1925): 1–3.

Goglia, Antonio. "Gli avvenimenti in Italia." *Polemica* 3 (June–July 1924): 334–37.

——. "Opposizione–Fascismo–Stampa." *Polemica* 3 (August 1924): 354–65.

——. "Verso la conciliziane." *Polemica* 1 (March 1922): 119–30.

Gramsci, Antonio. "La questione meridionale." *Rinascita* 2 (February 1945): 33–42.

Grandi, Dino. "L'idea fascista." *Polemica* 1 (March 1922): 100–03.

Gregory, Tullio. "Per i sessant'anni della casa Laterza." *Belfagor* 17 (30 November 1962): 700–13.

Grilli, Marcel. "The Nationality of Philosophy and Bertrando Spaventa." *Journal of the History of Ideas* 2 (1941): 339–71.

"Introibo." *Lacerba* 1 (1 January 1913): 1.

Jacobitti, Edmund E. "Labriola, Croce, and Italian Marxism (1895–1910)." *Journal of the History of Ideas* 36 (April–May 1975): 297–318.

Labriola, Antonio. "Undici lettere a F. Turati." *Rivista storica del socialismo* 1 (January–June 1958): 44–52.

"La critica." *Il saggiatore* 4 (July 1933): 210.

La critica. Vols. 1–11. Bari: Laterza, 1903–14.

Lanzillo, Agostino. "Alfredo Oriani." *Critica sociale* 24 (16–31 July 1914): 223–24.

La voce. Vols. 1–6. Florence, 1908–14.

Leonardo. Vols. 1–5. Florence, 1903–07.

Licitra, Carmello. "Proemio." *La nuova politica liberale* 1 (January 1923): 1–8.

Luporini, Cesare. "Il concetto della storia e la polemica intorno all'illuminismo." *Belfagor* 6 (31 May 1951): 249–64.

M. M. "Il regno." *Hermes* 1 (January 1904): 59.

Maffi, Maffio. "La religione della bellezza." *Hermes* 2 (May 1905): 42–46.

Manacorda, Gastone. "Giovanni Boine." *Belfagor* 5 (31 May 1950): 308–17.

—— and Muscetta, Carlo. "Gramsci e l'unità della cultura." *Società* 10 (January 1954): 1–22.

"Manifesto." *Polemica* 1 (February 1922): 2–3.

Marchiolli, Ettore. "La filosofia della pratica." *Critica sociale* 19 (1 October 1909): 301–03.

Marrucchi, Piero. "Il punto morto nel sistema di Benedetto Croce." *La voce* 3 (12 January 1911): 486.

Mastroianni, Giovanni. "La polemica sul Croce negli studi contemporanei." *Società* 14 (July–August 1958): 711–37.

——. "I principi del Croce." *Società* 17 (June 1961): 283–301.

Mattcucci, Nicola. "Dieci anni di cultura in Italia." *Il mulino* 4 (August– September 1955): 683–88.

——. "I giovanni, il fascismo, e la cultura." *Il mulino* 1 (December 1952): 667–73.

——. "La cultura italiana e il marxismo dal 1945–1951." *Rivista di filosofia* 44 (January 1953): 61–85.

——. "Un commento a Croce." *Il mulino* 4 (June 1955): 516–19.

"Matteotti." *Polemica* 3 (June–July 1924): 289–91.

Maturi, Walter. "Rileggendo la 'Storia d'Italia' di Benedetto Croce." *Cultura moderna,* December 1952, p. 13.

Milburn, Myra M. "Benedetto Croce's Coherence Theory of Truth: A Critical Evaluation." *Filosofia* 19, Supplement to No. 4 (November 1968): 725–34.

Momigliano, Attilio. "La critica." *La rassegna d'Italia* 1 (February–March 1946): 234–36.

Montale, Eugenio. "Testimonianza." *Belfagor* 17 (2 March 1962): 225–26.

Neal, Th., pseud. "L'idealismo e la sua guerra intestina." *Lacerba* 2 (1 September 1914): 328–31.

Noi, pseud. [Filippo Turati.] "La sinistra alla prova." *Critica sociale* 8 (1 August 1899): 182.

"Nota." *Critica sociale* 6 (1 April 1896): 110–11.

Orano, Paolo. "Le angosce della filosofia." *Polemica* 1 (March 1922): 253–66.

Orsini, Gian N. G. "Studi crociani negli Stati Uniti d'America." *Rivista di studi crociani* 1 (January–March 1964): 111–16.

Pagallo, Giulio. "La filosofia della prassi e la formazione dello storicismo crociano." *Giornale critico della filosofia italiana* 31 (April–June 1952): 218–40.

Papini, Giovanni. "I miei conti con Croce." *Lacerba* 1 (1 June 1913): 116–19.

——. "In quante maniere non ha capito l'Italia." *Leonardo* 4 (October–December 1906): 311–20.

———. "La necessità della rivoluzione." *Lacerba* 1 (15 April 1913): 73–77.

——— and Prezzolini, Giuseppe. "La fine." *Leonardo* 5 (1907): 257–63.

———. See also Falco, Gian, pseud.

Parente, Alfredo. "Avventura dello storicismo e il tramonto dell'egemonia crociana." *Criterio* 1 (January 1957): 80–84.

———. "Chi sono i fedeli di Croce?" *Il mulino* 4 (November 1955): 894–903.

"Parentesi." *Polemica* 3 (August 1924): 353.

Pareyson, Luigi. "Antonio Aliotta, L'estetica di Kant e degl'idealisti romantici." *Filosofia* 2 (January 1951): 141–49.

Pedrazzi, Luigi. "Il pragmatismo in Italia: 1903–1911." *Il mulino* 2 (August 1952): 495–520.

Pellizzi, Camillo. "Croce: l'ultimo della borghesia." *Gerarchia* 2 (1923): 1353–60.

Peritore, Giuseppe Angelo. "Piero Jahier." *Belfagor* 18 (30 September 1962): 560–65.

———. "Scipio Slataper." *Belfagor* 8 (30 November 1953): 705–15.

Pesce, Domenico. "Un'inedita lettera di Croce a De Sarlo su marxismo e vita morale." *Rivista di studi crociani* 5 (January–March 1968): 73–83.

Petrini, Mario. "Ricordando Luigi Russo." *Belfagor* 18 (30 September 1962): 560–65.

Petronio, Giuseppe. "Correnti culturali e di pensiero nella 'Critica sociale.'" *Rivista storica di socialismo* 1 (January–June 1958): 69–80.

Piccoli, Raffaello. "Benedetto Croce's Aesthetics." *Monist* 26 (April 1916): 161–81.

———. "Il programma del Partito Nazionale Fascista." *Polemica* 1 (February 1922): 50.

———. "La presenza della 'minoranze' liberale." *Nord e sud* 7 (November 1960): 54–58.

Plekhanov, Georgi. Review of *Materialismo storico . . .* by Croce. Reprinted in Italian in *Cultura sovietica* 2 (1945): 108.

Prezzolini, Giuseppe. "Io devo..." *La voce* 4 (February 1912): 756.

———. See also Sofista, Guiliano il, pseud.

Ragionieri, Ernesto. "Rileggendo la 'Storia d'Italia' di Benedetto Croce." *Belfagor* 21 (March 1966): 263–79.

Rensi, Giuseppe. "Le colpe della filosofia." *Critica sociale* 24 (1–15 July 1924): 203–6; (1–15 August 1924): 227–29.

———. "Le divergenze, l'errore e la malafede." *Rivista di psicologia* 15 (March–April 1919): 107–18.

Romanell, Patrick. "Romanticism and Croce's Conception of Science." *Review of Metaphysics* 9 (1955–56): 505–14.

Rossi, Mario M. "Il pragmatismo italiano." *Rivista di psicologia* 19 (January–March 1923): 8–23.

Rossi, Pietro. "Benedetto Croce e lo storicismo assoluto." *Il mulino* 6 (January 1957): 322–54.

Rossini, Wolfgang. "L'esperienza della Voce." *La rassegna d'Italia* 3 (January 1948): 36–37; (February 1948): 140–49.

Rotondò, Antonio. "Le storicismo assoluto e la tradizione vichiana." *Società* 11 (December 1955): 1011–47.

Russo, Luigi. "Conversazioni con Benedetto Croce." *Belfagor* 8 (31 January 1953): 1-15.

———. "Dal liberalismo al communismo." *Belfagor* 4 (31 March 1949): 211-16.

———. "I corsivi di Gramsci." *Belfagor* 15 (31 July 1960): 472-78.

———. "La terza forza e la storia." *Belfagor* 3 (31 May 1948): 350-52.

———. "Nuovi conversazioni con Benedetto Croce." *Belfagor* 8 (31 March 1953): 158-71.

Salvemini, Gaetano. "Coco all'Università di Napoli o alla scuola della mala vita." *La voce* 1 (1908): 9.

———. "La politica di Benedetto Croce." *Il ponte* 10 (November 1954): 1728-43.

———. Review of *La formazione della filosofia politica di Benedetto Croce,* by Aldo Mautino. *Il ponte* 10 (November 1954): 810-12.

Santarelli, Enzo. "La revisione del marxismo in Italia nel periodo della Seconda Internazionale." *Rivista storica del socialismo* 1 (October–December 1958): 381-404.

Santucci, Antonio. "Il tramonto della logica antica." *Il mulino* 2 (January 1953): 29-35.

Sapigno, Natalino. "Gobetti." *Rinascita* 3 (July 1946): 157-63.

Scalia, Gianni. "Dieci anni di cultura democratica in Italia." *Problemi del socialismo* 1 (March 1958): 214-26.

———. "Marxismo e pensiero contemporaneo." *Rivista storica del socialismo* 1 (October–December 1958): 604-15.

Segre, Umberto. "L'integrazione politica dell'individuo nello storicismo." *Rivista critica di storia di filosofia* 5 (1950): 25-39.

Siniscalchi, Franco. "Verso l'avvenire." *Polemica* 1 (February 1922): 12-16.

Sofista, Guiliano il, pseud. [Giuseppe Prezzolini.] "Decandenza borghese." *Leonardo* 1 (1903): 9-12.

———. "La critica." *Leonardo* 4 (October–December 1906): 361-64.

———. "La miseria dei logici." *Leonardo* 1 (February 1903): 5-7; (March 1903): 7-8.

———. "Risposta a Mario Calderoni." *Leonardo* 2 (November 1904): 7-9.

———. "Un compagno di scavi (F. C. S. Schiller)." *Leonardo* 2 (June 1904): 4-7.

———. "Vita trionfante." *Leonardo* 1 (1903): 4.

Solmi, Sergio. "Croce e noi." *La rassegna d'Italia* 1 (February–March 1946): 255-60.

Sorel, Georges. "La crisi del socialismo scientifico." *Critica sociale* 8, no. 9 (May 1898): 134-38.

Spadolini, Giovanni. "Croce e il mondo carducciano." *Rivista di studi crociani* 3 (March-April 1969): 229-34.

Spirito, Ugo. "Lettera aperta a Benedetto Croce." *Giornale critico di filosofia italiana* 33 (January–March 1950): 1-11.

Stella, Vittorio. "Interpretazione sull'utile e il vitale nel pensiero crociano (1950-1960)." *Giornale di metafisica* 17 (January–April 1962): 29-71.

Taddei, Marcello. "I profeti della stirpe." *Hermes* 1 (March-April 1904): 117-28.

Tarozzi, Giuseppe. "Per la libertà filosofica." *Rivista di psicologia* 16 (January–March 1920): 108-14.

Tormenti, Aristo. "Neo-idealismo?" *Pagine rosse* 1 (20 June 1923): 10–12.

Treves, Claudio. "Giolitti." *Critica sociale* 7 (1 August 1899): 190–99.

———. "Postilla." *Critica sociale* 24 (16–30 April 1914): 123–24.

Turati, Filippo. See Noi, pseud.

Ungari, Paolo. "Positivismo, neopositivismo e cultura socialista." *Rivista storica del socialismo* 1 (July–September 1958): 329–39.

Varisco, Bernardo. "La fine del positivismo." *Rivista filosofica* 8 (May–June 1905): 324–55.

Vasoli, Cesare. "Considerazione sulla Voce." *Il Ponte* 13 (March 1957): 390–401.

Vedrani, Alberto. "Contro le nuvole." *Critica sociale* 34 (16–31 March 1914): 92–93.

Vice, Il, pseud. "Postilla." *Critica sociale* 24 (16–30 July 1914): 223.

Vinciguerra, Mario. "Di croce e dell'equità." *Il ponte* 10 (July–August 1954): 1251–53.

———. "Incontro con croce." *La rassegna d'Italia* 1 (February–March 1946): 281–87.

Volpicelli, A. "A . . . un rivoluzionario liberale." *La nuova politica liberale* (January 1923): 108–9.

White, Hayden V. "The Abiding Relevance of Croce's Idea of Liberty." *Journal of Modern History* 35 (March–December 1963): 109–24.

Zagaria, Ricardo. "Bari." *La voce* 4 (15 February 1912): 752–55.

INDEX

Absolute, the, 149
Abstract, the, 29, 39, 49, 54, 63, 84, 91, 96, 97, 147; Hegel opponent of, 140
Abyssinia, 93
Academia Pontaniana, 68, 73
Action, 10, 127, 154–55, 158, 202n23; in Croce's thought, 118, 148, 150; essence of, 127; impetus to, 129, 164, 178n100, 190n56, 201n22; moral basis for, 67; political, 55; pragmatism philosophy of, 108
Action party, 41
Adowa, 112, 122, 197n26
Aesthetes, 121, 162
Aesthetics, 51, 105, 119, 148; 193n10, 207n56; and the new culture, 75–86; and struggle against positivism, 87–100
Agnoletti, F., 196n18
Albergamo, Francesco, 212n8
Alfieri, Vittorio: Timoleone, 24; 95
Aliotta, Antonio, 161, 194n31, 212n9
Ambrosini, Luigi, 90, 160, 208n67
Amendola, Giovanni, 157
Anarchists, 111
Ancien régime (Tocqueville), 87–88
Aneceschi, Luciano, 86
Anima (journal), 157, 158
Anticlericalism, 4, 6, 38, 48
Antideterminism, 112
Anzilotti, Antonio, 120
Arango-Ruiz, Vladimiro, 161
Ardigò, Roberto, 86, 138
Aristophanes, 1
Aristotle, 4, 169n42, 170n43; Topics, 18–19
Art, 54, 138, 186n165, 193n20, 194n31;

Croce on, 61–62, 73, 74, 77, 78–79, 80–83, 84, 86, 188–89n26, 207n56; cultural regeneration through, 100; in Cuoco, 28–29; of D'Annunzio, 99; Hegel on, 194n30; in Hermes, 103, 104; in Leonardo, 106; and philosophy, 141–42, 143; separation of, from philosophy, 50–52
Avanti! (newspaper), 112, 113, 132

Bacon, Francis, 168–69n24; Vico's study of, 13–14, 15
Bakunin, Michael, 112
Basso, Lelio, 112
Beautiful, the, 81, 147. See also Good, true, beautiful
Becker, Carl L., 5
Becoming, 5, 6, 50, 71, 142, 144, 169n42
Being, 71, 141, 142, 144, 169n42
Beleval, Yvon, 166n7
Berchet, Giovanni, 96
Bergin, Thomas G., 18
Bergson, Henri, 104, 106
Bernstein, Eduard, 67, 69, 129; revisionism of, 113, 128, 204n40
Bissolati, Leonida, 112
Bobbio, Norberto, 215n59
Böhme, Jacob, 106
Boine, Giovanni, 157, 161
Bologna, University of, 92
Bordiga, Amadeo, 205n41
Borgese, Giuseppe Antonio, 81, 102–03, 121; Croce's break with, 155–57, 159; "Ghost Ship, The," 102; Papini and Prezzolini differed from, 105
Bosanquet, Bernard, 194nn30, 31

235

Bourbon Kingdom of the Two Sicilies, 4, 8
Bourbon regime, 23, 30, 31, 172n*56*
Bourgeoisie, 127, 131, 132, 135, 178n*108*,
    187n*38;* Italian, 104, 111, 114, 115–16,
    117–18, 132
Bruno, Giordano, 42, 71

Calabria, 49
Calderoni, Mario, 201n*22;* attacked by
    Croce, 203–04n*32; Disarmonie econo-
    miche e disarmonie morali,* 203n*32*
Calò, Giovanni, 200n*3,* 212n*9*
"Campaign for the compulsory Reawaken-
    ing of Italy, The" (Papini), 108
Caramella, Santino, 182n*134*
Carbonari revolt, *1820,* 30–31
Carducci, Giosuè, 47, 92–98, 103, 109,
    119, 122, 184n*145,* 196n*18,* 199n*54;*
    compared with Croce, 155; enthusiasm of,
    for Crispi, 197nn*25, 26;* impact of, 198n*48;*
    Inno a satana ("Hymn to Satan"), 94, 95,
    96–97, 197n*31; Odi barbari,* 93; "Versa-
    glia," 97; writings published, 196–97n*19*
Carlini, Armando, 196nn*8, 15*
Cartesianism, 12, 18
Cartesians, 15, 17, 19
Castel dell'Ova, 49
Castelli, Enrico, 212n*11*
Categorical Imperative, 108, 203–04n*32*
Catholicism, 17, 34, 49, 56, 77, 92, 95;
    imprisoned by philosophy, 50; Vico and,
    169n*30*
Cavor, Count Camillo di, 40
Cecchi, Emilio, 200n*3*
Certainty, 14
Charles II, king of Spain, 12
Christianity, 6, 92, 93; prototype for
    Socialist victory, 126, 130–31; reality in,
    52–53; Sorel on, 130–31; and Vico's
    theory of early man, 17. *See also* Anti-
    clericalism; Church, the
Church, the, 3–4, 38, 75; antinationalist
    teachings of, 31, 32; De Sanctis's writings
    against, 52; Spaventa's polemic with, re
    freedom in schools, 37
Civil wars, 179–80n*114*
Civilization: founders of, 17–18; modern,
    105
Class struggle, 118, 130, 189n*38*
Clemenceau, Georges, 91
Codignola, Ernesto, 188n*21*
Collingwood, R. G., 170–71n*48*
Collucci, Tullio, 136
Common sense, 2, 7, 29, 30, 44, 54, 89;

and action, 164; collective will manifest
    in, 21; constituted *prius* of science, 170n
    43; defined, 1, 19; imposed by republi-
    cans, 24; of Southern Italian peasants,
    27; lack of, in Italy, 8; natural law mani-
    fest in, 18–20; origin of, 18; treasured by
    a people, 25
"Concerning Italian Positivism" (Croce), 110
Concreteness, 5, 16, 50, 65, 66, 67, 69, 138,
    147; in art, 79; in Carducci, 96–97; in
    definition, 146; essential to lay religion,
    120; good, true, beautiful as, 147, 148;
    hallmark of southern intellectual tradi-
    tion, 62
Consciousness, 6; and knowledge, 14–15
Conti, Angelo, 105
Conventions, 107, 108
Corradini, Enrico, 38, 103, 115, 116, 118,
    121, 207n*60*
Corsi e ricorsi. See Vico, Giambattista,
    corsi e ricorsi
Council of Trent, 52
Cousin, Victor, 32
Crespi, Angelo, 105, 135, 193n*10*
Crispi, Francesco, 93, 113, 122; Carducci's
    enthusiasm for, 197nn*25, 26*
Critica, La (journal), 88–92, 98, 102, 104,
    130, 133, 137, 162, 196nn*8, 13, 15,*
    202–03n*29,* 207n*64;* determinate point
    of view, 89, 91, 102, 128, 209n*18;*
    differed from *Leonardo,* 206n*53;* review
    of *Leonardo* in, 109, 110
Critica sociale (journal), 112, 113, 128,
    129, 133, 134, 135, 136, 204n*41*
Criticism: aesthetic, 79; Kantian, 67;
    literary, 50–51, 54
Critique of Pure Reason (Kant), 77
Croce, Benedetto, 2, 4, 7, 17, 26, 35, 55,
    56, 105, 114, 184n*146,* 188–89n*26,*
    196n*15,* 207n*64,* 208nn*12, 67,* 212n*9;*
    abandonment of transcendence and Her-
    bart, 77; aesthetics of, 193n*10,* 207n
    56; on art, 61–62, 73, 74, 77, 78–79, 80–
    83, 84, 86, 188–89n*26,* 207n*56;* attacked
    M. Calderoni, 203–04n*32;* attacked
    pragmatism, 203–04n*32;* authority of, 3,
    86, 89; autobiography, 98; belief in
    values, 59, 62, 67, 73, 77, 148; biographi-
    cal information, 57–59; on Borgese, 102,
    104; and Carducci, 92, 95–98; central
    concern of, 188n*21;* central purpose of
    mature thought of, 145; *La critica,* 88–
    92, 209n*18;* and D'Annunzio, 98–100,
    119–20; declining popularity of, 137,

155–64; and De Sanctis, 46–47, 56, 73–74, 83, 84–85, 182–83n*141;* difference between Vico and Descartes in, 77; discredited Lafargue, 65, 68, 189n *45;* on economics, 68; on education, 28–30; ethics in thought of, 150–51; Franchini on, 187n*11;* and Gentile, 70, 71, 72–73, 191–92n*94;* goal of, 84–85; at head of cultural renewal, 56, 57–74, 133–36, 156, 192–93n*4;* Hegel in thought of, 50, 77, 83, 85, 139–45, 147, 149, 194n*30;* histories of, were political statements, 192n*101;* history in thought of, 60, 61, 80, 83–84, 114–15, 133, 137, 143, 147–48, 151–53, 163–64, 188–89n *26,* 215n*59;* hostility to orthodox Hegelianism, 60, 61, 62; hymn to D'Annunzio, 104; idealism of, 55, 77, 134–36, 138, 144, 161; impact of, on Italian culture, 3, 10, 78, 88; on impact of Carducci, 198n *48;* influence of, revolutionary, 114–15; and Labriola, 58, 59, 64–65, 66–68, 69–70, 71, 73, 85, 95, 111, 125, 128, 134, 142; on language, 82, 194n*31;* and *Leonardo,* 109–11, 115, 118, 119; on literature, 73, 92, 96–100, 119; man in thought of, 81–82, 88, 149, 154, 155, 159, 164; and Marxism, 62, 68, 70, 72, 95, 118, 120, 127, 128–29, 132, 133, 210n*41;* and new culture, 75–86; and Oriani, 122–23, 207n*63;* otherworldliness of absolute historicism, 137–53, 154, 160–61, 164; and philosophy, 3, 120, 127, 137–39, 147, 161, 163–64, 187– 88n*16;* Philosophy of Spirit, 61, 80–81, 137, 191n*94,* 192n*101;* polemic with De Sarlo, 139, 189n*27;* reading of Vico, 71, 74, 82–83; realization that revolution against positivism becoming end in itself, 155, 158–59, 161, 163; and rebirth of idealism, 134–36; rejection of historical materialism, 65–66, 68–69, 70, 76; rejection of left Hegelianism and positivism, 197n*37;* rejection of Vico's cycle of history, 83; reluctant to accept idea of philosophy of history, 83, 84, 85, 87, 88, 143, 145, 152, 154; review of Masci's *Psicologia,* 202–03n*29;* on science, 61, 137–39, 143, 144, 188–89n*26,* 211n*7,* 212n*8;* search for faith, 70; Socialist period of, 69, 114–18, 131, 132, 133, 210n*40;* and Sorel, 123–24, 125–36, 205n*41,* 209nn*28, 32;* sought concreteness, 62; stand re nationalism, 121;

struggle against positivism, 60, 61, 62, 68, 88, 119–20, 129, 138, 211n*4;* study of history, 60, 61–62, 65, 72–74, 163–64; and Turati, 128; on the useful, 214n*58;* utopia, the, 210n*40;* values in, 59, 62, 67, 73, 77, 148; "worldly sciences," 52; writings, 59–60, 61, 65, 68, 70, 80; "Concerning Italian Positivism," 110; *Estetica,* 77–84, 86, 87, 88, 95, 96, 97, 99, 102, 104, 105, 125, 137, 138, 139, 147, 148, 150, 155, 157, 163, 194–95n *34; La filosofia de Giambattista Vico,* 156; "Francesco De Sanctis and His Recent Critics," 73; "History Brought under the General Concept of Art," 61; *History of Italy from 1870 to 1915,* 97–98, 192n*101; History of Naples,* 180n*120; Logic as Science of the Pure Concept,* 139, 142, 145, 148, 149; "On the Interpretation and Criticism of Some Concepts of Marxism," 68; "On the Materialist Conception of History," 65; *Philosophy of the Practical,* 139, 145, 149, 150, 204n*32; La Spagna nella vita italiana durante la Rinascenza,* 59– 60; *La storia come pensiero e come azione,* 148; "Sulla filosofia teologizzante," 149; *What Is Living and What Is Dead in the Philosophy of Hegel,* 140

Croceanism, 134, 152, 164, 194n*31;* reaction against, 157, 158–59, 160

Croceans (*Crociani*), 91, 135, 160, 164, 183–84n*145*

Cubeddù, Italo, 179n*108*

Cultura filosofica, La (journal), 212n*9*

Cultural renewal, 55; through art, 100; Croce at head of, 56, 57–74, 133–36, 156, 192–93n*4*

Culture, 1–2, 3, 4, 7, 41, 55, 88, 159, 164; and faith, 54–55; Gramsci's definition of, 1; impact of Croce on, 3, 10, 78, 99; and impetus to action, 164; lay, 84; national regeneration of, 45, 46, 75; Neapolitan, 41; necessity of changing, 10; Roman Catholic, 3–4; scientific, 13–14, 15

Culture, new, 47; aesthetics and, 75–86; generation of, is revolutionary, 2; need for, 96; vs. reformist socialism, 101–24

Cuoco, Vincenzo, 4, 9, 24, 25–30, 32, 34, 35, 56, 74, 163, 173n*62,* 174nn*70, 71;* definition of Patriot, 174n*69;* on education, 175n*82;* integrity of individual in thought of, 175n*81;* passive revolution,

Cuoco, Vincenzo (*continued*)
122; Providence in thought of, 27–28;
revision of Vico, 26; *Saggio storico
sulla rivoluzione napoletana del 1799,*
25–26; on Vico and Genovesi, 171n*54;*
view of Napoleon and Murat, 174–75n*72*

D'Annunziani, 102–03, 104, 111, 120, 162
D'Annunzio, Gabriele, 98–100, 102, 109;
attacked by Croce, 119–20, 123; egoism
of, 120; *Figlia di Joria,* 98; *Francesca,*
98; *Laudi,* 98; morality of, 199n*55; Pia-
cere,* 99
Dante Alighieri, 52
Darwin, Charles Robert, 12
Darwinism, 63–64
"De antiquissima Italorum sapientia"
(Vico), 14
De Maistre, Joseph, 174n*70*
De Mas, Enrico, 174nn*70, 71*
De Meis, Camillo, 39, 50, 60, 139, 188n*21*
"De nostri temporis studiorum ratione"
(Vico), 28
De Ruggiero, Guido, 91
De Sanctis, Francesco, 4, 5, 6, 41, 46–56,
61, 77, 87, 102, 104, 122, 137, 138, 144,
150, 163, 183–84n*145,* 188n*21;* 194n
30; biographical information, 49, 184n
147; Carducci different from, 93, 94;
concept of man, 120; "conscience of
the nation," 152; and Croce, 46–47;
56, 73–74, 83, 84–85, 183n*141;* "La
cultura politica," 54–55; and form
(concept), 186n*165;* Gentile on, 183n
142; as Hegelian, 139; lay religion, 186n
165; particularization of spirit, 56; political philosophy of, 47–56, 89; rejected
materialism, 76; L. Russo edited works of,
184n*146;* separation of art, 78; *Storia
della letteratura Italiano,* 96
De Sarlo, Francesco, 139, 189n*27,* 212n*9*
Decadence, 105, 132; in literature, 98–99,
100
Definition, 146–47, 148
Della Valle, Guido, 212n*9*
Del materialismo storico (Labriola), 65
Democracy: French, 132; struggle for, in
Italy, 112–13, 117, 129, 205n*41*
Depretis, Agostino, 58
Descartes, René, 11, 12, 18, 19–20, 62;
cogito ergo sum, 14–15, 53, 76, 77,
167n*9,* 182n*136;* difference of Vico from,
76–77
Determinism, 64, 66, 111, 134

Development (concept), 181n*129*
Devenir social, Le (journal), 65, 68
Dialectic, 164, 169n*42;* or opposites, 141–
42, 144. *See also* Hegelian dialectic
Dilthey, Wilhelm, 59, 187n*11*
Di Malherbe, Boileau, 85–86
Di Rudinì, Marquis Clemente Solaro, 113
Distincts, theory of, 142
Divine, the, 81
Divine Comedy, The, 51
Dogali, 122
Dovere, Il, 176n*86*
Drobisch, M., 58
Droysen, Johann Gustav, 187n*11*
Dualism, 144–45, 182n*136*
Duni, Emanuele, 171–72n*54*
Duse, Eleanora, 98

Eckhart, Meister, 110
Economics, 10; Croce on, 68
Edie, James M., 16
Education, 9, 30, 41; in Cuoco, 28–30;
hostility of masses to, 175n*82*
Egalitarianism, 152
Egoism, 102
Einaudi, Luigi, 204n*40*
Elite, 38, 39, 44, 45; cultured, 9–10; as
leaders, 28; Neapolitan, 27; in southern
Italy, 31
Elitism, 9–10
Encyclopedic humanitarianism, 140
Encyclopedism, 26
Encyclopedists, 91
"End of Positivism, The" (Varisco), 139
Engels, Friedrich, 31, 71; preface to *Das
Kapital,* 189n*45*
Enlightenment, the, 5, 6, 22, 62, 89, 95,
132, 140, 172n*54,* 173n*58;* link between
Positivism and, 91, 138; Neapolitan
thinkers and, 23, 26; Vico separated
from, 19–20
Epinay, Mme., 172n*54*
Equality, 38; in Socialism, 117, 118
Estetica (Croce), 77, 88, 96, 97, 99, 102,
104, 106, 125, 138, 139, 147, 148, 150,
155, 157, 163; dedicated to Carducci, 95;
designed to be complete statement of Phi-
losophy of Spirit, 137; impact of, 77–84,
86, 87; original formulation of, 194–95n*34*
Ethics, 150–51
Euclid, 107; *Elements,* 13
Evolution, 50
Existence, principle of, 50
Expression, art as, 80–81, 82, 83

Fable of the Bees (Mandeville), 141
Faerie Queene, The (Spenser), 78
Faith, 66, 195n*34;* constitutes culture,
    54–55; myth and, 125–36; need for, 73,
    75, 95–96, 124, 150
Fascism, 46, 104, 121, 122, 209n*32*
Fatti di Milano, 112
Ferdinand I, 24, 25
Ferdinand II (Bomba), 48
Ferraris, Carlo, 111
Ferri, Enrico, 133
Feuerbach, Ludwig, 34, 61, 191n*89; Das
    Wesen des Christentums,* 43
Fichte, Johann Gottlieb, 42, 76
Figlia di Joria (D'Annunzio), 98
Filosofia di Giambattista Vico, La (Croce),
    156
Fiorentino, Francesco, 76–77
Fisch, Max, 16, 18, 168–69n*24*
Fiume, 120
Fogazzaro, Antonio, 119
Form (concept), 51, 185n*164;* De Sanctis
    and, 186n*165;* in revolution, 178n*100*
Fortunato, Giustino, 205n*41*
Foscolo, Ugo, 95, 103
Fourier, François Marie C., 12
France, revolution in, 38–39
Francesca (D'Annunzio), 98
Franchini, R., 187n*11*
Frederick II, "Stupor Mundi," 12
Free will, 21
Freedom: academic, 37; barriers to, 6
Freemasonry, 109, 121, 196n*18*
Freemasons, 91–92
French, the, 5, 91, 92; in Italy, 23–24,
    25, 26, 28, 53; materialism, rationalism,
    optimism, 26
French Revolution, 23, 96, 126; Spaventa
    on, 178–79n*108*
Freud, Sigmund, 126
Frigessi, Delia, 110
Fuentes, Carlos, 3
Futurism, 104
Futurists, 162

Gabinetto de Psycologia Sperimentale,
    212n*9*
Galiani, Ferdinando (Abbé), 8–9, 171–72n*54*
Garibaldi, Giuseppe, 40, 95, 101;
    Carducci's hymn to, 92–93
Garibbo, Roberto, 205n*41*
Garin, Eugenio, 78, 105, 109, 187n*16,*
    188n*21,* 191n*89,* 211–12n*7*
Genovesi, Antonio (Abbé), 171n*54*

Gentile, Giovanni, 2, 33, 34, 46, 67, 77,
    105, 129, 139, 162, 179n*108,* 209n*20,*
    210n*40;* analysis of Marxism, 70, 72;
    biographical information, 70–71; collab-
    oration with Croce on *La critica,* 88–
    89; and Croce, 70, 71, 72–73, 191–
    92n*94;* on De Sanctis, 183n*142;* influence
    of Spaventa on, 177n*95;* influence of, on
    Italian intellectuals, 161–62; philosophy
    of, 185n*161;* student of Jaja, 188n*21;*
    writings, 71–72
Gentileans, 91
Gentiles, 17, 21, 47
Geometry, 29, 60, 106, 107; convention-
    ality of, 13–14, 15, 18
German idealism. *See* Idealism, German
German philosophy. *See* Philosophy, Ger-
    man
Germany, 135; discipline of, 162–63
Gerratana, V., 183–84n*145*
"Ghost Ship, The" (Borgese), 102
Gioberti, Vincenzo: *On the Moral and
    Civil Superiority of the Italians,* 42
Giolitti, Giovanni, 113, 123, 131
Giornale d'Italia, 132–33
Gobetti, Piero, 160, 200n*3*
God, 16, 21, 22, 45, 87
God–Man idea, 106, 107, 109
Goethe, Johann Wolfgang von, 3, 152
Good, the, 147
Good, true, beautiful, 16, 18, 168–69n*24,*
    214n*58;* as concrete, 147, 148, 149
Goretti, Maria, 16, 18
Government, limited, 30
Gradualism, evolutionary, 125
Gramsci, Antonio, 2, 34, 47, 55, 130, 139,
    183n*145,* 185n*161,* 186n*165,* 187n*181,*
    198n*47;* definition of culture, 1; effect
    of Croce on, 3; lack of publishers in
    Southern Italy, 207n*64; On Historical
    Materialism and Benedetto Croce,* 152;
    rejection of Croce's Olympianism, 154–55
Grazeadei, Antonio, 204–05n*41*
Guicciardini, Francesco, 186n*172*
Guyon, Mme., 110

Hebrews, 21
Hegel, Georg Wilhelm Friedrich, 6, 12, 35,
    42, 45, 60, 61, 62, 71, 76, 81, 118, 122,
    164, 177n*95,* 191n*89,* 198n*46;* on art,
    194n*30;* in Croce's thought, 50, 77,
    83, 85, 139–45, 147, 149, 194n*30;*
    De Sanctis's interest in, 49; historicism
    of, 149; on liberty, 36–37; *List der*

Hegel, Georg Wilhelm Friedrich (*continued*)
Vernunft ("cunning of reason"), 21, 141,
143; *Logic,* 49, 142; rationality in, 151;
and Risorgimento, 31; and Spaventa,
33–34; translation of, 176–77n*87,* 181n
125; Weltgeist, 7, 34, 43, 50, 52, 77,
104, 154; world in thought of, 72
Hegelian dialectic; inversion of, 7, 40,
42–43, 55–56; revision of (De Sanctis),
49–52
Hegelianism, 26, 77; De Sanctis and, 183n
141; Italian, 6–7, 31–32, 40, 42, 43, 44,
48, 111; literary product in, 51; orthodox,
43, 44, 49–50. *See also* Left Hegelianism;
Right Hegelianism
Hegelians, 4, 7, 73; and form 185n*164;*
historization of truth by, 60, 61; Mazzinian, 31; Neapolitan, 176n*86*
Heglian (term), 139
Hegemony, 2, 34, 55; Crocean, 3
Heine, Heinrich: *Zur Geschichte der Religion und Philosophie in Deutschland,*
198n*46*
Heraclitus, 71
Herbart, J. F., 58, 62
Herbartianism, 73, 77
Herbartians, 58
Hermes (journal), 102–04, 155, 156
Historical materialism, 63–64, 65, 66, 68,
117, 128, 129, 130, 135, 136; detached
from socialism by Croce, 132; and ethical
values, 67; Gentile and, 72; meaning of,
66; or Marx, 133; rejected by Croce, 65–
66, 68–69, 70, 76; Rensi's attack on, 134
Historicism, 4–5, 6, 7, 9; of Hegel, 149;
absolute, 137–53, 154, 160–61, 164
Historic Right (*Destra storica*) party, 58
Historiography, 60
History, 27, 54, 56, 76, 77, 87, 96–97, 111,
188n*24,* 211n*4;* is art, 61–62; autonomous from triadic dialectic, 144; common
sense is, 19, 27; concept of, 5–6, 7, 65–66;
in Croce's thought, 61, 80, 83–84, 114–
15, 133, 137, 143, 147–48, 151–53,
163–64, 188–89n*26,* 215n*59;* cycle of,
20–21; in Hegel, 50, 140, 143; human
autonomy surrendered to, 152; human
origins of, 16–18, 22; intellectual, Italian,
2–3; in Labriola, 64; materialist concept
of, 64, 65; as reality, 15; reason motor
force of, 36; sacred aspect of, 140, 141;
and science, 188nn*16, 21;* is spiral, 170–
71n*48;* study of, 5–6, 11–12, 59, 60, 61;
universal, 82. *See also* Man, as creator of

history; Philosophy of history; Vico,
corsi e ricorsi
"History Brought under the General
Concept of Art" (Croce), 61
History of Italy from 1870 to 1915 (Croce),
192n*101*
History of Naples (Croce), 180n*120*
Hobbes, Thomas, 11, 13; *Six Lessons to
Professors of Mathematics,* 166n*8*
Holbach, Baron d', 172n*54*
Holy Family (Marx), 97, 198n*47*
Homer, 23
Hughes, H. Stuart, 3
Humanism, 4, 6, 16, 31, 52, 76, 97, 152;
Croce's departure from, 84; De Sanctis's
impact on, 55–56; influenced by Cuoco,
26–27; lay, 34, 81; pagan, 92, 93, 95;
revolutionary, pre-20th-century, 11–56
Humanists, 7, 87; revolutionary, 30–32
Humanitarianism, 5, 151; encyclopedic, 140

Idea: as impetus to action, 127, 129, 178n
100, 201n*22*
Ideal, the, 12, 58–59, 141
Idealism, 7, 48, 100, 104, 212n*11;* of
Croce, 77, 138, 144, 161; Gentile convert
to, 71; German, 127; in *Leonardo,* 109;
and materialism, 76–77; rebirth of, 72, 76,
134–36; Rensi on, 210n*45;* and separation
of philosophy and science, 139
Idealist revival became nationalism, 120–
24
Idealists, 56, 111, 136; German, 71
Ideals: in revolution, 126
Ideas: grounding of, in reality, 50; and
politics, 73–74; revolutionary, 2, 4, 7,
16, 35, 87–88; value of, 107
Ideology, 127
Illusion of Progress, The (Sorel), 130–31
Immanentism, 10, 16, 21, 43, 56, 77, 78,
149
Individualism, 36
"In Memory of the Communist Manifesto"
(Labriola), 62
Inno a satana ("Hymn to Satan") (Carducci),
94, 95, 96–97, 197n*31*
Integralism, 133
Intellectuals, 2–3, 54, 77, 111, 186–87n
181, 205n*41;* and attacks on socialism,
136; attracted to Marxism, 56; and conception of life, 74; and Crocean idealism,
134–35; Croce's influence on, 133, 157,
161; Gentile's influence on, 161–62;
iconoclasm of, 10; and limits on man, 87;

and nationalism, 31–32; post-unification, 101–02; responsibility of, for culture, 55, 56

Intuition, 80, 81, 82, 83–84, 138, 142, 207n56; as form of knowledge, 148

Istituto de Studi Superiori, Florence, 102, 200n3, 212n9

Italia, L', 52

Italian Communist party, 205n41

Italian people, the, 94; alienated by revolution, 23–24, 26; resisted thought of intellectuals, 8–10; ungovernable, 12. *See also* Masses

Italian Socialist party (PSI), 111, 112, 113–14, 117, 125, 128; Croceanism in, 134; voluntarism in, 133

Italian thought, 7; influenced by Cuoco, 26–27; marked by resistance of masses, 8–10; oscillation in, 9–10; uniqueness of, 6

Italian unification, 32, 38, 39–41, 47, 48, 53–54, 58, 101, 122, 127. *See also* Nationalism

Italy, 4, 7–8, 40, 72, 76, 92–93, 95, 104; dilemma of, 54–55; governance in, 111, 116, 117; greatness of, 101–02; histories of (Oriani), 122; middle class of, 172–73 n56; place in hierarchy of Europe, 8, 42; war with Germany, 162–63. *See also* Parthenopean Republic

Italy, southern, 31, 205n41; civil war in, 179–80n114; lack of publishing houses in, 207n64; lack of unifying culture in, 8–10. *See also* Naples

Jacobinism, 26, 197n37

Jacobins, 12, 23, 91, 95

Jaja, Donato, 60, 177n95; influence of, 70–71, 188n21

James, William, 104, 106, 107, 108; *Principles of Psychology*, 202n23

Jesuits, 29, 37, 89; reviewed Vico favorably, 168n18

Judgment: historical, 149–51; philosophical, 145–47

Kant, Immanuel, 5, 13, 36, 42, 71, 76, 82, 198n46; categorical imperative, 108, 203–04n32; synthetic a priori, 53, 72, 76, 77, 97, 140

Kautsky, Karl Johann, 69, 129

Kierkegaard, Sören, 9

Knowing, 14, 28, 76

Knowledge, 4, 18, 29, 215n59; art basis of,

78, 81, 83; classification of, 83, 84; empirical, 145; historical judgment is, 150; new form of, required, 145; of no use in action, 148; and opinion, 169n42; and power, 168–69n24; Vico's theory of, 13–16, 22

Kuhn, Thomas S.: *Structure of Scientific Revolutions*, 170n43

Kulischioff, Anna, 63

Labriola, Antonio, 4, 31–32, 58, 59, 71, 75, 77, 83, 88, 102, 118, 129, 132, 143, 152; abandoned Herbartianism for Marxism, 62–67; and Croce, 62, 64–65, 66–68, 69–70, 71, 73, 85, 95, 111, 125, 128, 134, 142; *Del materialismo storico*, 65; discontent with, 135; on history, 64; "In Memory of the Communist Manifesto," 62; as Hegelian, 139, 144–45; and Marxism, 62–65, 68, 69–70, 72, 127, 128, 142, 190n56, 205n41; revolutionary antideterminism of, 112; *Socialism and Philosophy*, 70; and Sorel, 125; writings in *Giornale d'Italia*, 133

Lacerba group, 159, 160

Lacerba (journal), 158

Lafargue, Paul, 65, 68, 129, 189n45

Language, 13, 82, 194n31

Lanzillo, Agostino, 135, 211n52

Laterza, Franco, 184n146

Laterza, Giovanni, 123, 207n64

Laudi (D'Annunzio), 98

La Vista, Luigi, 49

Law: ancient, 17; divine, 5; eternal, 17, 20–21; reason is, 40. *See also* Natural law

Lay religion, 1, 4, 34, 52, 55, 120, 154, 160, 186n165; in Croce's *Estetica*, 77; and impetus to action, 164; new culture as, 75–76; politicization of, 162

Leadership, Italian, 72, 122; in elite, 28; political, 24

Le Bon, Gustav, 126

Left Hegelianism, 7, 31, 34, 125, 144–45; rejected by Croce, 197n37

Left Hegelians, 97; German, 40

Lega Democratica per il Rinnovamento della Politica Nazionale, 200n3

Lenin, Nikolai, 30, 181n131

Leonardiani, 105, 106, 108, 109, 111, 117, 118–19, 201n22, 206n53

Leonardo (journal), 90, 102, 105–11, 135, 156, 200n18, 206n55, 207n60; collapse of, 119, 121; differed from *La critica*, 206n53; pragmatic phase of, 108, 211n7

Leopardi, Giacomo, 95, 96, 99, 101, 102
Letteratura e vita nazionale, 1
Liberty, 35, 38, 117, 118; popular, 36–37; Rousseau's concept of, 40; in Hegel, 36–37
Libyan crisis, 157, 158
Life, 158, 164, 196n*31;* conception of, 73–74, 75, 150; in *Leonardo,* 105–06, 108
Limits, 1, 54, 87, 97, 109, 151
List der Vernunft (Hegel), 141, 143
Literature, 139; absence of seriousness in, 96; Croce's study of, 73, 92, 96–100, 119
Logic, 29, 144
Logic as Science of the Pure Concept (Croce), 139, 142, 145, 148, 149
Logic (Hegel), 49, 142
Logos, 144–45, 149
Logos (journal), 194n*31*
Lombardo-Radice, Giuseppe, 89, 163
Loria, Achille, 68, 111, 129
Lo Schiavo, Aldo, 71
Lotta politica, Le (Oriani), 135
Lovecchio, Antonio, 190n*56*
Luther, Martin, 126

Mach, Ernst, 106, 211n*7*
Machiavelli, Niccolò, 2, 52–53, 54, 69, 89, 93, 94, 96, 127, 151, 186nn*167, 172;* on conquest of a republic, 173n*62*
Maeterlinck, Count Maurice, 106
Maffi, Maffio, 200n*3,* 215n*8*
Man, 5, 7, 16, 20, 30, 40, 45, 52, 85, 87, 178n*100;* alienated, 43; Carducci's exaltation of, 97; celebrated in philosophy, 120; "conscious" and "unconscious," 30; as creator of history, 4, 6, 8, 9, 15–16, 17, 22, 23, 26, 105, 108, 163; as creator of good, true, beautiful, 16, 18; as creator of own destiny, 34; in Croce's thought, 81–82, 88, 149, 154, 155, 159, 164; early, 16–18; faith in, 95–96; goals of, 120; is godlike, 6, 16, 53, 81–82, 86; in materialism, 76; moved by faith, 127; natural equality of, 23, 27; need of, for sense of religion, 75–76; as omnipotent force, 97, 102, 105; place of, in world, 4–5; in Positivism, 86; set free from God, 94, 95; social world and language of, 13–16; in Sorel's thought, 125–26; stages of, in history, 20–21; theory of knowledge in, 14–15; in Vico, 168n*21*
Mandeville, Bernard de: *Fable of the Bees,* 141

Manin, Daniele, 101
Manzoni, Alessandro, 95, 96, 99
Marchesini, Giovanni, 138
Marchiolli, Ettore, 134
Margherita, queen, 92
Marinetti, Filippo, 158
Marpurgo-Tagliabue, Guido, 160
Martini, Carlo, 200n*18*
Marucchi, Piero, 159
Marx, Karl, 4, 5, 38, 43, 44, 68, 118, 141, 181n*131,* 194n*30,* 204–05n*41;* Croce on, 69, 73, 127–28, 163; and demise of utopian socialists, 133; Hegelianization of, 71, 191n*89; Holy Family,* 97, 198n *47; Theses on Feuerbach,* 118, 198n*47;* true, 133
Marxism, 1, 2, 3, 5, 47, 67, 129, 152; antirevolutionary theory of, 125; crisis of, 128; Croce and, 68, 70, 118, 120; Gentile's analysis of, 70, 72; German, 69; inadequacy of, 68; Italian, 31, 56, 69, 111–12, 125, 205n*41;* Labriolan, 62–65, 68, 69–70, 72, 127, 128, 142, 190n *56;* Sorel's contribution to, 126, 130; true, 133
Marxists, 1, 33, 34; and Crociani, 183–84n*145*
Marzocco (journal), 104, 105
Masaryk, Thomas, 128
Masci, Filippo, 110; *Psicologia,* 202–03n*29*
Masses, 28, 29, 35–36, 38, 54, 112, 122, 128; common sense of, 27, 40; in Enlightenment tradition, 19–20; hostility of, to education, 175n*82;* liberation of, 30, 36; southern Italy, 9–10, 27, 31; Vico's thought isolated from, 19
Materialism, 5, 40, 51, 56, 75, 91, 110, 111, 135; and idealism, 76–77; immanent, 144–45; rejected by Italian humanists, 7, 43, 76. *See also* Historical materialism
Materialists, 111
Mathematics, 13, 15, 145
Mazzini, Giuseppe, 41, 94, 101, 126, 176n*86;* on De Sanctis, 185n*151*
Mazzinians, 42, 48, 111, 176n*86*
Meaning, locus of, 120
Memory, 84, 195n*34*
Merlino, Franceso Saverio, 111, 112, 204n*40*
Metaphysics, 150
Michelet, Jules, 181n*125*
Mill, John Stuart, 9
Mind, 16, 76, 77, 140; Italian, 3–4, 181n *122;* world product of, 21
Modernism, 15, 104

Momigliano, Attilio, 89
Monarchy, 92
Morality, 30, 44, 132, 203-04n*32;* in art,
207n*56;* Christian, 94; in Croce, 151
Morra Irpina (now Morra De Sanctis), 48
Moses, 23
Murat, Joachim, 28, 39, 173n*65,* 174-
75n*72*
Mussolini, Benito, 33, 114, 121, 122, 131,
135, 136, 209n*32,* 212n*11*
Mysticism, 110, 119, 162, 201n*22*
Myth, 66, 141, 154-55; and faith, 125-
36; philosophy of history as, 164. *See
also* Ideal, the

Naples, 3-4, 12, 22, 24, 25, 26, 28, 76,
165n*3,* 180n*120;* "the calamity of the
South," 8-10; center of Italian Hegelianism, 6-7, 31-32, 35, 139; culture of,
4-5, 26-28; humanism of, 30; intellectuals
in, 4-10, 26; revolution at, 35; university
of, 8, 12, 32, 33, 41-42, 167n*9* Vichian
historicist culture of, 94
Napoleon I, 28, 30, 174-75n*72*
Napoleon III, 40; coup of, 32, 38, 39, 179n
108
Nationalism, 31-32, 91, 207n*60;* art for
sake of, 103; of D'Annunzio, 120; idealist
revival became, 120-24; of Italian Hegelians, 7; revolution for, 38-39; Spaventa
apotheosis of, 181n*131*
Nationalist party, 103
Nationalists, 121, 135, 136
Nation state, 6, 7, 31, 38, 52
Naturalism, 5, 88
Naturalists, 89
Natural law, 5, 6, 11, 23, 24, 27; in Enlight-
enment tradition, 19-20; as impetus to
action, 164; in Vico, 17-18, 22-23
Nature, 15, 20, 45, 87, 109; in Croce's
thought, 80-81, 144; in Hegel, 143-44;
in Vico's thought, 144
Nazionale (journal), 35, 36
Neal, Th., 121
Neapolitan Academia Pontaniana, 60, 61
New Science (Vico), 1, 14, 15, 16, 21, 22,
60, 82-83, 85, 156, 171n*52,* 181n*129,*
182n*136;* fourth book, 20; politicization
of, 22-23; publication of, 168n*19;* revi-
sion of, by Cuoco, 27
Nicolini, Fausto, 155, 156
Nietzsche, Friedrich Wilhelm, 9, 89, 99,
117, 120
Nothing (concept), 141, 142, 144

Nuova antologia, La (journal), 61, 90
Nuova Europa, La, 78

Odi barbari (Carducci), 93
Oldrini, Guido, 181n*125*
Olgiati, Francesco, 211n*4,* 214n*58*
Omodeo, Adolfo, 91, 182n*134*
*On Historical Materialism and Benedetto
Croce* (Gramsci), 152
"On the Interpretation and Criticism of
Some Concepts of Marxism" (Croce), 68
"On the Materialist Conception of History"
(Croce), 65
*On the Moral and Civil Superiority of the
Italians,* (Gioberti), 42
"On the Study Methods of Our Times"
(address, Vico), 13
Opinion, 164, 169n*42*
Opposites, 141-42, 144
Oriani, Alfredo, 121-23, 207n*63,* 211n*52;*
La lotta politica, 135, 208n*67; Political
Struggle in Italy,* 122, 123
Ortega y Gasset, José, 9

Paganism, 119
Pagano, Mario, 24, 25, 171n*54; Processo
criminale,* 173n*58*
Panunzio, Sergio, 209-10n*32*
Papacy, 31, 42, 47, 52, 53. *See also* Church,
the
Papini, Giovanni, 2, 38, 104-05, 108-10,
121, 157, 158, 159, 193n*10,* 201n*22,*
207n*60,* 211n*7;* "The Campaign for the
Compulsory Reawakening," 108; and
Croce, 109-11, 115, 118, 119; directed
Leonardo, 206n*55;* notion of action,
202n23; on socialism, 117
Paracelsus, Philippus, 106
Parente, Alfredo, 196n*8*
Parmenides, 4, 71
Parthenope, 24
Parthenopean Republic, 24-26, 28
Parthenopean republicans, 175n*72*
Particularity, 36, 138
Pascal, Blaise, 11
Pascoli, Giovanni, 119
Passion, 141, 149, 150
Patria, 39
Patriot (defined), 174n*69*
Peasants: education of, into proper role,
28. *See also* Masses
Peirce, Charles Saunders, 104, 107; "Illus-
trations of the Logic of Science," 201n*22*
Pelloux, Luigi (general), 113

Peloponnesian War, The, 16
People, the. *See* Italian people, the; Masses
Perception, 83
Petrocchi, Policarpo, 197n*25*
Petronio, Giuseppe, 70, 129, 134
Petruzzellis, Nicola, 62
Philology, 13
Philosophy, 26, 28, 29, 50, 54, 61, 95–
   96, 135, 215n*59;* and art, 141–42, 143; in
   Croce's thought, 138, 139, 140–53, 159,
   163–64, 188–89n*26;* essence of action in,
   127; German, 26, 35, 76, 129, 152; of
   Labriola, 64; last limit to free constitution
   of reality, 109; makes man creator, 105;
   modern, 4, 43; Neapolitan, 4; science
   must become, 45; separation of, from
   aesthetics, 51; separation of worldly
   sciences from, 52; in Socialism, 117–18
Philosophy of history, 7, 56, 65–66, 87,
   151, 153; Croce's reluctance to accept,
   83, 84, 85, 87, 88, 143, 152, 154; as
   myth, 164; of Oriani, 122; philosophy of
   practice as, 71
Philosophy of practice, 63, 71
Philosophy of Spirit (Croce), 61, 80–81, 191n
   94, 192n*101;* revisions in, 137; in Vico, 85
Philosophy of the Practical (Croce), 139,
   145, 149
Physics, 44, 143
Piacere (D'Annunzio), 99
Piedmont, 32, 37, 38, 39, 42; Italy fell to,
   40–41; monarchy of, 39
Piovani, Pietro, 171n*52*
Pius VI (pope), 23
Pius IX (pope), 48, 49
Plato, 13, 169n*42*
Platonic Republic, 28
Plekhanov, Georgi, 67
Poet, 96, 185–86n*165;* as creator and
   leader, 100, 103–04
Poetic wisdom, 83
Poetry, violence of, 162
Poincaré, Raymond, 106, 211n*7*
Political Struggle in Italy, The (Oriani),
   122, 123
Political theory: lack of, in Croce, 163–64
Politics, 30, 50–51; for Croce, 89; De
   Sanctis on, 52–53; ideas and, 73–74; and
   religion, 55; revisionism in, 133
Pons, Alain, 174n*70*
Popolo, Il, 131
Positivism, 26, 45, 62, 64, 68, 77, 102,
   104, 139, 155, 162; adopted as ideology
   by Socialism, 111, 112, 117–18; aesthetics

and struggle against, 87–100, 106, 109,
   111, 121, 155, 158–59, 161; crisis of, 85;
   Croce's antipathy to, 60, 61, 62, 68, 88,
   119–20, 129, 138, 211n*4;* defended by
   Treves, 135; denied need for sense of
   religion, 75; evolutionary, 128, 204n*38;*
   in Italian Socialist party, 133; Lorain,
   112; man in, 81, 86; reformist, 132;
   science meant, 138
Positivists, 61, 73; and art, 193n*20*
Practical, the, 214n*58;* in Croce's thought,
   149, 150; philosophy originated in, 151
Practice, world of, 1, 100. *See also* Philosophy of practice; Theory and practice
Pragmatism, 106, 107–09, 111, 133, 201n
   22, 211n*7;* Croce attacked, 203–04n*32;*
   made into a religion by Prezzolini, 107–
   08
Praxis: knowing possible through, 76, 77.
   See also Theory and practice
Prezzolini, Giuseppe, 2, 38, 90, 104–10,
   115, 118, 119, 135, 157, 160, 211n*7;*
   left *Leonardo,* 206n*55,* 207n*60;* notion
   of action, 202n*23;* on pragmatism, 201n
   22; and *La voce,* 121, 123
Principles: eternal, 164; first, 169n*42;*
   philosophical, 148
Probability, theory of, 29
Problem and solution, 148–49
Progress, concept of, 131, 151, 153
Progresso, Il (journal), 34, 36
Proletarian movement, 131, 163; struggle
   necessary in, 126, 127, 128
Proletarian revolution, 132
Proletariat, 64, 114, 115, 132, 135; mission
   of, 189n*38*
Providence, 40, 141, 151; to Cuoco, 27–28;
   human, 143; locus of, in Spaventa, 39;
   Vichian, 21, 22, 27, 141, 171n*52,* 172n*54*
Psychology, 9, 212n*9*

Radicals, right, 136
Rassegna contemporaneo, La (journal),
   90
Rationality, 141; and history, 151
Reality, 8, 12, 13–14, 15, 76, 138, 145;
   art as, 62; for Christians, 52–53; and
   definition of concepts, 147; description
   of, 20; emancipation from, through
   pragmatism, 108–09; flight of Neapolitan
   scholars from, 12; Gentile on, 71; grounding of ideas in, 50; and intuition, 83;
   philosophy the method of examining,
   140; and positivism, 91–92, 119

Reason, 35, 39; absolute, 36–37; age of, 8; "cunning" of, in Hegel, 21, 141; faith in, 151; in Kant and Hegel, 140; rule of, 40
Reasoning, 18–19, 143; concrete, 169n42
Reflections on Violence (Sorel), 131
Reformation, 126
Reformism, 129, 133
Reggio Calabria, 25
Regno, Il, 103, 116, 121, 156, 207n60
Religion, 5, 8, 9, 55, 57, 127, 150; as impetus to action, 164; imprisoned by philosophy, 50; need for, 75–76, 127, 129, 153; orthodox Hegelianism was, 43. *See also* Lay religion
Rensi, Giuseppe, 133–34, 210n45
Republicanism, 24, 32, 35–36, 39, 92, 94, 174n69
Revisionism, 204n40; Bernsteinian, 113, 128, 204n40; of Borgese, 156; first period of, in Italy, 133
Revolt: through art, 100
Revolts, intellectual, 102, 103, 104, 111, 121, 155, 158–59, 161, 162; of Neapolitan humanists, 30–32
Revolution, 2, 4, 9, 23–27, 35–36, 38–39; attempts to build "new culture" by, 9–10; components of, 178n100; and creation of nation-state, 38; ideals in, 126; in Italian socialism, 112, 113; meaning of, 179n110; passive, 26–27, 122; social, 38. *See also* Ideas, revolutionary
Revolutionary myth, 127
Revolution of the Saints, *1640.* 132
Rhetoric, 18, 164
Right Hegelianism, 122, 144–45
Right Hegelians, 7, 31, 50, 61
Risorgimento, 4, 6, 7, 42, 58, 75, 92, 96, 101, 177n95; and civil war in southern Italy, 179–80n114; conclusion of culture of, 54; Croce on, 115; developed as reaction against French, 26, 91; failure of, 122; generation of, 56; nationalism and humanism coalesced to form, 31; need for new, 102, 103, 118; not only an event but a culture, 47; philosophy of, 34–35; poets of, 95; sought by Croce, 114; Spaventa's ideas and, 46
Rivista critica del socialismo (journal), 204n40
Rivista d'Italia, La (journal), 90
Robertis, Giuseppe de, 206n55
Roman Catholic Church. *See* Church, the
Romano, Enotrio (pseud). *See* Carducci, Giosuè

Rome, 23, 47, 53–54, 58, 204n39; university of, 58
Rotondò, Antonio, 197n37
Rousseau, Jean-Jacques, 20, 178n100, 180n115; Spaventa's polemic against, 40
Ruffo, Fabrizio, 25
Ruggiero, Guido de, 2
Ruling class, Italy, 111, 117
Russia, 135
Russo, Luigi, 45–46, 47, 90, 94, 208n12, 209n32; to edit works of De Sanctis, 184n146
Russo, Vincenzo, 25

Saggio storico sulla rivoluzione napoletana del 1799 (Cuoco), 25–26
St. Simon, Comte Claude Henri de, 12
Salomone, A. William, 22
Salvatorelli, Luigi, 24
Salvemini, Gaetano, 2, 8, 61, 121, 157, 200n3, 205n43, 206n55
Sanfedisti, 25, 28
Santarelli, Enzo, 133
Satan, 97; invoked by Carducci, 93–94
Savonarola, Girolamo, 52, 186n167
Savoyards, 49
Schelling, Friedrich von, 42, 61, 76, 143, 198n46
Schiller, Ferdinand C. S., 108
Sciacca, Michele Federico, 212n11
Science, 28, 111; attacked by Prezzolini, 106–07; common sense dictated *prius* of, 170n43; in Croce's thought, 61, 137–39, 143, 144, 188–89n26, 211n7; in ethical state, 44–45; in Hegel's thought, 143–44; and history, 59, 60, 188nn16, 21; idolatry of, 91, 92; in Labriola, 64; of *New Science,* 22–23, 26; and religion, 55
Scientific methodology, 26
Scienza nuova. See New Science (Vico)
Scirocco, Giovanni, 86
Self-interest, 36, 38
Sentimentalism, 112, 114, 115, 118
Serra, Renato, 90, 155, 157, 160, 161, 196n13, 206n53
Sin, 52–53
Skepticism, 11, 15, 20, 78, 136, 164; problem of, resolved in Croce, 148–49
Smith, Adam, 20; "invisible hand," 21
Social atomism, 162, 163
Social contract, 40
Social order, new, 189n38
Social science, 60
Social scientists, German, 59, 61, 65

Socialism, 65, 67, 129, 178n*108;* attacks on, 136; Christianity prototype for, 126, 130–31; to Croce, 69, 131; as faith, 128; historical materialism and, 66; Marxist, 129, 133; nationalist, 163; nationalization of, 135; practical, 127; reformist, 101–24; and southern Italy, 205n*41;* Turatian, 117, 118, 129, 208n*12*

Socialism and Philosophy (Labriola), 70

Socialists, utopian, 133

Society: classless, 64; collectivist, 118; core of, 169n*42;* development of, 11–12; and freedom, 121; Italian, 111; made by man, 15–17; moral regeneration of, through socialism, 131; origins of, 16–18; rests on opinion, 164

Soffici, Ardengò 158, 159–60; *Fragments,* 193n*10*

Sollen (ideal), 140, 141

Solon, 23

Sombart, Werner, 129

Sonnino, Sidney, 132, 133

Sorel, Georges, 56, 66, 67, 70, 104, 107, 129, 141, 163, 204n*40;* contribution to Marxism, 126, 130; and Croce, 69, 124, 125–36, 205n*41,* 209nn*28, 32; The Illusion of Progress,* 130–31; impact of, on Italy, 209–10n*32;* journal: *Le devenir social,* 65, 68; permitted by Croce to write in *La critica,* 209n*18; Reflections on Violence,* 131; *Le système historique de Renan,* 131

Sovereignty, 40

Spagna nella vita italiana durante la Rinascenza, La (Croce), 59–60

Spaventa, Bertrando, 4, 5, 6, 32–46, 49, 50, 53, 56, 60, 62, 71, 73, 88, 93, 94, 137, 138, 162, 163, 178n*103,* 180n*120,* 188n*21;* accepted chair at University of Naples, 41–42; biographical information, 34–35, 36, 57; change from republican to monarchist nationalism, 39; and Croce, 84–85, 192n*3;* doctrine of ethical state, 33, 34, 37, 39, 40, 44–46, 161–62; and dualism of subject and object, 182n*136;* "error of," 45–46; and French Revolution, 178–79n*108;* and Hegelianism, 139, 177–78n*98;* idealism of, 44, 45; influence of, 33; locus of historical reason in state, 181n*131,* 182n*134;* mature thought of, 43–44, 45; on Oriental philosophy, 170n *43;* polemic against Rousseau, 40; political and intellectual in, 177n*95,* 179n*122;* rejected materialism, 76; revolutionary

ideas of, 179n*108;* science in thought of, 44–45; and Vera, 43

Spaventa, Silvio, 4, 5, 6, 34, 35, 36, 41, 42, 57, 60, 94, 177–78n*98,* 180n*120;* guardian to B. Croce, 58

Spenser, Edmund: *The Faerie Queene,* 78

Spinoza, Baruch, 42, 71

Spirit, 4, 6, 56, 85, 145, 149; art basis of activity of, 80–81; as creator, 71; in Spaventa, 44

Spirit, philosophy of. *See* Philosophy of Spirit

Sprigge, Cecil, 149

Stampa, La (newspaper), 90, 156

State, ethical (doctrine), 33, 34, 37–38, 39, 40, 44–46, 161–62; origin of, 39

State, the, 179n*110;* in Croce's thought, 162, 163; Italian, 179n*108;* in Machiavelli, 52; modern, 120; role of, 44

Stein, Lorez von: *Der Socialismus und Communismus des heutigen Frankreichs,* 179n*108*

Stoicism, 164

Storia come pensiero e come azione, La (Croce), 148

Storia della letteratura Italiana (De Sanctis), 96

Storia d'Italia (Croce), 97–98, 192n*101*

Strike, general, 130

Structure of Scientific Revolutions (Kuhn), 170n*43*

Studi storici (journal), 71

"Sulla filosofia teologizzante" (Croce), 149

Syndicalism, 133, 136

Système historique de Renan, Le (Sorel), 131

Taddei, Marcello, 103–04

Talmon, Jacob L., 40

Tarchiani, Nello, 200n*3*

Tarozzi, Giuseppi, 138, 193n*20*

Theology, 52

Theory and practice, 12, 20, 47, 77, 155; came unhinged without culture, 54; and Croce's demotion of science, 138–39; hiatus between, obviated by Marxism, 64; in Marxism, 71

Theses on Feuerbach (Marx), 118

Thiers, Aldolph, 48

Thing-in-itself, 140

Thought, 10, 43, 142; discarded for action, 158; Gentile on, 71–72; historical, 76;

in Labriola, 64; in *Leonardo,* 105–06;
modern, 33, 42, 53; process of, 140;
true act of, 147
Timoleone (Alfieri), 24
Tocqueville, Alexis de, 9; *Ancien régime,*
87–88
Tolerance, 89
Transcendence, 7, 17, 21, 22, 43, 85, 120,
144–45, 149, 151; annihilation of, 10;
negation of, 75–76
Transcendentals, 16
Transcendent values. *See* Values
Treitschke, Heinrich von, 162
Treves, Claudio, 112, 113, 128, 136, 204–
05n*41;* defense of positivism, 135
Triadic dialectic, 143, 144
Truth, 14, 16, 64, 107, 147; historization
of, 60; locus of, 20; in orthodox Hegel-
ianism, 43
Truths, 107–08; universal, 145–46
Turati, Filippo, 112–13, 128, 132, 134,
204n*40,* 205n*41,* 209n*32;* positivism of,
204nn*36, 38*
Turatian socialism, 117, 118, 129, 208n*12*
Turin monarchy, 39
Two peoples (doctrine), 9–10, 26–28, 31,
56, 92, 174n*71;* class differences between,
38

Unità, L' (journal), 157, 158, 206n*55*
Unity, absolute, 45
Universal, the, 151
Universalism, 91
Universals, 4, 80, 84, 108; science and
philosophy dealt with, 137–38
Useful, the. *See* Utility
Utility, 29, 107, 147, 149, 214n*58*
Utopia (word), 179n*108*

Vacca, Giuseppe, 179n*112*
Vailati, Giovanni, 201n*22*
Value: criteria of, 107
Values, 60; in Croce's philosophy, 59,
62, 67, 73, 77, 148
Varisco, Bernardo: "The End of Positivism,"
139; *From Man to God,* 212n*11*
Vera, Augusto, 32, 43, 139, 181n*125*
"Versaglia" (Carducci), 97
Vichian epistemology, 13–14, 16, 17, 19,
20, 22
Vichianism, 171–72n*54*
Vichians, 22–23, 24–25, 55, 94, 171–72n
54; legacy of, 30
Vico, Giambattista, 4, 5, 10, 29, 30, 32,

42, 43, 44, 45, 50, 56, 59, 61, 88, 107,
138, 141, 152, 164, 181n*131,* 182n*136,*
194n*31;* author of two peoples doctrine
[*q.v.*], 174n*71; Autobiography,* 165–
66n*5;* bowdlerization of, 22–23; and
Carducci, 97; and Catholic religion,
169n*30; corsi e ricorsi,* 7, 11–12, 20–21,
22–23, 26, 27–28, 131, 145, 152–53,
170–71n*48;* Croce's reading of, 71, 74,
82–83; "De antiquissima Italorum sapientia," 14, 168n*21;* death of, 22; "De
nostri temporis studiorum ratione," 28;
differed from Descartes, 76–77; early
philosophical orientation of, 12–13;
and Enlightenment tradition, 19–20;
error of, per Croce, 85; evolution of
civil institutions, 171n*49;* fitted into a
universal history, 76; knowledge in
thought of, 13–16, 22; man in thought of,
168n*21;* and mathematics as universal
language, 13; nature in thought of, 144;
natural law in, 17–18; *New Science,* 1,
14, 15, 16, 20, 21, 22–23, 27, 60, 82–
83, 85, 156, 168n*19,* 171n*52,* 181n*129,*
182n*136;* "On the Study Methods of Our
Times" (address), 13; and philosophes,
166n*7;* on philosophy and legislation,
173–74n*66;* providence in thought of, 21,
22, 27, 141, 171n*52,* 172n*54;* rationaliza-
tion, 151; recognition of importance of
history, 12; rejected materialism, 76;
revision of work of, 26; role of, in development of De Maistre's thought, 174n*70;*
science of, 26; study of Francis Bacon,
13–14; *verum-ipsum-factum,* 76, 77,
168n*18;* view of history, 5–6
Vienna settlement, 101
Villari, Pasquale, 61, 80, 184n*147,* 211n*4*
Vinciguerra, Mario, 78, 86, 89, 188n*24*
Virtue, 52–53
Vitalists, 163
Voce, La (journal), 90, 121, 123, 155,
200n*3;* breakup of, 157–58; chronology
of, 206n*55;* editors of, 186–87n*181*
Vociani, 121, 123
Volkmann, W. F., 58
Voltaire, François Marie, 149, 164
Voluntarism, 133
Vossler, Karl, 78, 138, 139
Vulgate, 16

Weltgeist, 7, 34, 43, 50, 52, 77, 104, 154
Wesen des Christentums, Das (Feuerbach),
43

What Is Living and What Is Dead in the Philosophy of Hegel (Croce), 140
Will, the, 141, 149; collective, 21, 44; general, 40; and intellect, 149–50
Words, 19
World, the, 72, 140; moves because of passion, 141; product of mind, 21; theory and reality of, 11

World War I, 163

Zanichelli (publisher), 196n*19*
Zarathustra, 99